C000022783

The Lucky Country

*Or are all Australians just Convicts with
Mullets and Tattoos?*

The Lucky Country

*Or are all Australians just Convicts with
Mullets and Tattoos?*

JAMES MCGUIRE

Published in 2011 by Antony Rowe
Publishing
48-50 Birch Close
Eastbourne
East Sussex
BN23 6PE
arp@cpi-group.co.uk

© JAMES MCGUIRE 2011

The Right of James McGuire to be
identified as the Author of this work has
been asserted by him in accordance with
the Copyright, Designs and Patents Act
1988.

All Rights Reserved. No part of this book
may be printed, reproduced or utilized in
any form or by any electronic, mechanical
or other means, now known or hereafter
invented, including photocopying and
recording, or in any information storage
retrieval system, without permission in
writing from the publishers.

A catalogue record for this book is
available from the British Library

ISBN 978-1-907571-12-1

Printed and Bound in Great Britain by
CPI Antony Rowe, Chippenham and
Eastbourne

DEDICATION

*For Sally and my family for allowing me to do
the trip of a lifetime*

CONTENTS

(Authors note: I have endeavoured to relate the stories I heard and the conversations
I had as accurately as I could, but have changed the names of most of those involved.)

CHAPTER 1

*The beginning: Australia nearly goes Dutch and I get
time off for good behaviour*

THE year is 1644, the month January and it's 4.21 in the afternoon, it's raining and Abel Tasman, having just had a nice smoke and put down his bong, has just received these instructions from the Dutch East India Company, the VOC:

'Both by word of mouth and through the perusal of journals, charts and other writings, it is in the main well known to you how the successive Governors of India ... have, in order to the aggrandisement, enlargement and improvement of the Dutch East India Company's standing and trade in the east, divers times diligently endeavoured to make timely discovery of Nova Guinea of other unknown eastern and southern regions ... the first was undertaken in the year 1606 with the yacht *Duyffken* ... on which voyage ... the unknown south and west coasts of Nova Guinea were discovered ... '

Nova Guinea is today Cape York in northern Australia and this quote, taken from the book 'The Explorers' by Tim Flannery records the first white European contact with Australia by a Dutchman, Willem Janszoon. There had been others who claimed to have had contact, including the Chinese some two to three hundred years before, but Janszoon's was the first that was undisputed.

So there I was sitting on a train going home to deepest darkest Sussex having just recently returned to work following a ten week break, six of which had been in Australia, pondering what I should do to remember this, my longest break from work since 1984. Given the thrill of being back in the rat race is second only to having my gonads sliced off, grilled and served to me, accompanied by a nice piquant sauce and glass of '82 Bordeaux (one of the best vintages ever), I have decided to relive my break by taking you, dear reader, with me around the east coast of Australia (batteries not included) which is where I spent most of my time. I was going to be a veritable Captain James Cook of the 21st century albeit someone who can't navigate, who does not come from Yorkshire and only likes to travel in comfort. But why Australia, after all I hadn't committed any crime? I shall return to this in a moment.

Australia is a land that, according to a friend of mine, was: "old enough, yet at the same time still young, as a nation, which was developing its own identity and that was willing to question the established order of things ... "or in other words its links to the 'Old Country' and that " ... it was a place still seen as being a land of opportunity." But there's also the view that some have that Australia being essentially a very large island (yes I know – Continent but I'm trying to make a point) is in places still stuck in the 1950's and 1960's and that has an insularity in outlook although it is good at sport and has Kylie Minogue, its greatest export to the teenage/middle aged male. Many also know it as a land that has so many unique features and interesting facts that you need a whole book just to name them, but just for a flavour I've listed some of my favourites:

The UK fits into Australia 33 times, the land mass is double the size of Europe, that the ratio of Australians to sheep is 1:7, hence the expression that Australia was built on sheep, that there are 24 million cattle and 40 million kangaroos (means that sex of an evening allows for choice which I think is not to be sniffed at), has over 1,500 species of spider, 700 species of reptiles, 6,000 species of flies, 25,000 species of plant life, the fastest growing tree in the world (the eucalypt), that has 21 of the 25 deadliest snakes in the world, including the world's deadliest, the Australian Taipan (genus *Oxyuranus* for all you who like to know these things) whose venom could kill 100 people with a single bite. Also the magpies in Australia are so vicious during the breeding season that they like to attack people and often the same person again and again so remember if visiting the place be prepared: draw eyes on the back of your head, use an ice cream container as a hat or even use tinsel because the shiny stuff is a distraction but above all 'have a heart' as one helpful guide tells you and remember they're nice 'family birds'.

It has 378 species of mammals of which some 80% are unique to the continent, 869 species of reptile of which 773 are unique, 20,000 vascular plants of which 75% are unique, and thanks to an Englishmen, a certain Mr. Thomas Austin, the Continent of Australia also has one of the largest rabbit populations in the world having been introduced there by him in 1859. It has the 2nd largest Greek population outside Athens in Melbourne, was responsible in 1964 for the very first surfing championship, that 24% of Australians were born overseas (compared to 10% in the USA and 6% in the UK); that there is an Aboriginal buried in Eltham near London by the name of Yemmerrawanyea who accompanied Governor Phillip on his return home. This is a Continent that also has the Big Banana, the Big Merino, the Big Pineapple, the Big Prawn and the Big Ned Kelly – all seriously large sculptures that serve some purpose I'm sure.

It also probably has the highest per capita male population with mullets and with every woman whose idea of being different is to have the same tattoo on the small of their back. I know, I made the last two up, but the rest is absolutely true. I had to go. This would be a trip that would result in danger, much travel, a lot of museums and history, wildlife in abundance, beer, nudity and sex (though the latter was going to be difficult given the restraining order that I am under). I would be leaving a miserable old git and be coming back a more youthful, slimmer, tanned version of my former self. This would be a trip that would also establish once and for all whether Australians are immersed so far up their anal cracks that they require a torch to find their way out, or not. For fear of upsetting any Australian who might be reading this, I would just like to mention that I have paraphrased a friend's comments here when I told him what I was about to embark on. He is a cricket fanatic and I suspect that some of this ever so slightly one-sided view may be tainted by the relative merits of England and Australia on the 22 yard surface.

So, I hear you ask, how did I wangle it? Well for the last 26 years I have worked in London, the US and Switzerland, starting off as a grandly titled 'Investment Executive' when I first began what my grandmother once referred to as "grown-up work" through to my current role as 'someone with an organisational box' in the corporate structure of a large bank. I'd now been working at my current firm for ten years sitting on my rather sumptuous backside (for reference I am a two saddler when it comes to riding a bike – one for each cheek) going through life's daily chores.

One of the benefits of working with the same company for so long was that after ten years there is an opportunity to take an extended leave sabbatical. For me that was going to fall in November 2009 and so the question when I found myself with this opportunity to do whatever I wanted for ten weeks was what I should do. This would be my longest holiday since I'd started working which had been shortly after man had invented fire. There were plenty of options to consider: should I be adventurous and take a backpacking holiday say across the Far East and slum it whilst communing with nature and the world? There was very little chance of that as the idea of hauling a backpack anywhere let alone to those far off places appealed to me about as much as having piles, so that was out. I am also at a stage in life when anything short of some element of pampered luxury (e.g. nice soft toilet paper, soap, satellite TV, room and bidet) was to be avoided. I could cross 'The Pond' and travel around the US but I had already seen a lot of it when I lived there as part of my job in the mid 1990's. Going to Europe wasn't particularly appealing either, not least as the weather would be less than pleasant. Of course I could sit at home and do nothing which would clearly be cheap, but I think my wife might have had a different view.

I took soundings from my friends as to what they would do which, aside from the already junked backpacking idea, ranged from going to some Pacific hideaway and just chilling out, or 'chillax' as I believe it is called today, going on a safari (nice idea, no air conditioning) through to climbing Mount Kilimanjaro because "everyone was doing it these days". Now in the past I'd thought that it would be nice to visit Australia and New Zealand and I knew a few people that were natives of the soil who were living and working in London and so decided to sound out their views on logistics and ideas. And November is of course the start of their summer which was another incentive to go given that England at this time of year always seems wet and mild. I don't know why they bother with the weather forecast unless it's just to tease us into thinking it might be sunny.

The big question in going to the Antipodes was whether I could do both Australia and New Zealand? Should I do the Outback? Should I do the Lord of the Rings bit, dressed as Bilbo Baggins, and go to New Zealand looking for Vladimir Putin, sorry I mean Gollum? More importantly what was I looking to achieve? Travel for me is about discovery and about learning more about the people and their history as well as partaking in the odd snifter or two, preferably without having to fork out a fortune.

The planning stage was next and for this I needed someone or something, like a brochure, that was reliable and that could guide me as to how I should proceed. So one windy and not altogether pleasant afternoon in mid February 2009 I entered a sparse and dimly lit travel agent (as in a shop not the individual – just thought I'd clarify!) which didn't immediately inspire me with confidence. My immediate thought was that my best bet would be just to take a brochure and peruse it on my own but the problem here is that I have never really bonded with brochures. I recall booking a farmhouse in France once for a family holiday and the descriptive was very appealing along the lines of 'This beautifully restored farmhouse situated in the pretty hamlet of La Grenouille overlooks a wide valley, has four spacious bedrooms and a pool' etc. Instead what we got was a farmhouse with a broken toilet, a pool that was so green that I could not see the bottom and everywhere there was mouse excrement.

I swallowed my pride and sat down with one of the agents and from there the outline of what I was going to do began. Australia is a land well known for its beaches and its almost horizontally relaxed attitude to life but this was not what I was looking for, not least as I'm not anatomically designed for beaches and I'm not that keen on doing nothing. So if I went to Australia I had to be active. My idea was to fly from London to Cairns in Northern Queensland and then travel by car down to Adelaide in South Australia with multiple stops on the way. I decided against the Outback for the simple reason that I just didn't fancy driving to a one horse town, staying in a pub/hotel and being potential murdered either by a lunatic hitchhiker-murderer (Australia has a surfeit of these) or bitten by one of the countless poisonous creatures that inhabit the Continent.

Trying to get a flight to fit my requirements was like pulling teeth out with pliers. If it wasn't the cost or the number of changes I'd have to make, it was the "we don't fly there sir unless there's a z in the month". I could of course take a really cheap option with one of the many budget airlines (the ones with outside toilets) but given that there would be more changes than I've had hot dinners and a suspicion that 'close to Melbourne' when referring to the airport was in fact more likely to be Alice Springs, that option was out as well, not least as one of my 'hates' about travelling is having to check luggage given that I'm convinced that whatever I put into the hold will never be seen again. It has thankfully never happened although the first time that I had to use three flights in succession to get to my final destination I hadn't realised that my luggage was checked all the way through. I looked a complete idiot when I went to remonstrate with the lost baggage people after the first flight as they informed me with in a tone that suggested the village idiot was loose again that it was already on the connecting flight and that if I didn't get a shift on, and I quote " … it would be enjoying cocktails by the pool and not me", What a funny man he was although with my shoe still inserted up his backside sitting down must still be a bit painful.

In the end it was sorted out and involved flying in and out of Sydney and taking an internal flight from Melbourne to Cairns with the net effect being that Adelaide was out of the picture. So far so good but then what looked like disaster appeared in the form of an email informing me that my flight had been cancelled. Cancelled, but its only May and I don't go till November, how can they cancel it? You know when you read a book or a newspaper, the bit that tends to 'sell' itself to you is the blurb on the back cover or a headline that seems to scream out at you such that as often as not you don't then look any further but just buy it, or maybe that's me (although interesting to note that the more upmarket UK papers now have tabloid-like headlines or teasers). Well so it was with the email cancellation, because if I had at that point bothered to read further I would have noticed, as I did shortly after but only once I had railed against BA and what utter bastards they were for causing me this angst, that all they had done was to re-book me on a later flight. Still it always feels good to SHOUT LOUDLY AT YOUR COMPUTER not least if you are, like me, a computer Luddite.

A few weeks before I was due to leave I had mentioned to a friend of mine who I'd been to school with, Chris, about my plans. I had travelled to the US and Spain with him in the past and suggested that he might want to come along for a part of this great adventure which he agreed to. Given my size and his it would be like Tweedle-Dee and Tweedle-Dum travelling together. So it was that the final plan was arrived at and it was that I would fly direct to Sydney, then drive along the coast to Melbourne, stay there for a few days, do the Great Ocean Road and then the goldfields in the Grampians, after which I would fly to Cairns and then on to Port

Douglas where Chris would then join me. From Port Douglas we would head down the coast stopping off on the way at places such as Magnetic Island and Airlie Beach, finally ending in Brisbane where he would fly back to the UK. I would then continue south taking in the delights of Byron Bay, Port Macquarie and then inland to the Hunter Valley and finishing my tour in the Blue Mountains at Katoomba.

It would mean staying at some 30 hotels, motels and inns on the way and lugging around my bags from room to room. If there is one thing I really cannot stand it is taking too much luggage on any trip and I have always as a rule looked to travel light. I once did a 2 week business trip to the US and only took a tote bag with me, which contained all I needed namely one set of underwear (turn inside out every other day), toothbrush, 5 shirts (wash at the end of the week), 2 pairs of socks (wash as per shirts) and suit. I stank like the back end of a cow by the end of the trip but at least I didn't lose my luggage which I think you'll agree is a moral victory for me. Unfortunately for Australia this approach to green travel or, in the lingo du jour, maintain a low carbon footprint, was not going to work. Still at least my car ran on unleaded and was fuel efficient so at least the drive to the airport would be eco-friendly.

By July everything was in place including pre-paying all the stopovers and the car (or so I thought). I was ready to go and so now it was a matter of waiting for The Adventure to begin.

CHAPTER 2

The journey begins: London to Sydney via Bangkok and things start badly

I remember when I was a small child and it was Christmas, only it wasn't because it was November but I was excited anyway and the nearer it got to the 'Big Day' the more excited I became, and of course more irritating to my parents. Well wind that clock on 40 odd years to an old, grey haired overweight man and bingo you get the picture of how I was feeling as the time to departure drew nearer. Then it was the Big Day, November the 2nd and time to go. My flight was due to leave at 5.45pm so, allowing for check-in and for the drive I had at least 4½ hours (allowing for traffic on Europe's largest car park, the M25) until my flight from the moment I left home and because I was going to be parking in Terminal 5's own car park, a mere 10–15 minutes from the actual departure area because as we all know, BA long haul all depart from there thus it would all hopefully be relatively painless.

In the end as there was virtually no traffic and I actually arrived just under three hours before my flight. "Not a problem" I thought, "gives me time to enjoy the lounge" (silver card holder don't you know!) " … and do a bit of pretend shopping." So I arrived at Terminal 5 where all BA flights leave from, don't they? I parked in the valet parking area, gave the keys in to the smiling attendants and boarded the shuttle. I was off and the lounge with all its accompanying luxuries was minutes away. Marvellous! At this point I got my e-ticket out just to be sure that all was in order, and there at the top, horror of horrors next to the flight departure details was Terminal 3. Brilliant! I'd parked in the wrong place, in the wrong Terminal and so instead of being in the BA lounge I was instead battling with my luggage to get onto the Heathrow Express which would be stopping at the correct Terminal adding at least another half hour on to the journey. Of course I could have gone back to my car, collected it, paid for the nanosecond I'd left it there but this would have involved two things which is an anathema to the male psyche: a) admit that I had made a mistake and b) admit that I had made a really big mistake because I couldn't be bothered to check. That wasn't going to happen.

Once I'd arrived at the correct Terminal, checked in, had my scrotum felt in security (I must stop sowing metallic studs into my underwear but a thrill is a thrill and it's all perfectly legal) I proceeded to do what many of us do when travelling abroad on holiday which is to look for something new to wear that will never be worn again, is usually quite horrible and costs the earth or else try to find an accessory that is special because it's in duty free like that must have Rolex I don't really want, let alone can afford, or that designer handbag my wife doesn't really need. I looked in the clothes shops, Paul Smith, Timberland, Pinks and so on but couldn't find anything and came to the conclusion that people of a certain size are perhaps not their target demographic (i.e. anyone with a waist over 32 inches and a neck size that would only be suitable for children). Even the shops that were selling real holiday wear were not much better. I could of course buy a pair of Speedos but I didn't fancy them being vacuumed up my backside the first time I went on the beach. As a last resort the thought of buying a 42" television, HD ready of course from Dixon's was tempting given that the in-flight movie might be terrible.

Duty free is also the place where there are all walks of life meet from couples like newlyweds , friends going on stag or hen weekends, families with boisterous children, children on a school trip which might be their first holiday without mum and dad, old couples reliving a past life and the business type in their neatly pressed suits. There is both a sense of real anticipation especially amongst the young with teenage girls holding hands and giggling whilst spotty boys try to act cool, mums and dads stressing over their young broods boisterousness, the old with contented smiles on their faces looking on as if to say "Been there, done that, now it's your turn" and the 'suits' trying to look very important with those blue tooth contraptions sticking out of their ears making them look like complete dickheads. Above all though there is a very palpable sense of excitement, the noise of conversations in whispered voices that in reality can be heard by anyone nearby and of the occasional wailing baby being fussed over by mum as dad looks away pretending that it was nothing to do with him (which for all he knows it may not). Above all, though, this pre-flight temple to materialism and fast food is like being in a sort of limbo land where we are all part of some type of slow-moving conveyor system that is feeding us through duty free to part with even more money before taking us to the departure gate. I wonder if it was all filmed whether it would resemble something like Fritz Lang's superb 1927 film, 'Metropolis', where instead of being the underground workers of that film, we are nevertheless in the hands of the airport planners and managers 'guiding' us through to the end (the flight). I know it's a bit deep and probably cobblers but I can live with that image.

Given the amount of time I had, and having hoovered up most of the food available in the lounge, I soon went to the next stage of the traveller which is the boredom of waiting for the flight to be called, incessantly checking the information board to see if the flight was boarding, delayed or worse, had been cancelled. So I resigned myself to another traveller's activity of checking and then re-checking that I had the ticket, my passport and all the details of the trip. On one family holiday I managed to leave the information relating to which hotel we were staying at home so nowadays I print off at least 2 copies of the journey with all the details, putting one in my check-in luggage (which of course is plain daft given that I could easily lose it as it holidays in sunny somewhere else but not where I am) and one in my carry-on. I am not a big fan of printing tree loads of paper but I am equally damned if I am going to get lost. Sorry all tree huggers out there, I promise to plant a tree like I did when my school came up with the natty slogan 'Plant a tree in '73'. My green credentials are as you will agree, impeccable.

I have always found that boarding a plane is quite an event, especially if it is a large one like a 747 not least when they have two entrances. It is a strange scene to behold as the world and his wife franticly gather all their stuff together, corral the kids, ready to board. At least one, maybe two couples will be bickering over who has the tickets and passports. All of us though are waiting for that the same thing: the lady (always seem to be a lady) who has the attention of all as she takes the microphone and announces that the flight is now ready for boarding with passengers seated in rows 900 through 850 or whatever and the rush begins. Once on board I, like everyone else, start to 'mark' my spot. This seat, this area, was now mine so all of you others can just p**s off! I then go through my ritual and something that I always do when flying long distance. This involves taking out a book (which I will never read), sweets (which I promptly lose somehow), a pillow and make sure my passport is readily available (and soon to be hiding with the sweets I can't find). Into the luggage rack goes my bag and then I sit down, only to then get up again because I've left my pen (never used but a 'just in case') in the bag. And then sit down and pull out the in-flight magazine to find out what films were going to be shown knowing full well that I'll probably sleep through most of them or, as has happened a lot, find that the video machine doesn't work on my seat. Once I've completed this I will then always take out the in flight shop magazine which is utterly pointless given that there is no chance of me buying anything, but it's all about ritual.

All around me I can see others going through their own rituals and I always feel an affinity to them, almost to the point that I want to compare notes to see if there is something that they're doing that I could do. Rituals should always be a transferable commodity. The last part of preparation is the 'look round' to see where the nearest child is. I've nothing against children, after all I've got my own (currently available on eBay), but when I travel, which is usually on my own, I've little desire to be near one. I'm still scarred from the flight I'd done in the US from Boston to Florida during the holiday season when the plane was a) full of babies; b) full of babies that were wailing; c) full of babies whose nappies were 'ripe'; d) full of kids screaming and shouting with excitement and last but not least that one, sweet little darling that threw up all over me just as the plane took off for the near two and half hour flight.

As with all air travel there are those who like it, those that tolerate it and those that hate it. Take off is a good time to observe these three creatures. The traveller who likes flying can easily be spotted as he or she is calm, has started to read their 4,000 page book freshly purchased from W.H Smith or if next to a window, are keenly looking outside as the runway disappears from view. Then there is the opposite traveller, the panicky one; they are a giveaway as the worry frown is all too apparent, accompanied by the looking straight ahead or down at their shoes, some also moving slowly back and forth as if in silent prayer asking "will we, won't we take off?" Then there is the tolerant traveller, like me, who is the half-way house. I'll cover all options: magazine/book ready to flick through, if near a window half look and then the sneaky move back and forth staring at an angle in order not to be mistaken for the panicky one. Once in the air the three creatures morph into one until the landing when we all revert back to type. However there is of course the moment when this all goes completely out of the door when the Captain announces that there might be a little turbulence at which point the rule book changes completely and we are faced with a different analysis of travellers. Cards on the table here I really don't like anything that just doesn't seem right and when planes start to move around, which I do believe is also referred to as yawing (I thank you), I start to get a cold sweat and begin moving back and forth looking straight ahead because I've now become a panicky one. The calm traveller has, depending on the strength of the turbulence, moved into the tolerant traveller mode whilst, in their seats, rocking for all that it is worth and looking around mouthing silently "can't you see, we're all going to die?" as if they were Edvard Munch's 'The Scream' is the panicky traveller. I recommend that the next time you fly that you have a look round at your fellow flyers and join in the 'game'.

A few weeks back I'd been chatting to one of my friends who is a frequent visitor to Australia about my route, and often flies via Singapore where he told me there was a great hotel in the transit area that for a small sum of money would be ideal for a shower given the stop-over was going to be about 2 hours. So that sounded like a plan and I duly bought some Singapore dollars. You'll remember that I said earlier that my flight had been rescheduled. Well I had clearly not taken this in and had also failed to register anything when checking in because as we came into land in Singapore the captain announced over the intercom:

"Welcome to Bangkok where the local time is … "

After a rather unpleasant hour in the airport which required going through two sets of security I re-boarded the plane and settled down for the next leg of the flight to Sydney which was just over eight hours, arriving in the wee small hours the following day, though technically it was the day after yesterday which in turn I'd missed because somehow when I crossed to the other side of the world someone or something had decided to steal November 3rd. This is something I will never get back and I now know how the average man and women on the street felt when the Julian calendar was changed to the Gregorian one morning on September 2nd 1752 when the day after became the 14th. What a pain if you'd booked a late summer holiday that covered those very days only to arrive at Ye Olde holiday home, unpack, have dinner, wake up the following day to find that you were late for work and then being asked by someone "How was your holiday?" Mind you it was much worse for the Russians who didn't adopt the calendar until 1918 at which point January 31st was followed by February 14th. Given that Russians have a liking for vodka I can imagine the scene after Ivan and his chums had been out for a celebratory drink on the 31st, only to wake up the following day and it was the a full two weeks later. "What a night, comrade!"

Chapter 3: Sydney

I arrive in Terra Australis Incognita the unknown land of the South and wonder what happened to the whales.

Day one: November 4th

It's an early May Sunday evening in 1770 and a party has just arrived back on HMS Endeavour from a fishing trip and Captain James Cook (although actually only a Lieutenant at the time 'Captain' was a courtesy title) noted in his journal:

'Sunday, 6th. In the evening the Yawl return'd from fishing, having Caught 2 Sting rays weighing near 600 pounds. The great quantity of plants Mr. Banks and Dr. Solander found in the place occasioned my giving it the Name of Botany Bay.'

Actually it was not until the mid 1840's that this spot, the first of note in his travels up the east coast of Australia in 1770, was called Botany Bay. It was originally called Stingray Bay and on most charts of that time this was the name seen. However, be that as it may Botany Bay was supposed to be the site of the first white settlement. In fact it wasn't and instead Port Jackson was (named after the then Home Secretary). Before I go any further, given that this was Sydney, I thought a little historical background to the place (and thus the beginnings of modern Australia) might be appropriate.

By the second half of the 1780's Britain had lost its American colonies through the cunning leadership of General Cornwallis who, and here I would just to put the record straight, deliberately gave them up when he heard one local refer to the toilet as 'the restroom' and had asked for a rubber to erase something in his journal and was handed a condom. It just wasn't cricket! This in itself was a disaster because America was a great place to send the less desirable elements of the British population (out of sight and out of mind and all that) but with the loss this was no longer a proposition.

And this was a problem. By this time in Georgian Britain if you were poor then life was hard and the law was increasingly stacked heavily against you and one of the main reasons for this was that Britain was in the throes of the Industrial Revolution and the protection of property in all forms seemed to pre-occupy those at the top of the social ladder. With no police force in place (it wasn't until the 1830's that Oxbridge types could partake in that hilarious sport of knocking off a Peeler's hat) there was a sense from the 'haves' that the population was becoming increasingly unruly (read for this the labouring classes). There is a very strong image of Britain around this time in a picture from 1751 by the sometime moralist and satirist William Hogarth called 'Gin Lane' that depicts seedy and debauched slum dwellers destroyed by the effects of gin. Ironically, given today's 'people who know best' predilection for telling everyone else how much to drink, there is another picture of his called 'Beer Lane' which is in direct contrast to the other and promotes a social order that is the antithesis of 'Gin Lane'. This growing dispossessed underclass is encapsulated by Robert Hughes in his book 'Fatal Shore' as being 'rag-pickers, bonegatherers or the swelling crowd of Irish casual labourers … old women who collected dog-turds … ' and so on. By the way what does one do with collected dog-turds?

"Hello Martha, I'm back from work."

"Hello, dear, I've got a special treat for you tonight."

"Oooo, what is it?"

"Fricasseed doggy-do a la Parisienne, with chips."

"What about mushy peas?"

"Sorry love, I couldn't get any. I did find some lovely nettles to go with this."

"Nope. You can't have doggy-do without mushy peas!"

And not to labour this too much it really was a real 'them versus us' situation resulting in more and more legislation to curb the excesses of the masses as observed by Hughes:

'Between the enthronement of Charles II in 1660 and the middle of George IV's reign in 1819, 187 new capital statutes became law – nearly six times as many as had been enacted in the previous three hundred years. Nearly all were drafted to protect property, rather than human life; attempted murder was classed only as a "misdemeanour" until 1803.'

Jails were becoming second homes to many. This resulted in a dilemma; if jails were full what could be a solution to ease this over-crowding? America wouldn't work so somewhere else needed to found. The First Fleet was to be the spearhead to all of this and ultimately led to over 160,000 men, women and children being transported. But as Tom Keneally points out in his book on the early convict colony, 'The Commonwealth of Thieves' the harshness of transportation bore little resemblance to the crime itself:

> 'Anyone reading the Old Bailey transcripts is struck by the imbalance between minor miscreancies and the ultimate, transglobal punishment of transportation. In modern terms, what happened with the Georgians was the equivalent of sending a shoplifter to some biosphere on another planet.'

It was so daft that many Welsh were sent to Australia simply for speaking Welsh and even people like the Quakers for having the effrontery to meet in solemn worship (dodgy types them!) As for what you could be found guilty for and receive capital punishment it was even more ridiculous as Hughes details where the law:

> ' ... prescribed the gallows for over two hundred offences ... ' ranging from ' ... burning a house or a hut, a standing rick of corn, or an insignificant pile of straw; for poaching a rabbit ... or even cutting down an ornamental shrub; or for appearing on the high-road with a sooty face.' That last one just is mind boggling – goodness knows how dangerous it was to be a travelling chimney-sweep at this time. It did mean though that some more sympathetic juries tended to recommend prison and not death.

This is the reality behind Phillip's journey to Botany Bay which ultimately was, according to Stuart Macintyre in 'A concise history of Australia', either:

> ' ... to get rid of a dangerous social problem, and the farther way the better. Others contend that Botany Bay had strategic advantages' or
> ' ... after the loss of Nantucket in the United States it would allow a

resumption of southern whaling. Most of all it offered two precious commodities, timber and flax.'

Criminality was not the only issue taxing the minds of the leaders of that period. There was also a growing simmering of political discontent which came from our Celtic friends most notably in Ireland and Scotland where many within the intellectual class began to express a view that basically told the English that it was time for them to go and for independence from the Crown. As an example of what I mean there is in Edinburgh, Scotland, a commemoration of this very thing called the Martyrs Memorial that remembers the men of the Scottish Political Martyrs who were found guilty of sedition in 1794 and transported. These men aspired to an independent Scotland and were against the Act of Union of 1707. In Robert Burn's poem of 1791 'Rogues in a Nation', there is another fine example of the feelings of the time with its scathing attack those who 'sold out' the Scottish to the English in the Act of Union in 1707 as can be seen in one of the verses (the word 'stell' translates as 'steel')

'What force or guile could not subdue,
Thro' many warlike ages,
Is wrought now by a coward few,
For hireling traitor's wages.
The English stell we could disdain,
Secure in valour's station;
But English gold has been our bane-
Such a parcel of rogues in a nation!'

I like Steeleye Span's version of it, but will remember to shake my fist the next time I listen to it and mumble something Gaelic to show solidarity. Although given that I'm not Scottish and given that the Scots continue to hurl abuse at us, the English, at all sports matches where England play and support ABE (Anyone But England) maybe not. Meanwhile, across the Irish Sea there was also a large amount of unrest highlighted by the United Irishmen's rebellion of 1798 (known in the annals as the Battle of Vinegar Hill) which was a resounding defeat resulting in many of its leaders and supporters ending up being transported. The battle though was a fine example of how the Irish should have asked the average

Englishman's view of the time about what they could expect from our garlic eating friends across the Channel, which was to never trust them. And why was that? Unfortunately the Irish had expected them to arrive with an army and were somewhat flummoxed when the French failed to turn up. Maybe the French took a wrong turning as they rounded the Mumbles in Southwest Wales something that rather amusingly really did happen in 1797 when Napoleon had decided it would be a good idea to invade England, so sent a small fleet which was expected to land near Bristol. This wasn't possible so they went on and finally arrived in Fishguard Bay, Wales. They successfully landed troops and weaponry but then things went pear shaped as the invaders were rather more interested in partaking of food and wine than fighting which didn't augur well for success and they duly surrendered. But the icing on the cake of this story is that although some of the French soldiers and sailors claimed that they were significantly outnumbered by the British Red Coats who, they said, had arrived in force and thus fighting was futile some say that the real story was that what they saw were in fact Welshwomen dressed in their traditional clothes (black hats and red/scarlet shawls) and had thus surrendered to them. Whatever the real truth and I suspect the latter, though funny, is probably just a good story, I've still some sympathy for the French if it really was them as I've met a few Welsh ladies over the years and I would probably have agreed with their decision.

For those being transported having most likely have already spent time in one of the prison hulks moored in the Thames, which was no picnic as they too were rife with crime and debauchery (if you weren't tainted before you were sent there, then the experience may well have 'turned' you), you might be forgiven for thinking that it would be better. No QE2 perhaps but certainly not what they had suffered so far. Unfortunately the journey itself was really unpleasant as conditions were usually cramped and the ships themselves fetid places. It was so bad that doctors had to be assigned to these ships and were paid to keep people alive. John Boyle O'Reilly, a member of the Irish Republican Brotherhood was one of the last to be transported in 1868 and gives a vivid his description of his voyage aboard the Hougoumont which I found in 'Fianna: A guide to Irish Ancestry':

'The smells were, of course, among the most notable feature of life on board. The combination of animal and human excrement, foul water from the bottom of the ship below pump wells which never came out, the remains of old cargoes and the perpetually rotten wooden structure of the vessel herself must between them have produced a dreadful stench, unrelieved by any kind of ventilation system in the ship. People were accustomed to this ashore in towns and villages which stank like an Oriental slum today.'

In respect of the First Fleet, of those that made, or more to the point survived, the voyage, and that made up the first penal colony were according to Project Gutenberg: 543 male and 189 female convicts along with 22 children. On the other side of the legal fence there were 14 officials and passengers (someone clearly booked the wrong cruise: "I said Austria, not bloody Australia"), 306 members of the ship's crew, 245 marines with 54 wives and children which gave a total of 1373 from an original manifest of 1420. They note that this was the net arrival at Port Jackson as many more died than were born and that in any event this figure may still not be accurate as crew musters were not kept at the time.

History books – or at least the ones I read at school – always talked about where this first colony appeared, i.e. Botany Bay. In fact the landing wasn't actually in Botany Bay and as Flannery explains Port Jackson was chosen as the main settlement because there was a need for the ships to be safe from the open sea and Botany Bay as Cook had pointed out, was not suitable for a settlement because of the lack of a decent harbour. Thus it was that Phillip decided to explore the potential of Port Jackson:

'On the 22nd January they set out on this expedition, and early in the afternoon arrived at Port Jackson, which is distant about three leagues. Here all regret arising from the former disappointments was at once obliterated; and Governor Phillip had the satisfaction to find one of the finest harbours in the world, in which a thousand of the line might ride in perfect security.'

And now the fun started. By mid 1700's Britain, along with the Dutch, French, Spanish and Portuguese, was looking to expand its tentacles globally to protect its trade. Where we took possession then in most cases the feelings of the locals was pretty much secondary (and in many cases these were the other colonial would be masters of the universe such as the French in India). However, with Australia as no other major sea-faring nation had laid claim, Britain went further in a brilliant piece of imaginative law-making because the Continent was claimed by the British Crown under full sovereignty using a new law to suit their purpose called 'terra nullius' (literally no man's land) which effectively said that until we appeared there was no one else who lived here. In effect they simply did not exist legally. It's quite an interesting approach to take really and for the Aboriginals, well they must have been somewhat puzzled by all this. They'd all gotten out of bed that morning, eaten their breakfast and wondered to the Bay for a spot of fishing only to find all of a sudden some bewigged chap, Captain Collins, holding a scroll and paper and, as recorded at the time and quoted by Keneally:

> 'As Phillip stood by, Captain Collins read aloud the documents signed by King George III and his cabinet which empowered Philip in New South Wales. Waves of august language rose and perched like birds in the tree: George III by the Grace of God, King of Britain, France and Ireland "to our trusty and well-beloved Arthur Phillip, Esquire". Never had a more exceptional claim of territory been uttered than in this commission ... and heard without comprehension by the no doubt observant Cadigal and Wangal clans of the area.'

And what the British had decided to have was, as Keneally goes on to point out the equivalent to declaring everything:

> ' ... from the Tagus River in Portugal to Trondheim in Norway. The claim also extended to all the country westward ... a greater distance than London to Moscow ... '

It still puzzles me to this day how the Western powers at the time exhibited such incredible arrogance and felt that they owned the world and that all else, that is peoples of the lands they looked to conquer and claim, were mere tools to be used. However, when reading the stories of the Conquistadors in South America or the British and French colonialists in North America, two things always come across: the West had the means to exact whatever it wanted due to superior weaponry and invariably the arrival of these strangers led to a massive increase in deaths of the indigenous people through disease. In Australia some estimate that as much as 50% of the indigenous people in and around the colony were dead within the first decade or so of the arrival of the First Fleet. It is very sobering stuff.

Australia could well have been a French colony as when Captain Phillip arrived a small fleet under Admiral La Perouse arrived at pretty much the same time. Just think on arriving at Sydney airport I might have been greeted with: "Bonjour, copain" instead of "G'day mate"! Perhaps that's one to keep to myself and not remind any Australian I would meet, or even an American for that matter. The name Australia has both a Latin and Dutch origin but it was not until 1824 that the Admiralty in London officially approved the name, even though it had been championed by Matthew Flinders as he explored much of the coast of Australia in the first decade of the 1800's trying to get it changed. However, back in London the Admiralty refused to change the name so that until then it was known either as New Holland or just New South Wales.

Of course the first explorers also loved naming places after benefactors or themselves and there are plenty of places that will tell you who this was such as the Torres Straits or Tasmania, the latter being named after Abel Tasman. Cook though was in a class of his own and much of the east coast is named after geographical features such as bays, brush or mountains like the Glasshouse Mountains in Queensland so named as they reminded Cook of the glass making chimneys in the Black Country back in England. I did read elsewhere that there is another possible reason that they were named this and that was because of the reflection from the sun on them when he was anchored in Moreton Bay. It must have been quite fun to be able to do that and one wonders what sort of thought process he went through, or did he have a book '100 top names for new Continents'?

On names, imagine if the Dutch had actually decided to set foot and claim it for themselves? There'd be names that required a great deal of throat clearing and spitting to pronounce them whilst at the same time the whole continent would be permanently swathed by a smog of weed and ladies of the night would be in legal abundance; well I mean have you ever been to Amsterdam? Speaking of names what in hell's teeth were the Pennsylvanian Dutch, the Amish, doing when they named two of their towns Intercourse and Blue Ball. I can just imagine that discussion between two stalwarts of this highly religious and upright community:

21

"So Brother Hans, what shall we name this town?"

"Well, Brother Cain, I was thinking that as I had great carnal knowledge with Sister Martha last night, so we should call it Intercourse in celebration."

"Well yes I suppose, It has a certain directness about it — what should we call the other town?"

"Ah I have thought of that as well. You know when it gets really, really cold and your lips, hands and feet turn blue."

"Err, yes."

"Well let's call it Blue Ball."

"Not shrivelled dick?"

"What! Do you take me for a pervert? Now where's that sheep?"

There's also a town called Beaver but I'm sure you can work out that Hans was probably responsible for that as well.

On naming things in Australia it was a habit, as Bill Bryson pointed out in his book 'Down Under', amongst the first explorers or men of substance that there would be a proliferation of places, rivers, mountains etc that would bear their name. It's fortunate that Captain Cook didn't get the bug to name everywhere after himself otherwise the 2,000 odd miles of coast he mapped might look rather the same on a map. In fact I only went to one town named after Cook and drive on one road, respectively Cooktown in North East Queensland and the Cook Highway in the same area. Equally there are a number places that are named as a descriptive of the place involved. By way of an example Mount Disappointment was so named by the explorers Hulme and Hovell who had hoped upon climbing the then unnamed mountain to see Port Phillip Bay but couldn't due to the trees and thus came up with the name, all very logical. Each state has a plethora of these names. I wonder what Koolyanobbing in Western Australia, Cock Wash in South Australian, Fannie Bay in the Northern Territory, Watanobbi in New South Wales and, by far the best Mount Buggery in Victoria (yes it really does exist at latitude −36 54 and longitude 146 45; I checked it on the website of Australian Geoscience), were named after? Alright so Koolyanobbing is actually an Aboriginal word meaning 'large hard rocks', but even translated it is slightly amusing.

Australia it always seems to be when I hear or read about it hot and sunny, a far cry from what seems to becoming a regular occurrence in the

UK of dull and wet summers (we went to Northern Ireland in August once to see the wife's relatives: we arrived in the rain and left in the rain without a break). So it was with a light heart and high anticipation, that I disembarked the plane on a slightly cloudy day. Never mind it'll be sunny tomorrow and the next day and so on. Being English though I have with a certain amount of justification I think a belief that bad weather and I are soul mates. Not this time though, this was Australia, land of the sun, the barbie and the stubby. Once through passport control (and not having my passport stamped more of which at the end) and having collected my case which I was relieved to see came out first, it was into a cab and off to the city. Almost to the second that the cab pulled away from the curb down it came. Here I was around the other side of the world and it was raining. Glad I packed just t-shirts and shorts. It really didn't help that the cabbie cheerfully remarked that this was the first day in a while it had rained and only yesterday it was 38 degrees and sunny.

I arrived at my hotel and checked in. The hotel was in the centre of the business district near the Circular Quay and the room, for an extra 150 zillion dollars per night, overlooked (with a bit of neck straining) the Sydney Opera House, situated at Bennelong Point. There's an interesting story on how this building comes about and one that is perhaps a warning that visionaries and politics do not mix. The idea to build it was thought of as early as the late 1940's by Eugene Gossens who was both the conductor of the Sydney Symphony Orchestra as well as being the director of the NSW Conservatorium of Music, although it is not until 1973 that the first 'official' concert is played (a performance of Beethoven's Symphony No. 9). Controversy dogged almost every stage of the development including Gossen's fall from grace when it was found on returning from a European trip that he had adult material in his luggage to the original designer leaving in a bit of a huff. The New South Wales government had put the whole project to a design competition and of the 233 entries the winner was a Dane, Joern Utzon. Utzon was a visionary but his ideas caused some consternation given that many of the design features were in every sense new, notably the shell-like parabolas, had never been tried before (the engineers took over 5 years to get them built), although his supporters emphasized that he was 'pushing forward the frontiers of the construction industry'. The costs ballooned and Utzon was effectively shown the door, although the fact that the design had been altered significantly left him feeling the finished article was no longer his. There is a wonderful description of the finished article which came from Beverley Nichols, the Australian writer, who on being asked about the Sydney Opera House replied:

' … [it] looks as if were something that had crawled out of the sea and was up to no good.'

The site where the Sydney Opera House is has a history of its own and revolves around an Aboriginal who is one of the most famous as regards the history of the First Fleet and the indigenous people. As the City of Sydney's Barani History of the Indigenous People explains:

'Bennelong, born c. 1764 of the Wangal people, is one of the most notable Aboriginal people in the early history of Australia. Also known as Wolarwaree, Ogultroyee and Vogeltroya, he was one of the first to live with the settlers, to be "civilised" into the European way of life and to enjoy its "benefits".'

Along with Yemmerrawanyea he too went to England and became a celebrity for a while, only to return to Australia and eventually die a broken man whose only comfort was the bottle. The more I looked into it and discussed it with those I met on my travels the more intrigued I became as to how attitudes had changed not least given the way that he was treated as almost a curio (according to the Barani History 'Much of the profile of Bennelong has been created by the writings of Judge Advocate David Collins … and Captain Watkin Tench … ' and 'They viewed him as an experiment in 'softening, enlightening and refining a barbarian'). And as if that wasn't bad enough, in death, Bennelong who historians today agree had tried to bridge the cultural and social divide (he'd even managed to avert a potentially lethal altercation between the indigenous people and the settlers after Governor Phillip was speared), was largely derided in death. The Sydney Morning Herald in July 1927 reproduced the story of him and when he died at Kissing Point in January 1813 the announcement of his demise in some ways summed up very succinctly not just what the white man thought of Bennelong but also of the indigenous people, something that endured for nearly two hundred years:

' … The principal Officers of Government had for many years endeavoured, by the kindest of usage to wean him from his original habits, and draw him into a relish for civilized life ; but every effort was in vain exerted, and for the last few has been little noticed. His propensity to drunkedness (*sic*) was inordinate; and when in that state he was insolent, menacing and overbearing. In fact he was a thorough savage, not to be warped from the form and character that nature gave him, by all the efforts that mankind could use.'

The Sydney Opera House has been the setting for many great events since its opening but there was one recently that was to say the least unusual. As I was looking into the Beenelong story in more detail in the wee small hours I thought, as I hit upon the BBC World News website, that it was April Fool's Day as I read that this iconic building was the setting to what was described by the singer Laurie Anderson as 'an inter-species gathering on a scale never seen before in Australia'. This turned out to be a concert for dogs using a cacophony of noises from whale sounds to violins. The report ends with this sentence from Anderson on being asked about what she felt said that ' … it was one of the best moments of her career'. No one knows if the dogs enjoyed it but a lot of dry humping of legs was reported.

After a short sleep, it was time to explore and I made my way to the most important part of any journey I undertake, that of finding the local bottle shop/liquor store/off license. Beer is essential when travelling and no matter where I go it is always the first thing I seek out. I am so shallow aren't I? I am not a big fan of just any beer – my taste buds are more susceptible to real ales or cider rather than lagers, given that the latter are: a) often drunk by men with Alice bands in the hair and who talk about only three things – cars, women and football; b) drunk in halves by the little lady on a night out (although nowadays I am not so sure about this). To be fair I do drink the stuff but only when eating a curry and only when I am beyond caring what it is I have in the glass in front of me as long as it says 4.8% alcohol by volume or more. This volume measure is also essential for me to know if a wine is good or not and I'd recommend 13%.

In respect of Australian beers my impression of Australian beer was that it was pretty much just Fosters, Castlemaine and VB (this is Australia's only true national beer which at its peak was around 25% of all beers drunk but has recently seen a decline to near 15% as micro brews have seen sales increase) and which collectively, to me, seem quite bland much like the mass produced beer in America that I'd avoided where possible. I only knew one English style ale called Coopers, which I'd tasted for the first time in Edinburgh a couple of years ago. Not knowing which to have I asked the shop assistant, Mike, and we got talking about what Australians tend to like drinking. In terms of the more commonly drunk beers (more lager in texture than real ale) he suggested that the best way to enjoy these was to first bring the beer can/bottle to near freezing point as it was the buzz from the bubbles and coldness that was enjoyed and not so much the taste, given that in respect of the latter there was none. I like beer cold but I do want to have a zing in my mouth afterwards so these were not going to work. However, on one shelf were stacked a number of Australian real ales and following his recommendation I purchased a six pack of a local brew called Lord Nelson Three Sheets. He also suggested that I should visit the pub where this was brewed, which for me sounded a good idea as it was an historic building, not too far from the hotel and most importantly served beer. History and beer at the same time, perfect!

It does seem to depend on where you live in Australia and as to what is drunk but I was pleased to see that micro brewers were gaining ground, although as Mike intimated it tended to be in the more metropolitan areas where incomes were higher and new immigrants with less traditional appetites settled. I have a strong liking for beers that are brewed by small producers not just because these beers tend to have much more care put into their production but also because they invariably have completely whacky names. When I lived in the US in Boston in the mid 1990's I used to knock back beers with wonderful names like Flying Dog, Smutty Nose, Loon, Harpoon, Black Mountain and so on, which were, as in Australia, usually regional, but very drinkable. Just on the convention that applies to naming beers, hats off to all those responsible for them. For me the best beer names seem most associated with real ale. I mean you can't fault names such as those in the UK like Dog's Bollocks and Fox's Nob, the latter a big seller in the hunting and shooting fraternity.

Having deposited the beer back in my room I had a look around Circular Quay. This is the main point for commuter ferries coming in from the outlying districts like Manley. Packed with commuters it was nice to watch them knowing that I for once was not one. The area contains a number of bars, restaurants and shops that all looked pretty pricey. There were the inevitable tourist booths that are a feature of any City or place where visitors are in plentiful supply. The booths were offering whale watching (something in my two years living in Boston, which is a prime spot for this, I'd always meant to do but never did), cycling (guided/ unguided) or harbour cruises. I walked on to take a closer look at with a mind to visit the Sydney Opera House. It could be that as I had arrived in Sydney not long after the city had been hit by a huge all enveloping red dust cloud some of which remained on the roof it was not as pristine as it could have been. Maybe I was just in the wrong frame of mind because it did absolutely nothing for me. I didn't even bother going in. I'm sure, or rather know, that for many it is interesting (one of my Australian friends thought I was nuts for not doing so) but for me it somewhat reminded me of the Barbican in London. The Barbican was built right in the heart of London on what had been a bomb site as both a place to live and also to enjoy the arts but for me it looks like a huge lump of concrete with no saving graces. In 2003 it was apparently voted 'London's ugliest building' in a Grey London poll.

I headed back towards the Sydney Harbour Bridge and came across the Campbell Storehouses, built in the 1830's, where ships from the Empire would load and unload their cargoes of victuals. Today, if you pay a small fortune, you can enjoy what I've no doubt is some very good food in the restaurants that now exist here. The area behind these warehouses is well preserved with many old buildings especially along George Street. Here the architecture is a mix of Georgian, Victorian, Edwardian and more modern buildings, but it seems with an emphasis on keeping some character. It was all very quaint but not surprisingly with in keeping with those parts of a city that are tourist 'traps' and the shops and cafes were expensive. No matter I wasn't here to buy anything and besides my stomach was grumbling loudly "Feed me!" so I repaired to a pleasant looking cafe for some nose bag. I was about to experience Australian service in all its glory.

You might be a bit puzzled by this comment but let me explain. I'd been told by some of the Antipodeans I knew in London that cafe service in Australia was not a hurried affair, but instead should be seen as part of the culture pertinent to the Continent, a flavour of the country and their approach to life in general. Fair enough, I was all up for that; when in Rome and all that. I sat down and promptly ordered my lunch. I say ordered, but the reality was that I rehearsed my order five maybe six times to myself whilst looking simultaneously in the direction of Belinda who was propping herself up at the order counter talking to her friend Brian who'd come in for a what was looking like just a chat, willing her to come over and take my order. The minutes passed and it seemed like an eternity was passing. Now, being English I am used to the service back home: it is invariably quick although a smile requires a Herculean effort, but no matter as I can be in and out of a cafe in good time, well fed and watered. It is a function and not a way of life in London. So here I was, stomach now protesting ever more loudly, in a cafe with just myself and Belinda and her friend Brian and then Meg who'd appeared from the kitchen, because that's how busy she was, and who now joined in the conversation they were having. I felt a sense of awkwardness begin to build up. What should I do? Should I get up, march over to the service counter, bang my fist on the top and enquire loudly as to the whereabouts of my order? Should I just leave and as I do so glare menacingly at the serving staff to show my disapproval of them? Maybe they were talking about me, playing a psychological game and seeing whether I'd crack and just start to beg them for food whilst apologising profusely for being English. I opted to just sit there and wait for my order to be taken which when it happened was a full twenty minutes after I'd arrived and sat down. The food's arrival took another eternity, but you know what, after all that when asked how everything was I responded "Lovely thank you" and when Belinda sort of apologised for the long wait, I said "Not to worry, I'm in no hurry", which of course was completely the opposite to how I actually felt. In all, this lunchtime feast took just shy of an hour, but little did I know that my experience today was bordering on 'fast' in terms of service, because the further I was from the large towns and cities, so life took on a whole new dimension such that the only time warp speed was ever heard was on repeats of Star Trek.

After lunch I continued my wondering this time towards the Bridge itself. The structure is fantastic and going beneath it and looking up at all the iron lattice work was almost mesmerizing. You can walk up to the top of the bridge with a guide, but that wasn't for me. I am not good with heights and the thought of ascending the walkway gave me the collywobbles. I had read the story behind the Bridge before I flew to Australia and in the Rocks Discovery Museum I looked at a photo montage from the turning of the first sod in 1925, through to its completion. The whole affair was hugely impressive, not least as the granite for the bridge came from the Eurobodalla country which is some way south of Sydney, and was transported by steamer from a town created for all the stonemasons called, imaginatively, Granitetown.

The Bridge itself was opened in 1932 and the story that went with it is both amusing and yet at the same time an aspect of Australian political life that has in one form or another continued to bubble under the surface. On the day in question huge crowds had gathered to watch the ceremony and listen to the speeches of various dignitaries. Just as the premier of New South Wales, Jack Lang, was about to cut the ribbon, he was beaten to it by Captain Francis de Groot who rushed forward on his horse and, wielding a sword, slashed the ribbon in two. Although this may seem to be the action of someone with a seriously unhinged personality (and initially this is what they tried to accuse him off later) it did have political undertones as de Groot was a member of a right-wing group, the New Guard which had strong fascist undertones and that was vehemently opposed to the perceived 'Red menace' as well as the Labor government led by Lang who was viewed by the Right as a communist stooge. My own completely unsubstantiated theory is as follows: de Groot was a bit bored listening to some puffed up local dignitary whining on about how this and that was going to be a major this and that to the community and that it was all down to the forward thinking politicians of the day that this was all achieved. Whatever the cause (and I emphasise my theory has yet to be proven) it probably added to the day's excitement and must have really upset the nominated tape cutter. No doubt they were an ornamental pair of scissors made especially for this occasion that even now his grandchildren are looking at and thinking how much more they'd have been worth on eBay if they'd actually been used. As for de Groot he was fined a fiver for his role. Although this was nearly 80 years ago, talk of the communist menace, Menzies' so called 'Yellow Peril' didn't go away completely although today the issue for some more nationalistic Australians seems more to do with a loss of their identity. No one I spoke to in my six weeks expressed any of these views to me personally and I suspect that it has more to do with a small but at times vocal minority.

The area around this part of the Bridge has a number of historic buildings. The Rocks gets its name from the rocky nature of the area and was one of the first areas in Sydney to be settled. The original inhabitants of not just the Rocks but of what is now called Sydney were the Cadigal people, who were part of the Darug nation. Tom Kenneally describes what the impact of the First Fleet would have on this almost idyllic existence:

'But their [the Cadigal] good fortune had passed. For longer than any other population of *homo sapiens,* the ancestors of the Aboriginals were genetically and culturally cocooned from the rest of the world, and were right to suspect the freight of these ships. Phillip's sailors, soldiers and convicts were walking incubators for viruses and bacteria barely before present on this coast. These micro-organisms too were looking for a new landfall and had the power to descend upon and mar the planet as known and cherished by the coastal clans.'

Today the Rocks is a genteel area of the City and one brimming with life from its restaurants and pubs to the rather splendid market I stumbled across later that evening, It's hard to believe that it had by the early19th century become home to a burgeoning underworld of criminality and poverty. As the century progressed so it continued to deteriorate prompting the well-to-do and law abiding to leave such that by the end of the century it was home to the most notorious slum in Australia, 'Frog Hollow'. There is an interesting parallel here with London because there was a similar pattern there whereby the rich moved west as the criminal class moved into what had been a more genteel east end. The nadir came in 1900 when plague broke out, although there is a debate still as to whether it was home grown or not (the lady in the Rocks Museum I asked said that in all probability it came via one of the many ships that docked in the wharves) but whatever it was it prompted the town's leaders to do something about the state of the area.

So today, looking around the Rocks, many of these buildings are actually 'modern' having replaced the slums of before. However, they, along with George Street, give this whole part of Sydney a more relaxed and unhurried feel. It is like walking back in time but where the modern is never far away. Although Melbourne has the oldest imported building, George Street, which appears on maps as early as 1791, has the oldest house in Australia built by Europeans, Cadman's Cottage (1816) which is a museum now (it was home to the convict John Cadman) which was a recommended visit not to be missed. Unfortunately no one told the museum that this was the case as it was shut and not open again until after I was to set off along the coast to Melbourne.

I continued on my way in the drizzle and soon came to the Garrison Church. The church, also known as Holy Trinity, was, not surprisingly, convict built and is quite a small structure but was the first in Australia constructed in this style. It was begun in 1840 and the foundation stone was laid by the first Anglican Bishop, William Grant. The church is dedicated to those who gave their lives fighting for queen, king and country. Down each side of the building are commemorative plaques remembering individuals of naval, army and air force units. Flags hang from the walls and the whole atmosphere is solemn. It is a thought that many of the early soldiers and sailors may originally been from convict stock or, especially in the case of the Irish, having left home to find a better life or get away from famine. Many who served were not necessarily doing it out of loyalty to the Crown. The character of the 'Digger' in the film 'Gallipoli' is not hard to find in the histories written up about the Australian other ranks' total disregard for their officers (unless you earned their respect) and their greater loyalty to their mates and Australia.

In his book 'Gallipoli' Andrew Moorehead recalls one such example. Following a particularly bloody phase of the initial battle the two sides agreed to talk about having a truce so that the dead could be removed and given a decent burial. This was no small meeting involving just the odd adjutant or two, but Mustapha Kemal the Turks' main man and some of his staff along with General Birdwood, the Allies' main man and his staff. As they were talking in a tent discussing practicalities a head popped around the flap belonging to a Digger and said:

"Have any of you bastards got my kettle?"

There is another fascinating short story taken from 'The Rebel Chorus' by Geoff Hocking about another person who gave their life but who also epitomized this attitude but in a different way, albeit 'bloody-minded'. His name was John Simpson Kirkpatrick and he was originally from the North East of England, a Geordie, who had ended up in Australia having been a merchantman who, having had enough, jumped ship. When the Great War broke out he enlisted and in 1915 was with the ANZAC's at

Gallipoli. His physique made him an ideal stretcher bearer and although he didn't work with anybody else he did have his donkeys. No matter the shells and bullets exploding around him and donkeys being killed he persevered to bring in the wounded. Almost inevitably he was killed, but here's the kicker. The top brass refused to award him a VC or any medal because it had been in the incorrectly applied for. Lions led by donkeys?

One thing I noticed as well which I came across in a number of other places was that the memorial tablets in the church for the those conflicts from the Boer War onwards contained the names of not just those who had died as is common in the UK but also those who had served in the various conflicts. In the case of the dead this was indicated with an asterisk or cross next to their name. I found this rather touching in that it showed a much greater sense of community, of that Australian 'mate', of togetherness. That's not to say that just commemorating the dead is wrong of course but it does seem to show Australians are as a nation much more open about recognizing everyone's contribution which seems to me right.

I came out of the church and walked north past a pub called the Hero of Wellington built in 1844, which according to my guidebook was reputedly used by smugglers in the 19th century via a tunnel from the pub to the harbour and was also a favourite for those friendly people in the local press gang ("Fancy a short cruise young man, full board and lodging included: now just look the other way while I thump you over the head"). I looked in and was depressed to see nothing particularly historic about the interior, unless the pokies (slot machines) were antiques. I was to discover on my travels that pokies were as common as mustard, but then according to the World Gambling Review in 2009 'The average Aussie will lose about $1,000 (US $679) on gambling each year. This means that Australians lose more money per adult at gambling than any other group on the planet. This number has increased 2 ½ times over the last 25 years. In fact, more money is spent on gambling than on sporting, cultural or entertainment events.' One of the oldest forms of gambling in Australia which is illegal in public is the game of 'Two-up'. Apparently it is a simple game, with its origins some say dating from the game of 'pitch and toss' from the time of the gold rush (some note that as early as the late 18th century a form of the game was played), where two coins are tossed into the air and the gamble is to call the outcome. It is I understand only legal in public on ANZAC day and was only legalised in casinos in 1973 initially in Hobart via a 'Two-up school'. The undercurrent of conservatism that my Australian friends say still exists may have a lot to do with this.

It was still raining but I was damned if I was going to go back to the hotel so carried on back towards George Street. From there I went to the Royal Botanical Gardens which were created in 1816 and 'provides for a pleasant walking experience' (so said my brochure). In fact before it became this it was more famous as being the first area in Australia to be cultivated by the settlers and originally had the name Farm Cove. The area itself covers quite a large area (around 34 hectares) and within this there is quite a lot to see – especially if you are into a bit of flora hunting. Unfortunately for you gardeners out there I know very little about what plants or trees are called outside of knowing what a daffodil is or a fir. That didn't matter though because as I walked around there were signs that told me what I was looking at. All over the gardens there are also markers that gave me a little insight into the history of the place such as the first garden in the colony and the remains of what is called the Macquarie Wall that was built to separate the Domain from the rest of the garden. This wall has its origins before the Royal Botanical Gardens in that it was started by Governor Bligh (yes him again) to stop people encroaching on the area where his residence was. Originally this meant there were in effect two parts to the gardens and the area that now surrounds the old Government House was called the inner Domain and the rest the outer Domain.

It is interesting that even with this barrier the very fact that there was a garden that all could enjoy was a much more enlightened approach to living together than that back in Britain. Governor Macquarie, like his predecessor but one, is seen by many historian as having a large dose of social awareness in the way that he saw those who were transported as people who should be allowed a second chance. It was he who encouraged convicts to become honest citizens and to turn over a new leaf. It was partly because of this that by 1821 he had to return in disgrace on some trumped up charges of abusing his privileges (the John Bigge enquiry: this also looked into how the colony was then faring from the perspective of the impact of released convicts). In reality he had upset not just some of the new entrenched interests, including those who had become very rich through either being members of the New South Wales

Corps (membership led to awards of land) or having powerful friends in London who saw any change in the status of the lower class as definitely not acceptable, especially if they had been transported to serve out a sentence.

Today the Domain is better known as a recreational area but in the past it has witnessed cricket matches in the mid 1800's, military ceremonial events, anti-conscription demonstrations (1915), anti-fascists rallies (1935), the launch of the Labor Party's 1975 political programme, the Sydney Festival, a speakers corner similar to Hyde Park back in London and, here's the really exciting bit, it was nearly the venue to accommodate the Spice Girls' 2008 world tour. .

As I was in no hurry I wondered slowly around, starting off in the rose garden, then on to the rare and endangered plants area, past the Cadi Jam Ora which tells of the struggle of the local Aboriginal tribe, the Cadigal, as they dealt with the new arrivals. At the top end towards the Bay is Mrs. Macquarie's point. This is home to Mrs. Macquarie's chair which is really a bench carved out of the side of the hill. She was the wife of Governor Lachlan Macquarie who was appointed in 1806. As is the case with anything that is highlighted in tourists brochures as one of those 'must see' sights the bench itself was surrounded (well not quite surrounded as you can only face on to it but you get my drift) by Japanese tourists clicking away and doing the V for victory sign. I have never understood why they do this but I am sure one day it'll be clear. As is usual when the Japanese are on holiday there are some specific things that I've noticed (and I don't mean this disrespectfully):

They all have cameras. I know it's a cliché but it is absolutely true. I walk past Buckingham Palace in London on my way to work and am sure that I am now in at least a dozen Mr. and Mrs. Watanabe's holiday snaps. Next time I must remember to smile. It's also a fact that they photograph everything. When I was in Melbourne later on my travels there was a young lady snapping pictures of designer shop signs. Hey, if that floats your boat why not! Also:

- The women of advanced years all seem to wear these rather large sun hats, the ones with a sun visor that looks like it has been stretched. Now I am sure again that this is entirely practical but forgive me for saying this but they do look ridiculous.

- There are at least 2 or 3 that still believe wearing Burberry is a fashion statement. I have nothing against the brand and I am sure that it looks very nice to some, but for me it does conjure up two images: the first is that slightly ageing but doesn't want to age lady from the sunnier parts of Europe and the second is the feral teenagers that blight our country.

- There is always a guide with her (I have never seem a male guide) umbrella. This is better than a badge I know but, and again forgive me for saying this, but the Japanese as a nation aren't, how shall I put it, that near to the sky. If a crowd of lanky westerners appeared, would they be able to see the umbrella?

- There is always a bus nearby. It seems to me, and again I can only really talk about London here, that they only do 'speed sightseeing' which entails getting on and off a bus all day, taking a few (well actually lots) of happy snaps and then repeating it all over again in a different location. Mad but I guess if it allows you to see everything good luck.

- The men seem to chain smoke. It is not just the Japanese of course. It seems every Asian man be they Korean, Singaporean, Indonesian etc has a strong affinity to nicotine and just to be balanced on this, the entire population of France, Spain, Portugal and Italy are seemingly born with a cigarette perched precariously between their lips.

The gardens overlook the Bay within which is sited Fort Denison which was built to house convicts shortly after the arrival of the First Fleet. If you go down to the Portsmouth in the south of England and look out into the Solent, you will see a number of forts called 'Martello Towers'. These were built at the time of the Napoleonic wars and were meant to act as a line of defence against any French attempt to invade England. In geographic terms the French were 50 or so miles away with a powerful fleet in the English Channel so you can understand the rationale. But here I was around the other side of the world and there in the bay was this fort, a Martello Tower. Napoleon's navy chief would have been pretty poor at navigating the English Channel if he'd brought the French fleet here on his way to Dover.

As I continued walking around the smells became captivating, a mixture of sweet aromas coming from the blossoms as well as ground such that my olfactory senses were finding it difficult to cope and I have a very large nose so you can see the problem. A small sign directed me off the stone path which took me through a small rainforest which emerged in the area that is the habitat of the grey headed flying fox, which is actually a rather unpleasant bat. They look cuddly but there was a sign that stated in no uncertain terms that these animals were not to be fed and if they bit you then you should seek medical assistance or contract rabies, whichever you preferred. Choices, choices, don't you just hate them!

On the other side of the gardens is Government House which has its origins in 1837 and was added to throughout the next 40 years. Looking at it I could just as easily have thought that I was at some grand country house in the home country. It was the seat of the Governor for many years and added to as successive ones took over. Unfortunately, I had chosen the wrong day to try to visit it from the inside as it was closed. Although it is no longer the seat of power (it was 'closed' in 1996 amongst much angst for those in Sydney who felt it an affront to the Crown after 151 years) it is used as a place of entertainment for such things as state occasions. The gardens here are dotted with trees that some Very Important People had planted from European Queens to Heads of States.

I have always been slightly bemused when I see photographs of someone like this in the paper with such booming headlines as 'King Rupert IV of Ruritania planting a tree to cement the bonds of friendship between his people and those of the peoples of Australia'. There's a tree in the part of the garden that is close to the Bay itself planted by HM Queen Elizabeth II when she landed in Sydney from the royal yacht. I bet she was thrilled to get off the royal yacht, have a spade shoved in her hand and then made to plant a tree dedicated to something or someone or even just her. Here's another thing whilst I am on this subject: what do they do with the spade that she has used? It's always in mint condition; do they let her keep it as some sort of memento like some kind of 'Kiss me Quick!' hat that you get from the seaside? Maybe she is a collector with a secret stash that will one day be put to use when the UK becomes a republic and then she can become a purveyor of fine quality spades, by appointment of course.

I spent a good couple of hours wondering around before making my way to the next port of call – the Justice and Punishment Museum. My guide book said it was 'well worth a visit' and that it 'contained many images of the criminals' and, which excited me the most, it promised to be a bit ghoulish. So I wandered over past the Conservatorium of Music which is housed in what were the stables for Government House. With a spring in my step and a light heart I crossed the busy Cahill Expressway and after a few attempts at getting my bearings I found it. From the outside it looked rather fun, housed as it is in the old court house. Up the steps in a couple of bounds to the entrance with my dollars ready; it was closed. So far I had been in Sydney for less than a day and three of the places I wanted to see were closed.

All was not lost though as my guidebook recommended another place of interest to the budding historian called the Hyde Park Barracks. This walk had two advantages in that it allowed me to walk up Macquarie Street and pass the magnificent Victorian buildings that line its side – the state library of New South Wales, the old parliament house, the old Sydney hospital and the New South Wales historical society housed in the Mint. Outside the hospital stands a magnificent bronze boar, Il Porcellino, which was donated in the late 1960's and is a replica of a statue back in Florence. It is supposed to bring you luck if you rub it. I always feel slightly self-conscious when I come across these sorts of things like wishing wells or lucky fountains. Do I partake or not? What should I wish for? What about all those germs? Being the generous sort I walked on and pretended that I had no money by patting my pockets frantically, just in case anyone was looking and thinking that I might be a tight bastard, which I am of course.

The Barracks are another Macquarie building. According to the blurb that you get once you have parted with your money, the Barracks were built between 1817 and 1819 by the very people who would occupy them – convicts. And who was the designer for the Barracks? Yes he too was a convict, Francis Greenway, which takes me back to that view about a sort of redemption to those who made an effort.

The Barracks contained everything to house and administer to the needs of the 600 or so convicts that could at any one time live there (some 15,000 passed through in the next 20 odd years). Originally a rather lonely building (within the Barracks there are models showing them from their beginnings to the later Victorian period), it in fact had kitchens, storerooms, cells and even apartments for those tasked with overseeing the convicts.

The Barracks were a great way to spend time and learn about not just the first inmates but also the evolution of what this place was used for once transportation had ended. On the top floor there was an exhibit that focused on the first occupiers, the convicts. I was alone on the top floor and it felt peculiarly weird. Here I was wondering around looking at where the men slept in hammocks (so close together you could easily touch the person next to you), reading about some of those who had been transported here represented by silhouetted characters looking ghostly in the half-light, knowing that this must have been a place of unquestionable hardship and yet for me it was 'just a tourist' site. In the dormitory two things struck me apart from the closeness of the hammocks. The first was that in the summer when it can get really hot it must have been stifling, not least as the ventilation system from what I could see was almost zero. The smell and just general filth must have been terrible, and having been to boarding school myself, although not nearly as bad of course as here, putting 'x' number of males in one room is a pretty unpleasant event.

The second thing that struck me was that the room had surveillance holes in built into the walls. Now, the most obvious thing that springs to mind is that these were put in to keep an eye on the convicts in order that nothing untoward happened, after all violence amongst them was not uncommon. However, I was told that there was another reason and this was to stop the inmates from, how shall I put it, playing mummies and daddies but usually where one of the participants was less than willing. On a more serious point the act of sodomy was seen as one of the worst depravities almost on a par with murder but was prevalent throughout the penal settlements and something that those in power wanted to stamp out. It was referred to in Latin as 'peccatum illud horribile, non Christianos non nominandum', or in English 'that horrible crime not to be named amongst Christians', but as Hughes points out it wasn't just the Establishment who despised it:

> ' … In the eyes of the law, sodomy deserved death; but in the eyes of social custom, especially the customs of the English and Irish working people, it was more than ordinarily loathsome.'

He goes on to say though that any serious analysis of what was going on had to wait until the 1830's when the whole matter of transportation was being debated by which time there were those that argues that it did no good and in fact added to the criminality and those that argued the contrary. There is a sense in the barracks though of the dreadfulness of existence with each convict having not just to look out for the warders but also for his or her fellow prisoner not least given the age of some of these people. Looking around this room it just felt so wretched.

The next part of the history of the building was equally depressing. The great Irish potato famine of the mid 1840's had seen many leave that blighted land. Most were poor and had little to their names but through sheer desperation looked for a new life that was better than the one they had. The second floor covered these people and specifically the women who came, either on their own or, upon arrival, separated from their men folk. In the show cabinets were reminders of how little these women had, from their meagre possessions to the almost hopelessness of their situation. Free yes, but in reality they were no freer than the indentured servants who first settled in the American colonies but with a big difference. The indentured servant worked towards paying for his or her freedom and thus no longer beholden to the master. These women, and looking at the stories many were not even adults, were it seemed to me slaves in all but name. They would have had to have taken whatever job was on offer, and given the times, they would have had little or no say in what this was. Women, as in so many other countries had few real rights and were second class citizens and it was not until towards the middle of the second half of the 19th century that women's voices began to be heard calling for equal rights through formidable women like Catherine Spence.

What I hadn't realised, though, was that in comparison to where these women had come from (and here the majority would have been from Europe) where women had no right to vote, save Sweden, that was not the case in Australia. In 1894 women in South Australia were granted the vote; in 1899 it was Western Australia, 1902 in New South Wales, 1903 in Tasmania, 1905 Queensland and finally in 1909 Victoria. Compare that to Switzerland where it was not until 1971 on a Federal level and for those women in the Swiss Canton of Appenzell Innerhoden it wasn't until 1990 but only after the Canton was forced to do so by the Federal Supreme Court!

But it was not just an immigration depot. By the 1860's it had also become an asylum for those who had become completely destitute or infirm. The Victorians were great moralists believing that it was society's duty to help those who were less fortunate. Altruistic perhaps and no doubt some genuinely felt that they were helping the less fortunate giving them a roof over their heads, educating their children and providing moral guidance through the church on a Sunday. However, you could equally see that for them a healthy and 'happy' workforce was an obliging workforce and thus disruption to production would not be an issue. I used to be slightly amused by the way that some of the workers lived: in a company house, in a company factory and then being paid tokens exchangeable only in a company shop. Victorians have always slightly puzzled me about their sense of what was or wasn't moral or acceptable. Top of my list of all time Victorian moralists would be none other than one of the 19th century's greatest Prime Ministers, William Ewart Gladstone who, it was said, used to invite 'fallen women' in for a chat. A chat about what exactly; maybe it was to discuss the cost of " … that'll be five guineas extra sir … "? Whatever it was he did live to a ripe old age and was PM shortly before he died so it must have been good for his health.

The final part of the Barrack's history is actually somewhat ironic. Having been the point of incarceration for convicts it was in 1887 converted into courts and government offices. The Museum brochure sums it all up:

> 'For more than 185 years the Barracks has had 50 different user groups, 28 of them legal or government departments.'

Outside the Barracks was another poignant exhibit although not easy to spot unless you have the guide. It is a simple yet moving memorial to the Irish potato famine represented by a number of bronze castings of people's belongings. The Barracks is an interesting biopic really of how the Colony develops and of who the people that were part of it came to be there. Although sanitized for the modern tourist I got a strong feel of the past and, deep down, a sort of sadness about what drove someone to leave home to find a new life only to end up no better off. Even the convicts, many of whom had been transported for the most minor of offences, must have felt an overwhelming sense of resignation knowing that in all likelihood they would never see their loved ones again. Maybe, and I am no psychologist, this is why some Australians today whose

40

ancestry this is, are so suited to living in the Outback where life can be pretty difficult or with the attitude so admirably demonstrated after the terrible fires in 2009 that killed so many and made hundreds homeless and just looking to start again with no self pity, just a thankfulness to be alive; admirable really.

Day two: November 5th

Having missed dinner the night before as a result of partaking of a couple of sharpeners followed by the 'I'll just have a quick nap' syndrome, I repaired once more down to Circular Quay for a bit of people watching over breakfast. The last thing I had done the night before was book myself onto a whale watching trip not because I really wanted to, but more because the only other thing that had appealed to me was a bike ride around the city that had worked out as a small mortgage in terms of cost, so I had an hour or so to kill before I had to board the boat. Oh and it was still raining.

I think 'people watching' is fascinating, especially if you are not in a hurry or just plain curious, and so I found myself a waterfront café, ordered my bargain breakfast (I am paying it off in instalments) and watched. The café was situated opposite one of the ferry terminals that service the outlying areas bringing in city workers and schoolchildren. I drank in the atmosphere looking at the names of places – Darling Harbour, Manly, Mosman, Watsons Bay, Parramatta, Neutral Bay, Balmain, Taronga Zoo and Woolwich – and wondering about the first Europeans who had settled there, why and what did they face when setting up homes. I can lose myself in time when in this mood and as I sipped my coffee wondered if they had had espresso machines back in 1788 would things have been easier?

The whale watching boat left from Circular Quay and thence to Cockle Bay to pick up some more punters and then out to sea towards Bondi beach. There weren't that many of us that actually boarded – the boat can take near a 100 passengers but I reckoned that we were maybe 20 in all, a mix of young and old. After picking up a few more at Cockle Bay (home to two of the ugliest hotels I have seen outside of France where this craving for a modernism and colours is a disease) we proceeded to the open sea.

At this point the first mate, John, came on the intercom, introducing himself and the crew as well as a whale expert from the University of

Macquarie. According to John she was the foremost authority on whales in this part of New South Wales; what she didn't know wasn't worth talking about. Also joining the crew was a character called 'Biggles' who was also a top whale spotter. The 'Expert' gave an introduction to what we were going to see this morning. The east coast of Australia is a main route for the humpback whale as it migrates down to the colder waters of the Antarctic to give birth and to mate. By law the boat has to be at least 100 metres from the whales and 300 metres if it is a calf. Having given us the introduction that was the last we heard from her as she busied herself with the sonar equipment and lunch. Still at least I now knew what is a permitted distance between a boat and a whale and I shall continue to use this when I'm back home, although as I live a good 8 kilometres from the sea, don't own a boat and am unlikely to encounter a whale even if I did, I'm not sure if I really will. But, as they say, it's always nice to know these things "just in case".

Once we got out the bay the water became somewhat choppy resulting in the retirement of two of our motley band who spent the next couple of hours revisiting breakfast. We sailed south towards Bondi and were told to keep an eye to the horizon to spot any jets of water from blow holes. Here's a little factoid about Bondi beach: 12% of all injuries are down to us, the British, a somewhat disproportionate amount but a statistic that makes me glow with pride: we are crap at surfing, sunbathing and anything beach related clearly which means we are actually quite good at being terrible. That I do believe is an achievement. John informed us excitedly that a mother and her calf had been spotted and that we were on track to see them. There was a buzz of anticipation amongst my fellow Captain Ahab's. Fingers were poised on cameras, a couple pointed animatedly to the horizon, the crew scurried about looking 'busy', John was calling the spotters and telling us that soon, very soon, we would see a whale.

We ploughed up and down, left to right, for hours it seemed and not one whale. Nothing; zip; rien; bugger all. Everyone's disappointment was palpable. However, John was not to be beaten by this (having told is that this never happens) and offered us all another free trip that afternoon as the chances of not seeing a whale at all were unheard of. So out we went again but this time we turned north towards Manly (named by Captain Phillip in honour of the way the local Aboriginals looked; methinks he may have been at sea without a lady for a tad too long). Of the original passengers only myself and one other had opted to go again; me because it had started to rain again and I didn't fancy walking around in it and he because he wanted to escape his wife who had bumped into a friend and wanted to talk about "the bloody grandchildren". On board also was a young couple visiting friends in the area who it turned out lived not a million miles from my village back in England close to where my rugby club is. You travel half around the world and end up meeting people who live 6 miles from you, go figure.

This trip was a little more successful and we did get to see two juvenile humpbacks albeit in the blink of an eye. We also saw a large number of flying fish which is simply too bizarre for me and a massive yellow tailed albatross, which got Biggles very excited to the extent that he could be seen talking animatedly to himself, or us, we weren't entirely sure. Now here's a queer thing. Not once did the sun shine, in fact not once did it do anything other than drizzle or rain, yet when I went back to my room my face resembled a somewhat ripe tomato. Now this could be down to a high level of unfitness or, as was more likely the case, I'd got sunburnt. This made me radically rethink my sun cream supply (I still expected that the sun would shine and all would be well with the world) from using a manly factor 12 to one that made much more sense which was factor spacesuit, also known as factor 30 and the lowest that can be acquired across the counter in Australia.

Refreshed and suitably 'after sunned' in the evening I decided that I would sample a pint or two of the local ale following the recommendation the day before about the Lord Nelson. Off I went back up to the Rocks, past the Garrison Church and arrived with a thirst at the pub. From the outside it reminded me of the type of building that you might see in the Cotswolds, having that similar large sandstone brickwork. Like the Hero of Waterloo this pub dates back to the 1830's but has less of the intrigue in terms of its history. Inside it was sparsely furnished but that didn't bother the clientele who were mostly city-types slipping in for a sharpener before going home. A far cry from the original regulars who would have been a mix of freed convicts and free settlers, along with soldiers and merchants.

The pub as mentioned brews its own beer and for me the choice was simple and that was a long, cool pint of ale.

"That'll be twelve dollars, please."

"Sorry?"

"That'll be twelve dollars please"

"But I only want a pint – I mean that's nearly eight pounds in English – I don't want to buy the place!"

Oh how we both laughed as I handed my money over with a sense of having been mugged in broad daylight. I drank that beer as if it were gold but there was absolutely no chance I was going to buy another. No way. On the plus side the six bottles of Lord Nelson's I had bought yesterday cost about half the price of a pint and these were cooling off nicely in my fridge back at the hotel. And if you're wondering it is a splendid ale and worth the cost.

I returned back down the hill and looked for somewhere to eat. I am not really a big fan of posh restaurants and so I looked for something that was simple. Around George Street there was a wide selection to choose from and I decided to go for Phillip Footes which offered a barbecue. Why not – it's Australia and this is what they do. On entering the restaurant I had to first buy my beer before ascending the steps to the barbecue area. This was a warning that I should have heeded in hindsight. Upstairs which was half under cover and half not, it was virtually empty I suspected due to the continuing rain, apart from a group of Japanese girls giggling away and two business types in deep discussion over a bottle of red. I went up to the meat counter and had a look; all sorts of meat cuts were on offer, from small to not so small. I was ravenous (whale watching is hard work) and so fancied a big juicy steak which I pointed to and asked the, what I presumed to be, waiter to have it medium rare.

"Mate, you can have it as medium rare as you want because you're bloody cooking it!" He chuckled and plonked a large piece of raw cow on my plate.

Clever concept this – I order the meat, part with a small fortune and then I cook it. That's absolute genius; not only do they charge a small fortune but save money by creating a DIY meal. I sent my compliments to the cook and left, walking back to the hotel via some of the back streets in the Rocks area that were a mixture of shops, houses and offices but with all maintaining a character that suggested 'old'. Throughout the world you can find cities that have these historic areas where there is a lot of character and just a pleasure to walk through devoid of those modernist buildings so loved by urban planners today. Bring me a cobblestone street, a Ye Olde Curiosity Shoppe and I am as happy as a sand fly on a freshly laid doggy-do!

Day three: November 6th

It was still fairly overcast but at least it wasn't raining yet. My first port of call was the Museum of Sydney which is housed in the original Governor's House (at the time because it had six rooms it was considered to be huge when compared to other abodes). It was the home of successive Governors' right through to 1846. On entering there was an area on the ground floor where I was able to see some of the original wallpaper, foundations and where the Governor contemplated the world whilst on his 'throne'. It is a 'fact' based on a rough straw poll I recently conducted, whereby men more than women see the lavatory as a quasi-study place but none could really explain why. I am of course part of this male oddity and enjoy a good 30 minutes sitting there, unhurried and relaxed, but can't tell you why this is any better than say sitting in the sitting-room (it's definitely not as comfortable as an armchair). Curious.

The building has three floors that combine both the modern with the more historical and is aimed at both adults and children. One of the exhibitions was of the pop artist Martin Sharp who is regarded as one of the leading lights of this genre. Sharp is maybe best known to the wider audience as one of the leading protagonists for keeping the funfair known as Luna Park open for the public (Friends of Luna Park) following the tragedy in 1979 when there was a fire on the ghost train ride that killed 6 youngsters. I learnt from one of the guides that there was a rumour at the time that highly unscrupulous property developers had paid for it to be set alight. It was an interesting juxtaposition between the sadness of this part of the exhibition and then the more fascinating aspects of pop art from record album covers, Tiny Tim, Disney, a homage to Van Gogh and so on. I have always liked pop art but never really taken much time to look at more closely so I spent a pleasant hour just sitting looking and talking to the guide about the influences that lay behind some of Sharp's work.

There was also recognition to the Cadigal people through a sculpture called 'The Edge of the Trees' which uses their voices in a clever use of sight and sound to take the listener on an imaginary journey back to before the first settlers. On level three I watched a video montage of the Aboriginal people called 'Eora' which means 'People'. It was all rather tastefully done.

I like the oral approach to telling history but there are limits and this came with the narrative history on show with actors reprising the stories of those who lived in the early years of the Colony. I have to be honest this type of history story-telling can drive me nuts as most of the narrators/ actors seem bent on hamming it up for that unknown agent who might be visiting. The one thing that drives me crackers above this though is when I turn up at one of those 'living museums' and the staff talk and dress as if I, the tourist, were stepping back in time with them. It just feels hugely embarrassing to me, I mean am I supposed to talk like they do, and it is usually in an appallingly rendered 'Olde English Accent' Even worse for me is when these people are so immersed in their character that if you ask a question about the background to the museum/exhibit/room I'm in they then go off into some rambling talk about how they had come out in 1800 and something from some unknown town in England to start a new life ... blah, blah, blah. No you didn't, you probably drove here this morning listening to the radio in your 21st century clothes, parked and then had an 'act like a complete cock' suppository shoved up your backside. You know who you are and I ask you to stop it now!

I left the museum and wondered back under the Bridge and headed to an area that was one of the main areas for ships coming in and out of Sydney called Walsh Bay. You can, if you fancy take a stroll around the heritage trail but I decided that I would instead just walk along Hickson Road which was built as a result of the need to stop the area flooding. In fact it was so bad at one point that as a result of the detritus that came ashore there was at least one recorded case of bubonic plague. The area is very much dominated by the arts as here there is the Australian Theatre for Young People, the Sydney Theatre Company and the Sydney Dance Company. There were also some particularly soulless apartment blocks including one that had a playschool adjoining the underground car park. As I reached the end of the road I passed an enormous cruise ship that looked like it was about to depart for other climes. These things are incredible when you see them for real and maybe it is fun being cooped up in one of those things for days or weeks at a time but for me the freedom that travel on land affords is so much better.

That evening I dined at the Orient Hotel on George Street. As I was eating, immersed in my own thoughts, I was besieged by a bunch of women who had just finished a charity event and were clearly a little worse for wear. One of them, Hannah, originally came from the north of England but had settled here in Sydney with her husband and two young children a couple of years ago. I asked her what she thought of the country and the contrast to the UK.

"It's brilliant. This is the best place to bring up a family, to work and to live. We live in Manly and every weekend we're on the beach all day and early evening. The climate is just perfect for that especially when compared to home … have you ever been to the north of England?" I have and it would be hard to compare the weather in somewhere like Scarborough to the picture she was painting. One thing she said that was interesting to me was to refer to "home" as being northern England. Was that a slip of the tongue due to alcohol or, as an expat, she was voicing what many first generation immigrants might still think whatever their nation of birth. There is another angle to this which is that today those who come to Australia do so for a variety of reasons but it seemed to me from what she was saying, and also affirmed by others I talked to, ultimately for quality of life. There are many definitions of what this might constitute but the common thread is that whatever the quality is, it is seen as better than where that person originated from. The '£10 Pom' was just one of these people.

Sydney has had many notables pass through the place and some, like Macquarie have left an indelible mark on the place and almost everywhere I looked there were constant reminders of this. There are also those who made a name for themselves but for all the wrong reasons. As I was thumbing through the various guides and books I had brought along a certain Captain Bligh, he of the Mutiny on the Bounty, leapt out of the pages for his role in what became known as the Rum Rebellion when he became Governor. This man, it seemed to me, was either a complete cock or was just in the wrong place at the wrong time. The story is another eye-opener on the early days of the Colony which by 1806 was in all but name a fiefdom of some very powerful individuals most of whom served in New South Wales Corp who it would appear had 'run, the place since. Bligh wanted to stop all this and reinsert the authority of the Crown so he decided to act by arresting the man he considered the main rabble-rouser, a powerful local figure called John Macarthur whom Hughes describes as:

' … a choleric man with a rage for gentility, who saw plots and insults everywhere and was as touchy as a Sicilian. He wasted half his time in imbroglios. Known to Emancipists as "Jack Bodice" – a nickname that reduced him to a rage – and to his administrative enemies as the "perburbator", he quarrelled furiously with judges, clergymen, sea captains and traders, and with a succession of Governors from Hunter to Darling.'

The simmering tensions hit boiling point in 1807–08 and at this point it starts to become almost déjà vu, or Mutiny on the Bounty, Part 2. Having been arrested and then rescued by his chums in the Corp, MacCarthur goes to arrest Bligh. Some stories have him hiding under the bed, some wearing women's close although that may have been because it was a Friday night and Mrs. Bligh fancied a bit of role play whilst others have him in full regalia, as if he was expecting the inevitable. After a period of house arrest he returned to England, MacCarthur was tried and in effect let off, and that's where the story ends. But does it? Australians are in my view very independent of mind and many bristle at the thought of being part of the Crown still; is this then the legacy of MacCarthur and his New South Wales Corp? I'd like to think so, but to be honest I go back to my original observation on Bligh in that he was indeed a complete cock and a man it seems so incapable of good relationships with anybody or thing that when he died even the worms eating into his corpse mutinied in disgust at him.

My visit to Sydney would not be complete if I was to leave out the most important event in the young country's existence. Australia as we know it today has only been in existence since 1901 with the Act of Federation. Although Melbourne was chosen to seat the first national government, it was Sydney that played host to the celebrations that brought Australia into being after many years of wrangling and debate which perhaps had as its high point a speech made by Sir Henry Parkes, known as the 'Father of Federation' to many, in his Tenterfield Oration which he made in on October 24th 1888 the gist of which was both a practical plea (such as better communication) through to bringing together the defence of the

Continent at a time when worries existed about German and Russian ambitions in the area, notably in New Guinea. The Federation came into existence at the stroke of midnight, January 1st 1901 and the celebrations were huge with many thousands lining the streets of Sydney and listening to the proclamation in Centennial Park within the Domain. To read the story of these celebrations is to understand something about the country today. It was about Australians uniting under a common flag and under a common leadership, of assuming nationhood. The Sydney Morning Herald enthusing about this in its lead of the following day:

'Sydney yesterday rose to the high occasion as only the capital of a great and noble country can rise ... Every man, woman and child wanted to see the procession and used the best available efforts thereto, but not so as to prevent every other person from obtaining his fair view ... Yesterday was the greatest day in the history of Australia, and everybody who was not absolutely prevented was determined to assist, however humbly, in its celebration.'

Given the average Australian's capacity for beer it must have been a very quiet January 2nd as everyone nursed their hangovers. As I travelled throughout the east I was to be reminded that although the events of 1901 are clearly hugely significant there were plenty of reminders that it was not an easy ride both getting there and until recently afterwards.

Chapter 4

*Sydney to Melbourne; the real journey begins, but no curry –
what horror!*

DAY four: November 7th

I woke early the following morning excited at the prospect of starting the real travelling part of my adventure. The car hire firm was located in a part of Sydney called King's Cross which is close to an area named Paddington, an area of Sydney built in the 1840's and full of a number of striking buildings many of which were renovated following a new influx of immigrants. It would have been nice to have visited as by all accounts it was, in places, very pleasant. Mind you I hadn't visited Bondi Beach either but that had more to do with my wish not to offend the local population with my body which is, and I live with it, not overly pleasant. I daren't sunbathe on a beach for fear that Greenpeace will want to pour water over me to keep my stress down so that they can get my re-floated back to sea. I also don't really like swimming in the sea since whaling is still carried out by the Japanese. One other thing as well that puts me off sitting too long in the sun is that because of my size whereby my stomach has a tendency to fold over itself I can end up looking like I am wearing a red and white hooped t-shirt after I finish. Not nice and certainly to be avoided by those faint of heart.

In the past the only other country that I had pre-hired a car was the US where, when I'd signed in, the rep would then give me the thousands of extra options like CDC (no idea), left toe damage premium waiver if looking left insurance or whatever. Anyway the point being that you get a lot of options but in total the extra cost is not a shock. Australia by contrast was incredible. I would have thought that when hiring a car anywhere in the world I'd by default paid towards the usage of said vehicle on the road. At worse I may have to pay the odd toll but no more and anyway I could always avoid those roads. Not in Australia though; for the privilege of being a driver on their roads I had to cough up 5.50 dollars per day. Now although this part of the journey was relatively short in duration, overall I planned to have a car for at least 37 days in all. Of course when I booked the car they don't tell me this, had they. But that wasn't it. There were even more additional costs including "Did you require an engine in the car?" and it was not helped by Clive who manically smiled non-stop. Either that or he'd glued his dentures in badly. Once I had given him the deeds to my house I was away. My first overnight stay was to be Batemans Bay which I reckoned was about a 4–5 hour leisurely drive which would allow some sight-seeing on the way.

The route out of Sydney can either be expensive or, if you ask someone in the know, cheap. Sydney, along with Melbourne and Brisbane, is surrounded by toll roads which are the most expensive I had come across. There had been a programme on the TV the night before about the companies that owned these roads – and specifically the one in Sydney. In simple terms the report inferred that they had a licence to print money and that motorists who have to drive in (and they interviewed a number) are essentially being fleeced. Luckily the route I took was the start of the Princes Highway and is toll-free. Mister tightwad strikes a home run for the UK!

Originally I had toyed with the idea of going along the Hume Highway which is much older in terms of history than the Princes Highway as I fancied following the route of some of the original pioneers (Flannery quotes one William Well who travelled here in 1844 and who moaned about the weather and about the lack of dietary options and the traffic which is a wonderful insight to the activity then of the early pioneers) but it would have meant going out of my way inland towards Canberra and not as I had planned, to stick to the coast. It's a shame in some ways as the Princes Highway is historically far less interesting. Originally called Highway One it was then renamed after the then Prince of Wales in the late 1920's. I bet he was overcome with excitement knowing that a road had been named after him. Having thus named it, the New South Wales government decided after many long meetings costing the taxpayer hundreds that The Princes Highway was too long; so they dropped the 'The'. Genius! Some things never change with how the public services spend our money.

My first stop on leaving Sydney was inland to Nowra and then north to the Fleet Air Arm Museum. The museum itself is situated on base at HMAS Albatross and was founded in 1974 by a group of enthusiasts. It wasn't very big and the housing was typical of the military style that we used to live in when I was a child; I believe the term is 'functional' although drab might be a better moniker. When I had paid I found that I was the only person there – I mean it is really off the beaten track and unless you are an enthusiast probably not something that you'll visit. I had a similar experience in Canada years ago when visiting an air museum near Toronto. I was 'Billy no mates' there as well, but as with then, today I was quite content to be on my own. After all it allows more time to browse and take in everything and there are no arguments and I can quite happily mumble sweet nothings to myself, a habit that as I grow older is causing some concern from those around me. It has its uses though such as back when I was living in the US and I was crossing Boston Common late at night I saw a man approaching with what I took to be a knife. My mumbling became much louder accompanied with the odd snort and he walked straight passed. I recommend it although today my mumbles were more of the "Mmm, very interesting" variety.

The museum houses planes from WWI through to more recent conflicts like Vietnam and Iraq and it was all a little formulaic until I came across the story surrounding the Royal Australian Navy's commitment in Vietnam that lasted around 4 years and cost the lives of 5 of those who served. As I went around the exhibit devoted to I listened to two recordings made by men who had served there: on one tape were the thoughts of home of a helicopter pilot not long before he was killed, whilst on the other was a recording of a live action flight in VC territory and the very audible noise of ground fire.

The Vietnam War in which the UK did not send any troops was a different affair here. Australia committed some 8,000 troops in all to the conflict with around 50,000 in all serving there between 1962 and 1972 when they finally pulled out. As with the US there was a huge anti-war movement that grew more intense when conscription was introduced. In total Australia lost some 500 killed, of which 200 were conscripts. One of the big issues that came out of the Australian's involvement was the question of where, as a country, did her allegiances lie and when Holt (the Prime Minister who literally ended up swimming with the fishes) told President Lyndon Johnson that Australia was right behind the US all the way it was seen by some as an indication that the country's role was subservient to the US. Menzies had promised Vietnam assistance (i.e. America) but some have since questioned whether he did this as he claimed (and his government) because there had been an overt request, or because the fear of communism and its spread was so great that he effectively committed the country without a request. In 1977 the Australian journalist, Graham Freudenberg, wrote about this episode, and what drove, in his view, the government to send troops to Vietnam. It came as a result primarily following a US request for naval support that Australia was not able to provide, but instead Menzies offered further 'special advisers'. This for Freudenberg was that:

> ' ... the crucial decision of Australia's generation-long involvement in Indo-China ... was made not because that was wanted or asked for, either by the United States or South Vietnam but because that was the only thing Australia could supply if the political aims of Australia's intervention were to be met ... (and) ... to get credit with Lyndon Baines Johnson.'

Whatever the reason it was an incredibly moving exhibit that brought a lump to my throat. I needed retail therapy to lift my mood and so as is my wont I then visited the museum shop. I don't know why but I love going to these shops, not because they have anything particularly nice but because I collect tat. Pure unadulterated rubbish that is always over-priced and quite unnecessary. In fact my family will only usually accompany me to a museum if it has a shop. So, it you ever want that special mug, T-shirt, fridge magnet or whatever, then feel free to call as I have plenty augmented today by that must have pint pot with R.A.N engraved on the side.

Back on the road again the countryside opened up either side of me. What I found striking though, was both how dry it looked and how much had been burnt. As I travelled throughout the east, including the tropical north of Queensland it was much the same and everywhere I went the locals were crying out for the rains. Each evening when I looked at the weather forecast the weatherman/women genuinely looked sad to report that the next day would be another 30 degree plus scorcher. Personally,

I was chuffed as hell given that the summer in the UK had been another washout for the most part.

The route down to Batemans Bay followed the Shoalhaven Coast and once I rejoined the Princes Highway at Nowra I passed through a number of very pleasant towns such as Wollongong with its Nan Tien Buddhist Temple, Keira and Ulladulla. As I came into Batemans Bay I passed the coastal stretch of the Murramarang National Parkland then crossed the Clyde Bridge and was there. Bateman's Bay was named by Cook in 1770 after Nathaniel Bateman, and although the area was explored by Robert Johnson in 1821, a big part of the district's growth was the discovery both of good timber and that the river Clyde was navigable and by the mid 19th century the Illawarra and South Coast Steam Navigation Co. was running regular services. Timber remained a major employer until the 1970's,

That evening I was booked into a hotel just off the main highway. It was to say the least basic but comfortable and backed onto the river where some locals were fishing. The whole effect was very pleasant and, even with the highway next to the hotel, remarkably quiet. I checked in and found myself suddenly immersed in a deep conversation with the proprietor who was an Indian by birth but had moved to Australia some twenty years ago. He was an incredibly proud man and told me that about his eldest daughter who was studying at university in Brisbane and how he hoped his other children would follow in her steps, which also got us talking about why he had come to Australia in the first place. He missed India, not least his relatives, but Australia for him offered a new start, a means to get away from the poverty of India, of becoming someone and of bringing up a family that would be able to have the opportunities that he had missed as a child. I asked him why he chose Australia and not America which seemed to me to be the epitome of somewhere that people went to make a new life. For him Australia was a more equal society where even if you don't succeed there is government support.

Is this what Australia is then, a watered down more user friendly version of the United States? Perhaps but over the course of six weeks I was to discover that there is a lot more to it than meets the eye and like so many countries in the world there is no easy one-liner to describe it.

Given the incredibly delicious smell of curry emanating from his sitting room which was right behind the check-in counter I had mentioned whether there was a good Indian take-away in town. Now Australians are rather like the British in many ways, not surprising given a shared ancestry in that, in sum, their food tastes are not overly sophisticated outside of the major conurbations. In fact I can say that with few exceptions most of the restaurants that I visited had dead cow as their main recommendation along with something done with a kangaroo and fish accompanied by rather sad looking vegetables. This predilection for meat was noted many years ago by Mr. P.E Muskett, quoted by Knightley:

'We eat meat and we drink tea ... Meat eating in Australia is almost a religion.'

So of course when I asked about a curry, *the* de facto national dish back in the UK (or at least in England), I had assumed that this would also be a number one choice here in Australia given our collective history. Back home the partaking of curry by me and my family every Saturday night is an institution. For myself, well I was brought up on the stuff whether home made by my mother or, when 'studying' for a degree in the early 80s, at one of the many Indian restaurants in Portsmouth where both food and alcohol were guaranteed after everything else was closed. Curry was in my blood. I needed a curry and fast. Well Mr. Singh was quick to dispel this. Australians it seemed preferred Chinese to Indian, something that he lamented. My heart sank: six more weeks without a rogan josh, pilau rice and poppadoms plus the obligatory ten pints of lager, this was going to be hard to do. Funnily enough if you ever chance to visit Ireland then you'll find exactly the same situation and in the 19th century it should be remembered many Irish left the Emerald Isle for Australia, some voluntarily others not so, although to be fair at that time there probably wasn't an Eastern Oriental Chinese take-away in downtown Cork.

Batemans Bay's is the first main town in Eurobodollashire (everywhere I went I was in some shire or other — a hang up from the old country maybe) which ends at Narooma. Eurobodolla is the local Aboriginal name and means 'Land of Many Waters'. The area has over 80 beaches, lots of rivers and lakes. It is also an area of much history revolving not just around the lumber business but also coal and gold of which the town is very much a part of. In fact the area became a part of the big gold rush centred in the Moryua district starting in 1851. On one of the trips

I had done in the US some years back I had visited an old gold rush town in California and read the stories about how men had flooded to the area hoping to be the ones that found the big strike. However, so many came and so many failed and reading through various articles it was abundantly clear that the only difference between California's gold rush and Australia's was the location. The same misery and hardships suffered in the US were evident here and I was to see this first hand just before I went to Melbourne in a town called Walhalla.

I had also read in my travel guide about all the activities that could be done in or near Batemans Bay, but I was only there for the afternoon and evening so instead of getting out my surf board I headed into town to see what was what, full of anticipation. This was my first 'real' Australian town and not really knowing what to expect I came to the main street that lines the estuary with strong sense of expectancy, but what hit me was how disappointing it was because it looked on first inspection that all there was were a proliferation of fast food takeaways which is so depressing. I'm not sure quite what I expected but certainly not this. These were interspersed with shops selling the usual souvenirs like 'Welcome to Batemans Bay; Crap Food is our Specialty'. Well it didn't really say that but you get the gist. The smell of fried food was over-powering. I had rather hoped to have a nice seafood dinner, not least as the area is famed for its oysters but short of having something swimming in fat it seemed unlikely that would happen. And mullets and tattoos were everywhere along with those ghastly singlets that Australian men wear as a mark of pride. No, they're not. Like a string vest looks ridiculous on an Englishmen when worn as the only piece of clothing above the trouser line, so too does the singlet.

I carried on walking, going further away from the centre of the town, past the shell museum (not the petrol company but a place devoted to shells: the excitement was almost too much to cope with and it was lucky it was closed) and just felt that I could be in 'anywhere town' in 'anywhere country' except that it was much hotter than many places I'd visited. I walked on for another three kilometres or so and eventually came across a very English village site, a game of cricket, but with a difference. Whereas in England most games are played when the weather is usually overcast and there is always the obligatory old couple sitting in their Austin Maxi wrapped up against the always present cold wind, this was on an Australian Rules Football pitch, the weather was hot with a cobalt blue sky, the audience mostly young dressed in t-shirts, shorts and flip-flops and, as if to add further to an almost perfect spot, the birds weren't the usual pigeons you get at home but cockatoos and king parrots. I stayed and watched just soaking up the atmosphere and listening to one of the most pleasant sounds, that of Australians hazing Australians.

By the way I have to ask an open question at this point. If the Australian for flip-flop is a thong, is the thong (worn by many an attractive woman with that 'must have' tattoo on her back) a flip-flop?

The only big downside I was quickly discovering about being outside in Australia, were the flies. They are unbelievable and a complete pain. As soon as I brushed one off fifty of its fellow bastards would replace it on self-proclaimed suicide missions. And their tenacity is quite incredible because they just don't give up. Somewhere in the mists of time when this country was being formed by the great god of the sky and earth he (or she) must have decided that, just for a laugh, not only would this be a country where everything that crawls or swims was designed to kill but, as if that wasn't quite enough, a special fly was created for no other purpose than to be the undoubted winner of the most annoying creature on this planet. The gods in heaven are no doubt heaving with laughter at this even today, and none more so when they see me, chubby cheeks, trying to fight off an infestation.

On the way back I walked on the side of the road where the houses were (the other side being the river and foreshore) and was struck by how small they were and, well, basic. Batemans Bay may well be a holiday resort but it also seems to me a place where there is a certain amount of lower income families living. However, as soon as I thought that this was the case there appeared a fairly large presupposing mansion with a neat garden, a large car and a pool. In Britain, and actually pretty much anywhere I have been in the world, the stratification of economic class is blindingly obvious from the project housing that is often at the edge of an American city to the impoverished shanty towns in so many countries. In all cases once through these areas it seems one enters a totally different world of manicured lawns, large houses or up market apartments. Throughout my travels in Australia I was struck by the lack of this separation, although this may be because I didn't enter the areas that it might be more obvious. However, I thought to myself whether this is the equality that Australians believe is part of their culture? Perhaps it is or perhaps it isn't but superficially it did seem so and I rather preferred it in some ways not least given that back in the UK we are inveterate snobs when it comes to both where we live and next to whom. It lead to another thought that I had and which again occupied my mind each time I arrived at a town that was reasonably built up, which was is it the same in the cities or is Australia much more about local community and if so is this just outside the metropolitan areas? Is there real social stratification between rich and poor? My own view after my travels was that there was much less outside of the main cities, partly due to the remoteness of some of the places where all had to muck and partly because many of those I met just seemed more concerned with living (and enjoying living) rather than worrying too much about keeping up with the Jones'.

That evening I did manage to find something to eat that hadn't been fried beyond recognition in a pleasant restaurant overlooking the river. I was lucky that through tiredness I had turned up early to eat because the last sitting was 8pm. This struck me as slightly odd, this being a tourist town, but then I thought that as it wasn't the tourist season maybe they just weren't busy. In fact I was to find out that pretty much anywhere I went, ex the three cities I visited (Melbourne, Sydney and Brisbane) and the larger towns, 8pm was 'late' to be eating. I had heard about the old days when Australia had very strict licensing laws that meant that getting a beer later than 6pm was nigh on impossible in a pub because those 'we know better than you' legislators wanted Bruce to go home to Sheila and the kids and be a family and not get drunk every night. Maybe this was why 8pm seemed to be late. I should just point out here two flaws in this legislation: firstly when Bruce went to the pub the bar would have been stacked deep with beer mugs which would invariably have been pre-paid for or just settled after the hour. The outcome was invariably the same as if the bars had been opened until the wee small hours except that instead of being plastered at midnight, many would be that way within the hour. I recall my own experiences when I was a student and more latterly in my rugby playing days, when chugging beer as quickly as I could was a guarantee that my body would turn into a quivering mass of rubber in short shrift. The second problem, especially in the Outback, was a clear inability to enforce the law rigidly, helped in most parts by a thirsty copper. In the UK there used to be 'lock-ins' whereby pubs would 'close', all the clientele would be seen to leave, only then to be readmitted via the back door to start drinking again. Australia was no different.

Now I am not one for going out on my own and painting the town red, not least when the whole place resembled a ghost town with shutters going up all over the place and 'closed' signs appearing in door windows, so I ambled back to the hotel to watch a little TV. Australian TV is, to say the least, interesting and quite the eye-opener. I'm not sure if they have as we do a watershed before which time adult programming is largely restricted, because if they do I didn't notice it. On one comedy stand-up show the number of times reference was made to both male and female genitalia even had me blushing and I'm not a shrinking violet by any means. I loved the fact that the news had interviews with Joe and Jo Public where the words "Bloody" and "Bugger" were used not in a derogatory sense, but more as an emphasis and on one report, even by the newsreader. I can't ever see this happening on the BBC, but if it did then what fun that might be as some stiff shirted newsreader told the Prime Minister that he was a "bloody idiot". I also loved the fact that on some channels the time a programme was supposed to start was really just a guideline such that a if it started half an hour later then 'no worries' because, heck, this is Australia; it was so wonderfully laid back.

Day five: November 8th

Today I was driving further down the Sapphire Coast (which begins after passing Norooma) on to Merimbula for a night. After a quick stop at Malua Bay to have a look at the sea, I headed for a town called Central Tilba which was a fair way off the beaten track and is situated close to Gulaga (Cook named it Mount Dromedary but now it has reverted to the Aboriginal name). The town is almost a living museum in as much as each house in the main street has been either carefully restored or just really well looked after. In its appearance it is a late 19th century town with wooden houses and beautiful trees, flowers and creepers (no idea what any of them were but the colours were tremendous from loud reds, deep purples, varied shades of blue, bright greens, sickly yellows and so on). As I entered the main street to my left was the Bates Emporium which has a frontage straight out of those early sepia photographs when cars had just been introduced and the local store had the only pump in town. In the window and all around were signs from yesteryear whilst inside alongside the modern conveniences of modern life, there was a feel of times gone by and all rather nostalgic.

As I walked down the main street there were a number of artisanal shops from the insanely expensive to the more down to earth. I could buy some wonderful leather outfits or a lovely hessian shirt in the 'are you aware that people in the world are starving' shop. These shops seem to be prevalent in the US, notably on the West Coast, where a couple (usually) haven't moved on from their anti-establishment view of the 1960's and are keen to sell anything that has 3rd World attached to it. In some ways this is very commendable especially if those who actually made the stuff were being paid the lion's share, but I bet they're not. Maybe it just eases their own consciences and for those that buy from them? All I know is that everything is invariably expensive and to ram home this hippy like idyll there always seems to be a surfeit of bongs or pipes for the partaking of illicit weed – so right on man.

At the bottom of the main street was the ABC Cheese Factory that had been established in 1891. I hadn't really thought that Australians would be big purveyors of cheese but in fact this part of the country produces a lot and it is not just of one variety. No sir, in fact at the ABC I could buy a wide variety of delicious sounding flavours:

Tilba Gold, Vintage, Applebox Smokem Cracked Pepper, Sun-Dried Tomato, Summer Herb, Tilba Trilogy and Italienne.

Right I thought to myself time for a bit of tasting. The factory shop is, well, somewhat basic. There are cheeses and other comestibles all around and of course the obligatory souvenirs. Being in a jovial mood, I advanced to the counter, mouth watering in anticipation, hands rubbing together as if on auto-pilot.

"Could I try some cheese before I buy it please?"

"No."

And that is where the conversation stopped. I tried one more avenue, showing deep interest in the factory itself.

"How much cheese do you produce here annually and does it get quite busy in the tourist season?"

There was silence, not even a whisper. I could have heard a flea farting 100 yards away due to the quiet. I needed an exit strategy, not because I couldn't just walk out which of course I could have done, but I need 'closure'. So I bought a stubbie holder which celebrated the Tilba Cheese

Club just so I could get the shop assistant to be pleasant. Nothing, not even a thank you; well lady if you're reading this I hope you're happy you miserable cow.

On the road again I stopped off at another seaside town, Bermagui. The beach was almost deserted aside from a young family in the distance who were all huddled in the shade under a large striped umbrella. I took off my sandals and walked onto the sand which, without my sun glasses on, created a fierce glare that made me squint. The sand was almost pure white and stretched left to right as far as I could see. As I walked the feeling of the sand in my toes was glorious – I mean here I was in the middle of an English winter, in shorts a shirt and no shoes, absolutely wonderful. All was right with the world. I don't really like beaches as I mentioned and one of my worst abiding memories was visiting Westward Ho in Devon when I was no more than a sperm and nearly being dragged into the sea by a huge wave on a particularly horrible day. But here, well it was bliss.

After having a breather I walked back towards the high street (which is essentially all that Bermagui has in terms of a commercial area) and visited the war memorial that sits overlooking the town. It's a quite spot situated at the top end of the town and as in Sydney's Garrison Church honours those who served and died. I strolled back down to the top end of the high street looking for a place to eat. It was no later than 10am but the pub was full to bursting; a bikers' convention it seemed had pulled into town. In front were there bikes as well a number of UTE's, old and new. I have to say that the new UTE has got to be one of the ugliest cars I have seen (they were originally developed in the 1930's as a luxury utility vehicle) and whenever I came across them on the road, or parked in town, invariably the driver was about twelve. I was told that the holy shrine of all that is UTE is Bathurst which had I had the time might have been fun to visit but it was much further inland than I planned to go. I wonder if it is like what I remember in my youth where the cars to own if you were a bit of a lad were either a Ford Capri Mk II or Ford Escort with a spoiler added at the back. And these too were driven by lads who just looked too young to drive but with two additions that I didn't see on a UTE: furry dice and his and her sunshades on the windscreen with Wayne (drivers' side) and Sharon (passenger side: never allowed to drive unless it was back from the pub when Wayne was too drunk to even light a cigarette).

As I passed the end of the pub I noticed a sign that said 'Bottle-O'. Not a big thing you might think but this was a drive-thru booze shop. Now Australia has some of the most draconian traffic laws concerning speed (at most 55mph) and drink-driving. Yet here you could drive your car, UTE whatever and happily buy some beer, spirits or wine from the comfort of your driving seat. Given that the Australian government is very keen to get across the 'no drink-drive' message it does seem a little odd?

I got back to my car, pushed my way through all the empty beer cans and grabbed the steering wheel and drove straight through a plate glass window of a shop before coming to a stop at the check-out counter. Actually I didn't really but that's what I imagined could happen if I decided to save on carbon emissions by drinking all the alcohol thus lightening the load in the car and thus also reducing petrol consumption.

Off I went again and stopped not long after in a lovely small town called Tathra. The town, like so many in this part of Australia, was initially settled in the first half of the 1800's and legally should not have been. As part of the control of free land grants and settlement the government of New South Wales had by the 1820's and 1830's defined those areas where land could be bought and sold as the nineteen counties. Tathra was actually outside of this but then there were by this time many new communities appearing, often without government sanction, in part reflecting the type of individual involved (free settlers through to released convicts) as well as the opportunities many sought in the land that, aside from the minor issue of belonging to the Aboriginals, was in their view theirs for development.

At the edge of the town, and overlooking the sea, is a garden of remembrance that also has a plaque commemorating the events of July 1941 when the USS William Dawes was sunk nearby by a Japanese submarine. The sinking ship was spotted by a young lady (Loma Stafford) who alerted the local military which then coordinated the rescue of the survivors. As I looked down from this spot I could see the Tathra historic wharf that served the community from the late 19th century until the 1950's and was part financed by our friends from Batemans Bay the Illawara Steam and Navigation Company. Today having been restored it houses a small café, souvenir shop and museum. The museum at just two dollars celebrates the area and had a couple of things that caught my eye, not least the chart showing how many ships had sunk in the area stretching from Sydney down to the Tasman Sea. Of more interest to me was that a large number of these had been sunk by the Imperial Japanese Navy. Although I knew that northern Australia had been heavily bombed, especially Darwin, and that with half of Papua New Guinea occupied there was a real fear of invasion, the fact that they had come this far south was new, reinforced of course by the plaque. I later read the story of HMS (HMAS was not used then) Sydney being sunk in Sydney harbour and the 3 midget submarines involved.

I arrived in Merimbula in the late afternoon and checked into my room which had glorious views of the bay. It was very pleasant to sit on my balcony with beer in hand (serving suggestion: 'Bloody Cold') and watch the world go by. That evening I ate the world's largest pizza whilst sitting outside overlooking the bay reading a book and drinking beer all on my own. It was a very pleasant end to a very pleasant day.

Day six: November 9th

Today was going to be quite a long drive as I continued down to Metung which is at the head of the Ninety Mile Beach. I was also about to head into my second state, Victoria. Here's a little useless information for you: Victorians used to have a nickname 'Gum suckers' as they used to literally suck the gum from the eucalypts before chewing gum. I'm not entirely sure how I might have reacted seeing some bloke sucking a tree. I once went on a nature walk in the Rockies which was led by what American's often refer to as an Earth Mother, a lady at one with nature, and who was absolutely fascinated by bear droppings ("Look guys, check the size of that stool. Real interesting don't you think?") and since then my policy has always to avoid potential weirdoes which to date I'm pleased to say has worked well.

The roads continued to be light on traffic making driving very pleasurable, not least if I compared it to, say, the autoroutes in France. I don't know how many holidays I have had that required a stress-fest of driving along these roads. Unfortunately as my family and I always had to travel during school holidays, which coincided with 'les Grandes Vacanes' when the whole of urban France ups sticks and leaves for the south, and when most of northern Europe heads to the sunny south, the very fact that we arrived alive at our destination was a feat of incredible survival. Let's be honest it is not in the nature of the French to drive sensibly unless that includes using the boot of your car as the front seat of theirs. Having said that, the Italians are pretty awful too as are the Germans, although with the latter it just tends to be flashing of the headlights as they are always seemingly in a hurry. However it is the Dutch and their damn caravans that really take the biscuit, driving with a slowness that would make snails look like Usain Bolt and always in my humble view driven it seems by a leathery looking individual accompanied by his/her partner and a load of blonde haired kids, all of whom are unfeasibly tall. In Australia there are caravans but they are far from traditional and often as not are converted UTE's or large trucks with a housing unit plugged on. I would also say that all things considered, ex the UTE driver, Australians are incredibly courteous on the roads.

I stopped off for breakfast at a town called Eden which is also home to a rather fun Whale Museum that celebrates the whaling industry which started in the 1790's. In the museum are various exhibits from the kind of boats used through to the tools of the trade. However, what got my attention was a skeleton of a killer whale named 'Old Tom', who (or is it which?) was part of the history of how the whalers worked in tandem with the killer whales. My image of the mighty Orca is of an ocean killer feared by man and beast alike, but here in the museum there was a completely different side to them. The relationship was based around the migrating baleen whales that came through this area. As the boats went out with the whalers in them, the killer whales would in effect herd the humpbacks towards the waiting harpoons. In some instances the killer whales would literally grab the boats lines and tow the whalers towards their quarry; looking at the teeth of Old Tom I could see where the lines had worn away the enamel.

Of note was that the link between these whales and man goes back thousands of years. Given that the area was originally inhabited by the Katungal Aboriginal people it was interesting to read that they called the killer whale 'Beowas' which was a word used to describe what they represented. The whales were their dead warriors who had returned and their stories talk about how, as with the more recent whalers, they worked together. All in all a quite extraordinary story akin to something like a shepherd and his sheepdog, although I'm not sure that I would have the whale on my lap after a hard day's herding.

The museum also had a lighthouse that used to shine over the bay from where I was told, as I paid my fee to get in, I would be able to spot the humpbacks as they migrated south and that this was a perfect time of year to do so. Given my luck at spotting them in Sydney I thought why not. So I climbed to the top of the lighthouse and lo there it was: a view so breathtaking that I can only describe it as truly awesome. There in front of me was whale upon whale breaking the surface to get a gulp of air before disappearing into the deep blue ocean.

"Yes, normally that is what you can see" said the guide "but today this sea fog looks set for the day."

Ah well, the museum was a nice diversion and following breakfast (please someone Australian explain to me why scrambled eggs and toast is always scrambled eggs infused with enough cheese to give someone a coronary?) I carried on down towards my destination. As I drove along there were constant reminders of the wildlife (dead kangaroos seen so far 5, dead wombats 3, dead snakes 2 and nude women 0) as well as the insects, and more specifically the cicada which has got to take an award for the noisiest living thing on the planet. The way it works is that maybe Mr. and Mrs. Cicada are having a little relationship issue and are angrily chirruping away to each other, when their neighbours join in, then before you know it, every cicada in Australia starts having their two penny worth. The other much more serious thing that is very evident both visually and through your nostrils is the devastation that bushfires have caused. It was only in early 2009 that well over 150 people had been killed in one of the worst natural disasters in Australian history, more of which later. The fires were helped in no small part by the sheer dryness of the place and time and time again I was reminded of this in the papers, on the news and in hotel rooms where guests were requested to be economical, to turn taps off in between rinses accompanied by constant reminders of how much water the area actually had in its reservoirs.

It was a long drive before I crossed into the State of Victoria. This is part of Australia that was the last to be settled in the south east corner of the country. The area is known as Gippsland after Sir George Gipps who was Governor of New South Wales from 1838 to 1846 and extends right down to Melbourne. It became a very fashionable part of the nascent colony in the latter part of the 1800's as a holiday destination. The area prides itself on the beauty of the countryside and the many lakes that are encompassed within its boundaries and as I arrived at Metung I passed through Lakes Entrance which kind of sums it all up. The Ninety

Mile Beach stretches from Metung all the way down the coast towards Melbourne and today is as popular a holiday destination as it was in past times.

One of the ways that genteel Melbourne folk would have travelled to the lakes by the late 19th and early 20th centuries was on the East Gipps Railway that was an addition to the railway that originally ran out of Melbourne to Sale. In 1888 it was extended from Bairnsdale to Orbost. On the way I kept passing the remnants of this railway and not far from a town called Nowa Nowa I turned off the main road in order to visit the historic (not my word but my guide's) Stony Creek Trestle Bridge which is now a part of the East Gippsland Rail Trail which stretches for some 90 – 100 kilometres. As I bumped along the dirt track to the bridge I suddenly felt rather pleased with myself because, you see, having paid an extortionate amount of money to hire this car, here I was 'off road' knowing full well that I was not supposed to do this. Still that'll teach them to charge me so much.

The bridge suddenly appeared from the bush and was quite impressive standing a good 100 feet high. I was the only one in the car park and as I looked at it I drank in the silence (the cicadas for once were quiet) and serenity of the place. I imagined Melbournians coming along this track on their way to some part of Gippsland to enjoy a holiday or just a day out, with their carriages being pulled along by an old steam engine. It must have been fun as they travelled up from the growing urban sprawl and then into the bush where there was always the chance to see kangaroos, koalas and birds of many colours and breeds. I commute to London from Sussex by train and it is nothing like this. The train does go through some beautiful countryside but once across the M25 it's just housing and the most exotic creature likely to be seen is the odd passenger with coloured hair and a body piercing or two.

Gippsland, as with other parts of Australia, also has a very dark side. Much of the area was settled by white people, many of whom competed for land with the indigenous population and who, it seemed to me reading about it, took any opportunity to commit some pretty terrible acts against them. The tensions between European and Aboriginal became inevitable as both fought to take what they wanted or keep what was theirs. The numerous books and studies on this part of Australia's history have titles that leave the reader with little doubt about what happened.

There are many stories about what happened in this part of Australia, and elsewhere on the Continent and there were deadly attacks on both sides. The brutality of some of these was staggering but one that stuck out was a chilling episode that Knightley talks about where:

'To save cartridges, the children were killed by a blow to the back of the neck'.

These events were not atypical and the issues between what were called by Macintyre the 'pastoral settler' and the Aboriginal continued right up into the 20th century. Not everyone I talked to was keen on getting into much detail on this subject and writing this book it is hard to both be cognisant that on the one hand in Australia today the vast majority of people are decent, hardworking and downright nice whilst on the other understand that these were dark days, the so-called 'Black Wars', when two cultures clashed head on and with such bloodshed. Is it because they are ashamed of what happened in the past? For me this is something that Australians today should not feel personally responsible in the same way as when Tony Blair stood up and apologised for the UK's involvement in slavery, I didn't feel that I had to go around apologising for the sins of my forefathers. However, the key is this business of talking about it, of accepting it as a part of history, of not ignoring it but, and this may seem a little sanctimonious, learning from it. In this I did find on my travels that on balance most Australians would rather talk about the cricket or football than this part of their history.

I arrived in Metung, which is set on a peninsular that to one side is bordered by Bancroft Bay whilst on the other side is Lake King, in the late afternoon. Metung was originally called Rosherville but went back to the Kurnai name that means 'bend in the lake' or 'hi-tree river bend' to some. The town has a catchy little motto 'Metung, too good to miss' which is accompanied by another that says 'Take a stroll around the village … there's something for everyone to enjoy'. I booked into my hotel for the night and did exactly that. The village is not large but is idyllic. I walked along the boardwalk that lines the marina which was packed with boats and small yachts. The village hosts a regatta once a year which goes back to the late 19th century and has a long history associated with the sea. The hotel I was staying at was part of this history in as much as it had been built in an area that used to be where flying boats would dock (if that is the right expression; maybe it's park. Here's a thought if a car can be double parked, can a flying boat and how do they paint the no parking lines?).

In the marina was a large rock, one of three that used to be sited here, that for the Aboriginal people that lived here represented fishermen who had been turned to stone for not sharing their bread by the women who were responsible for the social well-being of the community. There didn't seem a huge amount to do, and there weren't many shops open, so I wasn't quite sure what they meant in their tag line, but it was nevertheless a very pleasant place to unwind. I returned to the hotel having managed to locate the beer emporium and, following a quick run, sat on my veranda and admired the view out to sea. Well I would have done but for the trees. On the plus side though I spotted two king parrots, a magnificent colour mix of red and green, in the tree opposite bickering away and thought, momentarily of home. With a smile on my face I downed a couple of cold ones and thought to myself that I really must call the old ball and chain at home.

Dinner that evening was early and almost alone again. I sat outside to enjoy the dying rays of the sun and, having ordered, closed my eyes and just listened to the wildlife calling in the early evening. And then the evening was shattered by a guttural laugh to my left followed by the waft of a newly lit cigarette. I opened my eyes and there sat almost next to me were two women. And then the one that I reckoned had laughed started to talk, and talk and talk, but not quietly, oh no, even the birds in the trees were drowned out by the boom. I couldn't understand what they were saying as they were Dutch (or else just let loose a lot of spittle) but clearly the one listening was being talked at, rather than to, as she hardly spoke. What a rotten way to end the day.

Day seven: November 10th

I would have liked to stay a bit longer but I had been booked that evening into a hotel in the heart of the goldfields. The drive wasn't going to be long and I wanted to get their early so that I could explore the town that was described to me by a friend back in London as a 'must see ghost town'. I never look to pre-judge this instruction whether verbal or written purely on the basis that if I don't look into it I may well have missed something awesome or, as you'll read when I get to Melbourne, from time to time something that is so utterly mediocre that the effort to get there is completely wasted. Walhalla I'm pleased to say fell into the former category.

Walhalla is to the north east of Melbourne and is home to one of the great gold rush stories of the 19th century, coming about as a result of the discovery of payable gold in 1851 by Edward Hargreaves near Bathurst (I should have mentioned earlier that it is not just the 'home' of the UTE but also the famous for the Bathurst 1000, a petrol heads' nirvana) about 200 kilometres west of Sydney. This set in motion the rush to discover more and diggers from all around converged into the area. In the State of Victoria the Governor, La Trobe, offered a financial reward to anyone who discovered gold in the state. The impact of this was immense both in terms of industry as well as population which increased almost four fold from the 1850's into the 1870's. Walhalla was the site in 1862 when Ned Stringer struck alluvial gold (the town was originally called Stringer's Creek but the name changed in 1869). Walhalla was just one of a number of gold rush towns that sprang up in the area but none were as successful.

To reach Walhalla I drove through forests of eucalypts and pines along a windy road that had a sign post on every bend advising drivers to slow down to almost nothing. Not being in a hurry it actually made the drive very agreeable and allowed plenty of opportunity to take in the scenery. Just before I reached the town I passed the old Walhalla Goldfields Railway that was built almost at the end of the town's life in 1910; although built to service the mining industry it ended up being used by the townspeople to transport their goods and, in some cases, houses out of the valley where Walhalla sits. I pulled into the car park in the hope of hitching a ride along the valley floor only to find that it was closed.

As I entered the town along the only road it was if I'd travelled back in time; the buildings were not modern (though there weren't that many) and lined the main road which in turn cut a path through the valley. Either side were steep wooded slopes giving an almost Alpine feel to the place. It was almost as if I'd managed somehow to become fused into an incredibly picturesque postcard. I checked into the hotel (the Star Hotel) which is situated in the heart of the town. The hotel is not the original one which was burnt down in 1951 in one of the many fires that ravaged the town from its foundation to the closure of the mines in 1915 and then right on into the mid 1950's. I had arrived in blistering heat and I had heard that the fire alert warnings where one down from red and that extra care needed to be taken to stop a conflagration happening. And there is was again in my nostril as I'd stepped back into the street having deposited by bags, the unmistakable mixture of sweet smelling pines and eucalypts fused with burnt timber.

Walking back down the road from the direction I'd arrived I passed what had been the fire station which, given the propensity for things to burn down, was housed in a timber barn. Brilliant! Today it is a small museum that houses an old horse-drawn fire engine and some memorabilia including old photos of the crews that used to man the engines posing with a cup that they had won in some musical competition. The sepia photographs show these men in all their finery with their instruments proudly smiling at the camera against a backdrop of the town as it was. It must have been quite a place to live back in the late 19th century. Progressing on along the main street was the Freemason's Lodge, the old post office and most fascinating of all the old vaults from the Bank of Victoria which at one time or another stored the 72 tonnes of gold extracted from the mines in Walhalla and the surrounding districts (someone seems to have stolen the rest of the building but left the vaults, possibly the world's dumbest criminal?).

Next I walked up to a walkway (the old tramway) that overlooked the town and provided a panoramic view of what is an incredibly pretty village. Later that evening when I was looking through some old photos of the town I came across one that cannot have been far from where I had stood. Whereas today there are only a couple of dozen buildings, at the height of the town's history there were some 10 hotels, over 4,000 inhabitants at its peak, shops, 3 breweries and a huge smelter. Also, whereas there are trees everywhere just over 100 years ago the slopes were bare. The demands of the smelter were immense and towards the end of the life of the town they had to 'import' wood from other area because none was left. The ecological damage was staggering but, nature as she is, has today done a fantastic job of returning much of the place back to its natural look.

At the end of the walkway was Long Tunnel Extended Mine which today is still theoretically operational but in reality is a tourist stop. I haven't done much in the way of underground exploration, aside from a crawl around a tin mine in Cornwall, but this promised to be relatively easy. Again I was the only one there but far too early for the next tour so I bought a ticket and wondered off to the Walhalla Cricket Ground.

The cricket ground is not exactly easy to reach as I had to walk up a very steep path before reaching it at the top of a hill that (again looking at the pictures later) was one of the very few flat areas to be found hereabouts, made possible by the miners who in the 1880's cut the top off. I lingered for a while recalling what I had read on the plaque at the start of the ascent about how the MCC (not the Marylebone but Melbourne Cricket Club) had played here in 1911 when the future captain of Australian cricket, Warwick Armstrong was bet that he couldn't hit the Star Hotel with his first hit. There is one photograph in the hotel that shows spectators in all their summer finery, men in striped jackets and women with umbrellas to keep the sun off, watching as the game against the MCC was played. Then the cricket pitch was grassed and there were few trees; today it is a ghost pitch, grown over with the forest and bush once more encroaching at the edges. For a time it was also the home of the Walhallian Australian Rules Football team.

However, the story of the Walhallians legendary success on the cricket pitch is one that our present cricket team/rugby team/football team (delete as appropriate) might do well to adopt. They were difficult to beat because of one very simple ruse. Being sociable townsfolk a visiting side was always wined and dined the night before a game by the local bigwigs in the hotel they would be staying in. As Bacchus ruled the night the Walhallian team would excuse themselves early so, as they explained, that they could get to their homes which for some could be quite a distance. Fair enough but in actual fact they would camp that night on the ground, awaking fresh and ready in the morning. The following day their opposition, hung-over and laden with their equipment, would have to slog all the way up the hill to play arriving completely exhausted; what a great tactic.

This approach to gaining the upper hand, or not as the case may be, reminds me of the Swiss. Here is a nation that is situated in a country renowned for, amongst a few other things, its mountains. So what kind of army units does it have? It's got infantry, armoured, engineers and so on. There's nothing unusual about that, after all most armies have these types of units. But, and I really love this, until a couple of years ago it had a bike regiment. Not motorised you understand but a *pedal-based bike regiment* Pity the poor invading army as it drives over the mountain in its tanks to be confronted by one very knackered Swiss military cyclist:

"Vill you please vait until I haf mine breath back before ve fight?"

Mind you this is also a country that sells cheese with holes in it and to be fair hasn't fought a war since the Cantons tried to decide if Catholicism or Lutheranism was best for the Federation in the mid 19th century.

Having slogged my way back down hill I walked back to the mine, hoping that I was still the only one to be in the next tour. Alas it was not to be as there in front of me was a group of around 20 post pubescent Australian teenagers on a day trip. Now in the past I have had some pretty dreadful experiences back in the UK when a similar gathering has been at some tourist site, in a museum or just 'there', so my heart sank when I saw them. This was going to be hell and I wasn't looking forward to *that* individual who always seems to be part of these groups, the one who talks incessantly during the trip making sarcastic remarks about this and that to impress one of the girls or just his mates.

Before I went into the mine I watched a video showing the life of those who worked the mines, not just here but across the district. What came across to me was the youth of so many, of smiling groups of men and boys who looked as if they were about to go on a fun day out but in reality were to spend the next 10–12 hours chipping away at the rock looking for gold. Behind these smiles though I felt a sense of underlying sadness, almost as if those photographed had some expectation of becoming rich but knew that deep down this wasn't going to happen. But on there was also a sense of comradeship, of being in it together similar to those photos in books I have at home of the Pals Battalions marching off to fight on the Western Front in 1914–18. In both cases the hardship that these men faced whether working to keep their families on the breadline or, as with the Pals, seeing their mates mown down and killed in vast numbers, seems to me to be evident; the smiles hide a nervousness and anticipation of what might be than that of excitement or happiness. It is overwhelming sad but also a snapshot of the past that nowadays is much rarer to see. Later in this book I talk about the truly Australian concept of 'mateship', of being one together, and these sepia photos are a reminder that to an extent in this country at least it does seem to carry more gravitas.

I was soon joined by the others and then Gill the guide introduced us all to the mine taking us through its history from the start of operations in 1865 through to the final time the gold in any reasonable quantity was last mined in 1911. Founded by the Hercules Gold Mining Company (who didn't strike it lucky) and then taken over by the Long Tunnel Extended Gold Mine Company in 1867, the mine workings themselves were extensive and covered around 9 kilometres and were, at their deepest, nearly 950 metres. By the mid 1880's right up until its effective closure it was the State of Victoria's principal mine. Given the amount of gold that was extracted and its value even then (nearly 14 tonnes was taken out in the just under 50 years) the people who worked underground worked for a pittance considering the wealth they hewed out of the rock, but it was still a job many wanted to do because it paid 6 times the average wage of a worker in most other industries. Gill pointed out that the work itself was dangerous and that many miners died young from a variety of diseases or through workplace accidents, notably through the use of explosives. The video tells just a part of the story of how dangerous this work was and for nothing in many cases, but a cutting from the Sydney Morning Herald from 1851 gives an idea:

> 'Gold digging they imagine is but play – kicking the nuggets out of the sand with their feet. They find on arrival, it is exceedingly laborious and heavy work and that they will kick their feet and knock their shins against a good many rocks, before they see the specks – let alone the nuggets.'

The best job to get was that of a surface-man, someone who was past their prime in terms of being able to work underground, but, almost unbelievably, was also probably only in their early 30's. Life expectancy if you stayed in the mine was short so getting to the surface was regarded as both evidence of an ability to survive but also having 'made it'. I asked Gill more about this almost cheapness of life and on her advice I visited the Walhalla Burial Ground that is perched on the side of a hill. Now largely overgrown and certainly not a place to visit if unsure of your footing, it is the last resting place of some 5,000 souls, many of whom were unknown until the work of Yolanda Reynolds who spent two decades researching and cataloguing those buried there. And just as Gill had intimated many of the graves were of young men killed working in the mine or from one or more illness and disease. The graves were like reading a 'Who's Who?' of countries and as with everywhere I had visited or was to visit the religions were separated. I wondered how many of those in the graves had hoped that they were going to make their fortune on leaving their country of birth only to find that the reality was so much less kind. However it made me think about something that Australia doesn't seem to advertise well.

By way of an explanation the United States is still known as a country where people would go to seek their fortunes or to build a new life. It is repeatedly seen in the names of places, in films like 'The Godfather', in travel brochures that always seem to refer to Ellis Island and the role it played in modern America and so on. As I stood looking around the grave I realised that this was exactly the same. Here was America but in Australia. The town even had a Scandinavian name, albeit it was anglicised. Travelling around though it wasn't as easy perhaps as it is in the US to identify this early generation as for me at least the accents were just Australian (though ranging from slightly nasal to very nasal). Even the names of place are less obvious in Australia, although looking through my road map they're there. To many back home Australia is Fosters, Paul Hogan's 'Crocodile Dundee', the late Steve Irwin, Nicole Kidman and Kylie (and more recently her sister). I bet the only place people would associate with Australia's past is Botany Bay and with its people, Ned Kelly. The common theme is that both are to do with the Country's convict past. But Walhalla tells a different story. Ned Stringer wasn't actually Ned Stringer: he was in fact a convict on a 'ticket of leave' whose real name was Edward Randel.

This all represents a conundrum for me and remained to throughout my travels. Australia for some reason seems reluctant to advertise her past yet talk to the local shopkeeper or share a beer with someone and here the story is different. There are plenty of Walhalla's throughout the country with similar histories and stories of newcomers entering the country in search of fortune. Yes there are convicts, after all Britain sent thousands, but there are stories of success everywhere, of convicts taking opportunity in both hands and making something of it. There is a pride that from hardship so much has been achieved, a real sense that as a whole everyone benefits, which I have to say is not the same as the US. I should add that this slightly rose tinted look at Australia shouldn't be done without understanding the cost to the Aboriginals, but even here there seem to be huge strides in changing attitudes.

That evening after an early dinner in the hotel I got chatting to the owner. The re-building of this hotel and really of almost a rebirth of

Walhalla was down to a few really dedicated individuals who wanted to preserve a part of Australian history that is perhaps better known in places like Ballarat in the Grampians to the west of Melbourne than here. These were people who were proud of what had been here and what was here now and even though there were only 11 permanent residents in Walhalla, the pass through traffic now was at peak times huge. But what I liked about this hotel and the owner and his colleague working the restaurant and bar was that in my view for them commercialism was not the main driver but the love of the place. They also wanted visitors to the hotel to experience an almost 21st century-free sensation not just by having no A/C in the bedrooms but also giving the whole place a really strong feel of the past underscored by the reading room which contained an extensive collection of old photographs about the whole area which were fascinating. Sitting there later with a proverbial beer, I was once more transported to a time when Australia was becoming a nation where the gold rush was at its height and Walhalla was an integral part of that. But tonight as I sat here, it was quiet, almost as if the only things left to tell the story aside from the buildings, were the faces in the photos and the ghosts of those who had lived and worked here and whose mortal remains were in the graveyard. Either that or the beer was stronger than I had thought. I should mention before I close out this chapter that the teenagers who visited the mine with me were perfectly well behaved although they did keep looking at me which could have been because I am incredibly good looking or else questioning how someone with my girth had actually managed to fit through the entrance to the place. One question remained and that was I wonder if Armstrong ever hit that big six onto the hotel down below?

CHAPTER 5

Melbourne, home to the 'half house' and the most laid back human of all time

DAY eight: Armistice Day, November 11th:

> '15 February – Working up, the port with a very strong ebb against us, we however gained ground. The southern shore of this noble harbour is bold high land in general and not clothed as all the land at western point is with thick brush but with stout trees of various kinds and in some places falls nothing short, in beauty and appearance, of Greenwich Park. Away to the eastward at a distance of twenty miles the land is mountainous, in particular there is one very high mountain which in the meantime I named Arthur's Seat from its resemblance to a mountain of that name a few miles from Edinburgh … I have named the harbour Port King in honour of Governor P.G. King under whose orders I act.'

This passage is taken from another of Tim Flannery's books, 'The Birth of Melbourne' and is from the log of John Murray, Captain of the *Lady Nelson*, who in 1802 sailed into the bay (it was renamed Port Phillip by Governor King) and where today sits the entrance to Melbourne.

Melbourne is not a huge distance from Walhalla and the drive took around 3 hours with a short break for lunch in a roadway café in Yarragon. Given today was the day that commemorated the 'War to end all Wars' (The First World War and those since) it was nice to see, as I sat drinking my coffee, a group of smartly dressed uniformed children pass by wearing their obligatory sun hats (it was baking at over 35 degrees) and poppies. As the teacher passed I asked where they had been and he said that they had all been to a local town service remembering the dead of all wars and those who served and survived. I asked him if the children understood what the significance of the red poppy was and what they felt. He told me that for many children it was as much about remembering the community and about Australia's long involvement in wars that for many were fought in far off places the other side of the world.

"Were they proud of this or did they feel that it was something that they were made to do on sufferance?" This last comment was more of a reflection of my own upbringing when these sorts of events were seen by me and my friends as more of a hassle.

"No" he replied "many of these kids grow up knowing about the role of Australia, of the ANZAC's at Gallipoli and the incredible sacrifice made. Many of the kids have European backgrounds and whose grandparents or great-grandparents moved here in the 1920's and 1930's and some after the war so for them there is a strong heritage and one that many of their parents still honour and keep."

Back in London I was talking to an Australian who had moved to the UK in 1999 about this and had asked him if he was surprised about my encounter.

"Let me explain it this way" he said "on my way through to London I and a couple of mates decided that we would visit ANZAC Cove at Gallipoli to commemorate ANZAC day. The hassle of getting there was immense involving flights to Athens and then Holland back to Istanbul followed by a long overnight drive. We arrived in the early hours and after a few beers went to sleep. The service always starts at dawn and when we awoke I reckon there were 15,000 people or more there standing in total silence. Then the sun came up and the bugler sounded the Last Post which was then followed by the anthems of Australia and New Zealand. It was the most moving thing I have ever known and today it still makes me incredibly proud to have done it."

I asked him what was it that made him go and for that matter why many from those countries made the effort to travel to a place that was in a part of the world that was a million miles from home.

"It was about mates; it wasn't about the Empire but about sticking together, of brothers, fathers and sons often from the same town or village being as one. They knew that death awaited many of them, but they were with their mates. That's what counted." Interestingly in 2000 Steve Waugh took the Australian cricket team to Gallipoli and although some were concerned that it was a publicity stunt to somehow link the spirit of the ANZAC to a team that at the time was struggling, I'd like to think that it was more than that, after all there are photos showing cricket being played in 1915 at Shell Green and in my view those that went epitomised this Australian attitude to sticking together, of being proud of not just what they represented in the green floppy but what these men who had paid the ultimate sacrifice had done. It is worth remembering that in all some 8,000 ANZAC troops were killed at Gallipoli, no mean number given the size of both Australian and New Zealand at that time.

In Australia there are numerous Returned Servicemen's League clubs, like the British Legion back in the UK, but the difference is that many of those with memorials in front of the buildings I passed included names that could easily have been from towns in Italy, Germany and Eastern Europe and so on. Maybe that was that was it; maybe also it was as the teacher said that history in Australia was as much about the pride of a nation and the fact that it was much more ethnically diverse.

There is a sad epitaph to this remembrance of ANZAC day at Gallipoli. In 2003 there was an article in the Sydney Morning Herald talking about that year's commemoration of those who fought and died. At its peak this service, held each 25th April, saw as many as 20,000 attend to remember. However, as a new war raged in the form of terrorism and increased fears of Kurdish militancy, numbers had fallen to, according to this report just 8,000. Welcome to the modern era.

The quickest way into central Melbourne was via the M1 toll road, but having already paid a fortune to hire a car I was determined not to make a further donation so before I had left Walhalla I was provided with a route that would take me through the suburbs. It would take longer but turned out to be rather pleasant not least as I was in no great hurry. As I drove into the outskirts there were no high rise buildings with most being two maybe three storeys high interspersed with a more modern office block (but still no more than a few storeys) and to me there was once more a strong sense of Australia's colonial past represented by this architecture. As soon as I hit the Central Business District (CBD) it was a completely different world. As I drove past the Melbourne Cricket Ground it was as if the pavement had joined forces with the sky as huge buildings rose higher and higher. This was no hick town, no sleepy backwater. This was modern Australia, the country of today, showing its pride in itself through the buildings around me (and just for the record Melbourne has the largest percentage of the tallest buildings on the Continent with the Eureka Tower being the tallest). But even as I marvelled at the sheer volume of glass, there was still much evidence of older times, but, as with say Manhattan, I was under no illusion as to which century I was in. The suburbs may have been from yesterday, but the CBD was definitely today.

In some ways this contrast between the old and the new reminded me of when I lived in Boston in the US where my apartment overlooked two famous landmarks in the City – Boston Garden and Boston Common. One was a creation of the 19th century, whilst the latter was where in Colonial times farmers grazed sheep and cattle. As I looked across from my apartment to Cambridge on the other side of the Charles River I had on my right Beacon Hill and the Back Bay, parts of which date to the early 18th century: my very first apartment was where British officers had been billeted during the American War of Independence. To the left a large part of what are today Boylston Street and Newbury Street preserve their predominantly 19th to early 20th century feel. However, if I turned a full 180 degrees and looked out the back of where I was living (difficult as there was a brick wall and a Chinese family living the other side but I do posses x-ray vision) there was Downtown, equivalent to Melbourne's CBD, with all its modern office blocks. Although some old buildings existed such as the Post Office the emphasis was modern America. In this architectural vista was not just a part of Boston's history but that of when America was first colonised. Melbourne was the same.

Another key date in Melbourne's history was in 1835 when John Bateman of the Port Phillip Association in Tasmania surveyed the area with the intention of creating a township, never mind that the land in question was actually the home of a local Aboriginal tribes belonging to the Kulin nation alliance. Bateman from all accounts was pretty unscrupulous in his dealings with most people notably the Aboriginals in Tasmania where he was a prime mover in trying to corral them into a small area of the island. Tim Flannery has reproduced Batemans's diary entries for what became Bateman's Treaty. On June 8th 1835 he 'purchased' some 200,000 hectares of land from eight of the local Aboriginal Wurundjeri elders who in return received:

> ' … twenty pair of blankets, thirty tomahawks, one hundred knives,
> fifty pair scissors, thirty looking glasses, two hundred handkerchiefs,
> and one hundred pounds of flour, and six shirts.'

These were to be paid annually and Bateman and his heirs were to be granted the land in perpetuity. Ironically, the Treaty was annulled by the New South Wales government as this was already Crown land in their view, which of course conveniently omitted that fact that it was in fact the ancestral home to Kulin nation. However, as with other areas of the world where white settlers moved into, the indigenous peoples tended to have a completely different outlook on what land actually meant. Theirs was a life that encompassed living with the elements, with the earth and with natures' creatures. The way that they saw the land around them was more of a mutually inclusive relationship that encompassed life and death, whereby in return for it feeding them they showed a huge amount of respect for it. Many of these so-called treaties were dubbed 'trinket deals' (like Manhattan Island which was 'bought' for little more than beads). For those Europeans who travelled to these new lands the objectives that they had were more worldly and driven by a totally different set of standards. As elsewhere when these two elements of white settler and indigenous people came together conflict inevitably ensured. Through these deals consciously or not, these new entrants to the country were attacking the very essence of the culture and way of living that the indigenous people had been experiencing for millennia. It was so devastating that the Aboriginal population fell dramatically.

As a City (from 1847) Melbourne became a big beneficiary of the discovery of gold such that its wealth made it one of the richest cities not just in the Empire, but the world. In 1852 Antoine Fauchery arrived in the city and in one of his letters that Flannery quotes he describes the scene:

> 'The enormous number of newcomers to this little capital makes it an impossible place to stay in. Neither gold nor silver would get you a room there. A chair, a bench, cost more than they would at most splendid fireworks display, and barely half of this floating population that the English marine casts on to the shore every day succeeds in obtaining any shelter for a few days. Consequently, the other half sleeps in the open!'

As with other parts of Australia, as the population grew, this created its own tensions with everything from criminal intrigues to inter-communal fighting. In 1868 when HRH Prince Alfred visited the City, having been almost shot dead when he was in what is today the genteel Sydney suburb of Clontarf, fights broke out amongst the Irish Catholics who were not overly monarchist to put it mildly and their 'chums' of the Orange Order (Protestants) who were – so no change there then. The rise in crime meant, as it had done in Georgian England, more murders. Fauchery was witness to one outcome, a hanging, of one such deed and of the public spectacle that it was:

> ' … where I am living, they were hanging a gentleman guilty of murdering his workmate on the road to the mines. The crowd was dense round the gallows, and the ladies were handing each other, turn about, binoculars and field glasses, so as to miss nothing as they watched the victim's face.'

He went on to describe the condemned man's last moments on earth and imagined this man's anxiety as the time of execution drew near. This description reminded me of the women, Les Tricoteuse who, during the French Revolution, would sit and watch the execution of many of France's nobility all the while merrily knitting away. It's fair to say of course that at this time and well on into the 19th century public execution was a real crowd puller, a sort of day out for the family. Those about to be hanged were the stars of their day, albeit one slight snag, it was a one act show with no encore. One of the paintings from the period is 'The idle Prentice Executed at Tyburn', which shows huge numbers of people coming to watch. At the last public hanging in England in 1868, it was reported that some 2,000 came to watch a Fenian called Michael Barrett be hanged outside Newgate Prison. Although both events were reflective of what was going on back in England, Australians also loved a good execution as Fauchery described. It seems a somewhat strange way to spend a day but I guess there is no accounting for what some people enjoy doing. But I wonder, what do you wear? Can you buy a vuvuzela? Is it rude to heckle, or is that required? Do you clap the hangman for a good job? What if the rope breaks do you get your money back?

The City has always been in rivalry to Sydney. Melbournians are referred to as 'Mexicans' by Sydneysiders as they are 'south of the border' whilst the latter are seen as aloof and pretentious. It's one of the reasons that Canberra was chosen as the place for Australia's capital, sitting rather like Washington DC, in its own territory so that no one would be upset. It must have really riled Sydney when Melbourne got the 1956 Olympic Games and I have no doubt festered until they got it in 2000. Another sore point was that when Federation took place Melbourne was the first seat of government. Still at least Sydney had been the focal point of the celebrations that took place at the time as quoted by Keneally from the Argus newspaper:

> '*Argus*, 10 May 1901 – By the hand of royalty, in the presence of the greatest concourse of people that Australia has seen in one building, and with splendid pomp and ceremonial, the legislative machinery of the Commonwealth was yesterday set in motion … After a brief pause the Duke of Cornwall and York stepped forward once more, read a special cable of congratulations from His Majesty the King. And now Australia asserted herself, she had been suppressing her feelings to show that she knew how to behave with old world decorum in the presence of Royalty, but this message direct from the King himself, was too much – they simply had to cheer. And cheer they did. It was done without order or without concert. It was taken up time after time by sections of the audience; it ran round the aisles. And surged through the galleries; a hearty, spontaneous, irrepressible Australian cheer.'

I love that last sentence. To me it sums up what I was now seeing day-to-day as I travelled the country or as I today watch Australians as they play sport, serve me in a shop or just stop to talk to me. It's infectious and although my Australian friends and acquaintances are serious when it counts most just look to enjoy life to the full. Go to any place where Australians hang out in London and it's often there in spades, although to be fair most of those I know are now rather adept at moaning about the UK's propensity to have dreadful weather. Frankly it serves them right and anyway it stops them all developing skin cancer so perhaps a little more gratitude is required.

The hotel I was staying in was close to the main shopping district in Melbourne, the Treasury and Fitzroy Gardens, the latter being overlooked by the State Government Buildings. Reading my various guides there seemed a lot to do in the City from visiting the famous Melbourne Cricket Ground, the Immigration Museum and Melbourne Old Gaol to just enjoying some of the architectural highlights such as Flinders Station. I decided that my first port of call would be the gardens that, like the Royal Botanical Gardens in Sydney are filled with a huge variety of trees and plants. The gardens are dissected by Lansdowne Street, with the Treasury Gardens being the smaller of the two. The only real thing of note in these was the memorial to JFK in the form of an ornamental fountain and pond, the former of which was not functioning due to the water shortage. The Fitzroy Gardens are three to four times larger and contain a number of stops that the tourist is guided to by helpful signs throughout. The gardens themselves are very patriotic as they are laid out the design of the Union flag.

Now I have done plenty of 'follow the sign' type sightseeing only usually to be confronted by something that in reality doesn't live up to the expectation. In Toronto years ago I had visited a Titanic exhibition on the 'follow the sign' principle which also had those 'must see' invitational words (you know 'See the genuine toilet last used by Captain Smith when he took a dump' or as it should say 'this is a really crap exhibit and we fooled you'). Anyway, fifteen Canadian dollars later I calculated that there was more to see in the gift shop than the exhibition and that perhaps the marketing people had been somewhat over-enthusiastic in their descriptions. The Fitzroy Gardens are free so I am not going to moan about them too much but to be blunt the model Tudor village and Fairies tree fall right into the Captain Smith's toilet syndrome.

Anthony Trollope, when he visited Melbourne in the early 1870's, may well have been at this very place when he observed:

> 'These gardens are not in themselves well kept. They are not lovely, as are those of Sydney in a super-excellent degree. Some of them are profusely ornamented with bad statues. None of them, whatever may be their botanical value, are good gardens.'

In this piece from Flannery, Trollope does go on to admit that for the citizens the gardens are probably a healthy place to be. I bet he deep down wanted to also say that the Tudor village and Fairies tree were dreadful in some fruitful language, but as a Victorian gentleman kept things decent. Today the gardens have matured considerably and are well kept and although given the water shortage none of the fountains were working it was all very pleasant. Also on the plus side, I thought, there was always Captain Cook's cottage which is set in a small garden of its own and is genuinely his house that was originally located in Great Ayton in Yorkshire. There was a small entrance fee and the first thing that struck me was how small it was (the house not the fee, just in case you were confused!). It's minute and given the number of children living at one time in it very cramped. How could anyone live here comfortably? Outside is the garden which is supposed to be what it might have looked like when Cook lived there, but that too was tiny. So, I'd gone upstairs and done downstairs and the garden in all of 5 minutes. The only place left of course was the inevitable gift shop. This was situated where the barn would have been in the house's original location.

"Bit small isn't it?" I asked the rather bored looking shop assistant.

"Well, actually it's not all here."

"Sorry?"

"Well when the city authorities bought it in 1933 there was 40 feet missing when it arrived in Australia."

Three thoughts immediately crossed my mind: the first was the look on the cottage owners' face when he/she returned that evening after a hard day sheep herding in the Dales to find their home had gone and the second was what on earth do you do with 40 feet of cottage? Here's another thing that made me smile when it came to this inter-city rivalry between Sydney and Melbourne. You see Melbournians will tell you that this is the oldest European built building in Australia. Nope, that privilege goes to Sydney. Perhaps Melbourne city council needs to change their advertising to read 'Australia's Oldest Imported Building'. One up to Sydney methinks.

Having wondered around for an hour or so – it's amazing how much time I can 'lose' if my mind is free of everyday thoughts (although some who know me might suggest that this is what I am like every day) – I walked towards one of the city's most iconic buildings, Flinders Station, which is the oldest city station in Australia. So now it's one all then with Sydney. Although the station was established in 1854, the current building dates from the late 19th century and was built to a French Renaissance style being completed officially in around 1910. There is a saying in Melbourne 'I'll meet you under the clocks' which is a reference to the clocks above the main entrance. The station façade is eye-catching and reminded me of the Belle Époque buildings built towards the end of the 19th century such as the Ritz in London which was designed by Charles Mewes and Arthur Davis in a neo-classical style to give the look of an upmarket Parisian tenement at the time of Louis XVI. Looking at the departure board you could be forgiven for a moment thinking that you were at one of the large terminus stations back in the UK given the names of some of the destinations like Sandringham (Norfolk), Epping (Middlesex), Cranbourne (Dorset) and Sydenham (South East London). One wonders what might happen to these names if this country that continues to flirt with becoming a republic actually achieves full independence. Will they change the names? I doubt it, after all the Americans in the most part didn't and in fact in New England the majority of the county's still hark back to when the King's English was the lingua franca. Having pondered this and about how much a return fare from South East London to Melbourne might cost I went back outside and after taking the obligatory photograph off I went again to look at the shopping district along Swanton Street.

The street was like so many others in large towns or cities, filled with a mix of expensive shops and those that were more affordable to the likes of me, along with the usual mix of coffee shops (and it seemed that Starbucks had the monopoly). However, what stood out were not so much the shops but the people. Whereas I had a feeling in Sydney that the city was predominantly Anglo-Saxon in its genetic mix (though to be fair this was probably due more to the fact that I spent most of my time in one area), Melbourne seemed far more cosmopolitan. I asked a friend about this, he having returned to the city after 10 years in the UK, and he had noticed that not just that the city was more diverse, most notably in recent times with the influx of Asians from the Sub-Continent, but to an extent more vibrant because of this.

Sadly, there has been a darker side to this most notably in the seemingly random attacks on this community which some commentators have suggested as being racially motivated and not just about gangs as others have suggested. It is at this point that there seems to be a dichotomy between those in the country who welcome this influx of new immigrants as being a benefit to the country and those that hold on to some misguided concept of the past. And of the many people I talked to although not one condoned the violence there were one or two who seemed a little ambivalent about it, similar to the so-called Aboriginal 'problem'. Just going back to this diverse cultural mix that now exists in the city, it is perhaps ironic that it was here in 1901 that the White Australia policy that was in place for a large part of the 20th century was officially enacted from the Immigration Act of that year, but it also shows that, without ignoring the recent violence, this country has made great strides forward.

However, even with this and the new sense of confidence evident in many of the Australians that I met and know back in the UK, there is still a lot of hand-wringing as to what this really means and how this then translates in everyday life. I recently read an article about something called the 'Cultural Cringe', a term which was coined by A.A Philips about a perception that Australians felt that they were somehow inferior and that it was very evident in the arts and elsewhere in print and cinema and amounted to one long put down of a nation. The article went on to talk about how it wasn't class that differentiated Australians but accent. So much so that until the 1970's to read the news on ABC you had to have a British accent as it was seen as superior to the broad or general accent spoken by around 90% of the population. Mind you to be fair back in the UK when television was in its infancy and right through to the late 1950's, continuity announcers wore evening dress and spoke with cut glass accents. Today, and I know this is a little snobbish, but I really wonder what some of them are saying – but hey "thar's now't wrong wid regional accent lad"

On a much lighter note when researching this, I came across an article that was in a similar vein which revealed that there had been discussions in the newspapers about what was the image that Australia was trying to portray to the outside world. One such article by Kelsey Munro looked at a survey of 50 CEO's of small and medium sized business which appeared in the Sydney Morning Herald and comes straight to the point:

> 'Australians doing business overseas say their efforts are being damaged by tourism advertising that portrays Australia as the idiot in the global village, a study shows. A long line of tourism campaigns have used genial, laid-back stereotypes, from Paul Hogan's "throw a shrimp on the Barbie" and the notorious "Where the bloody hell are you?" to the recent "There's nothing like Australia singalong … " "being positioned as a nation of boofheads, serial barbecuers and boozers … "'

It's actually an interesting puzzle this. If I was to ask most Brits of my age what they remember about Paul Hogan outside of Crocodile Dundee and they'll say 'Fosters'; ask the same people to name other famous adverts along those lines and up comes those that ran for Castlemaine XXXX. No one can forget that great comedian Barry Humphries with his Sir Les Patterson and Dame Edna Everage. Most people know Uluru (though as Ayers Rock) and the Sydney Opera House. We all know where kangaroos come from and that Australia has lots of things that can kill you. Australians are good at sports and the sun always shines. But that's it; I can't think of one high brow cultural thing that comes from the land down under (Kylie aside) but that's the point I think. I know where this country is, and I was going to learn a lot more now I was here but was it important for it to have a surfeit of Reuben's or Beethoven's, to actually have a positive image.

Melbourne is sports mad like the rest of Australia and is home to both the MCC and the Carlton Club, both of which play in the magnificent Melbourne Cricket Ground more commonly referred to as the MCG. The ground dates back to 1853 and today has a capacity to seat 100,000 spectators making it one of the world's largest stadiums. Melbourne also is the home of Australian Football League which dates back 1897 when the Victoria Football League came into being. The AFL is the most watched sport now in Australia and is immense fun to watch. However, there are one or two questions that I have:

1. Why do the players wear the almost unbelievable tight shorts and shirts?
2. Why is there a baker at each end of the ground directing airplanes every time there is a score?
3. Why does the touchline official throw the ball over his head backwards – he could have someone's eye out (although if he did this in the UK no doubt health and safety would first have conducted an utterly pointless suitability study)?
4. Should AFL players be banned if they sport mullets – seems to me watching the game that there is a profusion of these?

When the AFL first came into being it was not to everyone's liking, with a reputation that bordered on legal thuggery, Flannery points quotes

John Stanley James' article of September 30th 1876 written under his nom de plume The Vagabond which appeared in the *Argus* and was penned by him after watching a not to friendly encounter between Melbourne and the Carlton Club:

'Football as now carried on here is not often rough and brutal between combatants, but seems to me to have a decided moral lowering and brutalising effect upon the spectators.' He goes on to talk about the injuries players suffer and then asks if it is all worth it: 'I think not, and hold that evil does not stop here, but that society is demoralised by such exhibitions … If an intelligent foreigner had been present, watching these young men clad in party-coloured garments running after an inflated piece of leather … he must have thought it the amusement of madmen. The spectators, who howled and shrieked and applauded, he would have thought equally mad … ' At this point he goes off on another lament about the way that players get injured, the language used (the umpire walked off in a huff and had to be replaced because of this abuse) and the generally ungentlemanly way the whole game was played, ending his piece: 'I consider that football as played last Saturday is a disgrace to our civilisation.'

Personally I think The Vagabond should have changed his nom do plume to something more akin befitting his delicate take on life. Perhaps if he had called himself The Big Girls Blouse that might have been more appropriate.

Melbourne is in more recent times the venue for the Formula One Grand Prix, which had been held in Adelaide, but which they nicked. I have to confess that F1 is for me the dullest event ever thought up by any so-called sports enthusiast. For me watching Michael Schumacker or Jenson Button or whoever going round and round a race track for two hours is only slightly less boring than watching grass grow and that's if it is on television. What sane person spends a fortune to see these stars drive round for a total of, oh I don't know, maybe a couple of minutes in that entire two hours?

The city is also the place for one of the most eagerly followed and attended events in the sporting calendar – the Melbourne Cup which will be 150 years old come 2011. It is like Ascot, the Derby, the Grand National and a soupcon of the Prix de l'Arc de Triomphe all rolled into one glorious event. Even in the rival city of Sydney there are big screens showing the days racing and everyone is dressed to the nines getting drunk; brilliant and not the least bit ridiculous and something that we should definitely embrace back at home. Beat this though, unlike the big horse-racing events back in the UK, the Melbourne Cup race day is a public holiday for those in the metropolitan area. Did I say that Australians had a relaxed attitude to life? It is also a day that not surprisingly sees a lot of employees in the outlying districts develop a serious bout of one day bubonic plague resulting in an inability to work.

I was reminded on reading up about this of a story that my wife's cousin recently told me about someone he knew who was very keen to go to some sporting event back in Ireland, so naturally he had called in sick. The day progressed well and as befits any sound Irishman, he had a really good time with plenty of the black nectar. However, being the loyal employee he didn't feel that taking a second day away from work was appropriate so duly reappeared the following day, slightly worse for wear, but keen nevertheless to get stuck in. His boss asked him if he was feeling any better. "Yes he was" he said and thanked him for his concern at which point his boss enquired whether it was the eighth or ninth pint that had acted as a cure for his sickness because unfortunately for said employee his boss was sat two rows behind him at the same event. Long story short, he was sacked and I was wondering how many Melbourne Cup aficionadas fall into the same category of being caught red-handed. Always, always check your boss's calendar.

As my hotel was near China town I decided that I would eat there that evening. Now Australia's beer as sold in a restaurant or pub as I mentioned before is not cheap. There is a way around this as diners can often bring their own into a restaurant and what is more, mein host will keep it in the fridge until needed. Just in case you dear reader missed this – they not only look after the beer for you, they will keep it cold and bring it to you as you eat and you know what, there is no corkage. Bless Australian restaurants because I can't imagine many places back home that would do this. As I have already lamented Australia is a nation that drinks a lot of lager that, as we all know back in the UK, only football players and those who like football drink because they are all girls. Luckily as with Sydney, the grog shops in Melbourne had plenty of choices of real ale and so that evening I was armed and ready with a 6 pack of Little Creatures Pale Ale (Freemantle, WA) and on the hunt for a decent Chinese.

Sorry when I say 'decent Chinese' I don't mean to impugn the character of a Chinese person, but as a descriptive of some fine oriental establishment where my taste buds could be assaulted by the aromatic tastes of China. You get the idea.

As I walked along the main drag in China town each of the restaurants had young ladies touting for business standing outside them. Again just for clarification to those of you who are now expecting a paragraph on some sexual encounter I was to have with one of these young ladies, they were touting for customers to go into the restaurant.

All the restaurants I passed had ducks hanging in the window ready for that favourite meal of mine, crispy fried duck with pancakes and hoisin sauce. I once had this for a starter and main course and pudding with some friends after a particularly 'long' day at Lords watching England lose to the Moldavian 2nd XI or some such team. Tonight I was going to treat myself and stretch the wallet on a banquet of untold delight.

I sat down and before I had looked at the menu and drank my first beer, a 'suit' opposite me on another table who had been, by the looks of it, having a good time somewhere else somewhat vocally recommended the dead something or other (might have been dog but this wasn't a Korean restaurant) with noodles, bean sprouts and flung floo wing wang, at least that is what it sounded like. What sold it to me, having enquired politely what it was like, was his fulsome praise of the collected mass of food on his plate:

"Mate, it's only the best bloody Chinese meal of my life! It's bloody brilliant! You've got to have it as well."

Well with a recommendation like that how could I resist? As for me I did exactly what he suggested (almost) and decided to order crispy duck which was excellent along with Mongolian black bean pork bellied thingy with rice, all a bargain at only one ingot of gold and my left hand as payment. As I munched away, savouring every morsel as it passed from my mouth to my ever expanding stomach, my new pal finished his meal. Oh and his rather large bottle of Pinot Beijing which was of an uncertain vintage. At which point he said in the direction of the waitress:

"Miss, miss!" the waitress comes over to him, all smiles, "this is the worst bloody meal I have ever had. I'm not bloody paying!" he said, but not in any threatening way, more just as a matter of fact.

Mind you it did seem a slightly risky thing to say I thought in a Chinese restaurant where the owner and his Triad friend, are merrily chopping bits of duck and pork with huge meat cleavers in the actual dining area. Still on the other hand it could just be that this was another example of the straight-talking Aussie that is so frequently heard of. Either way it made me shrink a little into my seat and assume that traditional English custom of pretending that a) I didn't exist especially as I sunk lower into my chair and/or b) that the other person didn't exist and thus it was really just a bad dream. The waitress to her credit just smiled at him and said little (aside from a few choice words that as a non-Mandarin speaker I'm unable to reproduce here), and asked him how he was going to pay. This somewhat flummoxed my new non-existent pal as I think he may have been expecting to have been allowed to just leave without settling the bill. After a slight pause he reached into his jacket, got out his wallet and proffered his credit card. And that was that. No drama, no angry exchange. He'd had his say and satisfied that this was duly noted, paid. I can't say I've ever seen a similar scene but I suspect that he might have been joking (and as already noted in a somewhat dangerous looking place) and if so then this is something I do recognise as being quintessentially Australian. There's no malice intended when this happens and in fact most times the culprit usually has a huge grin on his (and it usually is male) face and says "Aw, mate, it's just a bit of fun. No offence, just pulling your chain ... " or something like that. I wonder if that would work back home? I suspect not. As a post script as my now reinstated pal left he turned in the door before going on to the street and thanked all, whilst giving me a special wave as if to say that I should try this approach to bill paying. I'm English and thus not cut out for that sort of thing and although I toyed with the idea for, I don't know maybe a nanosecond and paid leaving an enormous tip (not necessary in Australia) just in case our man in the Triad decided it wasn't that funny after all but that as my pal had left I would be the 'Tourist Split in Half by Meat Clever as Other Diner Upsets Chef'.

Day nine: November 12th

Another glorious day greeted me as I left my hotel for what was going to be history tour day. Melbourne is full of interesting places to visit and my first port of call was the Old Melbourne Gaol. Based on Jeremy Bentham's 18th century Panopticon design whereby all prisoners could be observed more easily by the guards (ironically these too would have been in all likelihood ex convicts), it is a daunting place. As with other Victorian era prisons in the UK (e.g. Manchester's Strangeways or Pentonville in London) it was designed as being a place of hard penal servitude, where silence was 'golden' and no contact with other prisoners was allowed, even in church where each convict would sit in a cubicle where the only person they could see would have been the priest.

There isn't much left of the gaol itself, aside from a wing which is on three floors. The building was begun in 1841 and was the main gaol for the city until 1924. In the Second World War it was also used for housing PoW's as well as allied soldiers who had gone AWOL. Nearly all the cells have something about the history of the gaol in them, from death masks of convicted prisoners through to photos of inmates. The Victorians were absolutely convinced that someone was born a criminal and the use of death masks and brain autopsies was all to do with their fascination with the faux science of phrenology.

Perhaps the most famous inmate at the gaol was Ned Kelly who was eventually hanged in the prison. Kelly was what Australians call a bushranger, which basically is someone who was involved in criminality from stage hold-ups to horse stealing and cattle rustling. He was from what I have read of him some sort of believer in the need to move away from government and to be free to do what you wanted, a type of utopianism that was just not going to happen as the Crown extended its control. Hocking describes the type of people that were in this mould:

> 'In the bush, bands of similarly disaffected, often brutalised, young men created their own society; a society with its own rules and with quite unlawful means of survival. They took to the roads, robbing the rich and giving to the poor – and looking after themselves of course. They helped themselves to supplies from outlying homesteads, and took the best and fastest horses and earned fanciful reputations amongst the poor and convict classes for their refusal to bend to the demands of the oppressors.'

He goes onto describe some of them, nearly all of whom had some great names, like Bold Jack Donohoe, John Piesley, Bold Ben Hall, Captain Thunderbolt (there must be a fart joke in there), the 'Kings of the Road' and the 'Currency Lads'. The latter got their name, as Hocking goes on to explain:

> 'These fit and tall, stringy, well-fed muscular young men would never be considered the equal of the home-born Englishman – 'sterling' – and the English did their best to keep the Australians in their place; the very bottom of the social scale.'

For many Australians Ned Kelly was arguably the most famous of all bushrangers and was, and still is, seen by many as some sort of anti-hero, someone who bucked the establishment and died trying to achieve some sense of equality for the downtrodden. To many his life has taken an almost mythical existence, in some ways like our very own Robin Hood except that Kelly was real and as far as I know didn't wear green tights and hang around with a similarly dressed bunch of 'Merry Men'. If the Victorians were right on phrenology, then Kelly fitted the bill as he was born into a family of petty criminals (his mother was serving time when he was eventually executed) and almost from the start of his life he was involved in crime, culminating in the shooting dead of three policemen, one of whom Kelly 'executed' as described by Hocking:

> 'At first, Michael Kennedy was badly wounded and tried to make his escape, but Ned chased him for half a mile and cut him down. As he lay mortally wounded on the forest floor, Ned walked over to him and finished him off with a shot to the head.'

Kelly claimed when asked to justify this act that his was an act of mercy and tried to explain away this and other actions as a response to the way that he and his family have been treated by the state. As with others outside the law, Kelly looked to justify his actions, which still today resonate with many who have a critical view of the role of the state. His thoughts became known as the Jerilderie Letter as dictated in 1879 to Joe Byrne, one of the Kelly gang who would die violently in 1880. Reading it (which is not easy after a few beers) is to get an insight into what was a harsh way of life for those living outside the law and those that lived in the bush. At the time of the letter Australia was still six territories and Kelly looked to create a seventh, an independent area, free from the Crown, which appealed to many (although in the end very few actually followed him to the end). What the letter shows is that authority was also corrupt at the local level ('Farrell the Policeman stole a horse from George King and had him in Whitty and Farrells Paddocks until he left the force.') but it didn't matter if you were on the 'right' side of the law. In the trial of his mother and two others called Skillion and Williamson he bemoans the way that the jury was in effect picked in order to find them guilty ' … it seems the jury was well chosen by the Police as there was a discharged Sergeant amongst them which is contrary to law they thought it impossible for a Policeman to swear a lie but I can assure them it is by means and hiring cads … ' (there are echoes here of the Tolpuddle Martyrs who years before and been found guilty of illegally taking oaths and then been tried by and found guilty by a veritable who's who of the local gentry). He was quite particular about these servants of the Crown when they made arrests, most especially his own Irish countrymen:

> 'I have seen many as eleven, big & ugly enough to live Mount Macedon out of a crab hole more like the species of a baboon or Guerilla than a man … '

Kelly was eventually brought to justice following his capture at the Glenrowan Hotel in June 1880. He was tried and condemned to death. At his trial he was unrepentant and tried to justify what he had done as if it were more to do with his destiny and that ultimately he was not wrong and that only God could judge him. In the gaol today the gibbet (I was told this was the original one) had some flowers laid upon it which were dedicated to Kelly's memory. The room next door is where he waited for the sentence to be carried out and here too were more flowers. On the ground floor there was a poster of him dressed in a Guantanamo style boiler suit with the question posed as to whether he was a criminal or freedom fighter. I have to say it did leave an unpleasant taste in my mouth seeing this, but I guess one person's freedom fighter is another person's terrorist, or hero.

On the second floor, there was also the frame to which men, women and even children were tied to receive the 'cat'. Being decent and caring the Victorians (not the Australian ones, but the generic ones in case you are now totally confused) never whipped someone who had passed out. No, instead a doctor would be present to assess the recipient and (and here's the piece de resistance) would revive said person to get the rest of their punishment. As I said, they were very caring people.

The gaol was also the site of the first judicial public executions of Aboriginals in January 1842 when two were hanged for murder. As with other places I had visited and was to visit later, their story is told almost in a cursory way. Here were two men executed for breaking what was a white man's law and yet although the story told in the gaol was more aligned to the wider issue of clashes between white and Aboriginal it didn't go into any real detail about exactly why – the tensions of the newly disposed versus the newly possessed, the clash of cultures and so on. The Aboriginal was a postscript almost. It was rather like visiting the old prison at the Fortress of Peter and Paul in St Petersburg which brushed over the brutality of the Bolshevik. Even more odd, well to me at least, was that Ned Kelly was being portrayed as a freedom fighter and yet no acknowledgment as to what these two Aboriginals might have actually been. Were they freedom fighters too, or were they just criminals as Kelly really was? It was a shame not least as whilst I was there the place was over-flowing with schoolchildren who were being given guided lectures by some of the staff and I did wonder what they were focusing on. Was it the history of white Australia or that of the country as it was?

Writing this up brought me back to thinking about one of the people who I spoke to when in Melbourne that day. I was in a bar writing this journal when someone leant over and asked me what I was doing in the now familiar friendly manner I was rapidly coming to like that Australians have. I explained that I had visited Melbourne Old Gaol that day and was just making some notes about the treatment of the indigenous people by the British then and was trying to figure out where it all fit in to my view of the country today. He responded: "Yea, it was a real problem but then I guess then you were bound to get conflict. But it has got really stupid these days. You see anyone who can prove that they have the slightest little trace of Abbo in them, can claim to be above the law. Strikes me this country has gone too far. These buggers can do anything they want and it seems no one gives a damn. But you see it's wrong; it makes the rest of us resent them. Too many people see them as problem and to me that's because recent successive governments have been too keen to make amends for the past. It's right so don't get me wrong, because the treatment of them has been shocking, but where do you stop?"

"So what would you do?" I asked.

"Not sure mate; I think if those in power ever worried about what the average Aussie really thinks, then maybe we should just leave them alone and let them sort themselves out."

"But what about the social issues? Back home the only Aboriginals we tend to see, apart from those appearing in films with Paul Hogan, are often portrayed as social misfits sitting under a tree drinking, with badly dressed kids wandering all living in pretty nasty looking places or they are on tourist programmes dancing for the punters. Do you think that what your government is really doing is trying to hide a real contradiction in Australia between an aspiring nation, whilst 'paying' to keep the indigenous issue out of the headlines?"

"Possibly, but you know whatever they do it will always come down to a cultural division that is really hard to break."

With that he smiled, drained his beer and wandered off into the hot late afternoon sun. I have to admit I was quite taken aback by all this, not that it was said in a malicious tone or with rage. His use of the word 'Abbo' I found out on my return to the UK was not seen as particularly offensive and for a lot of Australians was quite a natural thing to say as for them it did not carry the racist overtones that many of us now feel it does. However as he talked I sensed that there was a lot of angst in his voice, of almost frustration that everything should be left alone. It was as if he was saying to me "Yes, we know it's wrong but what can we do?" But here we were some 167 years since the two hangings and the discussion now was not what law the Aboriginal should be ruled by, but more why bother if at the end of the day it creates more problems than it solves?

Having done the gaol there was, next door, the 'Crime and Justice Experience' in the old City Watch House which closed as recently as 1996 but offered a guided tour by a real member, or so I thought, of Her Majesty's constabulary. Was I to partake, given my dislike of someone hamming it up and pretending to be some character from whatever era/exhibit/gene pool? Absolutely! I may hate those amateur dramatics but entry was included in the price of the Melbourne Old Gaol entry and thus I was damn well going to get my money's worth.

The guide was a boot faced police sergeant with all the charisma of a block of wood and a grimace suggestive of someone struggling with dreadful constipation. I wasn't sure if this was part of the 'act' of looking tough, so if it was she was convincing. There were a few of us and we were herded into the 'charge room' and then everyone was given a charge sheet and told to read out what they had been brought in for. I was hoping that mine would be something exciting like Gentleman Burglar by night, the 4th Earl Didgeridoo by day, but instead I was drunk in charge of a bicycle which actually in retrospect was more appropriate. Among my fellow felons there was a rather well proportioned lady who was charged with GBH which had her in a fit of giggles (no I don't know why so don't ask) whilst three young Japanese ladies just smiled and bowed like one of those wobbly head toys some rather sad cat-loving people have in the back of their car or on the dashboard. Once done we were all led into the cell bock and then, as part of the experience I presume, the officer shouted loudly at us to get in one of the cells. We were then left in the cell without the lights on for 5 minutes to get a 'feel' for what it was like, which was that it was dark. That was it, nothing else, just dark and actually rather pointless. My fellow cell mates chattered away to each other (I seemed to have wondered into a Saga holiday group of uncertain nationality) when, as if by magic, the lights came on again. Wow, what an experience, and it certainly beat my trip to Mt. St. Helens in 1997 or for that matter anything I had ever, ever done. I can see now why there was no extra charge.

The experience ended with a quick visit to the women's exercise yard where the sergeant/actor then gave a quick overview of who would have been put in here. I'd almost felt like sticking my hand up in the air before she had said anything and shout "Please, please miss, was it, and this is a really wild guess, female prisoners?" but I suspect that she might have seen this as a tad rude so I held back and marvelled at absolutely nothing that could be described as interesting. Once that was done, we were unceremoniously corralled back on the street so that she could go back to the front and repeat the whole charade again.

Back in the real world I went in search of my next target and this time I was genuinely looking forward to it. Up until now try as I might I had yet to find a museum or gallery entirely devoted to the Aboriginal (the Museum of Sydney's display was limited) but I had been recommended by one of the hotel staff to visit the Koorie Heritage Trust Cultural Centre. I had been told that there would be a lot of information as well as artefacts about the first contact between European and Aboriginal people, the Koorie. The word Koorie itself is actually a catch-all descriptive of the Aboriginal people according to the Australian Cultural Centre. Around 1960 following discussions between the indigenous people as to what the correct collective term for them was (i.e. not Aboriginal) the name Koorie (also known as Koori, Kory, Koole, Kooli) was agreed as it was meant to be less offensive than using 'Aboriginal'. The trouble was that wherever one looked at the time in Australia there were different descriptive used given the number of languages spoken. This is still very much in evidence today so that there a names used such as the Murri in south and central Queensland, Nunga in South Australia and Yolnga in Arnhem Land to name a few.

The Trust's motto is 'Gnokan Danna Murra Kor-ki' which is translated as 'give me your hand my friend' which is very moving when you think about how badly these people were treated and still are in many quarters. Even today this still lingers as I was reminded of by a friend back in London who told me that in the Northern Territories the pubs will not serve them alcohol on 'dole day' as so many, so he said, got drunk and ended up fighting and are given the rather unpleasant sobriquet of 'stinker'. Maybe a trip to Newcastle in the north east of the UK or any major city centre for that matter might put this over-generalisation into perspective, but to be fair to him he was just highlighting the fact that it was precisely because of this view that many well-meaning non-indigenous Australians were still trying to decide exactly what was the right thing to do. The aim of the Koorie Heritage Trust is to further people's understanding and to provide an education about and awareness of their culture. Unfortunately there was little to actually see aside from a few paintings by an indigenous artist and a short history of the first encounter on the second floor. There was also the almost inevitable gift shop which seemed incongruously out of place. Neither of the two staff behind the counter seemed that keen to talk to me, both studiously avoiding any eye contact and given for once I was not about to buy an over-priced souvenir meant that I left without finding out more. It was only later that evening when I was mulling over how to describe this part of my day that I realised, on re-reading the information I'd got that I could have seen much more had I actually looked beyond my not inconsiderably large nose. More fool me.

Feeling in need of another lurch back into the earlier history of modern Australia I headed off to find the Immigration Museum. From the outside the museum looked anything but, based as it is in an unassuming building off Flinders Street and quite close to the Yarra River. As the saying goes 'never judge a book by its cover' because once inside it proved to be a fascinating hour's long glimpse into the development of Australia as a nation of many people of many nationalities. There were a number of exhibitions that each told a different story from the beginnings of immigration through to more recent times. As with Melbourne Old Gaol the place was teeming with kids all writing down notes in their notepads, filling the air with excited chatter interspersed with the odd expression of incredulity, most notably when I was in the Journeys Gallery, or Long Room of Old Customs House, which was in a huge room but that had a rather clever exhibit in the shape of a ship that showed how long it used to take to arrive here and how. To today's internet generation the very idea that anything as simple as flying would have taken days 70–80 years ago must have seemed strange. Here I got a real feel of who these first immigrants were ranging from those that moved here for a better life to those who sought some sort of sanctuary in Australia away from persecution back home. It was all very powerful stuff reinforced by some moving images and paraphernalia from those who had come. At least nine million people have come to Australia since the First Fleet in 1788, of which nearly 160,000 were not voluntary. All of this was very well told and I was especially taken by one passage in the guide that came with the entrance fee, as for me it said a huge amount about not just who came but, more to the point, what they had to face. It also goes to explain why so many today are, in short, bloody-minded about things, with a determination to get on with life, something that the more I travelled and the more I spent in the country I came across and admired more and more:

> 'Settling into a new country is not easy. Immigrants have to adapt to an unfamiliar environment and lifestyle, while maintaining aspects of their previous culture and way of life. Many newcomers spent their new lives in limbo, spending months in temporary migrant accommodation, committed to two year labour contracts. For

others, settlement has been far easier because they spoke English, or government had offered assistant land or home scheme. Generations of immigrants have had to adapt to a new climate, new landscape, new language, new currency, and new lifestyle, especially those who have settled in rural areas.'

In a footnote to this as I was writing this up when I returned home I discovered that the building that the museum is housed in was in fact the Customs House from where the White Australia policy which was enacted in 1901 was enforced. One of the many nationalities that had been at one point welcomed in to the country in the earlier part of the 19th century only to be then almost fined for being there through punitive taxation not of them but of their employers who used them and then, if that was not enough, to almost non persona grata were the Chinese. It was with a smile that I noticed that one of the leaflets I'd taken away with me had as its front cover the picture of a Chinese man with, in the background, his ancestors. The last laugh is on the Chinese as well given the importance to not just the world's economy but also the Australian's, just as they were well over 150 years ago.

I had one last stop on my shopping list of attractions and that was to visit the Queen Victoria Market which was located just to the north of the CBD and is, according to my guide book 'the largest and most historic market with over 1,000 stalls' in Australia. However, not surprisingly given my track record so far, it was closed so I don't know if it was as it claimed. So I had a cup of coffee just enjoying the late afternoon sunshine and watching the world go by. As I sat there with my steaming cup of latte (price on enquiry) I started to notice something about those who walked by me. Mullets and tattoos! There were an incredible number of men with either that eighties style of short sides and longish back hairstyles or worse, if there is such a possibility, those with decidedly little top cover who had pony tails. Added to this were those with tattoos, and here the majority were women. Maybe it should be each to their own, but why? The mullet is just, well, just so eighties and more suited to the Dukes of Hazard. As for men with pony tails, especially those of a 'certain age' cut it out! It is just wrong, Can you hear me "Wrong!" As for tattoos, maybe, but why are there so many, and why they nearly all the same? I decided that I from now on I would try to log how many times I spotted a mullet or pony tail as for me they are both the same and tattoo because, well, this is a country that had the shell-suit not been taken on by every Eastern European as a fashion accessory, might well have come last in the sartorial stakes. I would add at this point that yes once my hair was long but not mulletted (can the word mullet be conjugated?), I did once have a shell-suit which looked wicked man but I have never had a tattoo. I have thought about having a tattoo but given that my nickname when playing rugby was 'Squealer' on the basis that if ever I ended up at the bottom of a ruck or maul I would emit a noise akin to a pig being put through some pretty unpleasant actions me and pain do not mix.

Dinner that night was at the James Squire Brewhouse, There were three reasons I decided on this place. First, James Squire himself was an interesting character having been transported with the First Fleet and, on gaining his freedom became, amongst other things, the Colony's first brewer -some say that he was the favourite brewer of Governor King – a philanthropist, a policeman, a landowner and by the time of his death in 1822 a well respected member of the community such that his funeral was one of the biggest held in Sydney at that time. His name lives on in the beer which I may say is pretty darn good. To me this was something that underlined the difference between the punishment and treatment of criminals back in Britain and the attitude of some of the early Governors of the Colony towards providing for some form of rehabilitation. It also gave me a sense of what Australia could provide and why so many initially were attracted to settle here throughout not just the 19th century but also the 20th. Here's a little bit a trivia that I picked up when having a quick chat with a newsvendor from whom I had just bought a drink earlier in the day. On hearing my fine Home Counties cut glass accent (like the Queen don't you know!) he said to me as he returned my change:

"Do you know why we call you Whinging Poms?" To which I replied in the negative not least as he had not addressed me as 'sir'. "Well let me tell you" (at which point I thought to myself he would no doubt do something like roar with laughter and say that it was because we were all whiny pommy bastards given that the Australian press is not unknown to call us that whenever we lose any sporting event to them. I was wrong) he continued "It's to do with all those who came here from Britain, like the ten pound Poms, who couldn't stick it and went back home. Jeez they were nuts. Look at this place!" at which point he roared with laughter (not really but it sounds better). In fact POM is an acronym, depending on what article you read for either Prisoner Of His/Her Majesty or Prisoner of the Mother England.

Second they served crocodile and kangaroo and I thought well why not; when in Rome and all that. Third the pub allowed me to sit overlooking the street permitting yet more human observation and my tattoo, mullet and pony tail log to be built up. For those interested the crocodile meat I reckoned came from a chicken, but one with a very large set of teeth, no feathers and scaly, or at least it should have done given its taste. As for kangaroo, I gave that a miss based upon the cost being north of a million dollars and the barman didn't accept IOU's. And mullets, well I lost count as they passed in front of me. Sorry it's just ridiculous. I feel sorry for the local barbers, I mean these people with the mullets and pony tails are advertising your 'work'. Say something!

Day ten: November 13th

Today was going to be fun for two very good reasons. The first was that I was meeting up with an old Australian colleague of mine, James, who is so laid back that the term 'horizontal' is just not a fair description and the second was that we were going to drive north east to the Yarra Valley via the Dandenongs and into wine country.

I have always teased James that he was what the Americans call a 'trust fund baby'. This term is usually somewhat derogatory in nature as it implies, certainly in the US when I was there, some sort of horrible rich kid who worked for a hobby, not for necessity. My experience, though of most of the people I met who fitted into this bracket were that they were on the whole decent, upright individuals who wanted to work and be independent. James is just such a person although I can't be certain he really is a trust fund baby. He has a lot of hugely endearing qualities amongst which is a real joie de vivre and an infectiously positive outlook on life.

We were to meet outside the hotel I was at and so as he was a trust fund baby (allegedly or not) I kept a furtive look out for the most expensive car stopping ready to pick me up, maybe a Porsche or Merc open top.

I could sit there with the shades on and look real cool (or as cool as a beached whale can look).

"G'day James" came a voice from behind me. I turned and there he was, or rather 'it' was. The car, the expensive top of the range sports car I had imagined was in front of me. Except that it wasn't a top of the range sports car. No. Instead, peering through the passenger window sat James, Cheshire cat grin on his face, in a car that I would generously describe as being closer to scrap metal than an actual car. It was scratched and had dents all over it ("Sandra did those" he told me later – Sandra being his wife).

"Are we really going to get to the Yarra in this?" I asked "I had expected you to arrive in something, well a bit more like a car."

"Oh it's not my car, it's my mum's. I don't have one and anyway it gets from A to B … eventually."

Fair enough, so off we went out of Melbourne to join the Maroondah Highway which goes into wine country and originally served as the main route into Gippsland. Once out of the suburbs using the exorbitantly priced toll road (we did this not for speed or anything but because, as James put it "The toll pass is my mum's and I'm not sure she knows I've got it so it's free": big grin) we passed through some of the most beautiful countryside which fairly quickly becomes obviously wine country.

Our first stop was brunch at Domaine Chandon. As the name suggests there is a direct link to the French given that the house of Moet et Chandon established the vineyard in Coldstream in 1986. We ordered a glass of something bubbly each (horribly expensive) along with some nibbles and sat outside to admire the view. It was stunning, as stretched before me were rows upon rows of beautifully kept vines, both for the reds and whites identifiable by red and white roses, manicured lawns and in the near distance the Dandenongs. The Yarra Valley is well known for its Pinot, Sauvignon Blanc, Cabernet Sauvignon, Shiraz and Chardonnay varieties. In total there are 85 wineries in the area with the largest production being reds (about 65%). Economically it has two major contributions to make: one is the production value of the wines and the second is tourism. It's not new either as it was first seen as being a good place to grow vines in the late 1830's and even though it has been hit by phylloxera, had to focus on cheaper wine precipitated by the Great Depression and ultimately closed in 1937, it has re-emerged like a Phoenix from the flames and is now as important as ever.

One of the factors that make it ideal for cultivating vines is that the climate here is much less severe when it comes to heat and there is more rain. Mind you as I was reading this in their brochure sweltering in 35 degrees I realized that their definition of heat and mine were quite different. I should have taken on board what had been said by the weatherman on ABC's evening when he had said that the temperature in the next few days would drop and be mild settling around 24 – 25 degrees. In the UK this would result in a hose pipe ban, sun stroke, emergency directives from the government on how to stay cool (nanny statism is alive and kicking at home) and dire warnings not to go out for too long: here it's a question of relativity – mild in the mid 20's (in the UK a heat wave), hotter in the mid 30's (in the UK the beginning of the end of all ability to function) and then the much hotter mid 40's (in the UK a complete collapse in infrastructure and the end of time). As for rain there had been precious little, and this was a big concern.

We moved on, pushed to do so by an invasion of flies, towards Healesville and the Rabbit Brewery. As it was not yet open when we arrived a quick spot of midday snack was required by James. He ordered a pie ('Big Breakfast') which looked revolting but you should know, dear reader, that the average Australian is regarded as being a food 'sophisticate' so much so that in 2007 the meat pie was voted by 400 Australians as the most popular food in the 'Top Taste Lamington Poll'. The town itself is quite small but has this enormous brewery which actually is the old Little Creatures Brewery from Freemantle that was transported lock stock and (excuse the pun) barrel. The White Rabbit is the next venture of the Little Creatures Brewery expansion into eastern Australia and it brews a dark ale, which looks similar to a porter and tasted absolutely delicious.

Onwards and upwards as they say and back on the Maroondah Highway we headed for the Healesville sanctuary which dates back to 1921 (with the snappy name of the Australian Institute of Anatomy) and is set in 30 hectares and houses kangaroos, wallabies and other furry creatures native to Australia, some of which are endangered. I left the mortgage deeds to my parents' house in order to get in. First stop was the red kangaroos. The closest I had come to a kangaroo of any sort aside from road kill was watching Skippy the bush kangaroo when I was growing up (bet you didn't know that there were multiple Skippys and that many were female) so this was a first. I took a photograph and then another and another – I must have Japanese ancestry – before realizing that this was a little too much. It is odd how when one is on holiday the taking of photos becomes an obsession and that one is never enough. My wife is a great example of this and will merrily snap away at the same thing as if on auto-drive. By the way the one I kept was a real 'beaut' of a large male (balls like Christmas decorations) that had, as I snapped, just 'parked its breakfast'.

On to the 'Parrots in Flight' show with Les the Eclectus parrot and his mates. The birds are trained to come into the amphitheatre where the show takes place and then leave on cue and it was rather fun although they were joined by some pretty ugly black headed ibis. Next on the list were the mini kangaroos called potoroos, bilbies and the Tasmanian devil, which has a rather unpleasant Latin name 'Sarophiculus' or lover of death in English. In the reptile house were numerous venomous snakes, including the brown snake, which is one of Australia's deadliest creepy crawlies:

> "I killed one of those recently" said James as we looked at it, "my nephew was in the dining room and came out and said there's a snake on the window. Had a look and thought it was outside, until it moved."
>
> "Did you panic?"
>
> "Aw no, I just killed it with a spade and dumped it in the bin."

He said all this with a huge grin on his face and a very matter-of-fact way. If it had been me I would have probably required an immediate change of underwear, screamed like a soprano and run like hell; but then again James as I said is *very* laid back!

Much as all this was very enjoyable I knew that this part of Victoria had suffered hugely in February 2009 in the worst bush fires the country has ever seen. The first fire took hold on February 7th ('Black Saturday') and the last one was not brought under total control until over a month later. In that time thousands of properties were destroyed, towns disappeared – in Marysville 80% of all buildings were destroyed – 173 people died, hundreds were injured and thousands of animals were consumed by the flames. It wasn't helped by some of the driest and hottest weather (at one point the mercury hit 46 degrees) and winds of up to 100kmh.

Just looking at the newspaper articles of the time with titles like 'Bushfire survivors relive lucky escape' or 'Some drew life, others death' ('The Australian', 23rd September 2009) brings home to the reader the sheer terror that must have been felt by so many. There are stories of people not believing that the fires would get them, or dying trying to save their property. The fires leapt from tree to tree, house to house without stopping long enough for fire-fighters to create fire breaks or to bring it under control. In total at the peak, there were over 400 bushfires.

There were over 3,000 involved in fighting this and stories of selfless heroism like Peter Thorneycroft who saved the lives of 20 people in Kinglake by standing on the roof of the National Park Hotel and kept pouring water on the roof, dampening down hot embers as they fell. The Prime Minister made a public statement in Parliament about this, and for me this is again something that to me is a strong Australian characteristic:

> 'There in the papers today is the unforgettable picture of him [Thorneycroft] standing calmly on the roof dressed in a pair of shorts and thongs (flip-flops), no shirt as the sky blazed orange around him. The houses opposite the pub had all exploded, the witnesses say, and if Peter hadn't done what he did the pub would have gone up to. Peter says there's no one who's heroic, you just do it. Peter Thorneycroft is an Australian, he is a genuine Australian hero.'

This article appeared in the Sydney Daily Telegraph on the 12th February some 5 days after the fires had started, and has a powerful image of Thorneycroft standing on the roof of the pub. There are other inspirational stories such as the establishment of Blaze Aid by sheep farmers Kevin and Rhonda Butler who, having seen their fencing destroyed and then inundated with offers to rebuild, wanted to help other victims who were in the same position as them. The Department of Immigration and Citizenship awarded them, in November 2009, the Victoria Local Hero award, citing:

> 'Mr. and Mrs. Butler are outstanding citizens who inspire us with the passion they have for this country and its people.'

However, the one story from 'The Australian' for me that really sums up this 'bugger you' attitude, of a spirit of defiance and of being determined to move on, was about Ian and Julie Gilroy-Scott who live (note live not lived) in the hamlet of Callignee in the Strzelecki Ranges who lost everything despite the efforts of their nephew and four of his friends who risked their lives to save the house (they had to jump into a water tank to save themselves). When asked about what they had considered doing, Mr. Gilroy-Scott replied:

> "We always wanted to rebuild, there was no thought of not rebuilding. There are 6 of our close friends who are rebuilding. We see our neighbours now more than we ever did."

As James and I drove back to Melbourne I asked him about how the bushfires had affected his family and friends – his parents live in the Yarra Valley itself.

"We were lucky but we know people who weren't. It affects you no matter if you know someone or not as it was on the news everyday and the smoke and smell was visible and strong." For a brief minute or so, the smile had gone and we sat in silence. "And you know that three of the fires that gathered into major conflagrations were arson". I asked him why, which in retrospect was as dumb question because no one really knows why someone would want to do this and then somehow revel in becoming a hero as a result of something that they had created.

That evening was another new experience to be savoured. James was having a barbie with some friends and asked me to come along. This wasn't going to be the same as the experience I'd had in Sydney. No this was at a real Australian's home (although actually he is technically English), with real Australian beer and 5 tons of dead cow. His house could as easily been in one the new towns that were built around London in the 1920's and 1930's as the railways and tube lines were extended into the green belt, one storey, wooden flooring and with a nice compact front and back garden.

I went out the back and there in the garden was a furnace. I have never seen a domestic barbecue this big. I could have cooked a whole cow on it and had room for a pig. Unlike my pathetic little barbecue at home which uses charcoal briquettes, this monster was linked to the national gas grid. If anyone had been using their gas stove in the area when James put the flame on I'm betting that these would have gone out. Forget global warming, this was energy use at its highest level; ice caps gone;

glaciers, gone. Then the meat arrived, well I say arrived, more like was manhandled on to the griddle it was so large. This looked like it would take three days at least to cook.

As the evening progressed we had to retreat inside due to the incessant flies and other biting bugs that were buzzing around. Novel: a barbecue inside. Over a lot of beer and wine we all got talking about how Australia and the UK differed or had the same problems. We did all the clichéd conversations you have when Bacchus is in the house: politicians (wasters, liars), immigration (too much, social tensions), sport (England is dreadful, Australia is great and the Kiwis shag sheep – no argument there), the cost of living (too high, too many taxes) and so on. It was the kind of low brow debating that those of us who are regulars in life's existential look on life are really good at doing in the certain knowledge that we cannot actually solve anything. I don't know why I bother sometimes but it does make me feel quite good although I must buy myself a new soap box as the one I currently have has been worn out by years of trying to put the world to right. Anyway whatever the world was doing at that exact point in time didn't matter because once more I'd experienced true hospitality from a real Australian albeit James is actually English and his charming wife Irish, but who cares? Full of good stories, wine and enough meat to last me a life time I returned to my hotel and slept the sleep of kings. Well I didn't really as the meat was, how shall I put it, on a short-term lease in my body.

One last point about Melbourne is that when, in my younger days I had been 'forced' to watch Neighbours by my wife I came to know Ramsey Street, the setting for the soap. I didn't go there which was a shame in some ways but here I would just like to thank both my wife and also Melbourne for delivering the earth goddess that is Kylie Minogue to the world of maledom. Thank you Melbourne you shall not go unrewarded.

There is one final story that I think is a fitting end both to Melbourne and to the John Bateman story:

> 'Whitlam had prepared a little surprise. The founder of Melbourne John Bateman, the son of a New South Wales convict, had entered into some sort of sale treaty with local tribal elders, and when he took possession of the site of what would become Melbourne, he wanted to impress on the Aboriginals that the land was his and no

longer theirs. So he got a tribal elder to take a handful of dirt and pour it into the palm of Bateman's hand. At Wattie Creek reversed the process. He bent down, picked up some of the dry soil, took Vincent Lingiari's had and poured it into his palm.'

The quote is taken from Knightley's book and refers to the event in 1975 when the Australian government made restitution for the way that the land on which Melbourne is sited came to be owned by John Bateman. He was one of those ambitious early settlers who were, it seems, out to get what they could at any price to the local population. The pouring of the dirt into the palm of Lingari's was to put right a wrong that Bateman had done.

CHAPTER 6

*Westward to the Great Ocean Road and
where I find religion of sorts*

DAY eleven: November 14th

The following morning nursing a slightly sore head I collected my second hire car. By now my family was to be indentured servants for the rest of their lives in order that once more I could have the privilege of driving Australia's roads.

Getting out of Melbourne I was told was easy but then the people who gave me directions didn't realise that occasionally I am a complete idiot (or as my Antipodean cousins would describe it 'a boofhead') when it comes to road signs – for example I have been known to drive up one-way streets in France the wrong way waving 'hello' at those irate French drivers coming towards me, or to see a sign telling me to do this or that and then zooming past it only to realise that it was where I should have been. Mark you sometimes signposts can be confusing as they are when I left Melbourne trying to avoid the toll road. So it was I found myself reversing back into the traffic as I managed to get into the wrong lane only to be confronted by a number of very polite one-fingered salutes which, in the best of British, I acknowledged with a silently mouthed "Up yours too" followed by a smile and "sorry". After all I was brought up always to admit the errors of my ways.

The drive out of Melbourne would take me west and down to the Great Ocean Road through towns with some very British names like Torquay, Anglesea and Lorne, the latter being the official start. The Great Ocean Road was another one of those 'must see' routes that I had been told I had to do so I decided that to really enjoy this I would keep the distance between overnight stops to a minimum and get 'into' the area. My first night was to be Apollo Bay which I reckoned would take about three hours or so of comfortable driving and allow some stops in the Otway National Park.

I had gone, oh I don't know, half a mile from my backing into the traffic escapade when I hit an Australian M25 style traffic jam. Not just any jam, no, this one was one where the very crafty road planning zombies had managed to get six lanes of traffic merge into two from completely different directions. Complete chaos of course but, as with the UK, drivers were on the whole very happy to give way and let you join the snail pace flow. It took me just under an hour to do 3 miles just to reach the Melbourne suburbs and the car I was driving had decided that having the air conditioning on was contrary to its terms of contract. So there I was in traffic, in heat of over 36 degrees, grinding my teeth and looking for the birch tree twigs with which I could beat myself given the car was a sauna.

Once I did shake off the traffic things improved although not on the weather front. In fact by the time I had reached Apollo Bay in the early evening it had fallen by well over 20 degrees. The first stop was to look at the Split lighthouse, once known as the Eagles Nest Point and White Queen. I can understand the latter name as it does resemble the chess piece but the first, well there is probably a good reason but I haven't found out. The lighthouse was built in 1891 and formed part of an arc of lighthouses that were erected from the first half of the 19th century to help shipping in the notorious waters of the Bass Straits and the Tasmanian Sea.

I discovered that I could climb up the lighthouse that sat at the end of a pretty little lane which also had a number of the original houses that the various operators and their crew would have lived in. The guide, Fiona, was one of the very people that I had really wanted to meet; her great-great grandfather had been transported for refusing to serve in the Army. She wasn't entirely sure what the reason for this was, whether it was a war (she was in her mid 60's I reckoned so that it would have been around the time of the Napoleonic Wars and thus suggesting that he would have been amongst the first to settle here) or something else.

"How do you feel about this?" I asked.

"It's funny but I am very proud to be an Australian but just as proud to know that my links back to Britain are there and that for me is real history."

"And what about your great-great grandfather who was transported?"

"I don't know; it's easy to judge today what you think is right or wrong, but clearly he felt something didn't stack up for him and this is the result."

"So are you Australian or British?"

"Both; Australian at heart but with a sense of some Britishness which I feel is within many of us, like loving tea!" At this last comment she laughed more to herself in, what I felt was some sort of intangible romantic notion of what Britain was, less so than what it is like now. I'd have liked to have talked some more but were joined by a couple and so our conversation had to stop as she went into 'guide mode'

My father has put together a family tree from both sides of the parental family that goes back into time that I can only imagine but in reality feel very little sense of nostalgia about. History is history and unless I can find some tangible link, some sort of identification if you will with an event then on the whole it remains a dispassionate observation. Fiona's reminiscences and her link to a past imbued with British history were interesting, but as I travelled she would not be the only one I'd meet who talked this way. Most Australians I met, either here or at home, had memories or stories linking to the past and there was always a high level of clarity on this which I wish I could have in my own dealings with my past. This link to the 'Motherland' was everywhere I went and as soon as I got talking to someone invariably there'd be the "I have an aunt who lives in … " or "I used to visit there when I was child … " and so on. It felt at times like I was someone who at the height of Empire would arrive in some fly-ridden place and immediately be asked "What news from home?" I mentioned this to an Australian chum of mine back in London expecting some sort of deep, from the heart, comment full of pathos. Instead all I got was:

"They're just trying to be friendly. You need to get out more and stop play the psychologist. Australians have two things on their mind: sport and more sport!"

Just on this last point, a survey in 2007 that by living.australia.com confirmed this with the top 5 programmes watched that year being:

- AFL Grand Final
- Australian Tennis Open

- Rugby League Grand Final
- Election Debate: Rudd vs. Howard
- The Ashes

Just for comparison, showing that the UK is by far more intellectual and sophisticated in its viewing habits, here are the stats as detailed in the UK's 'The Guardian' for 2007:

- Rugby World Cup Final
- Coronation Street
- The Vicar of Dibley
- Concert for Diana
- Britain's got talent

So, in short, although the Australians undoubtedly love their sport they do at least spend a little time listening to political debate. Even worse of the top 10 most watched in the UK all bar 3 were fictional/reality TV. Alright so I won't quit the day job and become the next Jung or Freud, but I know I'm right, and anyway his family was full of convicts and I, having looked at my family tree, note that we probably sent them to Australia in the first place. Ah, those were the days (maybe I do after all have a nostalgic streak after all).

Apropos that last comment, I had a conversation recently with an Australian lady who had moved to France and asked her why some of her fellow countrymen/women could be a little 'chippy' when they moved to the UK. Interestingly she said that although *we* might think it hilarious to wind them up about their heritage (25% of all Australians can trace their roots back to convicts according to Buzzle.com), it is a tiresome and maybe slightly sensitive subject.

I arrived in Apollo Bay late in the day and drove through a bustling high street that had on the one side shops and restaurants and on the other the beach. It all looked very nice as I turned into the road where the motel was which could easily have had as its tag line 'The convenience of driving right up to your door' as that is exactly what I did. The trouble was that the room charitably could be described as basic with its Georgian plastic chairs, a bed that would have been too small even for a person of restricted height (you can't use the 'D' anymore apparently) and curtains that at best were minimalist in their use. There was also a rather odd opening to the outside not too dissimilar to that seen on a prison cell door which looked to serve no real purpose at all aside from being a large peep hole. As for the TV, well it must have been one of the first ones that were introduced to Australia in 1956 given that the cathode ray tube was at least eight feet long. Still it had a fridge for the beer so all was not lost.

In a particularly grumpy mood not made any better by the weather, I trudged around the town to find a restaurant that wasn't closed. I do quite a bit of travelling on my own and usually I like to eat in my hotel room to avoid the inevitable stares from other diners that suggested that I was obviously friendless and then find I'm sat next to either the front door (always happens when it's cold outside no doubt because the Maitre D looks at my somewhat large frame and thinks "Ah, a draft excluder") or next to the toilets from where the ambient smell was quite off-putting. In some restaurants the servers make a point of asking loudly if I am dining alone and then making an exaggerated effort to take away the cutlery from the spare place setting. However, here in Australia not once when I ate alone did I ever feel this or was hurried to move along so that they could have another sitting that evening. Perhaps they wanted to make sure that I supped all the soup they'd all spat in for a laugh, who knows, but whatever it was I didn't mind and besides some soups need a bit of 'body'.

Apollo Bay does have one major claim to fame which was that in 1936 the very first sub-marine cable allowing the use of telephones connecting Tasmania to the rest of the country was laid. Exciting stuff isn't it? One last point; Apollo Bay was another reminder of the fragility of the relationship between man and nature in all her forms. It too was devastated by fire in 1983 when the Ash Wednesday bushfires ravaged Victoria and South Australia. Until Black Saturday these fires were Australia's deadliest.

Day twelve: November 15th

I continued along the Great Ocean Road aiming for Port Fairy, another of the historic towns that dot this region. My first stop was another lighthouse (actually 'light station' for those aficionados of lighthouse spotting) at Otway. Imaginatively it was called the Cape Otway Light Station. Begun in 1846, it was in service by 1848 and is the oldest in Australia. The sea in front of the light station is called the 'Eye of the

Needle' and is where two masses of water meet (the Southern Ocean and Bass Strait) in a frenzy of white tipped waves and spray. This part of the Australian coast that starts where I joined the Great Ocean Road and goes on towards the border with South Australia is a veritable ship's graveyard. Estimates range from 600–700 maybe more and the need to have some form of navigational aid to reduce lost tonnage and people was the driving force behind the boom in light house / station building highlighted by such dreadful wrecks as the loss in 1845 of the SS Cataraqui with the loss of some 350 souls. Between 1801 and 1803 Mathew Flinders explored a large part of this Continent and in his journal 'A Voyage to Terra Australis' published in the year of his death in 1814 he pointed out the perils of this part of the world for mariners:

> 'Thus, speaking generally of the south coast of Terra Australis, it may be considered that during six or eight winter months, the winds blow almost constantly from some western point; and that gales of wind at south-west are frequent . The progress of the gales is usually this: the barometer falls to 291/2 inches, or lower, and the wind rises from the north-westward with thick weather, and commonly with rain ... '

He goes on in more detail but the bottom line was that these waters could be treacherous.

This part of the coast was, from all accounts, not an easily accessible place. In fact although Otway was established in 1848, it wasn't until 1919 that the Great Ocean Road itself was begun and took over 13 years to complete with Apollo Bay being the final town. Looking at the black and white pictures of that time it looked pretty inhospitable terrain but was work for some thousands of returning servicemen. The road's construction is a huge memorial to all those who did not come back to Australia having died in defence of the Empire as well as those who did. I should mention to avoid any letters of complaint that although Apollo Bay claims to be the first place that a communication cable was laid between the mainland and Tasmania that is not quite true as in 1859 the first cable was at Cape Otway, but it failed after six months and proved a very costly adventure.

All along this part of the coast there is evidence of Second World War and at Cape Otway one of the attractions was an old radar station which, although not much to see or write home about did act as a reminder once more of how close the Australians were to the Japanese threat.

As I sat in the café which was situated in the assistant light keepers' house, I was drawn to an article that I had downloaded from the internet the day before: it said that the first keeper was booted out after three months in charge for 'interfering' with the light. Interesting – I wonder what exactly that really meant?

The weather had by now brightened up as I headed to the iconic Twelve Apostles. These are all limestone rock formations created through erosion and are a magnificent sight. In the 19th century they were known as the 'Sow and Piglets' with Mutton Bird Island being the former and the smaller rocks nearby the latter. The name was changed in the 1950's in a flash of biblical fervour. No idea why as there are more than twelve and, well, I can't see the connection. I suspect that this had as much to do with the fact that church attendance in the 1950's was around 40% (compared to about half that today) and this name would have appealed more. It's an interesting thought based upon absolutely no proof but I like it. The formations have some great names: the Arch, London Bridge, the Gorge and Loch Ard. The story of London Bridge is quite amusing as it used to be connected to the mainland until January 1990 when that section collapsed into the sea leaving two rather, and here I use the description given in one of the many leaflets you can find relating to the rocks, 'bemused' tourists stranded. Personally if it had been me the last damn thing I would have been is bemused. I presume the conversation must have been:

"Oh look the rock has collapsed and we were almost killed. Ha! Ha! Ha!"
"Oh yes I am very bemused by this"

I don't think so, do you? I suspect that clean underwear was required all round. Having said that as I reminded myself once more that if they were Australian they do have the dubious honour of living in a country that, amongst other things that might do you harm, is host to 7 of the worlds' top 10 deadliest snakes. Now you may think as I do that this is perhaps a little unnerving. Well here's a quote in relation to the slithery things from 'Outback Australia':

'Let them enjoy their day as you enjoy yours!'

To be fair this is a guide about how to avoid being Mr. Inland Taipan's next victim, but come on, the deadliest thing in the UK is English pub food and you don't need a stick to beat that off, and it's not as if we humans are equipped with any deadly weapons on our bodies, unless you take into account morning breath. Maybe that's the answer if a snake were to attack, then huff on it and problem solved!

At Loch Ard I was reminded of the dangers that the early immigrants would have faced. On the morning of June 1st 1878 the SS Loch Ard with its cargo, crew of thirty-seven and seventeen paying passengers, foundered on the cliffs with the loss of all on board, save Eva Carmichael and Tom Pearce. Eva eventually returned to Ireland and the only memory left is the names of the seven members of her family that perished in the graveyard that is located near the disaster.

On to the Grotto which is accessed by walking down a concreted staircase – of course this is very natural, and somewhat reminiscent of Euro Disney. The Grotto is another one of nature's beautiful works and makes for one of those picturesque photo moments looking out through what is essentially an arch out to the sea. There were quite a few fellow tourists at the bottom, including a bicycle club, who were on the last leg of a trip from Melbourne along the coast all spandex and sweat, as well as an enormous lady of what I took to be of northern European extraction (pig tails, blond hair, round face complete with red cheeks) who was in animated conversation with one of the cyclists. As I was taking my photos ("smile please, and say cheese") I latched on to their somewhat surreal conversation:

"So where are you from?"
"Pardon me?"
"Where do you come from?"
"Ja, I am here in Australia to travel"
"No I meant where do you originally come from?"
"Ja, und I am in Australia"

This went on for what seemed hours and I am not entirely sure what the start of the conversation had been but I can tell you as I carried back up the steps, I heard

"See, we're from Melbourne; have you been to Melbourne?"

"Ja und travelling here … ". I could tell though that the enquirer wasn't English as she persevered without reminding the recipient of her questions that she should learn to speak English or, worse still, condescendingly talking slowly and loudly. However, as I walked back to my car I wondered at what point would the enquirer give up? At what point would she realise that there was a big dead end sign in front of her? I could understand it if they were drunk but even then you do tend to 'move on'. Maybe they're still there. It does put me in mind of something else that I find quite puzzling; working in a firm where German is widely spoken, can someone answer this question: If two Germans are in a restaurant in, a German speaking country with a German speaking waiter, but where they have a guest (for the sake of clarity – me) who is English, why do they order in English? Is it politeness because if it is, then stop putting your bloody towels on the sun beds before dawn so that no one else can use them. That my German friends, is politeness!

On and upwards towards my stop for the evening at Port Fairy which according to one informed source (alright Wikipedia but what the heck) was named not after some Victorian desire to foster good relations with the gay community, but after Captain James Wishart's ship 'Fairy' when he explored the area. Whatever the reason, it is steeped in early European settler history. Just the drive into town was quite dramatic. If, as I am, you are used to the narrow streets and roads in England, then Port Fairy is the opposite. The main street entering town was at least 80–90 feet across, may be more, but as I didn't have a ruler with me and am lousy at judging distance it could easily have been 10 miles across. It was wide, and I mean really wide and on each side, inter-mingled with the modern, were buildings that dated from the earliest settlement. It was in every sense a step back in time.

I booked into my hotel which was one of the weirdest experiences I have had yet. There was no reception area, no hotel entrance, nothing. Instead all that was there was a town house with a note saying that I should pick up the phone attached to the exterior and call to say I'd arrived. That was it; no credit card, no "can I help with your bags?" or even "can I turn show you have the lights work?"; by the way that is one of the most pointless offers of help to get when the concierge takes one to the room – I've been turning lights on and off for over four decades and I think I have got the hang of it or are hotel lights special? It was somewhat weird but rather in keeping with the atmosphere of Port Fairy. Port Fairy, as with so many of the places I had stayed at or visited from Sydney downwards was involved in whaling. From all accounts the industry here didn't last very long and an example of man's insatiable desire to take all from the environment without thinking about the consequences. It grew nonetheless thanks primarily to two individuals, James Atkinson and William Rutledge, who in the 1840's onwards encouraged people to come in and cultivate the land and set up business. In those days the name of the town was Belfast with only the port having the current name.

As I wondered through the town there was a real sense of the past from the oldest licensed pub still serving beer in the State (1844), to St. John's church (started in 1854) through to the 'modern' post office (1881). Walking in the residential area there were markers with old sepia photos of that house or street and it was hard to believe that anything had changed. I could easily have been standing here in 1900, save the presence of cars and satellite dishes. The houses were mostly of a single storey, some were made of clapperboard but most were solidly built Victorian brick structures with all having a small yet neat front garden and a profusion of colour from the trees and shrubs. This was the very essence of an old colonial town and almost everywhere I looked or walked it oozed with character.

Over a drink that night in the pub I got talking to the barman, who I reckoned to be in his early 20's, about why he was here, given the somewhat sleepy nature of the place:

> "Bang on mate. There's not a lot to do here, especially when it's not the tourist season. Work is pretty limited too, I mean I could try fishing or sheep farming but the money they pay won't make me rich! I mean if it's a quiet life you're after then we've got that in spades here. Everyone knows everyone, which is kind of nice and there's no real stress. I know there are more opportunities, and money, in the city, but you know I'm happy with doing this for the moment, after all what's the rush?"

Talking to Australians I know back in London about where they'd like to live in Australia (city or country) most said that although they'd like to have a pad in the country the reality was that to earn a decent living then being in one of the large metropolitan areas was the only way to achieve this – basically Adelaide, Perth, Melbourne, Sydney and Brisbane. That was it. The demographic profile of the country in 2009 from the Australian Bureau of Statistics website (which is a laugh a minute let me tell you), shows this loud and clear as nationally some 66% of the population lived in cities whilst in the State of Victoria the metropolitan district of Melbourne alone represented almost 70% of the population.

I had already noticed as I had been exploring Port Fairy that although there was much history there was also a definite sign that things were perhaps not so good today, a sense almost as if the town was passed its best. I am probably being a bit unfair on the town and I suspect that come the heat of the Australian summer the fact that it's on the Great Ocean Road and next to the sea might suggest a different picture. However, as I looked around the bar it was almost empty. Apart from myself, there was a group of youngsters who were on their way to Melbourne, some European tourists all trying to work out what 'please pay before you eat' meant and then no more than 4 or 5 locals. And this was peak time for the evening. In the street outside it was also pretty quiet and the only place where there was much activity was the high street, but even here some of the eateries were closed. Maybe it was just what I had been told before that Australians do most of their drinking and entertaining at home and that if I were to go into every back garden I would see this for myself. I'm not sure though if this was the case here because as I walked around one last time before turning in for the night I was struck by how quiet it was. If there was partying going on it was in the fashion of Marcel Marceau.

CHAPTER 7

*Roos, a twisted ankle and a hint of gold and
a touch of rebellion*

DAY thirteen: November 16th

The next leg of my trip was heading inland towards the Grampians to Hall's Gap and then east to Ballarat which was a town I was really looking forward to visiting because of two linked events: the discovery of alluvial gold in 1851 and the Eureka Rebellion of 1854, a seminal point in Australian history.

The drive wasn't going to be long so I decided to go across country and avoid any traffic that there might have been. As I drove along the back roads I counted the number of cars that either passed me or I passed; luckily it was no more than seven so no need to use my toes. It was a pure delight to be able to stop whenever I felt like and to drive as I wanted to so that I could soak in the sites without some lunatic using my boot as their front seat. As I turned a bend in the road shortly after passing through Dunkeld (for those who like to know the road it was the C178) I nearly reduced the kangaroo population by one; it was the first wild one I had seen and I've no doubt it would have been (drum roll here please) ... hopping mad if had hit it. I also came across some emus as they sipped water in a small pond which, as soon as I got my camera out, promptly ran off. It was all rather exciting given that my only encounter to date with the local wildlife had been either flat on the road or at a zoo.

In order to add a bit of excitement to my day I went off road towards a town called Mafeking, the last place in Victoria to witness a gold rush. My guide book said that there was a heritage walk and that you could see the old mine workings but I suspect that it lied to me because Mafeking doesn't exist. Either that or I can't map read. After some more fairly aimless driving, I rejoined the tarmac and sped towards Halls Gap, my rest-stop for that evening which sits in the heart of the Grampians, in a valley.

As I approached the Grampians (or Gariwed to give them their indigenous name) much of the foreground leading to them was flat and it seemed to take forever to actually reach them. As a budding geologist and one who is keen to share my knowledge with all I can tell you that they are made up of sandstone ridges that run north/south with steep inclines which are heavily forested with trees having such wonderful names as Stringybark and Red Gum covering some 168,000 hectares in all, making them the third largest national park in Victoria. Unfortunately the area has seen quite a lot of devastation, the latest being the fires of 2006 when swathes of forest were destroyed and which as I came into the park was not just very visible as but also I could smell it, a mixture of sweetness from the eucalypts tinged with the odour of burnt wood.

The area is now a designated national park, the third largest in Victoria, although I was quite surprised to learn that this was not until 1984. The first settlers here have been dated back around 20,000 years, the Ngamadjidji people, and the area is rich in Aboriginal culture (no less than 2/3rds of all Victoria's aboriginal sites are located here and for the record I failed to visit a single one). In fact it was that way until the first Europeans began to arrive in the 1830's ostensibly for water but then for farming.

Before I arrived at my night time stopover and having driven up an aptly named road called the Mount Difficult Road, I stopped at the Baroka look-out which offered a spectacular 180 degree view of the valley below including Halls Gap (where I was going to stay) and Lake Bellfield; given it was a beautiful day I could also see miles and miles into the distance … with a pair of binoculars. I wasn't alone as the whole place was teeming with school kids all, it seemed, intent on taking photos at exactly the same time as me and exactly in front of me, and if Apple representatives ever read this book I can assure you that you are very popular in Australia. Every child I saw was doing three things at once: listening to their iPod, taking photos and talking excitedly to each other. It made me wonder how they would cope if a time machine took them back to the 1970's when I was in my youth and when none of this existed (aside from the camera but even then nothing like the ones of today). Technology for kids then was two tins with a piece of string tied between them, and if they were Heinz Baked Bean tins then that was class.

Halls Gap was easy to find given that it is pretty much the only major town in the Grampians and sits, funnily enough, in a gap that was discovered by a Mr. Charles Browning Hall. The town is situated in the Fyans Valley and is the tourist hub for the area and is surprisingly small with only around 300 permanent inhabitants. It is small in every respect, the high street and restaurants huddled together in what is effectively a single row that can be walked in minutes. The whole town is surrounded by those steeply forested hills I'd seen earlier (or mountains if that is the correct terminology but given my degree is in history I'll stick to hills) and is literally a drive through in as much as everything is off the main road. As I wondered around, having checked in to my latest hotel, I bumped into a local out walking his giant of a dog. We acknowledged each with a polite hello.

"You visiting?" he asked

"Yes, from the UK"

"Which part?"

"The south, near Brighton; do you know it?"

"I used to live in Lewes when I was a kid but came out here 40 odd years ago for a pre-work holiday and decided to stay." I asked him why.

"The climate here is so much better and you've got space – loads of it. The lifestyle is just fantastic, I mean look at this place. I fell in love with the country straight away and haven't been back since."

"Do you miss England?"

"A little, you know like the beer and the weather; here it gets bloody hot and I haven't seen snow for years. I miss that, but then like I say my life here has been great and I've got more family here than back there."

"How did you find settling in with the locals; did you feel like an outsider and what about now?"

"Not really; back then they wanted people like me to come and provide skills – I was a teacher. Now I feel like a local and look upon myself as Australian. The only worry I have today is the fires, but then you learn to live with it."

He bid me farewell and wondered off. I was quite taken aback by this. I had this view that Australians didn't really like us English. To them I thought, we were arrogant, we were condescending and we all thought that Australian culture grew on a Petrie dish. Maybe some believe that but here was an Englishmen who had come to Australia and made something for himself. Yes, over 100,000 Poms did return to the UK in the post-war period but I bet many did this not because they weren't welcome but that they either couldn't adapt or that their expectations might have been too high. It also could have been that they just missed 'home'. There were two things that I got out of taking to him. The first was that if you made the effort in this country you would be rewarded whether through lifestyle, money or whatever and secondly was that on the whole Australians with their own strong sense of 'can do' will welcome you warmly if you make the effort.

I carried on walking in the warmth of the late afternoon through the forest with its sweet smelling trees, and thought to myself how odd it was that many young Australians leave the country because they see more opportunities in places like London than they see as existing in Australia. Yet I know talking to my British friends at home that many of us feel precisely the opposite and look almost romantically at places like Australia as not so much a place of opportunity, but where the pace of life looks to be so much more relaxed. It was something that I had felt before when I lived in Boston in the US. Here the day in the office seldom began before 8.30 am and by 5.30 most staff had left for home, the bar or the golf course to do some networking; a business dinner appointment was at 5.30, maybe 6.00 and done by 7.30 at the latest so you could get home to family or friends. The work/life balance just seemed to be so much better than the UK. Maybe it's an age thing, but as I get older I want to decelerate my life and here in Halls Gap I was doing just that. To finish my exploration I decided to run around some of the hills that surround the hamlet which would have been fine had some bastard not strategically left a large pothole in the road into which I manfully strode, twisting my ankle which resulted in me filling the air with words of no more than one syllable and that involved such things as travel and sex. However, I am pleased to report that it did make the cicadas shut up for a minute and I have little doubt that somewhere there was fellow tourist writing down in their journal that they heard the legendary Australian lesser spotted fat swearing bird.

That evening was a delight as I sat eating a pizza as big as a big pizza is (this one was huge, so much so that a fly called all his frigging mates to join him to land on it and do what flies do; I could have sworn one of them had an iPod) with, in front of me, the town park over-run by kangaroos feeding in the coolness of the evening. I mean does it get much better? Probably, but Kylie said she had to wash her hair that evening.

Day fourteen: November 17th

I woke very early to the cacophony of noise from birds trying to out-do each other in the "get up you fat lazy git don't you know it's morning?" stakes. Although I was eager to get to Ballarat I stopped to look at the MacKenzie Falls because my guidebook said I should. As it was early I was the only one there and, after descending the 30000 steps (or so it seemed but actually there are 260) came to the falls. I am not quite sure how to put this, but they were no Niagara. I mean they were ok and all that but, I don't know, perhaps the advertising is better than the end product. And before anyone gets all uppity about this I did enjoy the walk down and the schlep back up. Good all round exercise and more wildlife (starting to become a bit blasé about this aspect of my trip I think).

There were two options to get to Ballarat, the simple drive along the highway and be there in a couple of hours or, as I did, take a detour and head north east initially to Stawell for no other reason than it was not direct. Stawell it turned out was another picture book link with Australia's architectural past, with mixture of buildings dating from the mid to late 19th century, (it even has a clock that chimes just like Big Ben) and then, so it seemed to me stopping abruptly in 1950. It wasn't unpleasant at all, in fact quite the opposite. What is more there was a fully functioning high street full of shops, cafes and businesses; having seen at first had the effective death of the high street in many parts of the US and the beginnings of this in the UK due in no small part to the proliferation of huge out-of-town shopping malls, Stawell served up a treat.

Stawell does have a claim to fame that has nothing to do with gold. It is host to the 'Australia Post Stawell Gift' which is a running event and which dates back to 1878. I noted that the sponsor was the Australian Post and not our very own British Post Office because if it was then the finish would no doubt have been a) lost in the post, b) unable to complete as you were out or c) not able to do it until tomorrow. To be fair we have a wonderful post lady. The race is no small event and comprises 66 events held over three days culminating in the Easter Monday 120m sprint. It is worth a fair old bit to the winner, no less than 40,000 dollars.

Tradition is something I do like, not least when there is a link with the past. Where I live we used to have the Easter Monday walking races which dated back to 1903 and were a real part of the community. In the past hundreds took part and the roads around the village were 'littered' with young and old hobbling their way to the finish. It attracted great athletes such as Olympian gold medallist, Norman Stone, who competed in Melbourne in 1956 and more recently former UK number one Darrell Stone. By 2007 only seven took part and the winner was a 70 year old and as a result of the lack of participants and interest in the event it was cancelled in 2008. I wonder if Stawell just offered a medal (nice though it is) and a mention in that day's evening papers if it too would survive.

Stawell though has one tradition that it clearly keeps from the old country. Having done a wonder around and watched people park their cars next to the metres and then promptly not pay (unlike me) I found a nice looking little café on the high street and ordered an early lunch of baked potato, topped with cream cheese and a side salad and coffee. I am not entirely sure whether my diction was at fault or that there was just some terrible accident in between ordering the food and it arriving. When I say food I do so in a generous spirit because frankly it looked more like road kill on a plate, surrounded by some rotting greenery and a coffee that was an abuse of the trade descriptions act.

On the plus side it did make me a little homesick for the main course 'salmonella on a plate' often found at some greasy spoon cafes and pubs in the UK. The best for me in this category has to be a 'front room pub' in Edinburgh I visited years ago, after one or two wee drams with some locals I knew, where the menu was just 'Pie'. In front of us, on the bar, was something that looked like it could have been said 'Pie' but, on closer inspection, the abundance of fluff and what looked like something green on the edges suggested that eating it would not be very clever and that it may even have been the landlords cat; close call one way or the other.

Leaving Stawell I continued the drive north east heading towards Navarre and St. Arnaud. This region is called the Pyrenees named after the mountains that straddle France and Spain, and is another of the State's wine producing areas. Along with the Grampians the Pyrenees are the eastern part of the backbone of the Great Dividing Range. Unlike the Yarra, the wineries that dot this area are mostly from the modern era (1960's –1970's) as before wine gold was still the main industry. However, it wasn't the wine that intrigued me, not least as I know diddlysquat about it, but the French names as I had thought, nay hoped, that this had to be something to do with the early settlers and that I would find some sort of strong French connection as a result, maybe a baguette or two.

I arrived in Navarre full of anticipation. Blink and you miss it; it was not big and was no more than a drive through, with not much to see and looking at my ever useful guide book ('Rubbish Guide to Australia') it was historically primarily home to timber workers and sheep farmers. The only French connection was that in 1855 it was renamed Navarre after the kingdom of that name which straddled the Pyrenees between today's France and Spain. In 1589 the northern part of the kingdom was joined in what historians call 'personal union' with the French kingdom when the then king of that realm, Henry III became the French monarch as Henry IV. All very interesting of course but no sign of a baguette, not even a soupcon. No matter, just up the road was St. Arnaud which, on my map at least, looked like a major town given the name was in bold black letters. St. Arnaud was another one of those towns created as a result of the gold rush in around 1850 and was originally called New Bendigo Goldfied. But what about the name, was it a link to Saint-Arnaud, 47480 Bajamont, France? Had some mad Frenchmen fled from his native land and then founded the town and claimed it for the 2nd Empire of Napoleon III, nephew of Bonaparte and usurper of the 2nd French Republic? Sadly not, although there is a French connection in that is was named after Jacques Leroy St Arnaud who was a Marshall of France, the commander of the French forces in the Crimean War and French senator. The only other connection was that in the town there were a number of street names that were reminders of that conflict, but nothing specifically French. Quelle dommage!

It was now getting towards mid afternoon and I still had a fair way to go to get to Ballarat and my encounter with the Eureka Stockade. As I approached the town I decided to drive in along the Ballarat Avenue of Honour. The avenue was some 22 kilometres and along it on either side were over 3700 trees. There is a wonderful description which I came across on Ballarat's town website as to what this commemorates and underscores two very powerful messages:

'These avenues represent a new egalitarian approach in the commemoration of soldiers where service rank was not a consideration and are illustrative of a peculiarly Australian, populist and vernacular response to the experience of the First World War … '

The words 'egalitarian' and 'service rank was not a consideration' sent a shiver down my spine as I read it. In death and in the service of their country these men were all equal and bullets and shells killed and maimed irrespective whether the wearer of the uniform had pips, stripes or nothing. But here there was once more something that I'd already come across because this wasn't just about those who had died but also in honour of those who survived. The idea behind this came from Mrs. W.D Thompson who was a director of the local clothing firm of E. Lucas and Co and eventually led to a number of similar tributes appearing such that there are an estimated 128 of these avenues throughout Victoria all built in the 1917–1921 period. As I entered I passed through the Arch of Victory which had been unveiled in 1920 and stopped to take a closer look. The money to go towards this and that of the avenue had been raised by the 'Lucas Girls'.

The Arch itself is an impressive piece of architecture, consisting of two small towers and a centre piece of what I took to be an Australian army cap badge and inscribed with 'Avenue of Honour'. Just off the roundabout that it sits on were further memorials, one of which, the Temple of Remembrance, had all the names etched into steel sheets (as a book) as well as one for the 1939–1945 war. The number of not just dead but of those wounded amounted to an incredible 65% of all who served in the First World War. It was an incredibly moving place to be, although rather spoilt by the roundabout and the traffic. As I stood there deep in thought I recalled one of the most moving and emotional sites I had ever visited, the Ossuary at Douaumont which was erected to commemorate the dead from the battle of Verdun in the same war. The building houses the remains of over 130,000 soldiers' remains whose names are known only to their loved ones as well as being the place where over 16,000 graves are located. Big or small, memorials like this one in Ballarat are just so important to all generations both now and to come; they are a continual reminder of bravery and sacrifice by so many. There is a poem by Wilfred Owen called 'Dulce et Decorum est' which describes the aftermath of a gas attack and has as its last verse one of the

most memorable descriptions of what it must have been like to have been
in that war and what these men went through:

'If in some smothering dreams you too could pace
Behind the wagon that we flung him in,
And watch the white eyes writhing in his face,
His hanging face, like a devil's sick of sin;
If you could hear, at every jolt, the blood
Come gargling from the froth-corrupted lungs,
Obscene as cancer, bitter as the cud
Of vile, incurable sores on innocent tongues,---
My friend, you would not tell with such high zest
To children ardent for some desperate glory,
The old Lie: Dulce et decorum est
Pro patria mori.'

The poem was really an ironic take on the Latin verse of Horace that
in full reads: 'Dulce et decorum est pro patria mori', or translated 'it
is sweet and fitting to die for one's country'. By the time Owen had
started writing this the 'romance' of war had long gone and in 1918 he
also would become a victim in the 'War to end all Wars'

Ballarat owes its past to a humble blacksmith, Thomas Hiscock, who
found alluvial gold in 1851. Soon gold brought in thousands of miners,
known as diggers, from all nationalities and backgrounds eager to become
rich. Gold was hugely important to the Government as by the 1850's the
Colony was one of the worlds' largest producers. In fact even well into
the first half of the 20th century Victoria was still the largest producer of
gold in the country. As the population grew, spurred on by the gold rush,
tensions began to rise and standards, at least to some declined. Stuart
Macintyre quotes Catherine Spence who wrote at this time:

'Religion is neglected, education despised, the libraries are almost
deserted ... everybody is engrossed by the simple object of making
money in a very short time.'

The Government had also begun to be concerned about the effects of
large numbers coming to the Ballarat region. As Macintyre goes on to say:

'Seaman jumped their ships, shepherds left their flocks, labourers quit their masters and husbands their wives to seek fortunes … '

Above all the Government wanted to control the mining and make sure it, the gold, was theirs to control. As part of this licences were issued to all those diggers who wanted to work in the gold fields, which not surprisingly were highly unpopular. Into this came Sir Christopher Hotham who was appointed Governor in 1854 and who, as one of his first acts, instituted more regular licence checks and then started to increase the fee to initially one and a half pounds per month. With rumblings of discontent growing this was reduced but still left it above a pound. If they didn't pay – and many couldn't – then fines of five times that amount might be levied and failing payment of that, prison or some sort of unpaid Government work. Throughout the year grievances increased and by the start of summer these boiled over with the murder of James Scobie, a Scottish digger, who had been drinking and had unsuccessfully tried to gain entry to the Eureka Hotel, by the owner a rather nasty individual by all accounts called James Bentley, who was in the back-pocket of the local magistrate. Two more key events then followed, the burning down of the hotel and then on Bakery Hill on the 11th November 1854 the formation of the Ballarat Reform League which led a very vocal call for an end to corruption and licensing laws. The scene was set for confrontation and all would be revealed at the Eureka Centre where I was now heading

Finding the Eureka Centre was a bit tricky as I had expected it to be located bang slap in the middle of town. In fact it was more on the outskirts and meant driving pretty much through the town itself. Having spent time at the Arch of Victory I was now running a little late and was worried that, as with most things Australian, that it would be shut ("My goodness, it's almost 4 o'clock; time we closed"). Luckily it was still open. This was where history was made and to commemorate the actual spot of what became known as the Eureka Stockade was a circular metal sculpture that outlined the sequence of events as they unfolded. In the middle of this at the top of a flagpole flew the 'Southern Cross' flag, designed it is said by a Canadian miner called Henry Ross, which comprised a white cross and four stars at each point and one in the middle on a blue background.

The centre was much more educational in its layout and not the fusty type of museum that I am so used to; in many ways it seemed designed more with children in mind than adults. Was this a subliminal republican breeding programme, I wonder? I had arrived just as a bunch of youngsters were experiencing what it would be like being tried by Her Majesty's Government for their role in the three day Rebellion, for that is really what it was, an affront to the British Crown. There was a lot of hush as the 'judge' solemnly summed the case for the Crown up and then pronounced sentence. Anyway Mr. and Mrs. Rogers of 13 The Rise, Melbourne if you're wondering where little Johnny is, sorry to say they hanged him. But look on the bright side he had a really great day out.

The Rebellion was quickly suppressed by a large force or H.M's troops and police who cunningly went in early on a Sunday. However, the whole affair represented more than miners saying that they were not going to keep paying licence fees to mine for gold or countenance corruption in high places. This was about the rising new 'power' of the labouring class led by men with little liking for the Crown, such as Peter Lalor, an Irish Catholic with no love for the British whose brother had fought in the 1848–1849 United Irishmen's uprising. Hocking neatly encapsulates what Lalor felt at the time, but writ large could be any person working there at the time:

> 'For men such as Irishman Peter Lalor, the treatment of the ordinary working digger at the hands of the capricious English military troopers, the rough justice meted out by the unruly goldfields police and the determined execution of the Governor's decrees by corrupt magistrates soon brought to mind something that he had seen all too often before, and something he had travelled halfway across the globe to escape.'

In 1854 Australia was still 'new' but by now thanks to the gold industry not only were there the families of those who had been transported but there were also exiles from Europe, many of them republicans who had to leave due to the almost universal failures of the risings in Europe of 1848, along with a not under-represented number of English-hating Americans according to some accounts. Attitudes had changed amongst the working man or woman and it is worth bearing in mind the not too insignificant role that Chartists played in the Rebellion. There were many who saw the British Crown as alien to their ways and thus all authority vested in it likewise, men such as John Harpur who Hocking talks about in his book as someone who was regarded as being in 'direct opposition to the ruling elite' and who said ' ... we'll yet have men like Cromwell ... '. It struck me as rather puzzling when I read this as his father was from Kinsale and history tells us that Cromwell is hated by most Irishmen and women for what he did to them notably at Drogheda.

So how significant was the Rebellion? I came across this when researching the 150th anniversary celebrations, which was a quote from 'The Age' of the 3rd December 2004 by Ballarat-born Steve Bracks, then Premier of Victoria:

> 'I believe Eureka was a catalyst for the rapid evolution of democratic government in this country and it remains a national symbol of the right of the people to have a say in how they are governed. This means Eureka is not just a story – it is a responsibility. A calling to ensure we stay true to the Stockade's democratic principles and build on its multicultural heritage – because Eureka was thoroughly multicultural. Many believe that the events of Eureka were responsible for, or at least hastened, significant democratic reforms for the people of Australia. The principles for which the diggers, fought are universal – human rights, justice and tolerance. These priorities are as relevant today as 150 years ago.'

Although the Eureka had taken me on a whirlwind (I was walking fast as beer time was fast approaching and I was starting to get withdrawal symptoms) albeit fascinating tour through the events, including various re-enactments, the real treat for me was that the gift shop which was packed full of 'those things I bought on holiday but will never use/wear again.' As I paid I asked the shop assistant, Tim (it said so on his badge), replete with pony tail but as he was quite young and not going bald on any part of his head I let him off, what he thought about what had happened here and the children that were there today:

> "The kids seem to enjoy themselves because of all the activities they can do, but I don't know if they are really interested and this is one of those 'yeah right, seen that, tick box'."

"But what about you, does it have any significance for you?"

"For most of my generation" (he was in his early twenties I reckoned) "and I reckon any Australian it is right up there with ANZAC Day, which every Australian worth his salt celebrates, as another of those big dates in our nation's history. It's a proud moment in our development as an independently-minded country. Now that'll be four thousand dollars you English scumbag." I made the last bit up but I bet that was what was what he thought. Anyway I left my kidneys in payment for a top t-shirt with the Southern Cross emblazoned across the chest.

A last reflection on the Eureka Rebellion: Peter Lalor, a man who stood at the stockade and advocated the rights of the miners, a man who went on to become the Victorian State Parliament's Speaker, also used Chinese labour to break the strike at Clunes Mine in 1873. Interesting, a politician with no scruples; who'd have thought it? There was another irony in that his grandson would die as an officer of the British Crown serving at Gallipoli in 1915.

My hotel, the Sovereign Hill Lodge was situated overlooking the Sovereign Hill museum which was a recreation of a mining town at the height of the gold rush. A highlight held nightly was the show entitled 'Blood on the Southern Cross' which involved all sorts of excitements from a huge Peter Lalor to a burning Eureka hotel and included those well known participants in the Rebellion, the trapeze artists and acrobats flying across a huge circus tent which as all historians tell us was situated in the middle of the stockade. I reckon that it was nothing to do with the troops going in on a Sunday that did for the miners, but that swine Coco the Clown. It sounded all very exciting and I knew that I *had* to go there, but only after I'd finished my beer. Well, I would have gone but beer is for me a word that is only said in the plural form, and drunk accordingly, and although I did wonder around the museum (it was free and part of the hotel package, either that or I shouldn't have gone in through that hole in the fence) by the time I'd located a hostelry for dinner and beer(s) it was getting on and I had an early start the following day.

CHAPTER 8

*To the land of the banana bender, a swim with the sharks the
arrival of the Big Man*

DAY fifteen: November 18th

I was off to Queensland today, flying from Melbourne to Cairns and
then on to four nights in Port Douglas where I would be joined by the
Big Man, my friend Chris from those lovely days of school. The name
'banana benders' was not some sort of sexual fantasy or to do with a skill
involving a Uri Geller type ability to bend aforesaid fruit but was to do
with a jocular poke at the what the State was seen as by the others as the
Australian National Dictionary Centre explains:

'The term derives from the joking notion (as perceived from the
southern states of Australia) that Queenslanders spend their time
putting bends into bananas. The association of bananas with Queensland
('bananaland') is based on the extensive banana-growing industry in
tropical Queensland. The Queensland border has been called the Banana
curtain and Brisbane has been called Banana city.'

However, there was another somewhat less complimentary name for
the State before this due to the fact, as Knightley points out, that in 1922
it started to provide social security benefits for those who were unable
to work and because, as he described it 'Australians in work have never
really approved of governments giving money to those without a job' it
acquired the nickname 'the loafers state'.

The flight was early so my drive to the airport began just as dawn
was bursting out, if that's what dawn does. Perhaps I should ask her. The
route was straightforward along the Western Highway through pleasant
countryside which in places was covered in a ground fog, before arriving
at Tullamarine Airport where I dropped off my metal carrier with wheels
and looked for the QANTAS check-in. Thanks again to Knightley I can

tell you a little bit about the early days of the airline. It was founded in 1920 in Queensland by wealthy farmers and was named the Queensland and Northern Territory Aerial Service. The airline was based out of Charleville, south west Queensland and apparently the best (and only) place to stay was the Corones Hotel run by 'Poppa Corones'. He describes the time that Amy Johnson, world famous aviation pioneer, stopped off to refuel. She asked to bathe on champagne which was duly provided for her using 16 bottles and after she had gone 'Poppa renowned for making a prisoner of every penny, not only managed to rebottle the champagne … but somehow finished up with seventeen bottles.' You can perhaps forgive anyone who subsequently ordered one of those bottles being slightly puzzled by the taste. Corones was a wily old fox because having named the first planes he was given the in-flight food contract. Just remember the next time you fly the meal that you are served whatever class you sit in because it will be nothing like those that Corones served; Knightley tells the story:

> 'While the aircraft was refuelling at Charleville, his staff would rush on board with food form his hotel, white table linen and silver service.'

Although my flight was very pleasant (we arrived half an hour early) there was, sadly, no sign of that silver service of bygone days on board, although at least the sandwich I got did taste vaguely of the description on the packet. What it must have been like in those days; such fun!

I arrived in Cairns shortly after midday and the first thing I noticed as I left the terminal was the humidity and heat. The last few days in the gold fields had been warm, but not too hot and certainly not humid, but here I was, my first trip to the tropics since I lived in Borneo as a child and wham! The last time I had felt this humidity was in Singapore in 2006 and had wondered around Fort Canning where the big guns that were supposed to protect the place from the Japanese had been located (they all pointed to the sea and the Japanese crossed from Malaya using bikes) in blistering heat, evaporating all the time, so much so that when I stopped off to buy a drink a wag in the shop asked me if I'd just come from the swimming pool and had forgotten my towel. Cairns was exactly the same and so dripping with sweat and trying not to be noticed by the locals I found my new rental car.

To hire this one I had promised to give the car hire firm the first born of my children. It was black so ideal for soaking up the rays of the sun; it was also, in the politest of terms I can describe it, horrible. The only thing that didn't rattle or sound as if it was on its last legs was, well, not in my car. There were two options to get to Port Douglas. One was to drive along the Captain Cook Highway or to take a slightly more scenic route (according to my ever reliable AA Road Map of Australia, 2nd Edition there were more 'sights' to see). Not knowing which was best I asked the delightful lady at the car hire desk in Cairns as to what she would recommend. And here I once more encountered another Australian characteristic – humour yourself by playing games with the Pommie.

"Well you could take the Cook Highway but it's pretty busy as it's the only main road going north or you could go west along route one and then north towards Mount Molloy on the 81 where you turn right on the 44 which then takes you down into Port Douglas."

"Which is quicker?"

"Aw, if it was me, I reckon on taking the second. It's slightly further but it will be quicker at this time of day." She smiled and started to talk to the next in line.

So I set off not along the '44' which would have taken me along the east coast and directly to Port Douglas because as she had also said "It's really busy and will take you longer than you think" and instead found myself in second gear or whatever that low one is in an automatic going up this massive great mountain (to a pond dweller like me who lives below sea level anything over a foot is a mountain) following a huge truck going so slow that I thought I had hit one of those time warps I've seen in sci-fi films where everything seems to stand still. I mean when a snail passed me on the outside and seasons come and go, it was at that point I knew I was going really slowly.

On the plus side when I reached the summit the views of Cairns and the surrounding countryside were fabulous and for a moment all was right with the world. The sun was out, it was hot, the birds were singing and I had four more weeks, what could be better? Let me tell you then. Not going any further along this wretched road. It was after I'd reached Mareeba and turned towards Mount Molloy that I started to get a little edgy, a slight twitching above my right eye and a clear desire to take this piece of junk back to the lovely young lady and explain, diplomatically of course, what I thought of her quicker option. Mind you as I had already discovered the word 'quick' seems primarily one reserved for fast cricket bowlers than a concept that was a standard in Australian life. Perhaps my irritation was misplaced. Well not entirely, because the road into Port Douglas was hell with one hairpin after another and took what seemed to be forever to descend. I vowed never to come this way again and to never listen to an Australian giving directions to a place based on theirs and mine interpretation of busy and quicker.

Port Douglas is located in north east Queensland at almost the last point where a two-wheeled drive car can safely operate. The original inhabitants based on a study made by Dr. Chris Anderson were the Kuku Yalarij tribe who are believed to have settled here some 9,000 years ago. Their culture was intimately linked to the environment that they lived in – he termed it 'culturised' – with everything around them expressed in human terms. They had five seasons and I had arrived in what they called 'wungariji' or the 'hot time'. Just over a couple of decades ago it was a quiet village, no more really than a fishing port. Which belies its history because it was one of the most populated towns in Queensland in the late 19th century due to gold – it was to be the main town that 'serviced' the Hodgkinson River Goldfields, which when the latter ended declined only to become 're-born' in the 1980's as a holiday hotspot.

According to the Douglas Shire Historical Society the town was first surveyed in 1877 (to be exact July 1st: I like this sense of detail, very important though it doesn't say whether this was before or after lunch) and was variously called Terrigal, Owenville, White Island Point and Salisbury until some local brown-noser named it after the Queensland Governor, John Douglas. Not surprisingly gold brought in the people and like Walhalla in New South Wales, the population exploded to around 12,000 at its peak in the last decade of the 1800's. The demise of Port Douglas came almost as quick as its rise, and even though there was (and is) a thriving sugar cane industry, more of which later, by around 1960 the population was less than 1% of the peak. It lost out simply due to the advent of the railway and the Cook Highway which bypassed Port Douglas and the move of businesses and local government to Mossman which was then at the end of the link from Cairns.

As I drove into the spit of land on which Port Douglas sits I passed the Sheraton Mirage resort which dates from 1987 and was the beginning of the town becoming more than just a mere blip on a map. Continuing down the main drag (imaginatively called Port Douglas Road), to the right and left there was evidence of what Port Douglas is today – a mixture of resort hotels and new housing. However, at the tip, and really beginning with Macrossan Street was what I took to be the town as it was in its heyday. Admittedly a lot of the buildings were modern, but there was also much in evidence of its past. The old and new mix was well maintained, although there is a clear nod to the more financially comfortable tourist as some of many of the restaurants were both expensive and pretentious which I define follows:

- Over-priced starters with incomprehensible names like 'Stilettos of pate de Mont St. Michel a la Mode', which when it arrives is no more than some bland pate and toast.
- Over-priced main courses, also with stupid descriptions, that assume the diner has an incredibly small appetite (nouvelle cuisine is to food for me as Rudolph Nureyev would have been to rugby; pretty, but utterly useless). This arrives on a plate five times the size of your meal.
- Bottled water that costs more than the entire gold reserves that Gordon Brown didn't sell at the bottom of the market.
- A person (usually female) whose only role is to walk you to a table but heaven forbid will take a drink order from you.
- It is NOT a serviette – that is French – no, it is a napkin.
- Waiters/waitresses who refer to themselves in the familiar ("Hi, I'm Randy" being my favourite US greeting) or call themselves servers. Never knew that the Church was part of the restaurant experience – look it up if you don't know what I mean.
- 'Your server' who asks you how your meal was but cares not one jot. I have often felt like saying "It was terrible, but my friend bet me I couldn't eat it without vomiting" and then rush out of the restaurant retching all the way.
- When the bill arrives there is no attempt to conceal the service charge already applied or if not then being reminded so by 'your server'.
- And one last thing: please can someone somewhere explain why, when you sit at the table, there is often a plate already set in front

of you but which is then removed to accommodate the starter? It's completely bonkers.

Today Port Douglas' permanent population exceeds 6,000 and in 2009 Australian Traveller magazine rated it number three in its list of 100 Best Towns in Australia with populations under 45,0000 and if it's any consolation to the old inhabitants of the town, Mossman came 31st. I quite liked the make-up of the 12 panel judging panel as being described by the magazine as follows:

' ... we had fashionistas, grumpy old men, sports nuts, tourism industry experts, travel writers, and even some well-travelled *normal* people'. The italics are mine, because I love the idea that there are such people as 'normal'.

That evening I strolled to the centre of the town and popped into one of the oldest establishments that hadn't been completely destroyed by the 1911 cyclone, the Central Hotel, originally built in 1878. But as with Port Fairy, the Central Hotel had no character on the inside at all being replaced by plastic and neon. The menu on offer would have put even the worst road side café to shame back in the UK, unless I had a penchant for fries and increasing my already highly toxic levels of cholesterol. This led me to ask myself a question which was whether Australians 'do history'. It had struck me already that although accepting that the nation as it is today is still relatively young, outside of the main conurbations there was not much on show, and where there was it did seem fairly cursory. In some respects this is what I had felt, and still feel, about America although to be fair there is much more on show. Port Fairy was the closest I came to during all my travels to what I felt was keeping in touch with its history. The Central Hotel also disappointed me for another reason and one that I'd seen in Sydney at the Hero of Waterloo which was that for the sake of some sop to modernisation any atmosphere that might have been there had been sucked out. I guess I am showing either my age or that I am a snob.

As a footnote the town has three major claims to fame outside of its history and that is Bill 'I did not have sexual relations with that woman' Clinton and his wife Hilary 'I miss-spoke' Clinton visited the spot in 1996 on holiday, that Steve Irwin was killed off the coast near here and that newlyweds Tom and Eileen Longren were left behind by a reef operator in 1998 and their bodies have never been found.

Day sixteen: November 19th:

The following morning I made my way to the harbour to do something that had been top of the list of 'Things I must do in Australia' and that was to swim the Great Barrier Reef. Port Douglas is, as its tourism brochure tells you, the 'Closest Town to the Great Barrier Reef'. There were a few like-minded people milling about as I bought a ticket to go aboard the Calypso and spend the day snorkelling at three different sites. In all I reckoned that around 30 of us boarded and then set off to the first stop about an hour or so out to the reef.

Unlike the whale watching back in Sydney, I knew straight away that this was going to be much more fun and worth the kidney I had sold to pay for the ticket. On the way out I asked one of the crew whose name escapes me so we'll call her Sheila and who was serving morning coffee:

"Don't you ever get a little bored coming out here every day?"

"You're joking, right! Just look outside and around you. I bet you work in an office. Wouldn't you want to exchange that for this?"

"But what about the tourists like me, what are they like?"

"Look, I don't really care what or who they are. This is a great way to spend the day and be paid and apart from the odd chunderer most people on the boat are really relaxed. No stress, you know and the reef is so awe-inspiring and usually the weather is good so everyone is in good spirits."

"But as career can you see yourself doing this for a long-time?"

"I don't know and haven't really given it much thought anyway this is great at the moment; I'm young and got lots of mates here so I guess why worry what tomorrow brings, I mean, why should I? I mean if I save enough money doing this maybe I'll do the thing and travel to Europe and London of course" and with a grin she then said, looking me straight in the eye "You single?"

Actually this very last bit referring to my relationship status was what I wanted her to say but she didn't although I'm sure that was what she was thinking as she surveyed my lycra clad body (I was wearing my rather fetching 'stinger suit'). But on a more serious note, her attitude was further reaffirmation of the 'carpe diem' of Australians, especially the younger ones, I was meeting. She was right in so many ways and talking to Australians who come to the UK it seemed to me that with most it was to 'live' a little, maybe gain a bit of experience and see other countries before settling down back in Australia.

There is no doubt that there is a large, mostly transient, Australian population in the UK and according to the UK's Office of National Statistics there were, in 2009, 95,000 living in London, or to put this another way based on the Australian Government Census of the same year, just shy of 5% of the total population; in 2001 the Museum of London calculated the figure was just 0.25%. It has helped that sterling was nearly a 1/3rd less expensive today, but even so I can't see 5% of the UK's population moving abroad. I look back at what I did after leaving school and I fall into that dull pattern that many of my generation come from: leave school, take a little time off maybe but not too much, go to university then get a job, marry, have kids, retire and then die. There is absolutely no fun in that at all. I know today it is different and both my nephews both took a year out to travel, but the Australians, Kiwis and South Africans are the undoubted masters.

So back to the reef: what can I say about the reef that has not already been said or written about on hundreds of TV programmes or in books or magazines? It is unbelievable. The figures, which I took from 'Barrier Reef Australia' about this truly amazing natural wonder of the world, are quite simply staggering:

- It is about 2,300 kilometres in length stretching from Fraser Island to the south of Queensland to the southern tip of Papua New Guinea;
- It covers an area of some 340.000 square kilometres;
- It is home to hundreds of species of birds (215), fish (2,800), coral (400), echinoderms (star fish, sea cucumber – 600), turtles (6) plus dugongs, whales, clams and so on.
- There are 3,400 individual reefs and over 600 islands.
- It is home to some pretty unpleasant jellyfish including the not too friendly Box Jelly fish, sharks, sea snakes, stone fish along with toxic cones shells (it is highly recommended you do not put these to your ear to listen to the sea!).

Just on the Box Jelly fish, or as it is known in Latin *Chironex*, this is what I could have expected should I have been unfortunate enough to be stung by one of the little darlings that was writ large on a warning sign in Port Douglas:

> 'Severe burning skin pain. Sting marks are whip like and appear as burn marks on the skin. Adherent tentacles are often present. Victim may stop breathing and rapidly lose consciousness.'

I heard that surviving a sting was rare (although thankfully incidents were too) although recently a young girl surprised all when she recovered. I bore all this in mind because it was at Port Douglas that I had earmarked for snorkelling the Great Barrier Reef.

Tourism is not new to the reef and started in the 1890's although I have this image of Victorian women in their less than practical swimming apparel being towed into the water in the then fashionable (for modesty purposes) bathing machine. This is truly a wonder of the world and it is not surprising that in 1981 the area became a World Heritage Site. In their 2008 report, the Great Barrier Reef Marine Park Authority calculated that the economic value of the reef was over 5 billion dollars. In 2009 the World Travel and Tourism Council produced a paper that said the reef attracted 4.9 million domestic and 2 million international visitors annually and employed 54,000 people. Back in October 1802 Matthew Flinders wrote down his experiences when visiting here, describing the Great Barrier Reef thus:

> 'Different corals in a dead state, concreted into a solid mass of dull-white colour composed the stone of the reef. The negro heads were lumps which stood higher than the rest; and being generally dry, were blackened by the weather; but even these, the forms of the different corals, and some shells were distinguishable. The edges of the reef, but particularly on the outside where the sea broke, were the highest parts; within, there were pools and holes containing live corals, sponges, and sea eggs and cucumbers; and many enormous cockles … were scattered upon different parts of the reef … '

The somewhat odd description of 'negro heads' he goes on to explain as:

'The reefs were not dry in any part, with the exception of some small black lumps which at a distance resembled the round heads of negroes … '

But Matthew mate, if you had only gotten in the water! The sheer beauty of what you would have seen be it the coral, the fish or the giant clams would (and is) have been breathtaking, though not literally as you would have drowned. In the water there was an an almost surreal sense that none of this was real. If, like me, the only live fish you have really ever seen were some goldfish in a pond, the aquarium in the dentist or the odd minnow and stickleback in the local stream then imagine being in a world where you can actually reach out and almost touch creatures that mother nature seems to have taken a huge paintbrush to and during what I suggest might have been some drug induced psychedelic trip, created an explosion, nay a riot, of colours that leap out at you everywhere you turn.

It was quite simply one of the best experiences of my life and the tranquillity of floating in the water difficult to match, although as I said to Sheila when I related my experiences to her, beating Australia in the Rugby World Cup in 2003 and then the quarter-finals in Marseille in 2007 was still top of the list. I could have mentioned the Ashes but decided not to, after all that would just be too churlish but also because she couldn't have cared one way or the other as she, in a sweet put down voice just said "I like the footy" which, as every Australian aficionado of rugby knows is really called aerial ping-pong.

Just on sport as once more I have strayed onto it, I have always wondered why the Australians are, generally, better at most things athletic when compared to the British (not just the English). My Australian friends and acquaintances said that one of the most critical things to this disparity was that in the UK the weather was, as we all know, less than brilliant, whereas in Australia the opposite was true. But it is actually not that difficult to understand why when you look at what the government has done in terms of spending, including providing an organisation, the Australian Institute of Sport, to act as a conduit for potential talent. According to an article by Ross Tucker and Jonathan Dugas in 'The Science of Sport' this was mostly prompted by a desire to succeed more in the Olympics and it has since ballooned. Back at home the only thing I remember from my sporting days (and I was very sporty don't you know!) was a) who had the cigarettes and b) whose round was next. Had I been an Australian, who knows?

On the way back I sat in the bow area (yes my nautical knowledge is quite extraordinary) enjoying the sea breeze and sun, the latter being reflected back up in the sky by my whiter than white body (imagine the next time you see someone interviewed on TV and their face is lit up by someone holding a reflection device in front of them and you'll know what I mean) and just thought that Sheila was not just right, she was bang on. "No worries mate."

Sitting opposite me were a young couple with two very tired kids, who I learnt, were on the last day of their holiday before returning to Perth tomorrow. The husband it turned out was, like me, a commuter but with a difference. He was working in the iron ore business in the northern part of Western Australia and did a two-week on, one week-off shift. Iron ore is, along with other mining in Australia, big business and with the boom in Chinese growth as a major driver, according the Australian Bureau of Statistics in 2007, 90% of the extracted mineral is exported (60% to China in 2007 alone) and is dominated by just two companies, Rio Tinto and BHP Billiton. In all 99% of Australian iron ore comes from that State. I asked him what he actually did and whether he enjoyed it:

> "Well it's hard work and at this time of year bloody hot. I mean working in 40 degree heat is not much fun and given that I spend most of my time outside as an engineer it can get quite uncomfortable. I guess I'm more used to it now, but with the kids growing up the hardest part is leaving home and then not seeing them for two weeks."

I understood exactly how he felt as when I lived in Boston in the US my family stayed in the UK and I would only see them probably every 8–9 weeks at best. But equally as he said you just have to get on with it and go where the work is. I asked his wife what she thought:

> "Anthony and I feel it's the only option at the moment. You have to make the effort these days and, what with the economy, go where the opportunities lie. Yeah, I miss having him around and so do the kids but what can you do?"

Anthony added "I think the real drag for me working in the mines is that you can't really wind down with a tinny at the end of the day because the company has the right to breathalyse you whenever it wants and any trace of alcohol and you're out. But I earn a good wage and that's what allows us to do this sort of thing and visit her family back in Kent."

Now, I have the utmost respect for anyone prepared to go out of their way to help their family or better themselves financially legally, but, and here this is would be the crunch, do I forgo a large snifter at the end of the day (especially a hot one like today) or send the little darlings out to work up chimneys like our Victorian forebears did to make ends meet? We carried on chatting for the rest of the trip back to Port Douglas about life in general in Australia and there was no doubt that even with the fact that Anthony was often absent (and by the way the drive he said was about 10 hours to get to work from Perth) they wouldn't change it for the world. Paula liked going back to see family in the UK because as she said "I love the winter and the cold, but when I come back to Perth ... " she paused and gestured around us, pointing towards the blue sky dotted with small puffy clouds here and there, with sun blazing away and the blue, oh so blue water, and then continued " ... you see what I mean? We get this back home and I'd miss it too much if I left Australia for good."

I knew exactly what she meant, but with a proviso. British winters are like our summers and this is best summed up as being brief to the point of non-existent. Living in the UK we seem to have three seasons of weather:

- Fifty weeks of the year it is cloudy and invariably raining/drizzling.
- For one week men freeze trying to stay manly and women dress with forty layers of clothing to keep warm (except in Newcastle where clothing is not a must have, just an optional extra) as the mercury dips below zero and the liberal media worries about the new ice age whilst people go round saying "I don't remember it being as cold as this before."
- For one week the weather is dominated by blazing sunshine and we all worry about global warming. Men become primordial and, whilst sitting in the garden, bare-chested, in direct sunlight trying to encourage the barbecue to light in order to show (as men) our skills with fire, we then demonstrate our hunting and gathering skills by fetching from the fridge that last piece of shrivelled meat that we

managed to find in the supermarket, the one that says 'BBQ ready Chinese style ribs; 10% real meat', which once we have finished cremating it on the barbecue requires immediate burial. Never mind though because in true British spirit you're completely past caring having demolished all the beer in the house and the box of wine (we men are sophisticated beasts), our wives, who until now had been sunbathing using up all of last year's sun cream (Factor 0 because they "need to top-up their tan") have now decided they've had enough, fed the kids and put them to bed and are watching some awful soap that the female of the species seems to adore so much. Still it's good to be a man in the 21st century.

In 2009 the British Met Office forecast that 'the coming summer is odds on for a barbecue summer'. Given the gloom and doom that abounded with the credit crunch and the dreadful summers of 2007 (the wettest in 100 years) and 2008, this sounded like just the medicine Mr. and Mrs. Joe and Joanna Public needed. So what does the weather do? Absolutely what it always does – rain. So much so that it almost surpassed 2007. The Met Office has decided not to do long range forecasts as a result.

It is a fact, according to me, that the English are by and large obsessed by the weather. Samuel Johnson in edition number 11 of the 'Idler' (June 24, 1758) said of this that ' … It is commonly observed, that when two Englishmen meet, their first talk is of the weather; they are in haste to tell each other, what each must already know, that it is hot or cold, bright or cloudy, windy or calm.' There was a recent survey undertaken by Lloyds TSB of 2000 people in the UK which found that we spend, and this is almost unbelievable, six months of our lives talking about the weather. Here I was in Australia and all I could think about each morning was what the weather was going to do. I even wrote it down in my notebook as if it was some religious duty. On holidays to France my family would be driven nuts by my constant talk (they called it moaning but let's not split hairs) about the weather. Ok, so the statistic is not so unbelievable but I suspect that I spend more than six months. And for the curious in my forty-two days here it was sunny for 85% of the time, but I still grumbled about the other 15%. It's all about perspectives as we all know.

Back in Port Douglas we all disembarked and went our separate ways. It is always one of life's puzzles for me. Why is it that when the British go on holiday we are much less reserved and happy to break bread with the person sitting next to us, but as soon as we come back home it is the complete opposite? Is this a thing unique to us as some of my foreign friends suggest or worldwide? It's all very odd but true.

A final thought on this part of my Great Barrier Reef adventure (there was more when I got to Airlie Beach). The reef continues to be one of the world's most delicate ecosystems and the government is very keen that it remains in as good a condition as is possible. This means that licensed tourist boats are limited as to where they can go and what they can do and commercial shipping also has to abide by similar codes of practice. In early 2010 the Chinese bulk coal carrier Shen Neng 1 ran onto the reef near Great Keppel Island because apparently it was off course and without any permission to be where it was. It was the second major disaster for the Great Barrier Reef as in March 2009 another vessel, the Pacific Adventurer, spilt over 270 tonnes of oil off Moreton Bay. In both cases it is alleged that these accidents were down to the coal and LNG industries booming and the need, some say, for companies to 'cut corners'. Whatever the reason, I would hope that man's ability to destroy so much that is beautiful in nature, invariably for money, is not always victorious. Wouldn't it be a shame if not just the rainforests disappeared but also the reef or the vast Alaskan tundra and so many other places of outstanding natural beauty just for a few pennies more?

Day seventeen: November 20th

Today Chris was arriving in the afternoon so I had some time to kill in the morning so it was off to the Rainforest Habitat at the entrance to Port Douglas. This turned out to be a very pleasant way to spend a morning. There are three parts to the Habitat – rainforest, wetlands and grasslands. In each of these areas were native flora and fauna. I lost count of the number of different species of birds I saw from kookaburras to parrots, lorikeets, parakeets, cockatoos, cockatiels and the rare cassowary with its bone head. This bird is plug ugly to look at and rather like the crocodile seems to be a survivor of the dinosaur age. It has, amongst other things, a penchant for violence and uses its front claw as a weapon. In the 2007 Guinness World Records it is listed as the world's most dangerous bird. So that's snakes, spiders, sharks, stinging painful plants (yes really), reptiles, sharks and birds that can all kill you. However, only one person is recorded as having being killed by one, that of a 16 year old in 1926. According to Outback Australia though, the deadliest creature in Australia as measured by deaths per annum (or 2008/2009 – it was a bit vague) was, and I shouldn't laugh, the notoriously savage and dangerous, leviathan-like European honey bee!

Of all the birds in the Habitat the one that caught my attention the most was the black necked stork standing over a chick looking wistfully at his foot. This bird and his better half were the first pair to breed successfully in captivity. But, beat this, it took a total of seven years which included courtship and the building of a rather nice bijou residence before she said yes. Bless woman, so easy to please! Then there was Glen the Koala. Poor old Glen was perched in his eucalypt completely spaced out on the leaves (the reason these animals sleep so long is a combination of the toxins in the leaves as well as their 'medicinal' value) when along came the keeper, picked him up and then asked if anyone wanted their photo taken (for a mere fifteen dollars) with him, Glen that is not the keeper. Maybe he was so spaced out it didn't bother him; certainly the photo I took of him suggested it, the keeper that is not Glen.

On to the kangaroos next, along with the wallabies and ducks and a packet of food with which I was allowed to feed them with. It should be noted at this point that although this packet was not expensive I felt a complete idiot when I walked into the enclosure and saw that there were buckets of the feed all over the place for free. Another one of those Australian pommie jokes. Remind me to eat more kangaroo. The kangaroos, as in Halls Gap, were curious and very friendly allowing me to pat them and they were quite happy to take feed off my hand. At this point to break the sheer monotony of this paragraph and because there isn't much more to say about feeding kangaroos let me enlighten you upon the origin of the name. The myth that is often mentioned is that on arriving in Australian in 1770, Cook and his entourage when asking the Aboriginals (the Guugi Yimidhirr people) about this strange creature, what they said was translated as 'I don't know'. In fact the creature was the gangurru or gangaru which Joseph Banks, the botanist who travelled with Cook, anglicised to kangooro and thence its present form.

Here's another factoid for those hungry for more – in the gift shop and others I could have bought bottle openers, wallets and other such delights made from kangaroo scrotums. I didn't see any hopping around minus their testicles so I presume they are dead when these special items are removed from their bodies. And no, I didn't buy one not because of any sense of morality but simply because they cost a small country's GDP to purchase (sorry to anyone of a sensitive nature).

Next came the crocs, both estuarine and freshwater, which were menacing and I was quite happy to be perched well above where they were. This part of the world has signs on rivers, lakes, ponds and so on warning would be swimmers or general water users to keep an eye out for these relics of the dinosaur era. They looked as if they had been stuffed and put in the water or at its side on the banks but given that one of the warnings to campers was to keep at least fifty meters from the edge of any water where they might lurk I guess they move pretty fast. Some of these survivors of from the age of the dinosaurs can grow to be over seven metres but even with this I read that, sensationalism aside, crocs actually don't kill that many people in Australia, maybe on average one or two annually although there are some pretty nasty stories of those that have been victims. In the last eight years deaths have been mainly from people swimming in lakes (billabongs) or rivers although one unfortunate was snorkelling in the Gulf of Carpentaria. These crocs often have names given to them, like Goldie, a fourteen feet male that was responsible for the death of five year old Jeremy Doble in February 2009. That's a little weird if you ask me.

Attacks however, are becoming more frequent and there is an irony to this. Both types of croc are protected under Federal Law and have been for close to forty years but numbers have since grown dramatically which, with increased population and housing development as well as tourism growth, the potential for human contact has increased. It creates a conundrum for conservationists who come under pressure from those who would like to see numbers culled as to what to do. I did ask a young Australian friend of mine when mentioning that in the Northern Territory alone there were an estimated 150,000 of these friendly creatures and what she thought should be done. She is an urbanite so I guess her reply was no surprise as she said without batting an eyelid:

"Goody, more shoes and handbags!"

One side effect of this though has been a growth in the number of people working to create a 'balance' with nature by removing dangerous reptiles away from populated areas and for many the most famous was the late Steve 'Crocodile Hunter' Irwin. His memory lives on in the Australia Zoo outside Brisbane, which he ran from 1991 until his death and where his remains are buried.

Here are two final stories involving the croc. The first relates to a story which appeared a couple of years ago in the Sydney Daily Telegraph about two tourists who were on holiday in Queensland and who were trying to get one of these monsters to participate in a photograph. Now clearly you can spot immediately a flaw in their plan. Crocs are not known to be a) friendly and b) temperamentally suited to having their photo taken especially when, and here's the idiot quotient rising rapidly from mild to sky-high, one of them began to try to goad it to react, to get a sort of 'live action' photo. He was quoted as saying "I began playing with it for a photo". Playing; with a croc; which has sharp teeth and likes meat. Luckily for him he survived as the croc lunged for him but you have to ask, will humanity benefit going forward from their combined IQ which I suspect would put them some way behind a plank of wood. You decide. The second one is actually rather funny and involved a gentlemen of extremely limited forward planning but who clearly felt at one with nature once he had imbibed a sufficient amount of the silly juice. This man had decided that, having drunk more than was probably sensible, to ride a crocodile. The said crocodile, cutely named Fatso and some 1,800lbs, was not too impressed with this and began to tuck into the interloper resulting in some pretty nasty wounds. The bit I liked about this story aside from the sheer stupidity of the man's actions was the almost blasé way Sgt. Roger Haynes of the Broome police responded when asked what had happened and is in my view a classic case of Australian understatement:

'Fatso has taken offence to this and has spun around and bit this man on the right leg.'

Taken offence! I bet he was bloody livid having this drunken nutcase sitting on him and apparently the only reason the croc didn't have marinated man for dinner was because he was a bit sluggish. I just love Australia!

After a quick coffee I drove down the James Cook Highway along the coast to Cairns to meet Chris. It was actually a rather pleasant drive although as a single carriageway main road and the only one that links the northern part of Queensland to the hub at Cairns, quite busy. Outside of the road works in Melbourne, traffic so far had been light but along this stretch there were cars aplenty and signposts every 500 centimetres (or so it seemed) warning you to slow down, take a rest, to have a crap, to scratch your balls and so on. Australian road signs advising the driver of impending danger or giving some bit of advice are frankly just a little too much. I had met one Australian with whom I had bemoaned the 'nanny state' back home and how much freer it was here and didn't believe him when he said that in Australia it was just as bad. However, I'm not sure I'd go as far as the equating our very own nanny state with theirs. After all amongst many brilliant edicts was the one where a UK town council cut down a load of conker trees (horse chestnut) 'just in case someone was hurt'. However, where the Australians score hands down is their wonderfully straightforward way of getting safety messages across. Whilst in Australia I came across a number of hard-hitting, but to my English eye humorous, campaigns from the road safety campaign to stop people driving and using their mobiles in Victoria with a tag line that was 'Don't be a dickhead'. Another advert from the VicRoads was titled 'Gingas get fresh' which had the subtext; 'Every time you use your mobile phone whilst driving, gingers get fresh with gingers'. Better still was the anti-knife campaign that used 'Wanker' or the drink drive campaign that said 'Drink drive, bloody idiot'. I mean can you just can't imagine this is in the UK.

Now Chris is what you might term a very traditional Englishman when it comes to holidaying. I have known him since 1976 and in all those years, both at school and after, I would best describe him as 'particular'. This means that he can be quite fussy when it comes to certain things specifically: food (must be meat at least three times a day), cars (must be top of the range and no matter what the weather the A/C is always on), hotels (must have room service) and getting from A to Z (must not under any circumstances be on foot where avoidable). The next two weeks were going to be interesting because on top of all this Chris is a 'strawberry blonde' who gets sunburn just by looking at the sun; when he arrived the sun was high in a cloudless sky and by the time we reached the hire car (a short walk) I could see he was beginning to cook.

Day eighteen: November 21st

Being in the tropics not only can the weather be absolute bliss but it can also rain as if there was no tomorrow. We had planned to go the Daintree where all sorts of excitements awaited the tourist from rainforests to river tours. But as we left the hotel the leaden grey skies began to let loose huge globules of rain. I looked at Chris who was driving (he likes to drive as everyone else is incapable – another of his little 'particulars') and suggested that instead of doing the planned day out we instead trek north to historic Cooktown.

"Is it far?" he asked

"I don't think so. Once we get onto the main road from Mount Molloy it should be easy" I lied.

"Are you sure?"

"Absolutely' I smiled, 'hour and a half tops, maybe two" I lied for the second time.

The journey followed what was the Cooktown Developmental Road, now called the Mulligan Highway in honour of an early prospector. It was originally a dirt road that had been completely metalled in the last few years and was thus suitable for 2WD cars. It passed through some historic sites like Mount Molloy (copper) and Mount Carbine (wolfram) and, well actually nothing for mile after mile after interminable mile. After two hours and after passing the 5 millionth termite mound and the zillionth burnt out tree or bit of scrub with not even a whiff of a kangaroo or koala, I took over the driving. Up until now I had really quite enjoyed the drives I had done, even in retrospect the one from Cairns to Port Douglas, but this was dull, oh so very dull. It reminded me of a drive I had done years ago from Albuquerque to San Diego which put boredom on a new plain shattered only be being stopped by a US Border Patrol officer looking for illegal aliens, aka Mexicans (why do they call them aliens?), as I passed close to the US/Mexico border. I wasn't sure what made him suspect me of harbouring a car load of Mexicans, maybe it was the sombrero, the mariachi band sitting in the back of the car, the bottle of Tequila and my large black moustache that aroused his suspicions, or possible he was a complete idiot.

"On the bright side … " I remarked casually to Chris: " … at least it's sunny." Oh, how he laughed and how tears flowed down his cheeks. I then added, trying to get some sense of justification for the time it had taken "Well in the old days when the road had no tarmac I'm reliably informed that it took over 6 hours and look it only took us 3 and a half. And Cooktown is very historic because Cook landed here in June 1770." There was no response. When Cook landed, he did so because his ship, the bark HMS Endeavour, had been hold by the Great Barrier Reef requiring him take shelter. His log recalls the incident vividly:

> 'Before 10 o'Clock we had 20 and 21 fathoms, and Continued in that depth until a few minutes before 11, when we had 17, and before the Man at the Lead could heave another cast, the Ship Struck and stuck fast.'

The experience is also recalled by Joseph Banks in his journal which is quoted by Flannery:

> 'Our situation became now greatly alarming: we stood offshore three hours and a half with a pleasant breeze so we knew we could not be very near it: we were little less than certain that we were upon sunken coral rocks, the most dreadful of all others on account of their sharp points and grinding quality which cut through a ship's bottom almost immediately.'

Cook in his account then goes on to describe how they had then tried to refloat her:

> ' … but threw overboard our Guns, Iron and Stone Ballast, Casks, Hoop Staves, Oil Jarrs, decay'd Stores etc.;'

They continued attempts to get her moving but to no avail even though the load had been lightened by '40 or 50 Tuns weight'. The result in the end was that they had actually sustained some damage and then spent the next 48 days on the Endeavour River repairing her.

But the real history for many Australians is not that event however significant it was, but that now very familiar story as to its position in Australia's history and that was alluvial gold. As with some of the other places already visited, the town had grown dramatically as a result with the port becoming Queensland's second biggest. Incredible as it seems looking at the place today the population at its peak rose to 30,000 in the area. The Centre for Government of Queensland has an interesting passage taken from the 1876 'Handbook' of the town which stated:

> 'Cooktown, a newly proclaimed mining township situated on the northern banks of the Endeavour River, about 1,500 miles NW of Brisbane. Though the town has almost been born in a day, it will most likely take its place as one of the most important centres of the colony should the yield of gold continue.'

As with Port Douglas, so too Cooktown's heyday was short-lived and by 1947 the census shows that less than 500 persons lived there. However, for the present day tourist the guide map suggests that there is a lot to see. I was all for exploring but Chris needed to eat, so whilst he went off to eat a whole cow somewhere I looked round. There were very few people around and about and much of what was on show was within a very short walking distance of each. I started off at Fisherman's Wharf and then headed towards the centre of town passing the statue of Mick the Miner (commemorating the gold rush), the Milbi Wall (an historical perspective of the indigenous people built by the Gungarde), the Cook Monument, the Cannon which was provided by London to see off the nasty Ruskis (at the time the Empire was concerned about their intentions in this part of the world), Mrs. Watson's Monument (she survived an Aboriginal attack, another reminder of the issues of European settlers and Aboriginals trying to live together) the Queensland National Bank housing the historical society (closed), the Cooktown Hotel (originally called the Commercial Hotel and now nicknamed 'Top Pub'), the Cooktown Railway Station, James Cook Statue and at the far end of the town the cemetery with its divided burial areas of Anglicans, Catholics (at the height of the town's success it had its own Bishop, two of whom are buried here as well as a convent whose founding Mother Superior is also interred here), a couple of Jewish graves and the Chinese Shrine. The latter is a poignant monument for two reasons as on the one hand it reminds the visitor about how significant was the role that the Chinese played in this country's history and secondly because it commemorates all those who died but as there was no census on the number it is really a monument to those who were known and those unknown.

It was all very interesting but done and dusted in just over 20 minutes so I wandered back into the still deserted high street which was about sixty feet or more wide. I popped into the only souvenir shop and out of curiosity given the distinct lack of people (most of the town was in fact ensconced in the local watering hole) enquired as to what business was like and why the owner had set up shop here:

"This time of year it's real quiet and there's not much tourist traffic at all. But Cooktown has changed a lot in the last few years and more visitors come, partly because it is a gateway to the very north of the state, but also because there is a new awareness of the history of the place not just because Cook landed here but also the gold rush and also from the threat to Australia from the Japs in the war; this place used to be more than just a point on a map. The new road has made a big difference as well and anyway I love it here, it's just beautiful with or without tourism. Everyone knows everyone and it's a real community, not like the big towns and cities."

I bought some vital additions to my collection of tourist tat, namely a kangaroo themed beach towel and a stubby cooler which as you will appreciate will always be useful in the UK's warm climate, and then went looking for Chris. Together we went to the James Cook Museum that was originally St. Mary's Convent, built to serve the needs of the large Irish community that was in place in the late 19th century, in 1889. Within the museum there was an eclectic collection of things to see from the early days of the convent, the influence of the Chinese, local life and of course Cook. Looking at the old black and white photos of the nuns in their habits I wondered how they coped with the heat and humidity at a time when luxuries like air conditioning didn't exist. On the way out of town before heading back to Port Douglas we stopped off at the lighthouse on Grassy Hill.

The views today are not much different to those Cook would have seen in 1770 with swathes of greenery in all directions and I was lost for a moment in a world of imagination knowing that it was here that the great man himself came to survey the lay of both the mouth of the river but also the land itself. Mind you this illusion was quickly shattered as behind us, coming up the path was an excitable family of Italians talking animatedly to each other with the men doing what Italian men do best and that is holding onto their crotch as if these were about to involuntarily disengage from the rest of the body. I shouted at them: "Hey, Giovanni, Paolo leave your genitals alone, no one is going to steal them!" At least I would have done if they didn't look like they had 'connections'. Always best to err on the side of caution I say.

We rejoined the Mulligan Highway and headed back to Port Douglas, stopping only briefly to take a look at a true natural wonder in the form of a mountain completely made of black granite boulders. It was named the Black Mountain due to the black granite — very imaginative. I know that I have touched on this naming lark already, but come on 'the Black Mountain', is that all they could come up with? If I'd been in charge of naming I would have called it something like Devil's Mountain or Hell and Damnation Hill, something with a bit of oomph that gives the traveller a sense of foreboding as to what might the mountain have been; a place of devil worship? An ancient place of death akin to the Mayan sacrifices? Was it perhaps the scene of some terrible event that befell the early European explorers? However, I later discovered back at our hotel that there was indeed more to it than I in my rather lurid imagination could possibly have known. The Black Mountain is known to the local Aboriginals (Kuku Nyungkal also known as the Annan River Tribe) as Kalkajaka and is steeped in great mystery with one translation being 'mountain of death' and another being 'the place of the spear'. The whole area is for the Aboriginals a significant cultural site and forms a part of their Dreamtime stories whilst for some non indigenous people a place of mystery. I think they should rename the whole Black Mountain National Park as Kalkajaka.

As I walked back to the car, I was confronted by two Aboriginals who were the worse for wear. Neither seemed to be that interested in either me or Chris and if anything, there was an air of sadness as we looked at each other for a brief moment. One of them shouted something, but not in any way aggressively and then stared at his bottle as if willing the alcohol to come out. That encounter was one of the very few I had in six weeks with indigenous people to my knowledge; this is their country but yet in large parts of Australia you wouldn't know that an indigenous population exists.

I won't bore you with the details of our drive back but suffice to say that as with our outbound journey the word excitement was not in evidence.

Back in Port Douglas I had more good news for Chris. Tomorrow we were going to move south and stay for a couple of days on Magnetic Island in the Whitsundays. I had a big build-up motivational speech ready:

> "It'll be great; two days of doing nothing and just relaxing. I looked at what there was before I came out and the hotel we are staying at has two pools, is bang next to the supermarket, which means you can get your snacks almost on tap."

This last bit was to get him in a positive frame of mind because Chris likes to snack, often between snacks, usually either biscuits or meat or both at the same time washed down by lashings of milk. So this build-up to our next port of call was pretty good.

I continued "There's just one small snag."

"What?"

I looked away at the ground and almost mumbled "It's about 300 plus miles and we need to get a ferry ticket, and this leaves at 2.30 or thereabouts, so we need to be away early in the morning."

Now Chris is a tolerant person, except when driving, and usually takes most things in his stride. Yes he has his 'particulars' but overall he is a nice chap. However, he is not big on early mornings, or for that matter a good timekeeper. And did I already mention he likes his food? So here was a small conundrum: we had to leave before 8 a.m., drive for another day and forego any stops on the way in order to get to the ferry in time. That evening over dinner little was said and I felt a foreboding for the following day.

Day nineteen: November 22nd

We were away early and it was very quiet in the car and I could sense that Chris was not best pleased with having to be on parade at a time that for him didn't exist and worse still miss out on breakfast, although I suspect he snuck in some biscuits before meeting me, but just wanted me to feel really bad. The drive itself was not overly eventful as we drove down the Bruce Highway aside from the fact that it was hard not to miss the largest industry in Queensland, sugar. On either side of the highway there was plenty of evidence from the fields themselves to the narrow gauge railways that are used to haul the cut cane to the processing plants.

The First Fleet had brought sugarcane with them but it wasn't until 1842 that the first refinery was set up just outside Sydney to refine imported canes. In an article called 'Australia's sugar industry' Robert F. McKillop charted the history of the industry from the First Fleet through to today and according to him, and others, 'The father' of Australia's sugar industry is regarded as Captain Louis Hope who established a plantation near Brisbane where '… He opened the first commercial sugar mill.' Since those days the sugarcane industry has become a big business in Australia and according to CANEGROWERS is worth at least $1.5-$2.5 billion annually. In all 'the country produces 32–35 million tonnes of cane per year, which when processed, equates to around 4.5–5 million tonnes of sugar' most of which is exported (around 80%). That's a lot of sugar cubes.

Back in the 19th century as the industry took hold there was a need for workers and given that there were not enough whites to do this (far too busy trying to find gold) the country started to bring in immigrant workers from the surrounding Pacific islands (referred to as 'kanakas'). As with some of the early European settlers in the New World at the end of the 17th and into the early 18th century, many of these Melanesians were indentured servants. In 'The Labor Trade in Melanesians to Queensland: An Historiographic Essay' Doug Monro looks at this whole area and notes that in the period 1863–1904 over 62,000 came on £6 per annum for a three year contract. Other historians note that there was no possibility of land or for that matter much else as such at the end of their term. It wasn't restricted to Pacific Islanders as many of the indigenous people also found out notably in northern Queensland. One policy that stood out was what became referred to as 'blackbirding'. This involved the use of nefarious means to get these people to work on the farms and in the mills either through false promises or straightforward abduction.

The Melanesians, like the Chinese before them, were a solution to the problem of not being able to provide cheap white labour. However, as with the Chinese, resentment began to grow and by the late 1870's the government in Queensland started to move against them with restrictions as to where they could work and what they could do. Monro stated that although this form of 'circular labor migration' was initially welcomed it soon changed by the 1880's as the fore runner to the White Australia

Policy began to become reality. In 1901 the country became a Federation and one of its first acts it enacted was the Pacific Islanders Labourers Act, which came six days before the official enactment of the White Australia policy. The Act put restrictions on Pacific islanders entering the country, the issuance of licences for those that were there prior to the Act and worse still the forcible repatriation of many, with no suggestion of compensation. More Acts followed all, as seen from today's perspective, with huge racist undertones. In essence, if you were not: a) white and b) European, then tough.

Macintyre discusses this in his book and points out that although many were allowed to stay, there was still huge discrimination and just like with the indigenous people, what these policies effectively did was to almost try to make then second class citizens in society. For the Aboriginal it was arguably even worse as they simply did not by this time (late 19th century) 'officially exist' such that as Macintyre points out even the Australian Natives Association related not to the indigenous peoples but the new white settlers.

There is another story about the sugar cane industry that makes Mr. Thomas Austin of rabbit fame not the only person to have made a huge mistake that generations have subsequently had to deal with. In 1935 the non indigenous cane toad was introduced into the country in order, it was hoped, to eradicate the beetles that were happily munching their way through the crop. Although some warned against it, growers prevailed and so it was that the toad as Tina Butler described in her 2005 article called 'Overstaying their welcome; Cane toads in Australia' became one of the most invasive creatures in the world to hit any country's ecosystems such that the World Conservation Union put them at the top of their list of the most destructive pests in the world. So what about the beetles? After all that was why the toads were brought in and although clearly not funny it is nevertheless one of those Homer Simpson moments as Butler explains:

> 'As it turns out cane toads cannot jump very high, only two feet actually, so they did not eat the beetles that for the most part lived in the upper stalks of cane plants. Instead of going after beetles as the growers had planned, the cane toads began going after everything else in sight – insects, bird's eggs and even native frogs. And because they were poisonous, they began to kill would-be predators.'

Now they have become a real problem and also a sport. In a country that loves to excel at all things competitive there are regular 'games' that involve golf clubs (in Queensland there are 'tournaments of 'Cane Toad Golf) and cricket bats and other such adventurous sporting themes. There are also other uses now being proposed including food and sportswear. In the case of the former a Mr. John Burry a game meat processor was interviewed on ABC in January 2010 and said:

'As someone said to me a couple of days ago, it's a case of turning lemons into lemonade.'

His marketplace would be China because the only way that Australians would eat it was if it was in a pie. Yum! Yum!

I also mentioned clothing. According to an article in '9 News' by Evan Schwarten you could also wear the toxic chap if you wanted as one Queensland firm had decided to turn those toads killed in the big Toads Day Out 'fun day' into golfing gloves this year. According to one of the organisers of the event, Lisa Ahrens:

'Apparently there is quite a market for toad-skin golf gloves in Japan.'

I know that Australians have had some issues as regards their historical dealings with the Orient, but trying to poison the peoples of these countries over dinner or the links is a bit much.

The drive along the Bruce took in a number of quite large towns including Innisfail which is the centre of the Cassowary Coastal Region. The sugarcane industry is very much part of its history as well, and by the late 1800's there were three mills in the town. Today it looks weary and we stopped for lunch in what was a fairly run-down part. The ubiquitous UTE was everywhere and seemed to once more be driven by young males (plus mullet and tattoos). On the subject of cars, on the news last night I'd watched an item about 'hoons' and the problems that they were causing in Australia. My initial reaction was what were Geoff Hoon, the UK's erstwhile Secretary of Defence, and his family doing to the Australians before I realised that they were talking about predominantly young males who used roads as race tracks and who performed stunts like handbrake turns and burning rubber. Hoons are for many Australians not much better than primordial gutter life. Over the last decade various laws have been enacted curtailing the activities of these people (who apparently are aged between 17 and 25) from fines to confiscation of their car. In Victoria, over 10,000 cars have been impounded since the law came into effect in 2005 with many being as a result of speeding or even having their stereos on anti-socially loud. The majority of those falling into this demographic are male and invariably in a lower economic bracket. There is a slightly lighter side to this as with any law that is quite draconian it can often catch out the most innocent of people. However, I am led to believe that there is another reason for this behaviour and it has less to do with being anti-social but more with sex. Yes sex! Basically men get off on their cars and here they mean any man. Hard to believe I know but apparently some of the wise and wonderful in academia think that this is a causal factor in not just hoons but the generally aggressive way that the male drives. It leads me to think that the next time I get in my car should I wear protection like maybe a mac? It brings a whole new meaning to putting the car into gear, putting your foot down and then just at the last minute applying the brakes. I also wonder what car makes for a good lover. Should it be small like a Mini or big like a Porsche Cayenne? Does brand make a difference? If it were a French car would it last longer than if it were English (not that we have a car industry which probably explains why we as a nation are seen as lousy lovers)? Why though stay in first gear if you can go much faster in fifth and get there quicker?

As we continued towards Townsville we hugged the coast passing through some beautiful scenery, not least the area just north of Ingham where we had a magnificent view of the Garringon National Park and of Hinchinbrook Island. Arriving in Townsville my job was to locate the departure point of the ferry using the map that I had carefully printed off before I left home. After the third circuit of the town we two males eventually decided to ask for directions. I know it's incredible but we were in a hurry and tempers were beginning to rise. Interestingly where we asked for directions was opposite the departure point so I'm guessing that the person who gave us them was wondering why two simpletons were being permitted to drive. Now any women reading this will no doubt say that this is typical male; that is we would rather get lost than admit that we need directions to anywhere. Well, in part I think that you are absolutely correct, but here's my take on why we don't until it is absolutely necessary. We don't like being told by you that "You should have turned left there" or "wasn't that the road we just came down?" We know but we don't need reminding by the person WHO HAS NOT DONE ANY OF THE DRVING SINCE WE ARRIVED IN FRANCE.

The ferry terminal was small and there were only three other cars waiting to board the boat that would be our lift to Magnetic Island. It was quite a pleasant trip, not long, and gave me and Chris (clicking away as if his life depended on it) an opportunity to take in the coastline. The approach to the Island said one thing to me: 'Thunderbirds are go!' Here was Tracy Island in all bar name, an image made so much stronger by the buildings at the entrance to Nelly Bay and by the flora of the Island. I was fully expecting as we arrived at the jetty to be met by Brains or Virgil or whoever, and then whisked off to the International Rescue HQ. Instead as we left the boat we got lost again (once more my fault) which was actually really, really dumb as to get to the hotel all we had to do was to drive off the boat and turn left (first left mind not second or third). Once we had negotiated this seemingly easy task we found that rather than being given just rooms for the two nights we were to stay, we were both instead given apartments complete with washing machines (for the little lady should she come as well).

My first plan of action after dumping my bags was to do a jog having been cooped up in a car for most of the day, but where? The resort had a number of helpful leaflets on what to do (it even had one on Brisbane which although very nice was a fair distance away; it would be rather like a hotel in London advertising Paris). I picked one that looked like fun. It was a seven kilometre round route that took in the hill that overlooked Nelly Bay and then went down into Arcadia and thence back to the resort. It was described as being 'moderate' and suitable for anyone who was healthy. I reckoned it would take an hour or so, after which I'd be in fine fettle for dinner and a sun-downer.

The Oxford Dictionary defines the word moderate thus: 'average in amount, intensity, quality, or degree … '

Well to the utter, utter cretin who compiled the leaflet let me tell you something. You need to add an addendum to it advising those wishing to take this route that a crampon attached to both shoes along with a survival kit and a compass might come in handy. It started off easy along Mandalay

Avenue and the residential area of Nelly Bay but as I began to ascend I found that at best I could just about heave myself from rock to rock. No running, no jogging, just a lot of fruity language. It wasn't helped by the heat, my attire (rugby shorts/shirt/socks) and those infuriating flies. As I struggled up, a young family descended as if they were mountain goats, smiling all as one at me and said in unison or so it seemed "Not far to go, mate". This too turned out to be a gross distortion of the facts as it took over a week to arrive at the summit, or at least that is how it felt. On reaching the top of what I believe was Mount Cook, a mere 493 metres above sea-level I stopped and took in the sights and sounds. I had arrived in a small slice of heaven. It was so quiet, aside from the birds and the wind gently blowing through the trees consisting of eucalypts, hoop pines, stringy barks and many more almost justified the tourist website's exhortation:

'Just twenty minutes … from Townsville and you could be in what many consider Paradise!'

When I had showered I sat on the balcony of my room and drank in the view as it looked straight out onto the bay itself, with the Island enveloping it from either side. As for the sunset – brilliant although I did have my beer goggles on by then so it could just be that the pool lights had been turned on.

Day twenty: November 23rd

Magnetic Island got its name from Cook and his belief that the Island had a high iron content that was upsetting his compass. Maybe the real reason is to be found in a wonderfully entitled tome called 'A Rudimentary Exposition on the Induced Magnetism of Iron In Sea Going Vessels And its Action on the Compass, In Different Latitudes, and Under Diversified Circumstances' by William Walker, R.N in 1853:

'Seaman, however, are generally persons with a limited amount of what is usually called education … ' and then about reaching the rank of Able Seaman he goes on that his ' … limited amount of education disqualifies him from graphically describing the principles of his art to another.'

Or perhaps Walker was a man whose own self-importance far outshone his actual abilities because had Cook, a man from very humble beginnings, been around at the time this was written I wonder how he might have reacted reading this. I suspect that Mr. W Walker, R.N may have had the wrong letter in his last name.

The Island, affectionately known as 'Maggie' by the locals, is not huge with nearly two thirds of it being a national park. It enjoys 320 days of sunshine per year and the island has been associated for a long time with the main indigenous people the Wulgurukakaba who named it Yunbenun. Unfortunately for them, the conflict between their traditional way of life came up against the needs of the European settlers who found the island to be a rich source of hoop pine and of granite, which in turn led to the establishment of Townsville. The last permanent indigenous people who lived on the island had left by the late 1920's, though I was pleased to hear that some are now returning.

This was a place that needed serious exploring and having met up with Chris for breakfast I hired a bike to cycle the Island. I am quite a proficient cyclist and since retiring from Rugby at the sprightly age of forty-two, have spent most weekends 'a-saddle' (though to be fair for anyone following from behind it must be quite difficult to see the saddle as my backside does envelope it somewhat) so I thought that this would be easy. But Magnetic Island is far from easy when it comes to cycling as it offers some pretty nasty climbs and a lot of sand towards its tip at West Point. And the bike I had hired was low in the number of gears and weighed a ton. I left Chris as the deposit in the event I stole it; why is everything so darned expensive?

I set off to West Point full of beans. After the first hill in 31 degree heat that enthusiasm had somewhat dissipated. However, I soldiered on and after a good hour arrived at the tip of the Island having negotiated a nasty stretch of sandy road, very sweaty and almost completely knackered. However, in front of me was a sight that would pass any audition for 'Most Picturesque Site for a Postcard'. There was blue sea, by now a blue sky, white sand everywhere and a small patch of green within which were half a dozen palm trees under which was the shell of an old launch. This idyllic scene was somewhat shattered by the discovery as I cycled back of a grave with, in front of it, an explanation about how the island had been used as a place of quarantine for amongst other things those suffering from yellow fever. The grave itself was of an immigrant who had died in 1900 at the age of just 23 years.

On to the other side of the island and Horseshoe Bay which, from what I could see of it, was more a spot for the 'young' (i.e. anyone younger than me) and was full of those really annoying bronzed youths and their sun-bleached blonde girlfriends. I'm not jealous of course given that my body is also a temple, albeit one of doom rather than one that will get the ladies all 'hot'. I once told my wife that if all else failed in life I could become a gigolo. She laughed and hasn't stopped since. It's one of life's mysteries that not looking like George Clooney puts me in the box marked 'probably lousy in bed'. I mean if "Get lost you fat bastard" was a come on from the ladies then I, my friend, would make Casanova look like an 'also-ran' in the ladies stakes.

It would be quite easy to imagine living here and when I met up with Chris again at the same restaurant I had left him at 4 hours previously (yes I do believe he had stayed there eating the entire island's food supply for the year) he was chatting to a very pleasant lady who had done just that. She lived half the year here and half in Sydney, basically following the heat of the sun rather like the wrinklies back in the UK who do the same in respect of wintering in Spain. I looked at some property prices and for very little you paid a lot: there was one on sale in Nelly Bay probably no bigger in space than my humble abode back in Sussex, but would set the prospective buyer back a cool 2.1 million dollars. Mind you the views were pretty spectacular across the bay, there was a pool, the forest around was teeming with wildlife like the koala right on the doorstep and of course the little matter of the weather. I thought about buying it but with the possibility of being bitten to death by a death head adder decided not to.

The island does have one growing problem as I discovered when I went to get a towel for the pool and asked the young receptionist what it was like to live here.

"Oh I don't live here; I catch the ferry from Townsville every day."

"Would you want to live here though?"

"Yes and no. I mean on the one hand it's really peaceful and all that, but to be honest there's not much to do once the lights go out. I mean if you want a night-life then ok there is some but it's pretty limited. I mean where I live right now may not be the flashiest place but there's so much more to do at night and at the weekends … " and then without taking a breath and looking at me with some intent continued … "but if you're old then it's probably quite nice with all this quiet."

I don't know if she was actually referring to me but I understood what she meant. Although very young children can receive a preliminary education on the island, beyond that they must commute to Townsville. There, away from what I guess can be quite a claustrophobic existence on the island, they can see what maybe to them a much more exciting world.

Tourism is not new to the island and Picnic Bay gets its name from those Victorians who would come on day trips to eat, drink and be merry whilst trying to avoid the odd person wondering around with bubonic plague (remember the island was a quarantine area). In the first decade of the 20th century it grew with the start of regular ferry services thanks to Robert Hayles who saw the potential in the island. Aside from being ravaged by Cyclone Althea in 1971 (90% of the islands houses were destroyed or damaged), the island remains an attraction on the Queensland tourist map. The resort we were staying at sat on the new ferry terminal which had been built in 2003 as a means to increase the number of visitors as well as holiday home buyers. I asked the receptionist how business was both in terms of trippers as well as those who wanted to buy an apartment as a holiday home.

"Not too busy; we're only about 20% full on the rooms at the moment but the domestic season hasn't started yet. We've sold some condos but there are still quite a few empty. I guess the economy hasn't helped much."

This lack of occupancy was noticeable not just looking around the pool at the lack of people, but by the number of cars in the car park. I counted seven in all including ours. Australian tourism has been suffering for a couple of years in part due to the credit crunch but also due to the strength of the currency. It is not just overseas visitors though but also domestic ones. The Australian Tourism Forecasting Committee's year-end report in December 2009 highlighted some of these issues such as domestic visitors in Australia falling over 6% in the year (a sharp fall from its mid-year forecast) and although not as bad a still 0.5% fall in international visitors. This last figure does compare favourably when looked at globally but even so it is still not good. It does suggest an improvement in the next few years but not spectacularly and let's face it you can't visit everywhere. On the plus side I was pleased to note that the visitor from the UK was the highest in terms of economic value, and ironically given their treatment in centuries past, the Chinese were the largest growth area in terms of visitors, not least the gamblers who I was told fly in (or cruise on 'whale boats') just to go to the casino and nothing else.

After a dip in the pool, which was like taking a warm bath, I rejoined my fellow intrepid traveller for a tour of the island by car. Two minutes later, or so it seemed, we had arrived at Picnic Bay and decided to eat dinner there. Given that it wasn't that late (around 7pm) the restaurant-come-bar was surprisingly empty aside from a few bush stone-curlews and a single rather unhappy looking possum. We got talking to the owner, Antonio, as to why it was so quiet.

"You see that jetty over there … ?" Antonio gestured towards the front of the restaurant that faced the sea at a long wooden jetty that went out about 200 to 300 metres out into the bay " … well that's where all the boats and ferries from the mainland used to come in. Of course being in front we were in the perfect place to pick up custom especially from day-trippers looking to watch the sunset over a couple of tinnies and a pizza. When they completed the new terminal at Nelly, business just went down."

"So what are you going to do?" asked Chris.

"Not a lot I can do; this has been a family-run place for over 10 years but we can't make it work anymore so we're thinking of closing for good. It's sad but that's progress." This last comment carried with it a huge dose of irony. As a post script to this that shortly after I returned to the UK, the restaurant was gutted by fire and I guess is now closed for good. Still, like Antonio said that's progress.

Day twenty one: November 24th

Today we were back to the mainland and on our way to Airlie Beach which was, according to the town's website the ' … gateway to the Whitsundays, Queensland's pristine 74 islands.' Originally called Airlie, someone worked out that the area had some beaches so guess what, the word 'Beach' was added. You know I should really get into the naming lark, seems to be pretty easy to me. The Whitsunday's by the way were so named as they were 'discovered' by Cook on Whitsunday 1770. It was a relatively short drive punctuated only by Chris's need to eat more meat at some ghastly fast food emporium where I ordered a Double Piece of

Cardboard with Fat Laden Potato Sticks and a Large Flavoured Sugar Drink that actually was just ice. As we arrived in Airlie Beach I recalled something that Simon had said to me back in London as we were planning the trip.

"You know that are as you travel further down the Gold Coast you're going to hit schoolies week."

I had no idea what this was until he explained the phenomenon to me. If you are American read 'Spring Break' for 'Schoolies Week'. The event began life in the 1970's at Broadbeach in Queensland but has since spread including such places as Surfers Paradise, Byron Bay and as far as the Great Ocean Road in Victoria. There is no real equivalent in the UK, except if you included Cornwall where all the Hamish's and Jemima's take daddy's car and drive down to the west country to daddy's west country weekend holiday home for a bit of posh persons shagging and drinking. Schoolies is a big event that attracts thousands of teenagers who have left high school. The event is massive by anyone's standards and involves partying along with a higher than usual level of drinking and drug-taking. In a survey carried out by the Centre for the Study of Sexually Transmissible Diseases, La Trobe University Melbourne, in 1997 some 2/3rds of boys and 1/3rd of girls expected to have sex with the most promiscuous from NSW and Victoria. Most of the surveyed audience also expected to be drunk and a sizable percentage 'stoned'.

Some welcome it, some hate it and there is no doubt that although the majority of kids enjoy themselves without causing problems, a number don't. There are official schoolie events which are for all to enjoy but are free of any stimulants and all have to prove that they are leavers and not, and I do like this description, 'Toolies'. This latter group are those deemed 'too old for school' (tool) or in other words those who should be wearing slippers and tucked up in bed with a hot cup of cocoa. There is another group which goes by another glorious name, 'foolies'. These are pre-schoolies and really should also be in bed tucked in by mummy and with teddy.

Now when I booked this holiday something must have resonated with Simon. Maybe it was my fearsome good looks, my youthful manner or maybe it was the fact that I am in fact a sad old git. Whichever it was he had booked Chris and I into a hotel that, although not entirely schoolie free, was nevertheless more for the gentile customer. I remember him continuing the conversation about schoolies week with:

"Well schoolies week can be pretty noisy and I just thought that given your age you might want something a little quieter so I booked you in a hotel which tends not to have many of these kids staying."

Charming I thought, I'm only forty-something, I'm still a dynamo on the dance floor, a real party animal and I can keep up with the best of them. I was recently on a trip to New York where on the last night the 'youth' suggested it would be great to go on to a night club for a few beers and a boogie. Not wishing to seem old and fuddy-duddy I went along. On someone's phone there is a photograph of me fast asleep in what was apparently quite a noisy nightclub. I guess Simon was absolutely right.

In front of the hotel there was a small schoolie event going on in a tented off area but actually it wasn't too bad and from what I could see and hear the kids were on the whole well behaved. One thing that I was told when souvenir T-shirt buying was that many events try to make shop owners provide discounts on their merchandise almost as if by not doing so you were somehow being unfair and while some didn't mind others as this particular person told me that he "Would be buggered if I do it". Interesting thought, provide a discount or have anal sex?

According to Jeremy Pierce writing in the 'Courier-Mail': 'The schoolies class of 2009 is worse behaved than a rowdy, drunken sporting crowd, according to statistics ... .' This comment was predicated on the number of arrests made (Surfers Paradise was the worst) and were mainly alcohol related. The piece goes on to say that the 2009 event led to calls for schoolies to be cancelled in future. It quoted the Gold Coast Mayor Ron Clarke as saying that the schoolies were 'a blight on the city' and he was backed up by many residents and businesses. But here's a thought, if you don't want the kids there don't rent them rooms! I have to say that all the time I bumped into any of these kids I had no problems; they pretty much kept themselves to themselves and left me alone and in Airlie Beach itself there were according to the local police no real issues.

It is a fact of life that, and I can certainly attest to this, if you give any teenager access to alcohol, the opposite sex and a disproportionate sense of freedom – many will not have fled the nest for so long or ever – some are bound to get out of hand. The statistics suggest that it is a problem, but since the government took on the responsibility of managing the event following the violence in 2002, there seems to be a much higher level of both control and organisation.

Day twenty two: November 25th

The forecast the night before had suggested rain today but no matter as the previous evening I had decided to re-visit the Great Barrier Reef and had booked a day trip on a Super Maxi 80 called 'The Ragamuffin' (originally launched in 1979 as the 'Bumblebee') and was, and here I once more use my nautical knowledge, quite long at just under 30 metres. It had a crew of around 14 all wearing lovely pink polo shirts and today would have just under 60 paying punters. The boat has quite a history having won the Sydney to Hobart in 1988 and 1990 and winning various other races or being well placed (whatever that means). The trip would take me and my fellow 'reefers' to Blue Pearl Bay at Hayman Island which according to the Queensland Tourist Board was 'the epitome of tropical paradise'. The last time I had been on anything this size was sailing a few years ago during Cowes Week. This hugely popular annual racing event is top-notch in the social calendar and attracts those stereotypes we all know: the men who seem to have one arm tucked permanently under their jacket, blue blazored with a cap set at a jaunty angle and their wives/girlfriends gamely trying to keep their recently quaffered hair from blowing this way and that. Today though was totally different. For a start casual wear was order of the day; secondly no work was required unless anyone really wanted to and thirdly, unlike when I was at Cowes, the sun was in fact shining. My fellow passengers were an eclectic bunch and ranged from some better off schoolies, a variety of nationalities through to some slightly less agile seniors having a second, possibly third, honeymoon. It was all very friendly and relaxed.

Having applied Factor 3000 to my puce white arms and legs I took in the sun and fell into conversation with Nicole from Seattle who was travelling with a friend who had been at university with her at, I seem to recall Berkeley. It was California anyway. Both were rocket scientists but Nicole was setting up her own software company and this holiday was the precursor for when she returned to Seattle in order to try to get some serious fundraising under her belt so that she could take the business further. Her friend whose name escapes me had just finished a PhD in chemistry and was now looking to find work. To my right were another couple, Rob and Rhoda, of whom the latter was on her last day of her holiday before she had to go back to the UK, Her friend was in the middle of an 18 month youth leadership course and was as he put it "Having a blast."

It's a fascinating world that we live in from the coincidence of the Worthing couple who were on the abortive whale watching excursion in Sydney through to meeting people that I probably wouldn't do back in the UK not because they don't exist, but because I know few people outside of my industry and because I'm a confirmed miserable bastard who can't be bothered to meet interesting people. As such this was pleasant with a capital P, passing time just chewing the fat, although I have to say that when Nicole started talking about what her software could do (steady there, I do mean her *IT* software) I began to hear a faint buzzing in my ears as the information passed from one side of my head to the other without registering. I fully admit that I am a technophobic and when someone starts to talk bytes, mega or otherwise I assume the appearance of the village idiot with no more than an inane grin.

The Bay was somewhat crowded and there were a lot of lithe, well tanned young Australian males strutting around like peacocks in front of a gaggle of blond, bikinied and as equally tanned young females. It was time to get out my secret weapon, by which I don't mean I would put a sack over my head and body and pretend not to exist. No, this secret weapon was the 'stinger suit' worn by brave souls like myself to protect against the friendly jellyfish (stingers). These stinger suits are fine for those of you of a certain build but when wrapped around me looked, well … put it this way, even the fish looked scared, although the ladies were swooning all over the place (or vomiting, it could have been either). And just so you know the picture taken of me, should you ever see it, wearing this was done just as the temperature dipped below freezing for a nanosecond, hence the 'shrinkage'.

Apropos this stinger suit one of the crew related a story about one poor soul who, like me, followed all the advice given in terms of stinger protection but had gone that extra mile by also wearing diving gloves, a full head protector, full face mask and diving socks. Prepared as he was he dived into the inviting ocean only to land face first onto a stinger, although as Sandy pointed out:

> "Of course he was lucky as it wasn't a box. If he'd landed on that little bastard he'd be dead." How reassuring I thought as I prepared to enter the water.

The Bay was the perfect place just to float around and unlike the previous trip up at Port Douglas there was no swell so the ingestion of sea water was fairly minimal. But just like there this too was incredible with all sorts of fish and coral to look at including, according to my diary, one fish that was at least three foot long and a foot high; or it might have been a small shark or a very small person with a diving suit on. I even saw a leatherback turtle lazily lolloping in the water. I mean can you beat this? I so easily can get lost in a world of my own when in this environment. It's not like visiting an aquarium because here on the reef I could reach out and almost touch the fish, and it seemed that they were as curious about me as I was about them as they swam right up to my goggles. As I continued to swim around I felt the urge to have a fish platter that evening for dinner.

We must have spent a good two hours in the Bay, including lunch which was all very nicely done. As with the crew of the Calypso, those on the Ragamuffin were as helpful and cheerful and the captain, George, with his huge handlebar moustache was a font of information about the boat and the reef which had I actually been listening too I could tell you more about.

Once back in Airlie Beach 'the epitome of a beach town' I had a wonder round. There was a real mix of the old and the new once more. The former was best seen in the area that we where were staying with its immediate post-war style architecture and low storey buildings. This contrasted with the proliferation of high rises that engulfed the town and reminded me of 'Any Old Town' on the Costa del Sol. It is a sad state of affairs that modernity often comes at a cost in terms of aesthetics. It is all about being higher and higher so that you can have hundreds of 'me too' looking apartments that often lend little or no character to the place. Airlie Beach is a nice place to rest ones weary body and I sat down on the u-shaped curve of the beach itself and just took in the view. The sun was beginning to set against a sky filled with grey and white cotton ball clouds with a gentle breeze blowing through the palm trees and giving yet another idyllic image for me to lock away in my memory bank. The only real distraction came from the tented-off area where the schoolies were beginning to prepare for that night's entertainment and there was an audible hum of excited voices with that nasal twang and that odd way of phrasing everything as if it were a question. It does beat that really annoying habit of people who say "like" after every word but only just. Speaking of odd phrases have you ever heard an American say: "I'd like to say" or "If you will."? I'd like to say what? You just have so why would you "like to say" and "if you will", if you will what? What have you Americans past and present done to the English language?

Outside our hotel there was a decent selection of eateries and the one that we chose was, appropriately, a seafood one. We were a little concerned as it was still early by Australian dining times and that we might not get a table. It was 7.30 after all. We needn't have worried as far from being full we were the only customers and they were in the process of closing. Never mind they could 'fit us in'. Even with just two people to serve and even though we opted for one course only, I could have swum to Hayman Island and back before the food arrived. I have tried to get an answer from my Australian friends as to why service is so slow. I mean it's not bad in the way that the French sneer at you or the English hardly acknowledge your existence but come on. The answer I got from most of those I asked was basically 'what's the hurry? This is another Australian trait that I was still finding puzzling but on reflection it does seem right somehow. If the food was hot when it eventually arrived by camel from somewhere in this vast Continent and the beer was cold, so does it matter how quick it comes?

Day twenty three: November 26th

"Morning Chris, sleep well?" I always like to start a bad news day with a positive start. Put your intended target at ease and then sneak in the bad news.

"Yes thanks. Breakfast?"

"Well to be honest, although that would be really nice we have to drive, oh I don't know a few miles today so maybe worth starting now."

"How far?" Chris asked in a distinctly resigned tone.

"Around 500 miles" I mumbled.

This was getting to be a habit and to be fair Chris did take it well as I let him drive and even had the window closed so he could enjoy the A/C more. Very thoughtful of me I'm sure you'll agree. It was again rather pleasant though just to sit there and let my thoughts run away with me. When I go cycling back at home I quite often go around Brighton with its mix of buildings and communities from the Regency end around Kemp

Town to the more modern developments near the station. I like to ponder what it would be like to live in some of the houses I pass. Well here I was doing it again. Many of the houses were raised which I presumed was to avoid flooding given this was still the tropics. Some were right on the road and could easily have been something I might have seen in the Sussex countryside save that there were palm trees, eucalypts, sugar cane fields and of course no real traffic.

We stopped at a typical service station where the food was, to put it delicately, guaranteed to kill you within ten minutes of ingestion. The service though was fantastic full of "darlings" and "what can I do for you" all with a smile and that lack of urgency. Next time you visit a motorway service station in the UK see how long it takes a) to get your food and b) a smile when paying for it. The ladies behind the counter were lovely and interested in what Chris and I were up to.

"Do you like it here?" Kim asked (she being the one serving at the counter)

"It's great, so much nicer than even I had thought it would be."

"That's Australia for you. You know our motto is 'no worries mate' and that's what it is like."

I'm sure she then asked me if I wanted the dead Road Kill Pie oozing fat or the chicken salad sandwich which interestingly was minus any salad. Or chicken. It reminded of when I was in Zurich a few years ago and I was out with some colleagues in the local beer hall and ordered, as the healthy option, a Wurstsalat, or to the non language speakers out there, a sausage salad. On its arrival it had a lot in common with what I was currently attempting to eat in that there was absolutely no salad save a small gherkin. To be fair the sausage was enormous though I was a little concerned that some donkey had been an unwilling donor. We ate outside for about ten seconds before the flies found us. On the plus side moving back inside, I was once more able to add to my mullet and tattoo sightings.

By late afternoon we were in Agnes Water which consisted of what appeared to be a shopping area and houses. It all looked very pleasant. Our resort hotel for the next two nights though was about a mile or so out of town on the way to the Town of 1770, more of which later, and situated next to an area that was being developed I assumed for either holiday homes or as a resort. Buildings were half finished and it had the feel of having been abandoned back to nature as grass had begun to grow where builders had trod and bits of timber, brick and plastic sheeting lay strewn on the ground. I don't know if it was abandoned but when we checked into the resort hotel it was quite empty bar a few families. It was just like Magnetic Island all over again and I suspect that the issue was once more the drop in tourism.

The rooms themselves were enormous and were really one bedroom apartments complete with laundry facilities in a small annex and dirt cheap. That evening we decided to 'eat in' as one other appealing factor was that on the balcony each apartment was equipped with a barbecue. As Chris tried to buy all the meat from the local supermarket I managed to grab what looked like a quite nice piece of chicken that once I had cooked it (I did it in the oven as my skills on the barbecue are primeval) had the flavour and texture of rubber. Never mind at least it was less expensive than going out.

Day twenty four: November 27th

Agnes Water is part of the 'Discovery Coast' which I now know thanks to Queensland Travel 'stretches from Bundaberg and Bargara in the south through to the town of Rockhampton and Yepoon in the north and incorporates the Islands and reefs of the Capricorn section of the Great Barrier Reef stretching from Lady Elliot Island in the south to Heron Island and Great Keppel Island in the north.' It is major domestic as well as foreign tourist destination and for the most part it did seem on first glance as being able to keep the historic from being too overwhelmed by the modern although if our resort hotel was anything to go by, this was under threat. Agnes Water is a town surrounded by national parks and is very popular as a destination for Brisbane's and Sydney's middle class professionals.

There didn't seem to be much in the way of places to have breakfast so we decided to drive on to the Town of 1770 which as its tourist blurb told me: 'What an unusual name for a town, you think. Well, the Town of 1770 (Seventeen Seventy) was named after the year in which Captain ... James Cook first landed in Queensland.' How exciting!

The Town of 1770 was small, very small. These days it is very difficult to get a house in the town and in all there are currently only 250 dwellings. However, once more I had entered somewhere that, aside from a sign alerting the unwary to the threat of estuarine crocodiles, was another slice of perfection. The trees were in blossom and flowers were in abundance. There is not enough space to write down all the colours but take it from me the reds, pinks, yellows, blues and so on were in stark contrast to the grey and brown colours of an English winter back home. It was truly beautiful aided by yet another clear blue sky and the warmth of the sun. The town comprised of a harbour, a shop, a cafe and a booking place for various trips to the Barrier Reef Islands 'a short 23 miles away' as well as other water based activities. All sounded too strenuous for both of us so we repaired to the cafe and tucked into some decent scram. I could do this every day given half a chance.

As Chris demolished his meat with a side order of meat I had a quick look round to see what there was to do if you didn't want to overdo the exercise. We were in luck as next to the cafe there was a small office which was home to the LARC (lighter amphibious resupply cargo) cruises that had two tours, one that went along the Eurimbula National Park up to Bustard Head Lighthouse, a restored heritage listed site that enabled one to discover the 'tragic history of murder, suicide, abduction and drowning … ', whilst the other took one around Round Hill Creek that allowed you to 'experience the peaceful solitude and changing moods of our tropical paradise.' Both sounded great fun but sadly as much as I would have liked the first option this was not available today so I booked us both onto the 'Afternoon Cruise'.

Given that this didn't depart until late afternoon we returned to Agnes Water to chill out. The trouble is when I am on holiday I find it incredibly difficult to do nothing so whilst Chris went off to his room to sit under the A/C and cool down, I wondered down the beach. It was deserted. No one, not a soul; I was king of all I surveyed so I took off my shoes and walked onto the sand. The next time you put the oven on at home leave it to heat up and then stick your feet into it, and then you'll experience what I did with the sand. I have never in my life experience such heat. You couldn't even sit down unless a towel was between you and the sand. I lingered for a few minutes, having put my shoes back on, and decided that I would go and get changed into my running gear and 'do the beach.'

Some ideas should be left just as that, an idea. Running on sand is never easy, but with the mercury touching forty it was uncomfortably hot, not helped with my once more sensible choice of wearing a heavy cotton rugby shirt and socks. I ran towards the only part of the beach that had surfers and swimmers – most without stinger suits and all horribly young and buff. It looked so tempting and given that the speed at which I run at will never lead to a four minute mile I envied them as they rode the wave crests in on a deep ocean blue sea. As I headed into Agnes Water from the beach I passed through a very pleasant palm-tree shaded area full of people have al fresco picnics and all looking relaxed. I had a strong desire to stop and join them, not least as someone shouted out:

"Mate, it's too hot to run. Come and have a cold one."

I suspect that if this had been back in the UK the welcome I'd have received would not have been quite along these lines. No, I said to myself, I am an Englishmen (and an adherent to the 'mad dogs and Englishmen go out in the midday sun' way of life) so I carried on through the bottom half of the town which was dotted with small shops and some nice little houses, but nothing hugely ostentatious, helped by the fact that any new development was restricted. If it hadn't been so hot I would probably have enjoyed it more but by the time I wobbled back to my room the only thing on my mind was to sit under the A/C for a good twenty minutes and slowly expire. However, Chris and I still had adventure ahead of us that afternoon with our appointment with the LARC so we set off to the Town of 1770 once more. There were two of these monstrous vehicles originally used in the Vietnam War by the Australian army and like the 'Duck Tours' now seen in many cities in the US and Europe that use old DKW's, the LARCs are land and water friendly, were painted a garish pink and named in honour of two of Cook's crew as the Sir Joseph Banks and the Dr Daniel Carl Solander. We were joined by a young family of mum, dad and two rugrats who were very excited to be going on the 'big pink thing' as one of them put it. Now if there isn't a double entendre to be had there then my name isn't James M. McGuire but I kept it to myself and just chuckled to myself with a reminder that one day I really ought to grow up.

The next hour was a sheer pleasure made more so by the captain of our intrepid craft, Paul, who had been a marine engineering consultant until a few years ago and, having built himself a house in Agnes Water, did these tours for, it seemed to me, not money but because it was just fun. He was full of information from when Cook first arrived (the channel out of the bay is very much as it was over 200 years ago), to the wildlife (we passed by pelicans, terns and over stingrays and other fishy things) to the ecology of the Eurimbula National Park. An abiding memory for me was the sight of a man, with his dog, fishing on a large sand bank in the middle of the bay as the sun set behind him almost as if he had been paid to be there just so that tourists like me could gush about it afterwards. Either that or he was stranded and all that waving was nothing to do with fly fishing but calls for help. I wonder if he is still there or has he been rescued?

Day twenty five: November 28th

We checked out early and headed off further south towards our next destination which was Hervey Bay. It would be from here that we would then go to Fraser Island. Given it was a short drive we decided that a 'must do stop' was Bunderberg, famed for its rum. Bunderberg was another place where map reading and me didn't mix and we managed to pass over the same bridge at least four times as we looked for the all important distillery. The city itself was quite large so getting lost was easy to justify – I mean there were lots of roads, and as once again I was darned if I was going to ask for directions. The distillery itself was on the edge of town in what looked to be a somewhat run-down area and was not as large as I had imagined it would be. Unfortunately when we pulled up the guided tour of the site had just left and there would not be another that day so we contented ourselves with the souvenir shop to buy things celebrating a drink that neither of us touched. Completely daft but at least the lady at the checkout came from Hassocks not too far from where I live so I was able to reminisce with her about home whilst parting with five billion dollars to pay for a t-shirt and stubby holder.

As we drove down Route 3 (no I've no idea why it's important you know the number of the road but as I've written it in my notebook it stays) which turned out to be a good call as it took us through a number of small hamlets all with their pie shops and pubs. To me the Australian pub is so different to that back home and feels like a throwback to an earlier era like the 50's and 60's. Although I didn't partake of the amber nectar in many I did poke my head around the odd door or through the odd window which, along with my extensive research of Australian pubs through watching the odd episode of 'Home and Away' or 'Neighbours' sort of confirmed this view. I actually quite like them, even the one in Sydney where I had a beer called the Mercantile Hotel that had tiles of green along the outside that would not have looked out of place in a Victorian toilet, (although I'm not quite sure how given that is was re-built in 1915 by the brewers Tooth & Co). I would just like to say that I mean this is a positive and not negative way; there was a certain character to it that you just don't seem to get nowadays.

Back on the road again, we soon pulled over for some lunch in a cafe come souvenir come arts and crafts shop which went by the delightful name of 'Sticky Beaks'. It was by now in the high 30's so sitting in the shade was a must and very nice it was too.

"Chris, do me a favour, take a photo of me will you."

So he went to the side of the road and prepared to do an action shot of me eating my lunch (David Bailey please move over, you have met your match) when out of the corner of my eye I saw 'it'. 'It' was about eight foot long, with a forked tongue darting in and out of its mouth and fangs that would have put Dracula to shame. I froze. What should I do given that all my primal instincts were going into overdrive? Do I run? Do I scream for help? Do I stay put?

"Chris, Chris! There's a bloody great snake in front of me." I whispered loudly (if that isn't an oxymoron).

Just as I had finished whispering this, sweat pouring down the side of my cheeks as a sense of panic set in the lady of the establishment came out with my coffee and, seeing me as white as a sheet, reassuringly said:

"Aw that's just a tree snake, it won't harm you. Now if you go out back of here then that's where the browns are, they're real nasty." And off she went back inside with a smile.

At this point Chris came back from the side of the road and asked what the fuss was all about. I told him about the forty foot snake with the three heads and how I had valiantly fought it off with my bare hands when said lady reappeared, this time with Chris's milkshake, and he asked her about the snake and whether it was as I had described.

"Little tiddler, no more than six inches I reckon." Not from where I was bloody sitting it wasn't lady! Bloody monster: at least seventy feet long.

We arrived relatively early in Hervey Bay and booked into our hotel that overlooked Hervey Bay itself. Hervey Bay is pronounced Harvey Bay and

I make no comment on this given that back in the UK we have places like Bicester and Shrewsbury which are not always pronounced as they look. It got its name in 1770 from Captain Cook who named it after Lord Augustus Hervey, the Earl of Bristol and Cook's boss. He was also apparently a bit of a ladies man and had a nickname which was the 'English Casanova'. I know the burden of having these nicknames thrust upon one; after all many call me the 'George Clooney of England', although it's pronounced 'Jabba the Hutt's Younger, Fatter Brother'. In the 1870's the area was briefly overrun by smorgasbord-eating Swedes (how many countries have a people named after a root vegetable?) and renamed Aarlborg. As with most of the places visited or passed by so far, the sugar industry was big here. Apparently it is now one of the fastest growing cities in Australia. How jolly exciting; I couldn't wait to see it!

Having dumped my bags I went to check the sailing times for the ferry tomorrow that would be taking us to Fraser Island. At the check-in desk I was assured that if we turned up at 8.30 am the following morning we would be in plenty of time for the coach that would take us to the ferry terminal. Excellent, this would be very hassle free as it had only taken my five minutes to get to the desk from our hotel and what's more we could leave our car here for the two days we would effectively be On Fraser Island.

Back at the hotel I hired a bike (I say bike but more like one of those bone-shakers beloved of our ancestors) and cycled north along the esplanade towards the Colonel Gardiner Memorial Park. Thoughtfully the town council had provided a cycle path that permitted the cyclist to avoid all roads and would thus take me all the way to the park. It was a warm, sunny, late afternoon offset by a cooling breeze coming off the sea which given that the cycle path was well shaded made cycling very pleasant. Every so often I passed an open area where families were gathering for barbecues – this was something I had seen in Airlie Beach, but there it was mostly groups of young people. Here it was whole generations, with the elders sitting on chairs or on rugs while grandchildren played, dad sacrificed something on the barbecue and mum prepared all the extras like salad, bread and drinks. When I lived in the US and played rugby on a Saturday a similar thing would happen; the day (and it was invariably a whole day) was about family and there would be picnics, kids and wives and girlfriends, boyfriends for the front row, all enjoying a good day out.

As I cycled along I noticed for the first time since I had left Melbourne a truly cosmopolitan mix of shops, cafes and restaurants from Italian to

Middle Eastern to Indian and so on. All of the cafes and pubs (and there were plenty) were beginning to fill up with people all enjoying the last rays of the sun whilst supping the odd ale or two. It has always struck me as strange that the UK still appears to be one of the few countries in the world where many towns and cities view drinking outside as almost a taboo; it's better than it used to be but there are still those council Nazis who feel that because a small minority act like total idiots, then de facto we all do. Mind you one thing in Australia that is different to the UK and actually is something that we do have is that children are not allowed in pubs.

At the point where I met the park itself, the cycle path ended and I was then required to rejoin the road, but given that this whole area was residential traffic was very light. Once again though as I cycled the various streets there was no way I could determine that Wattle Street was made up of those in a lower economic class to those that lived on Banksia Street. As in the other towns I had explored to date, there was a mixture of architecture, some nice and some clearly the domain of the mullet-haired tattoo covered male of the species. Actually, the last comment is a bit unfair because the more grandiose houses are probably full of middle aged men with pony tails and trophy wives. No, that's not fair either as I have now just classified all Australian males as either being mullet-haired and tattooed, or pony tailed. To put the record straight then, I would suggest that there are some houses in Hervey Bay that are abodes of these types, but not all. Happy now?

The evening was approaching and according to my watch it was beer o'clock so I scooted back to the hotel but this time via the road which turned out to be rather better than I'd expected as from the park back into the main part of the town I gradually moved from residential through to the more commercial area as I neared the hotel. However, it wasn't busy in the sense that I felt that at any second a moron would cut me up or that if I took my eyes off the road I'd knock into someone trying to cross the road without looking. In all the cycle had taken me a couple of hours and by the time I returned the bike the sun had begun to move down behind the hotel which, from my room at least, gave a splendidly romantic view of the marina and of the shops and restaurants that lined the sides. As I supped my first cold one my thoughts were taken up by the next stop on the tour, namely Fraser Island. This island, the largest sand island in the world, was recommended to me as a 'must see' stopover on my journey so I was quite buzzed when I went to bed at the thought of going there.

Chapter 9

*We go green on Fraser Island, discover Eliza Fraser and
end up being trendy on the Sunshine Coast*

Day twenty six: November 29th

Anyone who knows me will tell you that I am calm, am even tempered and absolutely top when it comes to political correctness. I am also an inveterate liar when it comes to describing myself in these terms, so to set the record straight aside from being a miserable git I also have a slight temper. This can be set off by the most minor things from not being able to find my wallet – why do people ask you when did you last see your wallet/lost item? If you knew that surely it would not be lost – or else more major things like the little jobsworth that confronted me as I presented the tickets for Fraser Island as Chris parked the car.

"Good morning, can I check-in for two please?"

"You're late."

"Late for what?"

"For checking-in. The bus is about to leave for the ferry and you're going to miss it, because you should have been here at 8."

"But last night I checked with your colleague and she said that we should be here by 8.30. It's 8.25 so we're not late. Anyway the bus is still here and my friend will be back in a couple of minutes once he's parked the car."

"The bus is leaving with or without you. Nothing I can do."

"We'll I'm not late and I have a reservation on this ferry to take us to Fraser Island so the bus will have to wait."

The glare that she gave me and the blood spitting out of her mouth (metaphorically if any of you are worried that she'd burst a blood vessel) told me all I needed to know. She was a complete cow of the first degree and anyway I had won because the bus driver who was cut

Drink and Drive, Australian style

Tilba, where cheese tasting is not allowed

Walhalla where Australians first learnt to cheat at cricket and hoard all the gold

Great Ocean Road: the views are spectacular although the Twelve Apostles are perhaps not what I'd expected

The Arch of Victory at Ballarat, a poignant reminder of Australia's sacrifice in service to the Empire.

The Eureka Stockade where Australia could have become a republic

Fraser Island – a 'green' approach to tourism?

A 'moderate' walk in the Blue Mountains

from a completely different cloth waited for Chris to return. The ferry departed from Round Heads at 9 a.m. according to the timetable and the bus journey to this terminal took just over 20 minutes. I have already told you about the television programmes that start at some point but not necessarily at the time in the programme schedules. Well, so too the ferry as it stayed exactly where we joined it as the clock approached 9.05, 9.10 and then 9.15. So, you little cow, we we're too late? I felt like ringing her up and ask what exactly we were too late for: was it too late for the ferry to leave bang on time, half an hour late? Maybe she wasn't really an Australian but some new arrival from some public service 'Help Desk' from back home which are invariably staffed by people to whom 'politeness and customer care' are just four dirty words.

Fraser Island is the world's largest sand island measuring in total some 1,840 square kilometres. In his book, 'Princess K'gari's Fraser Island: a history of Fraser Island' Fred Williams retells the legend of how the island was formed, quoting Olga Eunice Miller who learnt it through the oral tradition handed down to her through the generations. In this legend Beiral who was the great god in the sky sent down his messenger, Yendingie, to make the land. When he reached Hervey Bay he was joined by the beautiful white spirit, Princess K'gari who helped him. She liked what they had done so much that she wanted to stay and, after pleading with Yendingie, got her wish but as she was a spirit he had to change her form:

> 'So he changed her into a beautiful island and then, so she wouldn't be lonely, he made some trees and some flowers, and lakes so that she could see into the sky. He made beautiful creeks and laughing waters that were to become her voice. And as well as birds and animals, he made some people to keep her company.'

The people of course were the Aboriginals who comprised, according to the Williams, three main tribes which were the Ngulungbara, Batjala and Dulingbara. These tribes were all part of the Kabi Kabi people who lived along what is now called the Sunshine Coast. Kabi I found out is more to do with the language group than a specific single homogenous tribe. The area was also a central point for one of the major Aboriginal festivals, the Bunya Festival and of Dreamtime. Dreamtime is central to their culture and is all about how the world and all that is part of it was formed and how the

Aboriginal people live in harmony with the spirits in all their forms. One source that I looked into to understand this was The Aboriginal Art and Culture Centre in Alice Springs which tells the reader of the origins of this and how we all come from the 'Ancestor Beings' who were the bringers of knowledge and it is from these supernatural beings that the world and the sun as we know them today originate and here there is a similarity with the story of Fraser Island in that these 'Beings' formed everything that we see now in the same way that Yendinge did. For the indigenous what is around them and specifically the land ' ... is not just something that they can own or trade. Land has a spiritual value ... '

Although not unique to Fraser Island, the Bunya festival wherever it is held is steeped in tradition and is about renewal. The Bunya tree and its nuts were central to all of this and were eaten by all who attended. Williams describes the harvesting of these:

> ' ... harvesting could be a hazardous procedure. A full sized cone would weigh as much as 4 kilograms and when it came plummeting down from 15 meters it was a lethal missile.'

But as I discovered later on my travels these corroborees were more than just a food fest; they were a time when tribes would gather to celebrate (and for Fraser the radius according to Williams was up to 250 kilometres), there would be no fighting except in competitions, singing and story-telling and for some their first journey from boyhood to adulthood. However, as white settlers moved in so cultures clashed and these festivals and the traditions that the Aboriginals had held were deemed, for want of a better way of describing as being in the way, not least as the Bunya tree was a prized bit of timber ripe for cutting down. To the Aboriginal this would have been one of the biggest insults given that these trees were owned by a tribe (literally such that only they could knock down the nuts) or individuals and passed on to new generations in the same way we pass on prized possessions to our children. I learnt of the impact of this on the Jarowair people whose tradition of initiating boys into manhood was held at a ceremonial site called Gummingurruand (this is situated west of Brisbane) from there they would go to the Bunya Festival. By 1890 or thereabouts the logging industry saw this end as the peoples were dispersed to other parts of the colony. It took the

Queensland government nearly 120 years to hand this land back to the Aboriginal tribes.

In respect of the European history of the island, the Dutch are thought to have been the first to have visited Fraser in the early part of the 16th century and recent excavations at Indian Head have unearthed a number of bongs to support this theory. Both Cook (who called it the Great Sandy Peninsular) and Flinders (the Great Sandy Island) charted the island, convinced that they were seeing a spit coming out of the mainland. It wasn't until 1863 that the first white settler actually made the island 'home' and this was an American entrepreneur who went by the glorious name of 'Yankee Jack' Piggott. As with other places I had already visited the story then takes an all too familiar path. What Piggott wanted was the lumber, already identified twenty or so years earlier by Petrie as valuable, as a result of the needs created by the Gympie gold rush which began in 1867. These trees, initially the kuari pine but soon many others like the blackbutt were ideally suited to the needs of industry and so Fraser Island's trees meant money. The Aboriginals were not even considered and so there are no surprises than as to who lost out and what had been a thriving, albeit fluctuating Aboriginal population either worked for the loggers or left. The industry was in effect a death sentence for a way of life that had existed for thousands of years and the last Aboriginals who had lived on the island left in 1904 when the mission was closed.

However, I was more surprised to learn, given how verdant the is island today, that it was not until 1991 following a campaign by FIDO (Fraser Island Defenders Organisation, also known as 'The Watchdog of Fraser Island') which showed the huge damage that logging was having (including a picture of students standing on a 4 metre wide stump) on the ecology of the island that it stopped. Following this campaign in 1992 it became a UN World Heritage listed site with the Island's future being the responsibility of the state government. The founder, in 1971, of FIDO was John Sinclair and he suffered a huge amount of intimidation as he faced down not just the logging industry but also the sand-mining industry that had begun in 1949 (this was eventually closed in 1976). He is still at it today and FIDO is as active as ever.

The island has been of interest to tourists for over 140 years and there are records of visitors as far back as the 1870's, but it was not really until the 1950's that you could stay here when Sid Melcham began tours and built some basic accommodation. In 1962 Island Airways was formed by Sir Reginald Barnwall in the hope that he and his partner could then develop the island into a fishing tourist spot and the following year much of the area that is now built on was given over to this project. By the 1970's the northern part of the island was a national park and over the next twenty years although more development took place campaigning led to, as mentioned in 1992, it all becoming a UN recognised part of the world such that much of the island remains protected. One of the few areas where people can actually live is Kingfisher Resort where we were headed is one. The resort was established in 1988 in an area called North White Cliffs and covers over 160 acres. I read on the FIDO website that today there is increasing pressure being put on the Queensland to allow more developments like these but to date they have mostly said no which has kept the island's total permanent population at under 150.

The day was clouding over as we slowly chugged across the Great Sandy Strait that separates the mainland from Fraser Island. The only cars allowed are 4WD which were all tightly packed onto the car deck. The crossing took about forty odd minutes and arrived at the end of a jetty that leads up to the resort. First impressions are always important for me and from the ferry the resort looked like the perfect 'green' getaway, nestled as it was within the vast swathes of greenery that covers the Island. The beach to the right and left of the jetty was a bright white, not the colour I would have expected being brought up on the browns of sandpits as a kid and the stinking seaweed infested, off-white, off-brown sand found on the beaches back at home. It looked like we were going to have some fun helped by the fact that the cloud was not as heavy here as when we started.

At this point everyone who was afoot was expecting, as detailed before departure, to be met by the resort train (think any seaside town sightseeing train and you get the idea). We all looked out, laden down as most of us were with our luggage, but no one appeared.

"I guess they forget," chuckled the really helpful crew member I passed as I dragged my case passed him. This, my man, was not a time for humour.

The walk wasn't a long one to the reception area but by now the heat had picked up along with the humidity so that by the time Tweedle-Dee and Tweedle-Dum arrived to check in we resembled two mobile showers. The reception area was akin to walking into a huge cavern with a ceiling that was at least seven miles high. In front, stairs led out to the swimming pool area which was already busy even though it was still morning. On the left and right of the stairs were the restaurants, respectively the Maheno and Seabelle, whilst just behind the reception desk, a raised walkway went to the first floor rooms, whilst another pathway led to those that led straight out onto the brackish water hole behind the main building or the road in front. Chris's room was ready but mine wasn't so we decided to get a late breakfast/brunch. This is after all a resort hotel so they will have food on tap, no problem. We tried the Maheno.

"Table for two please" Chris asked

"I'm afraid we're closed until lunchtime in about an hour."

No matter and we sauntered over to the Seabelle. It wasn't difficult to notice that this was closed as well given that no one was around and there was absolutely no sign of food in the buffet area. So we asked reception if there was anywhere we could grab some breakfast.

"Sure. Go up to the Shopping Village and you'll find the bakery."

So off we went, stomachs grumbling with impatience for food, and breezed merrily into the bakery. Grabbing a menu, Chris and I perused the available grub. Good, they had bacon and egg butties; we'll get a couple of those. Nope, they too had stopped serving breakfast because they had run out of food. Now I don't wish to appear picky or anything but it does seem a bit of a poor show that breakfast 'runs out' in a resort; it's like an aeroplane having to land because it has run out of fuel because no one thought it would be necessary to fill it up with enough to get it from A to Z.

There was little we could do so Chris disappeared off to his room whilst I decided to have a quick wander around. The Kingfisher Bay Resort was pretty large and comprised not just a main building but also cabins and villas along with a shop, estate agent, petrol station and a couple of bars and restaurants set in the forest. All very self sufficient: but think about it Mr. I Own the Resort, no breakfast with all this available, not very sensible. The whole resort rose up from the beach into the forested hills with fauna and flora in abundance, and lots of sand. It is quite a weird experience to think that this island is just one big sandcastle.

Walking up from the main resort area towards the Dingo Bar (closed) I came across the Kingfisher Heights Estate, expensive but aesthetically pleasing private homes that had some quite magnificent views. It must be fun of an evening to sit outside with your pre-dinner snifter and just see the beauty of nature all around you, right on your doorstep. So if you have a couple of million dollars to spare pop into the estate agent and you too could be a proud owner. Returning back down the hill I deviated from the road and followed the Beevillbee Walking Track that goes around the back of the resort. The smell of pine, of eucalypt and of heat (by now it was in the low 30's) almost took my breath away. Either that or I was completely drained from the humidity. Whatever it was, the walk was very enjoyable and by the time I returned to the front desk my room was ready.

Having deposited by bags I headed back towards the beach. It was now quite sunny and the wind was whipping up the sand and sea spray. Walking southwards I passed mangrove trees that hugged the beach which in turn were themselves surrounded by huge eucalypts, something that you tend not to where I live. I had been told that sharks were prevalent in this area so that explained why there were no surfers (apparently sharks, the ones that like to eat you for breakfast) can operated in 3 feet of water so probably not a good idea to go for a paddle.

After a good hour or so I returned suitably refreshed to the main resort area and trundled down to the pool to expose some of my seriously hideous flesh to the sun whilst simultaneously given every child in the area nightmares about the possible existence of two-eyed ogres. As I soaked up the rays, I read the story a Scottish woman called Eliza Fraser who is central to the island's history. She and her husband were aboard the Stirling Castle (he was the ship's captain) which was wrecked some 200 kilometres north of where I was now lying. Two lifeboats were launched, one of which ended up with just one survivor in New South Wales, whilst the other came ashore at Waddy Point which is near the northern part of Fraser Island, carrying a heavily pregnant Eliza (the baby did not survive), her husband and some of the remaining crew.

Where they had landed was the home of the Kabi Kabi. Initially it appears all went well and they traded goods with the local people for clothing. However, a number of the crew decided to walk south and depending on which version of events is correct either forced Eliza and her husband plus two other crew with them, or left them. In any event stage two of this saga sees the party set upon by another tribe who took their remaining clothing and separated the men (who were put to work) and Eliza who it seems was treated quite harshly. There seem to be various versions of what happened next as well. What is certain is that the already ill Captain Fraser died fairly soon after. Some suggest that he died with a spear in his back, and this was 'confirmed' by Eliza saying that he had died in her arms, whilst others say that his health being poor he had died of natural causes. However, as she continued to build on her story, her claims suggested that he was in effect murdered. This claim and that of her treatment had consequences for the Aboriginals and according to FIDO amongst others:

> 'Eliza told stories of Aboriginal cruelty, savagery and brutality. She made much money by such tales but, although the truth of her stories has been refuted by many, they had the effect of creating a paranoia of Aborigines amongst the white settlers. One of Eliza Fraser's legacies was that there would be many massacres of the very people who had helped her ... '

Meantime some of the survivors of the trek south and sharks alerted the authorities when they arrived at Bribie Island. Here Lieutenant Charles Otter, under the direction of the commandant Captain Foster Fyans, ordered a search party to go and find the others. Step forward one Irishman John Graham, a convict who had been transported for theft in 1824. His story is as fascinating as that of Eliza Fraser. He was sent to Moreton Bay in 1826 for another offence. The following year he managed to escape and ended up on the run for the next six years, living with the Kabi Kabi and becoming fluent in their tongue and knowledgeable in their customs. Believing that his sentence was over he returned to town and was promptly incarcerated for another four years.

Otter asks for volunteers and a number of convicts including Graham step forward. He is credited in most histories with the rescue (if that is the right word) of Eliza and he did this by stripping naked and convincing the Aboriginals holding her that she was Mamba a reincarnation of his dead wife. He himself was known as Moilow and had been already welcomed in by the Aboriginals as a reincarnation of a dead elder. Mamba was the name given to Eliza as Flannery explains in his book 'The Explorers', because the Aboriginals believed that she was the reincarnated spirit of a recently deceased local woman whose skin had paled at death.

On their return Graham was feted as a hero (and given his freedom) and Eliza became a sort of national hero on her return to Sydney. A few months later she married Captain Chrisander Green and returned to England where she died in around 1858, but even here no one is actually certain and some say that she and her husband lived out their years in New Zealand.

Not everyone liked Eliza, not least as her stories (and these were told to audiences as a sort of 'An Evening with ... ') got more like an 'X' rated version of 'Boy's Own'. Harry Youlden, who was a survivor said in his story of the events written some years later, that she was 'a most profane, artful wicked woman' though others defend her putting her exaggerations down to the trauma of the ordeal. There are others who also say that another convict, David Bracewell who also had lived with the Aboriginals and had been called Wandie, was in fact instrumental in her rescue but he, for whatever reason, is not credited. There was one aspect of this whole story that had me intrigued: why given all the issues between the white settlers and the indigenous people were the latter so willing to accept people like Bracewell into their midst. Was it because of the Dreamtime and the Aboriginals strong animist beliefs? Was it because Bracewell and others were not in a group and most likely more reliant on the Aboriginals' help than the other way around?

So why is it called Fraser Island? In 1842 Andrew Petrie, whilst searching for Captain Fraser's grave, confirmed that what had originally been thought of as a spit of land was in fact an island and he thus named it after Fraser. Unfortunately as a post script he was also the first to notice the quality of the wood on the island which would become the key to the interest that the white setters would have in the island.

That evening was to be a food lovers' delight as Chris and I decided that we would try the buffet. To be honest I don't know why I really bother with these as they invariably have food on show that would not be far out of place in a Saatchi sponsored gallery under the title of 'Food?' by some famous artist known mainly to those pretentious so-and-so's that infest Notting Hill, Chelsea and Islington in London. It is also usually lukewarm at best and tastes like rubber with the consistency of glue. However Chris likes them and who was I to argue? Well my fellow gourmets, tonight's bill of fare was not going to disappoint. It was, and I am being charitable here, only slightly better than a cup of Bovril. Cards on the table here, I hate Bovril and for the life of me cannot understand why anyone would like it but, and here's a little snippet of interest, when the stuff was first marketed by its Scottish inventor the biggest buyers were the French army. Ergo, thanks to this concoction the French have lost virtually every war since; so much for the Auld Alliance or is it hooray for a rather crafty fifth columnist, one John Lawson Johnston! Poor Chris given that he'd looked forward to the delights of unlimited supplies of meat, of beef, chicken and pork and feasting and wassailing until dawn, well perhaps not the latter. His disappointment was tangible. Mind you he got a nice new pair of slippers when he chose two bits of 'beef' that came with a tread.

Day twenty seven: November 30th

One of the attractions of the island is the ability to drive around it in 4WD cars. However, as an alternative, there is also the option to take a trip on one of the massive 4WD buses, either to spot dingoes or to see the beauty spots, including driving up the world famous Seventy-Five Mile Beach. I have always wondered why some places are deemed famous whilst others aren't. I mean who decides that say the ruined castle with its beautiful Norman church is less world famous (or not at all) than this beach? Do you suppose every year governments of the world send their tourism ministers off to a remote island so that they can then pronounce on what is to be world famous the following year? There is another possibility though that is if a guide book refers to something as 'world famous' you just assume it is, no questions asked. I shall tell my local Parish Council to make the necessary arrangements and soon Bramber, once part of the much larger Norman fiefdom of the Rape of Bramber, owned by William de Broase, Anglo-Saxon slaying pal of William the Conqueror will soon be a tourist hot spot for all seeking excitement and adventure.

Chris and I had opted for the beauty spot tour which was to leave from the shopping village. This tour sounded the business as it would take in all the highlights that the island had on offer including the Central Station, Happy Valley, Eurong, the Maheno wreck, the Pinnacles, Seventy Five Mile Beach, Eli Creek and much more. This was going to be fun with a capital 'F'.

However, this is Australia where nothing is as straightforward as it seems and Fraser Island's tour of the beauty spots was about to fall into this pattern. Duly on time we turned up to join our group of fellow nature lovers. All seemed to be functioning smoothly as the throng of people gathered in front of one of the island's tour guides.

"Everyone for the Dingo Tour please board the bus."

"Is this day one? Ve haf bought tickets" asked a well tanned leathery skinned oldster with a very heavy German accent (I work with Germans and I know one when I hear one – the clicking of heels is also a clue).

"No, everyone for day two of the Dingo Tour mate."

"But ve haf tickets for the tour" insisted the intrepid traveller

"I heard you, but this bus is for day two."

"Ja, und ve haf tickets."

"Yes you do but this is day two not day one. Do you have tickets for day two?"

"But ve haf tickets und ve ver told to come here. Ven vill zis be please?"

"I dunno mate, I am only looking for those on day two."

"But, sir, ve haf tickets und ver told to meet here."

At this point the by now the somewhat flustered guide looked straight at the man, and by the way if looks could kill then this guide would have been my number one on the list with the most murderous in the world, and said in a somewhat forceful tone:

> "I don't bloody care whether you have tickets or not. I am only interested in day two people so if you don't mind can you now move aside unless you have the right ticket."

As fire flared from this man's nostril, our German friend turned to his friends who had been earnestly listening to the conversation and uttered something that if I spoke the language fluently may have been a bit too raw for this book. Better to be a shrinking violet in these circumstances so at this point I shied away, as did Chris, given that both of us were on the verge of asking said guide whether he was taking the beauty spot tour and might well have received the same sort of invective. The question remained, though, as to what we were supposed to do. There was at the designated time still no sign of our tour leader. Having been here a few weeks already I was not too stressed out but Chris was a bit tetchy; he definitely hadn't as yet acclimatised to this "no worries" approach.

A few minutes later a voice summoned us to a massive tank-like 4WD bus which could seat around 40 people. I had originally thought that the 4WD experience on the island would be in a Jeep or Land Rover. I have only ever done off road driving once in the past and this was in a Second World War Jeep in the Arizona desert with a maniac called Bob who, having made a pile on Wall Street, suffered a heart attack and then having taken a long hard look at his life had moved to the desert for, as he called it, "a quieter life". I hope that the screams of sheer terror that emitted from my mouth as we drove over what seemed to me to be vertical drops didn't upset the quiet life he expected. Anyway, with this monster there was no chance that we would end up doing that. Our guide corralled us into the bus and introduced himself: "Hi, mine name's Darren and I will be your man of action today. We will see the island as many might have seen it a long time ago from rainforest through to the wonders of the sands. Today we will also see the rich trees, bush, lots of sand and hopefully the odd animal or snake and I hope that you go away with the same sense of satisfaction I get from being privileged to do this every day." As it was to turn out we hit the jackpot with Darren who, until he came to the island, had been a reptile handler, or in other words the loony that comes to your suburban house or garden and removes the deadly snakes or nasty crocs that have appeared uninvited to the barbecue. And so we set off to the first stop, which was the Central Station.

Central Station had the distinction of being where it all began for the logging industry whilst at the same time being the effective beginning of the end of the Aboriginal way of life on the island. As we approached the heavens opened and within a matter of seconds we were all drenched to the bone. Marvellous, a day in the rain, sitting in a bus with a bunch of fellow 'steamers' (it was still hot so everyone was beginning to look like they were evaporating) all trying to avoid getting double pneumonia. However, not to be undone by " … a little rain, this is nothing you should see it when it really gets going … " Darren gave us all a short talk about Central Station and its role in the islands timber industry. Having done this he then strode off towards the forest and along the board walk built next to the wonderfully named Wanggoolba Creek. Like lambs to the slaughter we all followed. I've always wondered what it would have been like to step back in time to when the dinosaurs ruled the earth and kids hadn't yet discovered Facebook? Well here by the creek it was if this had happened not least as here was the world of the ancient fern, Angiopteris, which Darren informed us had the largest fronds in the world. I half expected a T. Rex or Brachiosaurus to appear and this image was all the more pertinent as Darren did tell us that part of the BBC's series 'Walking with Dinosaurs' was filmed here. With the rain pummelling the canopy above us and cascading through it in torrents there was a definite primeval feel to this place.

Rejoining the bus we moved on towards Seventy Five Mile Beech and as we did so Darren went into over-drive in describing everything around us pointing out some of the more interesting trees like the satinays which were to be logged in thousands as they were of a much higher quality in shipbuilding, the kauri pines, brush box, blackbutts, the palms (piccabeen), kauri and hoop pines, the broccoli plants, the scribbly gum trees so named as the marks left by moth larvae on the trunk were originally mistaken by the early loggers as Aboriginal writing, and the smooth bark apple tree that sheds its bark to create a compost. All the while Darren continued to negotiate the 'beast' through some pretty rough terrain as if it was second nature (which given he had done the tour many, many times probably was). Along the way we also passed a number of Aboriginal middens which were strewn with shellfish, a link to the past that had now long gone. Darren also pointed out certain trees that had been marked by the original loggers to delineate where tree felling was to take place. The man was a walking dictionary of facts and figures about the island that were so numerous I was having a little difficulty keeping up in my notebook. As we bumped along the pitted sand road (not sure how this bus fits in with the eco theme as it belched out thick black smoke into the canopy above) Darren kept stopping and pointing out a lizard or some other creepy crawly which would have been great but as he and those of us in the front were the only ones who could actually see it was a bit unfortunate for those at the back. Mind you on the plus side though a few of those at the back were some of our dear European cousins and by the sounds of their guttural noises were none too pleased either. I'd have had more sympathy with them but given that most of them probably gave Great Britain null points in the Eurovision Song Contest frankly they deserved it.

By now Chris had changed nationality and was in fact a bona fide Japanese tourist snapping away as if his life and whole raison d'être for being relied on it. I am a little snap happy as is my wife especially when she is with her extended family, but neither of us comes anywhere near

Chris who was beginning to get friction burns from not just the photos but from the videoing he was doing as well. To be fair to him, his photos will be a better aide memoire than some of mine that often feature me looking as if I have just stepped in something nasty. Looking at my Australian photo album I really can't figure out what possessed me to 'pose' literally at arms' length and thus basically have most of my less than Adonis-like features hogging the frame with whatever it was I was trying to get in the picture almost impossible to see. Hang on I remember why now: it took me until almost the end of my trip to work out how the self-timer worked.

Then it happened, the piece de resistance, the highlight of the tour albeit we had still a good three hours to go. We were just passing a picturesque rubbish dump when Darren slammed on the breaks resulting in everyone shooting forward in their seats and a declaration of war from the back of the bus.

"Over there, in the corner. Can you see it?" Darren whispered (pointless really as the bus was making enough noise to wake the dead).

Those of us at the front and luckily for Chris and me on the left hand side peered out in the direction that Darren was now pointing. What was it? Was it a snake perhaps or a special type of tree which is found nowhere else? Maybe it was Eliza Fraser? It was none of these but instead a very rare sight, none other than a Fraser Island dingo scavenging for food in the bins. I know very little about dingoes given the fact that they're not exactly native to the shores of Britain, although lately it is rumoured that wild panthers and wallabies now are, so maybe it is too. Aside from the odd nature programme, always it seemed, narrated by David Attenborough, there would invariably be long shot of a cute bunch of cubs playing with accompanied by his dulcet tones imparting snippets of information about how they mate, eat and socialise followed a shot of the pack crunching on some bones of a long dead animal. The only other time that dingoes had featured prominently was the Lindy Chamberlain case and the abduction of baby Azaria in 1980. Outside of this my knowledge bank was empty as I reckon most of the rest of those in the bus. But not for long as the font of knowledge on all things flora and fauna, Darren, elucidated:

"The Fraser Island dingo is still viewed as the purest of its species in Australia (about 98%) as, unlike elsewhere, there has been little cross contamination with dogs. But there is a real problem that has really begun to be an issue here which is that dingoes are wild animals but people seem to want to feed them. This can and does result in the animal losing its desire to hunt and then becoming a nuisance. They may look friendly but they are not pets and you have to treat them with respect. One of the biggest problems is that as people start to feed them they lose their hunting instincts and unfortunately start to hang around areas where people are."

The dingoes, *Canis Familiaris Dingo*, on Fraser Island are not large in number and, according to some, roam the island in packs, scavenging for food whatever that might be. Warnings are laid out in black and white for anyone who is camping to hide food or bury it, similar to advice in connection with bears. But of course people can be dumb and there have been instances of dingoes being given handouts and, no real shock, attacks because, as one ranger was quoted as saying "The message just isn't getting through" that these are wild creatures. But the increase in people and the access that they have to the island and thus to an animal that is by its nature territorial has increased. To put this into perspective in a 2001 article called 'Dingoes of Fraser Island', John Sinclair wrote, in the light of the death nine years old Clinton Gage, about how the dingoes of Fraser Island would appear to have lived with the Aboriginals for thousands of years and that the latter, he argued, killed them only if they were a threat, something that even when the Europeans first settled also continued. However, the current problems are due to the rapid growth of tourism. In the 1970's the numbers visiting were around 5,000 which by the early noughties had risen to some 300,000. This is where he sees the problem lying – people wanting to have that special photograph started to entice these animals and as a result attacks increased. Unfortunately Fraser Island has continued to see with, a more recently in 2007, an attack on a four year old boy. In this latter episode the Climate Change and Sustainability Minister for Queensland was quoted in the Brisbane Times as saying about the dingo that had attacked the child that it had 'lost all wariness of humans.'

There are two losers in this: on the one hand is the dingo which has been hunted down and 'culled' (in recent times this has been quite frequently) on the island to stop these attacks happening and then there is, on the other hand, those of us who would prefer to see these animals in their natural habitat as wild creatures to be admired from a distance. Let's face it you wouldn't get out of your car to feed a lion at a safari park, so why then would you do it with the dingo?

On we continued hitting each rut in the ground with a jolt and at points almost, so it felt, feeling like we would tip over. In places, due to the overall dryness of the underlying sand, the bus almost didn't make it up some of the more challenging hills, although it may have been due to Chris and myself given our combined weight. All the while that Darren was negotiating the sand road he continued to jabber on pointing what that was or gems such as the reason the sand in places was so white was because all the nutrients had been taken out of it by the fauna. So now you know too and will be able to impart this vital bit of information at the next soiree you attend, although I am not sure how you might engineer the subject to sand.

We entered the Seventy Five Mile Beach and started to head north. The only thing strange about this whole thing was that instead of a metalled road we had just sand. As far as driving is concerned the rules applicable are the same as any road with speed limits and driving on the left. Everywhere there were 4WD, some loaded with locals from the mainland on a day's fishing expedition, whilst others were packed with tourists. Driving on the beach sounds like a bit of a wheeze, but as Darren pointed out many that come to the island and then take their 4WD out onto the beach just have no clue. As we made our way north I could see what he meant as we were passed by speeding vehicles bouncing along the sand. In fact, according to the State government, the number of accidents, in just the last six years, that have been serious exceeded 120 with in excess of 100 casualties. In nearly every case the reason has been attributed to inexperienced drivers (one fatal accident was as a result of the driver of a Landcruiser swerving to avoid a wave at high speed) speeding or being overloaded and thus being awkward to handle. A few weeks after I returned back home there was another fatal crash which led to calls by some for those who bring 4WD cars or trucks being required to have a licence to drive this type of vehicle.

We arrived at Eli Creek next and it felt as though the world and his wife were there. The Creek itself was swarming with locals as well as tourists, the latter including ourselves having been disgorged their loads onto the white sandy beach by three of these monster buses. As an option if I'd felt really adventurous I could fly up and down the island in two small turboprop planes (just to clarify though not at the same time because that would have been really clever) for a small sum. Now I have no real love of flying but see it as an evil necessity to get from A to B so the thought of taking the kind offer to fly was not overly tempting. I was also acutely aware that some years ago when flying one of these small planes from Pensacola to Tallahassee the pilot/steward took one look at my manly body and asked me if I could sit in the middle to "balance the plane". I am sure someone out there can tell me all about why this has to happen, but for me all it said was "Don't bloody move otherwise this plane will fall over because you're a fat bastard." So I politely declined the offer to do a fly-by of the island.

Eli is a freshwater Creek that dumps millions of clear water into the sea everyday and the water itself may not have seen the light of day for hundreds of years having been filtered through the sand (thank you Fraser Island info website for this exciting factoid – my knowledge is almost dinner table worthy). I schlepped through the water which was crystal clear along the gully through which the Creek ran keeping an eye out for a) crocs, b) snakes or c) sharks that had lost their way and were looking for lunch. Back on the bus we moved on to the next beauty spot, the multi-coloured sands (seventy-two have been recorded) at the Pinnacles. Our arrival there coincided with the rain returning again which was unfortunate as the Pinnacles were supposed to be spectacular due to the colours caused by oxidisation as a result of iron being in the soil. Having taken millennia to form, all I could see was dull yellows and dark oranges. All in all it was a little disappointing, but I can always look at my layered sands from the Isle of Wight (Alum Bay) and pretend that they came from here.

All was not lost though and even though the sky was dull, there was a Dutch couple with their two children getting incredibly excited (I could tell they were Dutch due to the amount of phlegm being ejected from their mouths as they spoke) as they scampered around taking photos of absolutely everything. Even Chris, who by now found that the bunion on his finger had grown to the size of a tomato from his own almost maniacal snapping, could not match their determination to create a collage of the Pinnacles in all its glory. I do hope that is has pride of place at home in

Holland next to their 'stash'. I have one question though as an apropos of 'nothing in particular': why are Dutch people usually so tall? Is it because in days gone by so much of the country was below sea level so that genetically they grew to be able to keep their heads above water? It may explain why the Spanish Hapsburgs, once rulers of the place and who in my humble opinion are nationally much shorter, worried that they would drown should any of the dykes be breached. If any historian is reading this I think it is worth exploring, much better than waffling on about the Eighty Years' War.

Darren called us back aboard the bus and off to the next site which we had passed on the way up, which were the remains of the Maheno. This is an iconic wreck that appears in all the brochures it seems of the island which, given that it represents an heroic failure may seem strange to some but the story is quite amusing. The keel was laid in Dumbarton, Scotland, in 1905 and the ship, considered quite luxurious in her day, carried well-heeled passengers between Australia and New Zealand across the Tasman Sea. During the Great War she was converted into a hospital ship and by the 1930's was passed her best such that in 1935 she was sold to the Japanese as scrap. So far, so good and the Japanese duly came to pick her up and tow her back to Japan to be broken up. On board the Maheno they left a couple of brave souls, brave because there was no steering on the ship as they had decided to disable it thus, as we shall see, opening things up for potential disaster because as the Oonah which was pulling an unseasonal cyclone hit them. One wonders if the Captain of the salvage vessel was fully aware of the situation.

"Ah, Captain-San, the weather seems to be changing. Do you think we should worry?"

"No, First Mate-San, everything is fine".

"But Captain-San the wind is picking up and the waves are getting higher."

"I know, but you know we have nothing to worry about. Watanabe-San is on the Maheno and he will control it if things get a bit rough."

"But Captain-San, he has no steering."

"Borrocks!"

Due to the weather the Maheno broke loose and ended up on the shore where is it is today between Happy Valley and the Pinnacles. Originally the salvage company planned to refloat her, even leaving someone on board to stop anyone claiming the ship as bounty. This person, Darren thought, was the quarantine officer – he must have had a whale of a time! So there is the Maheno stranded on the beach when a local dignitary has a brainwave. He decides that he will get married on the tilting ship. I wonder how he broached the subject to his intended before they tied the knot: "Darling, great news, we are to marry on board a luxury liner!"

"How lovely" she must have cooed "you really are a real romantic; a wedding and a sea voyage. I'd better pack my trunk."

"Ah, yes, but there is a slight problem. The ship is actually not on the sea. In fact it's actually beached on Fraser Island. Oh and our honeymoon will be to guard the ship from anyone claiming it as booty."

"Borrocks!" she replied. I suspect the marriage may well have been quite short.

Sadly for the Japanese the ship was not refloated and stayed put and some say that the crew of the Oonah had anyway been too scared to go ashore as they thought that they might be the local Aboriginals main course. So it stayed put and at this point the boys of the RAAF enter the scene, seeing the wreck as an opportunity to practice their bombing techniques. Darren might have been yanking our chains as it were but he said that the percentage of ordinance that actually hit the Maheno was around 1%. There is a final story involving the Maheno which was that it was also used by the 'Z' Special Unit commandos for demolition practice during the Second World War, as part of their preparation for an attack on the Japanese originally in Rabaul, but following the changing tides of war was then switched to Singapore in Operation Jaywick in 1943. The raid was another 'Boys Own' adventure but, unlike Eliza Fraser, the men who took on this mission that resulted in significant damage to seven enemy ships were real heroes who put their lives on the line in order, it seems, to give a morale boost to the war effort. All 14 who took part returned safely although an attempt to repeat the raid in 1944 in Operation Rimau, which included 6 of them, failed resulting in their deaths.

The ship today is an eerie skeleton of metal made more so as I looked at it due to the grey skies and little spits of rain. Rusted, covered in barnacles and now in pieces it is a protected site which prohibits any climbing over it. It looked tiny when compared to today's luxury 'cities on water' I wondered what it would have been like as it was originally with its Edwardian passengers, the men walking on deck with their ladies.

Thankfully just as I had visions of Kate Winslett and Leonardo Di Caprio suddenly appearing on the remains of the bow with probably the most annoying song in the world courtesy of Celine Dion filling the air, Darren called us back on board.

We continued to retrace our tracks from earlier and headed south passing Happy Valley on our way to Eurong. I asked Darren how it came to be called this. The story could have been taken from some guide to 'Great places for to get very drunk'.

"Happy Valley got its name when two brothers turned up to settle there. At that time the island was alcohol free and so, not wishing to be alcohol-less the brothers built a still and made their own. The area soon became the only place on the island to go and get wasted, attracting not just the loggers but also the early tourists. It was a great place to drink and just do nothing."

I have only ever once tried liquor that came from a still (potcheen) which blew my head off, turned my stomach inside out, and resulted in me growing breasts and then not being able to talk coherently for days (some argue that is still the case). The stuff is vile but I guess when needs must you aren't going to be that fussy and given the stories of how the Island became more of a hippy hang-out it does make for a good story. Eurong was owned by the Fraser Island Resort which paid a cool 27.5 million dollars for what is essentially a hotel, a shop and some holiday homes that can only be accessed via the beach or a fairly bumpy ride in the forest. This was to be our lunch stop and once more the dreaded buffet. It didn't disappoint and was as awful as any I have tasted to date.

One final note on the diesel spewing 4WD buses, which with the best will in the world could hardly be seen to be in line with the eco-friendly intentions of the island. In the late 1990's and into 2000 there were serious investigations and probability studies being undertaken to see how feasible it would be to have a light rail laid to reduce the reliance on these monsters. John Sinclair in an article written in February 2010 for 'randomKaos' pointed out that Frasier Island was quickly becoming a major ecological issue such that for him 'It is therefore surprising that once it was listed the Queensland Government has allowed it to become so degraded that some people are now arguing that it needs to be placed on the World Heritage in Danger List.'

The 4WD for Sinclair is the major problem (outside of his view that those tasked with managing the island are too 'preoccupied with recreation management') with its 'mobilization of sand', or in other words the compaction of the substrata and subsequent water erosion which is resulting in huge displacement. Parts of the island have been badly affected by this, even where they are not directly driven over as a result. The light rail is for him and FIDO a possible solution. The debate about whether it is right or wrong to have a light rail has been going on for over a decade and one of the outstanding questions for those in favour and those against is whether or not it would reduce the impact of tourism or actually not just increase it (by increasing the numbers of visitors) or, worse still, lead to further development. It does seems like an eminently sensible idea having a light rail not least as in recent years tourist numbers have hit 300,000 per annum which, using FIDO's data comprises almost 800,000 effective days (in other words most people stay a few nights). That is an awful lot of human traffic being taken round the island hiking through the forest and generally adding to what is worrying conservationist, a pretty damaging footprint.

The island is beautiful without a doubt and this bus trip we were on did nothing to dispel this. I asked Darren what he thought about the impact of the 4WD on the island and the light rail proposals:

"There's been a lot of talk about the light rail and I'm all in favour of it"

"But what about the viability of doing it, I mean how would you operate along the beach for example?"

"Difficult one to answer, but with this old thing spewing smoke into the air and with tourists numbers as they are something needs to give. Seems that if you want to preserve this place as it is today you have to do something. Just look at what there is around here. "

As I write this I thought back to when we were at Eli Creek and the three full tourist busses, two planes and countless 4WD vehicles dotted around and then the words of Sinclair. Was the State more interested in preserving the ecology or a strong desire to make money?

Eurong was quite nice and although there was little to see it did have direct access to the beach, which if you are one of those people who like being a) eaten by sharks or b) stung to death by jellyfish is going to be right up your street. By now the sun was blazing away in the sky so all was right with the world again. I wondered across into the only shop and browsed amongst the tanned, inevitably blonde, youngsters. I mention this last point because yet again I found myself looking more at them than the goods on sale (all souvenirs at remarkably competitive prices such as the Fraser Island mug on sale for more money than the average person makes a year), not just because they were mostly incredibly supple and good looking, which is very annoying when I know that the only reason people look at me is to debate how many branches I hit when I fell out the ugly tree, but also because they all seemed to have visited the same tattooist. As with most of the tattoos I had seen to date all the females had a very similar flowery design on their backs just above their bums whilst all the males looked like they had all seen some advert for Air New Zealand with the Maori markings and decided en masse to have virtually the same design tattooed on their arms. Long live individuality!

Darren summoned us once more and off we went to the next beauty spot, Lake McKenzie (or to give its Aboriginal name, Boorangoora). This is a freshwater lake some 100 metres or so above sea-level that is one of a number of so-called perched lakes on the island. Perched lakes are huge bowls of rainwater collected over the eons that is unable to drain away due to the compacted plant life and sediment at the bottom (Fraser Island has upwards of 1,800 millimetres of rain yearly). Going back to the arguments over the ecological state of the island, Fraser has over 40 lakes and is home to just over half of the known perched lakes in the world as well as having barrage lakes (caused as a result of sand dunes blocking waterways) and window lakes (those below the water table). The trouble is that they are, where accessible, very popular as places to stop and in the case of Lake McKenzie, to swim in.

A study called 'Effects of tourism on Fraser Island's Dune Lakes' by Wade Hadwen and others, highlights what they see as the problem. The conclusion of the document was pretty clear, especially where it concerned the clear water perched lakes. Tourists in short could be causing shifts in the ecosystem by swimming in these lakes. In simple terms with all the deodorants, perfumes and other things we put on ourselves along with just being a foreign body to the ecosystem we are destroying the balance of nature by introducing more acidity into the water. Looking back I can see why there is concern because as we turned up the place was swarming with people sunbathing or swimming. FIDO in an article called 'Tourism Threatens Lake McKenzie's (Boorangoora's) Survival' also drew attention to another major issue with the lake:

'In just 30 years this swale has almost filled to overtopping. Tens of thousands of tonnes of sand and detritus washed off the roads that carry tourists to the lake and from the car-parks, picnic and camping areas have accumulated here.'

The article also talked about the way that the rules governing what tourists may or may not do were being flouted including, it says, pictorial evidence of back-packers camping illegally and of someone enticing a dingo for food. In FIDO's view the Queensland Parks and Wildlife agency were not doing enough to protect this island. When I reflected later on the day as a whole, although it was undeniably great fun and certainly something that I was privileged in some ways to do it did seem at odds to what I've always thought of as eco-tourism. To be balanced recently the Queensland Department of Environment, National Parks and Wildlife has it seems cottoned on to the concerns expressed and are now actively working to address the impact of tourists on these lakes. Unfortunately for anyone reading this who expects me now to say that I didn't swim I have to disappoint you, but at least I had forgotten to put deodorant on so did make a small, albeit unintended contribution to maintaining the pH balance.

Over a cup of tea and biscuits a few of the guides reminisced with some of my fellow eco-warriors on some of those that they had taken on tours mostly involving people who were so stupid that they had failed the exam for village idiot. One story made everyone smile, coming as it did just after a snake had been spotted sunning itself in the late afternoon sunshine, and involved Darren and an Englishwomen who as it was to turn out was a credit to our great nation.

"So there I was talking to a couple of tourists about the island and what it was like to work here when this lady comes up to me. 'Excuse me' she said, 'but can you tell me what type of lizard that is over there? I was going to pick it up and bring it to you but wasn't sure.' I looked to where she was pointing and just couldn't believe it; there is the undergrowth no more than 10 feet away was this lizard. Except it wasn't a lizard; no it was a death adder."

Someone piped up about how they had read somewhere how snakes tended to be wary of humans and only attacked if threatened or stepped on. Darren agreed but then went on to explain the death adder approach to this and just how stupid this woman was, and boy she was really stupid and as I said, a real credit to the Motherland.

"The death adder is a nasty little bugger and is actually more aggressive than most of its fellow reptiles. If you piss it off, and that can mean just getting near it, it can lunge at you and you don't want that unless you have the reactions of a super hero. The strike of one of these is fast, really fast at something like 0.2 of a second and unless you get treatment pretty quick it's bye-bye." At this point he then smiled broadly and said "And of course, as I told the lady, who was by now a little stunned, snakes unlike lizards, don't have any bloody legs."

Back at the Resort we de-bussed and went on our separate ways, travelling buddies no more. It is one of life's great mysteries that when I go on something like a tour, whether like this or as my wife and I did in 1989 around Europe, that I have a good rapport with those around me chatting away about trivial things like where we come from and what we do and, of course, we must keep in touch after this which we all know will never happen. Even should we see each other later that day in the bar or restaurant it's as if a switch in our sociability make-up has been turned off. It is either that or the more likely answer, which is that everyone does keep in contact but not with me because I smell or something. I can see them now in the resort bar all drinking and being merry with one person keeping an eye out for me, rather like a meerkat, in order to warn the others of my approach.

It had been a day of mixed emotions. On the one hand I felt very privileged to have had this opportunity to see one of the world's true natural wonders in the world (and don't forget I had already been twice to the Great Barrier Reef so this was like having another helping of my favourite pudding) whilst on the other hand I felt that commercialism had in many ways become intrusive. Deep down the same feeling came out on the Reef but here at least it did seem that the volume of tourists and boats visiting were being better managed. Fraser Island, or at least the part I saw, though undoubtedly beautiful, has lost something in that it seems to be that there is a philosophy that has more in common with packing them in.

Chris and I repaired to the Sand Bar for dinner which was a short walk from the main area and had advertised a pizzeria, bistro and cocktail bar. The buffet last night was still in the back of our minds, not least as we were looking forward to not having hot food that had been stewing away under a hot lamp for an eternity and had more in common with an alien life force than food. Chris and I almost ran, alright waddled but it was impressive, to our destination with what we expected to be a gourmet meal. The taste buds were all fired up, the molars and incisors were honed for an epicurean delight which we had as yet to experience here. We should have known better. The only thing missing was a golden arches sign or pizza hut logo. Order, take a ticket, sit down and wait until our number flashed up on the board above the kitchen hatchway. As for the cocktail lounge well I guess we'll leave it as another misrepresentation of the fact as my definition of what a cocktail bar is clearly is not the same as those who run the Resort. I know that we weren't here on Fraser for the food (well I wasn't but I can't vouch for Chris) but come on at least put some effort into what you serve. Disneyland Paris does a better job and their food is, in my experience and opinion, truly terrible.

Day twenty eight: December 1st

Today we left Fraser Island and headed south once more down the Sunshine Coast towards Noosa where we would be staying for a couple of nights. This was a driving day and although the weather was pleasant and sunny there was not a huge amount of time to stop and admire the scenery. The only place we did stop was Maryborough which is a typical colonial style town and where we had lunch and lazily watched the world go by over a toasted sandwich and coffee. The town or more accurately one of the oldest provincial cities (it was established in 1847) in the country, has a fair bit of history attached to it and where we had parked was close to the old industrial area near the Mary River. Here, in the Wharf Street precinct was an area that saw a hive of activity back then and well into the last century where not just industrial concerns such as sugar and engineering (both of which are still extant) but also immigrants landed. It is quite hard to imagine what it would have been like then with its noise and smell as today there was no real hustle and bustle with an air instead of calm. Traffic, both human and mechanical, was very light and even the shops looked empty as we wondered around before driving off again. It is hard to believe that this city could have been a potential capital of the state when I look around but it is actually I think better for it as it retains a lot of the charm and character that I had already seen elsewhere on my travels.

We returned to the Bruce Highway refuelled and keen to get to Noosa. On the way I started to read about a phenomenon in Australia, the Grey Nomads. What had initially made me curious about these particular travellers, and hence my break with scenery watching and onto more cerebral things, was due to a programme on the TV that I had watched that had been about the rising numbers of retirees driving the roads of Australia. A Grey Nomad is defined as being anyone over 50 years of age who has decided to pack it in and take to the road. These people are not an insignificant part of the population and are actively supported through websites and blogs set up by fellow travellers. They also have been nicknamed 'SKIN' which is in long-hand 'spending the kids' inheritance now.' They are not unique to Australia and in North America are referred to as Snowbirds and Grey Voyagers but they are different.

Whereas it appears that in the US and Canada these age groups take on a migratory tendency (for example the flocking of the old to Florida in the winter) in Australia they really get the miles, sorry kilometres under their tyres. The numbers, given size of population (remember it is about 22 million) are huge and it is estimated that as many as 390,000 recreational vehicles are out and about. The number of vehicles being sold each year to support this is on the rise as more take the view that "We earned it, we'll spend it."

As I had been driving around we continued to encounter a regular number of large 4WD, from campervans through to trucks that seemed to have had a living area attached to the back, most of which invariably had huge tyres and some not far removed from ex army troop carriers. All, without fail, were loaded with everything you could think of for someone who was most clearly not about to go on a two-week break. Some of those we passed had what looked like half a builders yard attached to the side from spades to ladders to hoses, tyres as well as bicycles. This wasn't your typical caravan that is all too painfully present on the roads back on Europe. Many of these vehicles looked far from comfortable and most had a real lived in look about them; the image of a VW Campervan being driven by students too broke to have anything more expensive immediately came to mind. They all had one thing in common in that they were being driven by some very leathery old man or women, usually smiling although that might have been due to wind or the denture glue sticking their mouth such that they could only given an upturned half-moon leer, and without a kid in sight.

These Grey Nomads are more than just a statistic though and there have been a number of studies to establish the impact that they have on local communities, most notably those in remote areas. One I read with interest was a collaborative study by Annette Maher, Rosemary Leonard, Helen Hayward-Brown and Jenny Onyx where they looked to examine the relationship these people had with mainly rural Australia. Reading through some of the key points of this study I came to realise that the Grey Nomads have more than just a social impact and that they also have a very substantial economic one too through their sheer number. The study highlighted the way that rural communities have been under 'threat' for over two decades as their relative wealth has declined along with populations. These Grey Nomads have become a possible life-line for many of these communities as a result, although there is a flip side in as much as they can also be a burden on a small town's resources (healthcare especially). As such in some parts of Australia in response to them some towns and rural communities are looking at ways of creating some sort of supportive infrastructure. One I came across was just outside Maryborough where we had just been where a couple of businessmen have set up RV Homebase which according to the chairman, Peter Shadforth, provides:

> 'Caravan and motorhome owners have long struggled with integrating their RV with their lifestyle, and juggling the logistics of managing their residential home while travelling, and our village has been designed to eliminate many of the traditional headaches the grey nomad community faces.' In essence this village would act as a base from which the Grey Nomads would then be able to explore the State whilst still having somewhere to return to.

In the UK and across Europe there are camper clubs and Australia's nomads are no different in this respect; however, the amount of blogs, or tips, being posted is quite incredible as I discovered when looking into this topic. Some postings just tell others what to look for from attractions to offering practical advice whilst others help those that are about to embark on what I guess could be termed almost a second childhood. The pictures on the web, as well as the TV programme I'd watched, showed everyone looking relaxed and happy, although I suspect this had as much to do with the amount of alcohol that was in evidence. Australia it would appear is a place of opportunity even when the grey hairs are multiplying and the wrinkles make a person look more like a walnut. It's a big difference to how we seem to treat our more senior members of society back in the UK where they are usually packed off to some residential home in order not to spend all your inheritance.

Day twenty nine: December 2nd

Noosa, which means 'shady' in the local indigenous dialect, is as with so many townships in this part of Queensland firmly rooted in the history of both logging and then the discovery of gold in the Gympie fields in 1867. The first visitors to the area were the Gubi Gubi and it is from their language that the more anglicised name 'Noosa' comes from, possibly from 'noothera' or 'gnuthuru'. Noosa's 'white' history goes back to 1828 when our friend from Eliza Fraser fame, Wandie wonders into the area having escaped for the umpteenth time from incarceration. By the 1860's the loggers had arrived and when gold was discovered around Gympie the area became a hive of industry. We had arrived the day before in good time and found the hotel which was just outside the centre of the town and, I am pleased to report, was also bang opposite a drive thru booze shop. I was set then, but Chris would have to forage further afield for his daily meat ration. We had arrived as it rained and today looked like it would be no different with the sky full of foreboding grey clouds and a whiff of wet in the air. As I have already told you I am particularly anal when it comes to the weather and I knew that today the Sunshine Coast would be anything but, although I had some help from last night's weather forecast which had some slightly dishevelled nice chap who looked like he had just escaped from an old people's home and invaded the television studio waving his arms everywhere and repeatedly saying "Jeez" before every sentence. I think this may have been the farming channel because I could have sworn that one of the presenters had some corn husk sticking out of his mouth.

My first port of call was Hastings Street which was in the middle of town and where we had eaten the night before. I'd read one of the glossy magazines in the hotel foyer that suggested that this street was very 'cosmopolitan' although what that really meant I was not entirely sure. Up until now with the exception of Sydney and Melbourne the places I had been to retained an element of character, with the mix of the old and the new. So when I entered the main drag in the town my reaction was one of almost total dismay. This wasn't my impression of Australia at all; it was like a rather poor cousin of one of the more swanky streets of the world like New Bond Street in London or Fifth Avenue in New York. There was no character at all and for me I felt that Noosa's image was just not right, almost plastic and in every sense sterile. In the glossy at the hotel it enthused about what one could see, including a French Quarter, but all the while brand names, all European or American, were shouting out from all sides of the street. It was as if they, the town council, had decided that any character that the place had had was not relevant and that blatant commercialism with brand names and upmarket shops and restaurants was the way to go. Just as you have places like Surfers Paradise (another horrendous blot on the landscape) which cater for the younger person, so Noosa is a town for an income bracket that comes with an expensive car and watch. Looking in window of the local estate agent I too could be the owner of a bijou residence with three square metres overlooking a house that overlooks the sea for a cool five million dollars. The glossy had had very little on the history of the town so I wondered what the demographic profile of a place like this might be today. Was it going to be a town that had a wide range of people wandering its streets: who were the 10,000 or so who lived here permanently? I got a strong feel as to the type of people that the good burghers of Noosa wanted from 'Noosa Style Living' published by 'STYLE Living Magazines' which I think neatly sums up what Noosa was about given that the magazine:

> ' ... is specifically targeted at the AB demographic both residential and visitors to the Noosa region ... This is the reader predominantly over 25 years with an annual income in excess of $50,0000.Noosa Style Living reaches the most affluent of visitors targeted by our advertisers through our select 4, 5 and 6 star hotels ... '

So let's be clear about this; they are only interested in the upper middle class and middle class and not C1, C2, D or E, or in other words anyone who was deemed too poor to be of importance. They also quite liked the 18–26 years old bracket, the so called Y generation as well as old farts like me from the X generation. Who thinks this up for goodness sake? Walking along Hastings Street was pretty much as per the magazine implied in its demographic breakdown as it swarmed with people dripping with designer this and designer that. Even a sandwich cost a king's ransom and it didn't even have gold leaf on it. The shops were all, bar a few, expensive as were the restaurants. But Noosa is like this because both the well healed of Sydney and Brisbane have made this one of their favoured destinations whether as a holiday or as a second home. Each year Noosa hosts over 250,000 visitors all I have no doubt with money to burn. Even walking along the boardwalk that faces onto the beach all the properties, hotels and restaurants that lined it oozed money. And as for the young: the place was a seething mass of bronze and blonde (again!) and although this was schoolies week these were those happily spending mummy's and daddy's money.

Don't get me wrong, I have nothing against places like Noosa but I feel, rightly or wrongly, that these sorts of places exhibit a high dose of superficiality, not least in those ridiculous shops that have about three items of clothing hanging in them and are staffed by some skinny shop assistant whose social skills would make a Trappist monk appear like a party animal and with everything at eye-wateringly high prices. Some places can carry it off like Monaco or Aspen, but here it just doesn't look right. It looked un-Australian. Bring me those mullets, tattoos and singlets any day compared to the plastic wannabe towns.

All was not lost because as luck would have it Noosa has one very bright spot which I now headed for with renewed vigour in my step which was Noosa National Park which was situated within an area called Noosa Heads. It looked as if it could offer an escape from the rampant commercialism and a chance once more to commune with nature. I was also quite keen to visit here not just because of the hippy in me, but because this park was in many ways the antithesis of Hastings Street. The park was initially gazetted in the late 1930's but at that time was a fairly small area (today it is around 4,000 hectares). Over the years there have been continuous battles between those who wanted to develop the area, including the Noosa Shire Council which wanted to build a road along the coastal part of today's park, and those who believed that it was essential to protect not just this area but, as has been done, the much larger 65, 000 hectares that now comprise both Noosa National Park as well as Cooloola National Park to the north. Reassuringly conservationism, which has been spearheaded since 1962 by the Noosa Parks Association, seems to have the upper hand today but there is still pressure from those who want to build. I found out later that Noosa National Park is the most visited park in Queensland with well over a million coming annually. Were they, like me, more interested in maybe spotting the odd parrot or koala or were they here because there were a couple of bays where surfing was supposedly fantastic.

There were a number of different routes that I could take including via a couple of the bays that surrounded the town. The clouds looked water-laden and ready to burst but it was still humid and far from cold so, come rain or sunshine, I set off on the first path which took me along Little Cove, past the Witches Cauldron, above Tea Tree Bay and after skirting Dolphin Point, Winch Cove and Fairy Pools. After a few more strides through the bush I arrived at an extremely blustery look-out that gave a great panorama of a very angry looking sea with the waves crashing onto the rocks below with the white horses riding them in giving off a salty spray that I could taste on my lips. Up until this point of my walk I had bumped into few other people, and most of those I had done so were joggers so no time for any chat and the odd surfer with their board. I didn't mind although it would have been nice to gauge their views as to how they saw this park and the whole issue of population pressures in areas as popular as Noosa clearly is. As I was enjoying nature in all her glory once again not having to talk to anyone was not an issue; in any event I was still trying to 'cleanse' myself of all the 'bling' back in the town. As I stood there gulping in the ocean air, refreshed by the strong wind two rather elderly women appeared, slowly jogging up from the path that I'd just been on, dressed head to foot in designer label clothing and with enough jewellery on them that I was surprised that they were not accompanied by security guards. As for make-up and hair styles two words suffice: layered and blond. Added to this both were carrying those coffee mugs that allow one to transport ones drink safely without burning ones had. Here I was, one with Mother Nature, and there they were, completely out of place almost as if someone had cottoned on to my thoughts about Hastings Street and decided to send these two ladies to remind me that this was a wealthy town and I shouldn't forget it! It could also have been that in fact both were Americans on holiday themselves who were only doing what is de rigueur to do in the US which is to look one's best exercising whilst nursing a cold cup of coffee. It was time to move on before I threw them to Poseidon as a gift to appease the anger of the gods and abate the raging sea.

From the vantage point I was at I descended towards Chrisandria Bay and started to walk along its long beach which was almost deserted but for one corner which I could see in the distance where surfers were out in force. The wind whipped up the sand around my feet and legs, stinging a little in the process whilst above me soared one of the biggest birds I think I have ever seen (and no, it wasn't a plane). I'd noticed it some way in the distance as I came onto the beach, but at that time it was on the sand presumably scavenging or just puffed out after a long fly from somewhere. My immediate reaction was that it was an albatross because I'd already seen one in Sydney on the whale watch and as that one was big, ergo this must be one too. It was more likely a whistling kite (*Haliastur sphenurus*) as I was told later, but I'll stick with albatross as I was near the sea and Coleridge's The Rime of the Ancient Mariner had sprung to mind. As I mused to myself about this, passing the carrion that the bird had been feasting on I looked towards where the surfers were and saw in the distance a sight that even today brings a shudder to me.

Let me just explain the reason for this comment. Back in 1980 Brighton became the first towns to open a nudist beach. At the time I was at boarding school and the only nudity I had seen then was that of other boys in a time when there was a certain innocence about sharing a bath or shower area and doing what we used to call the 'cock watch', or look for the boy who had developed three legs overnight. So one Ascension Day holiday a group of us thought it would be a wheeze to spend the day on the nudist beach, fully clothed of course, leering at the assorted flesh that might be there and hoping that some pretty young filly would strip off near us, prompting the male beach tradition of lying on his stomach and drilling for oil. Unfortunately the only nudist we saw was a very old man who was well past his sell by date in every respect but which nevertheless left all of us, innocents as we were, a little traumatised. Wind the clock on and we're back at the beach at Chrisandria Bay when there, right in front of me was that old man again, except of course it wasn't him but someone else with not a stitch on. Worse still, he had two friends, one male and the other female, who were both emerging from the waves. I was in a predicament as there was no way to make a large detour around them. I had to make eye contact, but with whom? The men, flapping away in the wind (flapping is probably the wrong word, but I am being generous) or the woman whose breasts were creating a wake behind her as she emerged from the surf. It had to be one of the men.

"Hello, cold is it?" I cheerily asked as I passed by before realising that by just saying that I might have inadvertently impugned their manhood. It's at this point that I wondered what the etiquette of a meeting like this should be. What sort of greeting should be made? Here are some of the options I should perhaps consider using next time:

- Nod and smile at the man as I look down then up.
- Drop immediately to the ground saying "I am not worthy".
- Start by giving a big thumbs-up and then follow this, clapping all the while, looking around for that imaginary crowd as if to say "Look at *that!*"
- Sing the Hallelujah Chorus
- Say "I've got one of those but only smaller" as a sort of ice-breaker
- Give the woman my phone number with a suggestion she brings the twins along but 'wrapped'.

I hastily made a retreat by walking back into the body of the park and thought to myself that they were probably German and wouldn't have understood anyway, so that was alright.

My goal was to end up on Sunshine Beach which I had been told was even swankier than Noosa Hill where we were staying. To do so required a fair bit of scrambling through the brush and on a path that at times was fairly steep resulting in my already sweat drenched shirt getting wetter and further beads of sweat stinging my eyes. Maybe those ladies I had met earlier had the right idea after all. Once more I passed some more fabulously named places like the Blowhole (sounds promising on a lonely night), Devils Kitchen and just beyond, redemption in the guise of Paradise Caves. This was the coastal track and just before descending onto Sunshine

Beach there was an incredible vista of the town that sits on it; as far as I could see (by now the sea spray was creating a white haze obscuring the far distance) the houses and, I presume flats, spoke in large dollar signs. Here I could have a spectacular property that was almost on the beach but only if the bank manager was feeling very generous. I cut back across the park stopping briefly at 'The Lookout' which afforded views of absolutely nothing but trees and more trees. But something struck as I had been walking around was that for the first time in almost four weeks of being in Australia this was the first time that I had not heard the cicadas; in fact there was almost no noise from the wildlife and scant evidence of it, apart from the exceedingly ugly Australian brush turkey of which there were plenty (oh, and my albatross/kite). This bird is no relation to the American turkey but was clearly designed by the same committee who came up with the camel having been asked to design a horse. It consisted of a big black feathery body, bald red head and yellow wattle and looked utterly inedible. I had hoped to see more than this after all that's what was in my guide but aside from the turkey, dead fish and albatross there was nothing. I presume it must have been a collective day off for the wildlife, or else they were in the same bar as my fellow travellers from Fraser Island.

I plodded back into town as the clouds once more began to gather following a brief burst of sunshine. Instead of going along Hastings Street I went along the beach itself and started to notice what looked like bits of jelly washed up on the sand. It looked pretty unpleasant, like miniature versions of 'The Blob'. Intrigued I wondered over to the lifeguard station to ask what these things were.

"Blueys mate; nasty little bastards" replied the ridiculously over-tanned lifeguard who was relaxing in a deck chair

"What are they?"

"Jellyfish, washed up by the tide. They swarm offshore but get pulled in because they're so close."

"Can they still hurt you?"

"Shit, yeah!" he said with the broadest of grins. Not an uncommon reaction I was finding when talking to the 'locals' about what could do some serious damage to your health. And so once again I was faced with the reality of Australia in that not only do they have almost every poisonous thing alive but, and this is really too much, even when these little dears are dead they can still do some real damage. There must have been a real glitch when the person in charge of dividing the creatures of the world out amongst the vast place that was Sahul (modern day Australia, New Guinea and Tasmania) before it all divided or else that person must have had something against Australia. Although throughout my stay I never felt really uncomfortable, always at the back of mind was the big question: "If I touch it or go near it, eat it or drink it, look at it in a funny way, will it then kill me?" I manfully made straight for the boardwalk and carried on away from the water's edge to avoid any chance of an affirmation of my fears all the while keeping a close eye on where the water was breaking on the beach. It struck me as I watched the sight of workmen replacing the sand with new 'clean' sand that there were a lot of people swimming or surfing without seemingly a care in the world. So another discovery – your average Australian is a) completely nuts, b) immune to pain and death or c) doesn't care less – no worries. I like to think that c) is probably the most likely. Having nodded to myself on this last point, I returned to the question of the sand and what exactly they were doing. As it happened one of the workman was standing on the boardwalk, orange attired from head to foot with an impressive lollipop sign complete with a red line trough a silhouette of a walker, obviously tasked with warning pedestrians that the creatures on the beach weren't in fact sharks but were diggers, so I asked him what the reason behind all this was.

"Buggered if I know; seems like the council have more money than sense. Mind you" he said, gesturing "look around and you'll see why they do it I guess. Bloody waste if you ask me. All these people with too much money, our politicians are keener on them than us working blokes. Next they'll ask us to paint the bloody sky blue every time it goes grey. Do you follow my drift?"

Indeed I did. Put bureaucrats or politicians in charge of anything like spending money on useful things that a community might need and they will do their upmost to spend it on something stupid. It doesn't matter where you go, they are all the same. In Queensland there had been a lot of hand wringing and mud-throwing over the proposed desalination project that so far had cost over a billion dollars but was not working although as Mike O'Connor in the Courier Mail ruefully observed:

'The good news is that while the plant is closed, it's saving money. The water that it produces when it's actually working costs $730 per million litres to produce, while the water from the dams cost about $200.'

Over in Melbourne the local authorities came up with a whizzer of an idea to combat violence that was alcohol related. This involved spending 17.6 million dollars on 30 'civil compliance officers' to act as arbiters of peace. As Chris Berg, who wrote about this in the Age pointed out, it seemed daft to spend all this money on something that the police were more than qualified to do. However, as he wrote, and this is where there is just the whiff of silliness in the air, other ideas to stop late night boozing included a proposal to stop people hailing cabs on the street on Friday and Saturday nights. It doesn't finish there and the Ministry of Stupid Ideas takes a bow with its decision in New South Wales to ban alcohol being served for 10 minutes each hour. Then there was the National Wine Centre project in Adelaide. Here the problem was one of spending an awful lot of money, then losing it and costing the taxpayer a bundle and then having to sell it on because it appeared no one in government had identified the actual business need, let alone demand. Going back to the plant, I leave the last word on this to O'Connor commenting on the political need versus the practical requirement of the desalination plant:

'The reason the plant is about as reliable as a politician's promise is that it was rushed into service to meet a political need ... politics, however, ruled and the Government declared that it wanted it built and quickly because, out in the 'burbs, the voters were getting restless.'

My man on the boardwalk sighed loudly as I walked away no doubt pondering more of life's great injustices or else when it was time for a beer. I carried on with my own thoughts and wondered into Noosa Sound which is a spit of land between Noosa Heads and Noosaville (you'd have thought that the town's founders might have been a little more adventurous in naming places or maybe it was late on a Friday and they all had to get home). To live here I would have needed serious money especially for a house which backed onto the mouth of Weyba Creek. It was all very neat with beautifully kept fronts and plenty of colours coming from the trees giving off aromas that were delicious. That was until the heavens opened again. I don't ever recall seeing rain this heavy in my life and to see a street that had a minute previously been bone dry become a flooded mess. It was quite extraordinary and yet at the same time utterly spellbinding. I took a photo of the 'view' and looked at the image in my camera; the houses opposite me on the other side of the road (about seventy feet across) were barely visible but those behind and on the high ground above Noosa Sound had become invisible. Steam rose up from the heated ground adding further to the sense that I was still very much in the tropics. It was over in about ten minutes and it almost felt as if it hadn't happened at all as the surface water quickly disappeared down the drains and the pavement and roads, still steaming but this time from a reappearing sun, started to dry off. I was soaked to the skin but loved every minute of it and, ladies, if you are looking for a wet t-shirt contestant may I throw my hat into the ring; I looked fabulous with my 'moobs' on show to the world.

That evening Chris and I had a splendid meal in one of the oldest restaurants in Noosa, Maisie's Seafood and Steakhouse. The restaurant today sits in quite a busy area of the Noosa, but looking at the photos hanging on the wall this used to be one of the few buildings around when there was little to call a town. In the restaurant the menu provided not just a long list of delicious sounding meals but also the history of the restaurant. It was built in 1920 for Jiddy Massoud on Gympie Terrace (the name of this part of town is a direct reference to the Gympie gold rush) as 'The Favourite' and was the first eaterie in the district. By the Second World War it had become very popular, not least as one of the most unusual drive-ins I have ever heard about. Given that the cafe was situated right on the edge of the ocean, it was ideally placed for amphibious craft which were driven up to the cafe so the soldiers could get their food. Fish was the main food served with up to 60lbs per day being cooked when really busy, which in turn also resulted in a lot of smoke belching forth giving it the nickname of 'Smokey Joe's'. Maisie, after whom the current restaurant is named, was Jiddy's daughter and worked there for much of her life. She had a wonderful view on life in the cafe and that in general and it is worth repeating because it would be so rare today:

'If people had money they would pay for their meals … if they didn't the food was free.'

The owners for the last 20 years or so are Ziggy and Julie Fiegl and for me as I looked around at all the photos hanging on the walls they have kept the spirit of what was here before. It really was one of the nicest places I had visited so far and it was so unlike the rest of Noosa; this had a real family feel about it, with no sense of pretentiousness, no hurry, no smell of money, lots of character and history and just a plain old well loved restaurant. I loved it and went back to the hotel with that contentment one gets when everything is just right.

The historic connection that the name 'Gympie Terrace' has is now under threat by some local residents who would like to rename the place Noosa River Esplanade because, as Mr. Laurie Stevens president of the Noosaville Association was reported in the Sunshine Coast Daily as saying:

'It's not a gold miner's holiday place any more, it's a vibrant and family orientated tourist area.'

Having now seen Noosa for myself, I would not disagree with his point about Noosa being a tourist area but it would be a crying shame if that happened because the name Esplanade has no connection to what was here before all that jewellery and perma-tan arrived in those expensive cars. Gympie Terrace is a part of the history of what made Noosa a town, maybe not so much as it is today with all its plastic, but nevertheless having an importance that a change of name could consign to history. After all this is more than a name that refers to the miners of 1867 who worked the goldfields because it is also about the growth of what had been a small fishing hamlet into what it is today. It's about the early struggles of those first settlers and of the problems they posed to the local indigenous tribes and it is about more recent events like the Second World War. Esplanade is so often associated with nasty little sea front hotels, characterless little cafes and cheap souvenir shops with 'kiss-me-quick' hats. If I were to change anything about Noosa it would be stop the gentrification of the area by rich out-of-towners.

One story caught my eye that evening as I was trying to reduce my luggage by drinking a couple of cold ones which I discovered in an article in the 'Australia Weekly' from August 2005. The article had appeared at the time the film 'Downfall' was released that covered the final days of Hitler and the Third Reich. In their research they had discovered that Hitler's last secretary, Traudl Junge, who had been with the Nazi leader in the bunker almost to the end and who had said that he was 'a kindly thoughtful man' had been to Australia a number of times after the war. One place that she had visited was Noosa Heads and in this article they had penned, was a photo of her sunbathing. Accepting the vileness of what the Nazi's did, I couldn't help wondering what she made of the place back then, perhaps making comparisons to the totalitarianism in Germany with the freedom of Australia, and whether the people she met knew who she was and how they might have reacted.

So was Noosa for the rich or was that just my idea? A snippet I'd read the previous evening on this from the official Noosa guide is the best summary I could possibly have had for this point:

'Noosa tourism still remains the major industry and developers are still building noosa holiday accommodation for the visitors that are coming to Noosa from all over Australia and the world. A population cap of 50,000, no high rise development permitted and very limited land available for development should protect Noosa for future generations to enjoy. *It also leads to some of the fastest rising property prices in Australia …* '

The italics are mine, but given the median cost of a house being over 640,000 dollars (units were above 500,000 on the same measure) I suspect that, with the Queensland average salary at around 63,000 and this median cost being almost twice the average mortgage for the State, then I believe I may well be correct.

Day thirty: December 3rd

Today we were heading for Brisbane, my third state capital and Chris's first. Sadly this was his last full day in Australia and it did seem a bit of a shame to have to drive for a large part of the day but there were some diversions to be had on the way including the glamorously named Glasshouse Mountains more of which later. As I was checking out I mentioned to the receptionist that we were planning to avoid going down the Bruce Highway all the way and instead were looking to stay as much as possible on the back roads with the objective of doing a big half-moon loop into Brisbane with the intention of getting her feedback.

"Aw, that'll be real nice. The scenery is lovely; you'll really enjoy the drive. It'll be so much better than just going down the Bruce which can get a bit dull at times, with all that traffic."

I thought about this for a minute and inwardly smiled to myself, responding, almost with incredulity at her comment on the Bruce:

"But everywhere, well almost everywhere, we have been has been really pretty. Your roads go through some exceptional countryside and as for traffic it only has been bad once and that was leaving Melbourne. We dream of this back in the south of England which is so congested these days that even on Sundays it seems the whole world is out in their car. I think that you are really lucky to have this as your backyard."

She looked at me, smiled angelically once more and replied

"Maybe; sure the beach is great and we get the sun but after a while it does get a bit, I don't know, dull. It's great for a holiday but not that exciting out of season."

"But how can you get bored with this?"

"There's not a lot to do around here unless you're in the tourist business."

This was déjà vu from what I had first heard in Port Fairy and it struck me as she said this that in Australia for the younger generation leaving the countryside or smaller towns and hamlets and moving to the City was the only way to get some sort of life. For those of my age who are getting to a certain age when getting up to go to the toilet at least three times a night is now standard, the pace of life is preferably slower and we're doing the opposite. But there is a wider issue that is taking up quite a lot of print regarding this and it has become a real issue in recent years because there have been some sizable demographic shifts.

Although many of the young look for the bright lights of the city, there are those both young and old who are looking to move away. In a similar vein to the Grey Nomads and their meanderings, there is a phenomenon in Australia that, having been such a small issue had by the 1980's started to be noticed and has also become a much talked and written about social phenomenon. In simple terms those leaving the cities and looking to downsize or discover some sort of idyll are becoming much greater and the impact is now being felt in communities throughout Australia. There are two descriptions applied to those who are moving back into the bush, or at least into the Australian hinterland and those who are moving to the seaside and respectively these are 'tree changers' and 'sea changers.'

Nick Osbaldiston from the Queensland University of Technology has done a lot of research into this shift. In his view one of the problems, certainly for those moving to the coast, is that these destinations are being 'loved to death ... and as development takes off that the aesthetics of the area are actually becoming transformed into mini-cities and mini-metropolises'. Of the towns that he identified Noosa was one and Byron Bay where I was due to go to was another. Interestingly he went on to say that those original sea changers are finding that 'their idyllic locations ... ' [are] '..too commercialised and lacking authenticity.' What was also interesting in what he had to say was that the dreams some had were 'leaps into the unknown'. As with the Grey Nomads the worry was also that these sea changers and tree changers would be seen as outsiders and a pull on the resources of the local communities but unlike the Grey Nomads these people were here to stay. In Noosa concern was recently expressed by Bob Ansett in 'Friends of Noosa Report – February 2010' that although the holiday season had gone 'very, very well' there was a worry that they needed to maintain a population cap. However, the policy on development not just in Noosa but along the Sunshine Coast was not being considered with the local populations in mind. In Australia the impact that this has had and could have is now as much an environmental issue as it is about housing and amenities to support expanding towns. Studies show that the movement of people out of these urban areas is not just about retirees but also a sizable minority who have little or no positive economic impact such that they might have had and so were putting a further strain on the local economy as they were not adding 'value' per se but were in simple terms becoming more of an economic millstone. In the 30 years to 2002 alone some one million Australians moved out of the metropolitan areas and given the prediction of population growth by the National Seachange Council which will see it rise to 35 million by 2050 the potential stresses are building.

These places need to grow to survive, or at least attract the money in, but they are caught between a rock and a hard place as it has led to wholesale changes in the character and demographic make-up of many town or hamlet and not always to the better. To survive these places have tried to adapt and to do this many had completely transformed themselves, for example Byron Bay where I was to be in a few days is a classic example, as Peter Murphy pointed out, this town had:

' ... transformed from its seaside industrial character, based on an abattoir that was operating up until the early 1970's along with a Greek cafe that closed at 6pm and a couple of rough pubs, into a kind of ersatz yuppie, 'waxhead' (surfie) and hippie paradise.'

To get out of Noosa was a relatively straightforward thing as we could have opted for driving back onto the main highway or, as we decided to do, via the coastal towns that have become satellites and Noosa 'wannabes' going south. It started off quite well as we meandered out of Noosa Sunshine Beach then along to Castaway Beach, Peregian Beach, Peregian Beach South and finally Coolum Beach. All of these mini-towns were very similar in lay-out with rows of apartment blocks interspersed with shops and restaurants. The latter were over-flowing with young well tanned people (children and adults alike), many equipped for the surf, and the odd pale looking tourist although given the lack of bright red men and women I concluded that there were no British, given our propensity to resemble fresh lobsters whenever exposed to that bright yellow disc in the sky.

On the subject of that yellow disc and skin it is a serious matter in Australia, so much so that one cannot buy any sun cream that is less than factor 30, given the strength of the sun and levels of UV radiation. Amongst those I talked to in Australia there is a much greater tendency amongst them to get an annual check for signs of skin cancer and it is not surprising given the statistics of the incidence of this disease with, according to the Cancer Council, some 1,700 dying each year from it in the country making it the world's top place for this form of cancer. In 2006 the Federal Government launched the National Sun Cancer Awareness campaign directed mostly, but not exclusively, at teenagers and each State now spends a lot of money advertising about the problem to bring the awareness levels. So once more I totted up the danger level of living in Australia: reptiles that kill (and some of the deadliest to boot), plants that could kill, dead sea creatures that could kill and now the sun.

Once we had negotiated our way out of Coolum Beach we headed towards Yandina which would allow us to avoid the Bruce Highway and also give us another opportunity to drive on some of Australia's almost deserted back roads. The countryside was a mix of forests and farmland interspersed with the odd hamlet with its pretty one storey houses and, invariably, a petrol station/pub/store all rolled into one. We stopped for lunch in Mooloolah in a cafe-cum-antiques-cum bric-a-brac shop. All very practical because as a customer in the cafe waited for their food or drink, they could spend dollars in the rest of the shop buying Auntie Mabel that Art Deco light she'd always wanted (made in China but don't tell her) thus giving the owner a win-win situation. There was actually something of an English tea room feel in the cafe part, almost as if instead of having the steak sandwich we should really have had tea and crumpets. It was all rather twee but very pleasant and many of the antiques were a microcosm of Australian history, with crockery, glassware, silver, brass, pictures and so much more from the country's past many baring the symbol of Empire on them. I do wonder how places like this stay in business and what sort of pass-through customers they get but it didn't seem to bother the owner who just "loved it here". There's a lot to be said for a pace of like that makes a person happy rather than being trapped in some dreadful non-existence that the rat race for so many has become, including yours truly. There was a chance though that he might have also been on 'happy pills' given that his smile was a tad lop-sided and he had a slight glint of farawayness in his eyes. As we left I felt envious and, as I always do when somewhere that suits my temperament, imagined living here myself without having to commute too far, enjoying the views and just being, as my kids would say, chilled.

The road had by now started to climb and we were driving along a ridge with on the left side in the distance the greenery of Bribie Island whilst to our right were the Blackall Ranges. This was bliss and at this point I could almost have done my Snow White impression and sung a little ditty but I think Chris might not have appreciated it given he was the designated driver and was being especially vocal at the audacity that others had of driving on the road at the same time as we were. After a brief stop at Bald Knob Road (yes you're right it was solely because the name was funny) to get a long distance photo of the Glasshouse Mountains we eventually reached the park itself depositing ourselves at the main tourist viewing area that provided a fantastic panorama of these weird looking formations. The Glasshouse Mountains are sacred to the Aboriginal peoples and played a significant part in the Bunya Festivals of the area. According to the legends of Dreamtime the peaks are part of a story and each of them represents a character in that story. The peaks are Tibrogargan (father), Beerwah (mother), Coonowrin (eldest child), Tunbubudla (twins), Coochin, Ngungun, Tibberoowuccum, Miketeebumulgrai and Elimbah.

Numerous books and websites tell of this legend, and here is one version from the Sunshine Coast tourist information website:

> 'The legend tells of Tibrogargan noticing that the sea was rising and calling out to Coonowrin to help his pregnant mother gather the young children together so that the family could flee from the rising sea. Coonowrin ran away in fear and Tibrogargan, incensed by his son's cowardice, followed and hit him so hard with a club that his neck was dislocated. When the seas retreated the family returned to the plains. Coonowrin, teased about his crooked neck and ashamed of his behaviour, went to Tibrogargan and asked for forgiveness but the father just wept with shame. Coonowrin then approached his brothers and sisters to ask forgiveness but they too could only weep with shame, thus explaining the area's many small streams. Tibrogargan then called Coonowrin and asked why he had failed to help Beerwah. He explained that he felt she was big enough to look after herself, though he did not know she was pregnant. Tibrogargan then turned his back on his son and still gazes out to sea today, refusing to look at his son who forever hangs his crooked neck and cries. Beerwah, the mother, is still pregnant, as it takes time to give birth to a mountain.'

The Europeans first came upon these formations when our good friend Captain Cook saw them in 1770 and described what he had seen and why he had named them the Glasshouse Mountains in his journal of May 17th:

> ' ... they are remarkable for the singular form of their elevation, which very much resembles a glass house, and for this reason I called them Glass Houses ... '

There is also another reason that they were named Glasshouse Mountains which was because the plugs of trachyte and rhyolite (lava) that formed them glinted in the sun. Whatever it was methinks that Cook might have had a couple of sharpeners before he saw these mountains because for the life of me the only thing I could think of were that they looked like huge green termite hills, like the ones we had passed on the road to Cooktown although obviously a tiny bit larger. They were a magnificent sight and were surrounded by forest on all sides. The mountains have attracted people for decades and many have climbed the peaks to get a view of the surrounding area. On Empire Day 1912, 'The Queenslander' had a story about one such climb up Coonowrin by a group of hardy individuals (I wondered if the two women in the party were dressed in those long dresses of the period or had worn something more practical) who, once they reached the peak with their Union Jack had:

> ' ... all gathered round and placed the flag on the old staff, after having lowered it ... Three cheers were given, and the dinner gong was sounded.'

This was the stuff of Empire – cheering the Union Jack and no doubt at dinner then toasting the King and Queen. I doubt very much that it would happen like that today. However what made me chuckle was the dinner gong summoning all to have some food. It made me wonder how they got their dinner up to the top along with the gong. Did they perhaps have a butler who had staggered up the mountain earlier in the day with all the accoutrements and food and had set the table in preparation for them mounting the summit? If my theory is correct then all I can say is that the butler must have been one heck of person because to my somewhat untrained eye in the matter of mountains and difficulty in climbing, these didn't look simple although no doubt they'd be deemed 'moderate' by our man from Magnetic Island. It's a far cry from today's climbers with their energy bars but it sums up a bygone era and a connection with Australia's colonial past where Empire was still celebrated and the niceties of the time observed (the article had gone into great detail of how they had been put up the night before by a friend who from the description sounded like he/she was a member of the local gentry).

Some of the Aboriginal people are, perhaps not surprisingly, less than happy with the way that these sacred mountains have become a tourist venue with little mentioned about what they mean. Even here at the viewing area there was little to tell a visitor about the story that I related earlier or the depth of the perceived spirituality they hold for the local tribes. To the Aboriginals they are more than mere mountains and with so much of their Dreamtime there is a mysticism that surrounds them. In another story about the mountains that featured in the Sydney Morning Herald from April 1947 there is an example of what this mysticism is and why today Aboriginals campaign for respect to be shown. The story concerned a man called John Petrie and his son Tom who had announced their intention to climb Mount Beerwah. Although they were 'beloved by the native tribes of Queensland', the local tribes begged them not to climb as it was home to the 'great Spirit ... who would punish by blindness anyone daring to look at him.' Neither John nor his son heeded the warning and consequently climbed Mount Beerwah. John fell blind shortly afterwards. Was this just a coincidence or something more mysterious linked to the mountain itself, who knows? However, apropos nothing in particular and with no explanation as to why, the paper reported that a railway station district had been named in honour of the Petrie family. Well that's alright then; lose your sight and then have things named after you.

We continued on our way to Brisbane which would be Chris' last night in the land 'built on sheep'. Once more I was navigating which I would have thought Chris by now would have realised was like giving the village idiot a Rubik's cube and asking him/her to complete it. Yes, we got lost but I am pleased to report that this time it was genuinely down to poor sign-posting and to a not too clear one-way system. The hotel was one of those anonymous chains that have less character than a plank of wood. The rooms in these places are often designed it appears by people who are convinced that having some completely awful modernist painting (usually a print) hanging on the wall, dreadful colour schemes often black on white or some other really horrible combination, minimalist furniture usually comprising of a chair, hard back, a small person-sized table packed with trendy magazines telling me how to 'enjoy' myself at some overpriced trendy restaurant or nightclub and a T.V the size of four football pitches that actually only has two decent channels. Worst of all are those hotels in Europe that not only have all of these 'facilities' but have decided that, for some reason that I have yet to fathom, native English speakers are only interested in watching Eurosport (aka football) and BBC News 24.

Tomorrow I was going to be on my own again for the last two weeks of my adventure and that evening Chris and I reminisced on our time together. Although I was excited at the prospect that my journey still had some days to go I was also sad in some ways to see him go. We ate close to the hotel and close to an avenue of shops I had passed earlier that day as I got my bearings (i.e. located the local bottle shop) where I was completely thrown by a shoe shop that in its window had twenty or so gollies on display. Here I was, in a country that many have accused of still harbouring racist views, and this shop was full of dolls that in the UK would now rarely if ever be seen. I went into the shop which turned out to be owned by an Australian-Chinese lady.

"Those gollies you have on display in your shop window, aren't they seen by people here as offensive?"

"What those, no" she replied. "Why do you ask?"

"I was just curious because if I owned a shop back in the UK and had these I could be in trouble if someone decided that they were offensive."

She looked at me almost in disbelief: "No-one has ever commented on them. Many shops have these on display and no-one takes any offence. They're just toys; nobody has said to me that this is wrong. I think that they look quite nice, don't you?"

There is no doubt that Australians talk in a matter-of-fact manner and what she had just said was symptomatic of this. I told an Australian friend of mine who lives in the UK about my encounter to see what he thought. Given that he had been living in the UK for a number of years and thus had been exposed to the way things are today, where you can't say "boo" to a goose for fear of offending someone, his response was intriguing and was also slightly ambivalent about the whole issue:

"Well back home we see things in a different way to what I'm now used to here. My parents and their parents are of an older generation that sees no reason to change what is culturally theirs. For example you'll still have references to 'Paki' for anyone who comes from the sub Continent as well as what you back in the UK would see as some really derogatory terms for the Aboriginals which to the average Aussie are just as it ever was. The thing is most people who haven't travelled out of the country don't see it as an issue. To them, it's how it's always been and I guess for many how it always will be. Take those gollies, to most people back in Oz they're no more than what the lady said, toys. We don't try to read in too much to what we see or hear. Maybe in the UK you are more sensitive to it because of the British Empire of which we were a part but not responsible for, I don't know." I asked him if he felt uncomfortable when he visited his parents back in Australia at this attitude. "Not really; sure I'm more aware of it and yes I know that for some it does seem offensive but like I said, in Australia much of the use of language has less to do with deliberately trying to cause offence than just being how it is."

There is a conundrum in this. On the one hand Australians are as already noted, friendly and outgoing people who will happily strike up a conversation about almost anything and yet on the other hand there is also this unwillingness to change certain habits. I think a part of this maybe goes back to the cultural cringe and the sense of identity that Australians see themselves as having. It has only been 35 years since the official end of the White Australian policy and in that time immigration has risen and many older Australians see it as a threat to their way of life. It's as if the mantra is "Come to Australia but be an Australian" or in other words this is how we live life here and you're welcome to join us but don't try to change it. More recently there have been heated discussions about who should be allowed to come and live in Australia and about having quotas as once more there is a fear in some quarters that allowing too many in would irreparably damage their Australian culture. However what exactly is that culture? Is it Anglo-Saxon and Christian? Is it something specifically Australian like the 'digger'? Is it even tangible? Personally I don't think there is a straightforward answer and certainly not one that is simple and to the point, but ask any Australian what epitomises their culture and invariably the answer will involve the sun, the sea, cold beer and barbecues but very little else. For most of my Australian friends there is seemingly a lack of real introspection that to me is one full of angst and acts as a mask or deliberate block to discussing what potentially is an uncomfortable issue.

CHAPTER 10

*Brisbane with the windmill but no wind and a bloke
called Petrie writing all that Aboriginal history.*

DAY thirty one: December 4th

Brisbane was named by Lieutenant John Oxley after the Governor
of New South Wales Sir Thomas Brisbane and is the capital city of
Queensland, a State that came into existence in 1859 having separated
from New South Wales. The split from all accounts was less than
friendly such that when the new Governor, Sir George Ferguson
Brown, examined the Treasury he found just seven and half old pence.
The details on this are kept by the Queensland Treasury and there is
quote that I really thought showed quite how desperate things were
from the 'North Australian, Ipswich and General Advertiser' on the
27th December 1859 which read:

> 'Some burglar broke open the room in the late Government
> Resident's official premises, but now used as the Treasury Office,
> and stole a cash-box which only contained seven pence in coppers.
> The man is a fool as well as a rogue, or he would have waited a
> better time, until some revenue was collected.'

Indeed he should have, because if he'd have done this at the end of
1860 he would have taken over 170,000 times more money.

Before the European settlers arrived, the city was the home to the
Jagera and Turrbal Aboriginal tribes whose lives were to be turned
upside down in 1824 when the first convict settlement came into being
at Red Cliffe Point, known to the Aboriginals as 'Humpybong' or 'dead
houses'. This settlement moved the following year and was sited near
today's William Street, which was close to where I was staying and thus

heralding the beginnings of the Moreton Bay Penal Settlement. The first arrivals were a mixture led by Lieutenant Henry Miller comprising 15 soldiers and 30 convicts. According to government records by the 1830's this had grown to over 1,000 convicts and 100 soldiers but by 1842 when the settlement officially came to a close was back to around 200 convicts. Convicts sent here were real recidivists, people who had committed yet more crimes and thus were deemed to require a much harsher form of punishment. It was basically a huge open prison surrounded by countryside that was at that time inhospitable to the settlers although as was discovered in the story about Fraser Island, there were those convicts who preferred to take their chances than to stay. When Oxley arrived and first explored the area one of the first people he spotted on the shore was an escaped convict called Thomas Pamphlett who along with three others had sailed north from Sydney and had been living with the local tribes for some months. No doubt as Pamphlett was English he was on a deck chair, trouser legs rolled up, wearing a holey vest and with a knotted handkerchief on his head reading the 'Daily Mail' and muttering "bloody foreigners" at anyone who cared to listen. Or not as the case may be.

On an excellent website called 'Brisbane History' there are a number of reminiscences written by people of either their experiences of the city as it was when they lived there or as it was when first settled by the convicts. One description by Archibald Meston (1851 – 1924) of how the area would have been when these convicts moved to Moreton Bay gives a vivid image of the terrain:

> 'All the site of Brisbane was covered by thick timber and heavy undergrowth, with patches of scrub, and all over the site of the Botanic Gardens, right round the river, was thick heavy scrub, with magnificent pines, beautiful bean trees, splendid tulip woods, and red cedars, also a fair share of stinging tree ... all South Brisbane frontage was also covered by dense scrub, the ridges at the back ... being timbered by light forest ... the original site of Brisbane, even as seen by me in 1870, was not attractive.'

As a penal colony it was not the nicest place to be holed up given that there were no afternoon teas, bands playing in the park or quaint dinner parties to go to and very little opportunity to do much else outside of the daily drudgery of being a convict with the exception on Sunday when they would have to go to church. The hours were sunrise to sunset. It was, in a word, harsh. "Well" said Josiah Pinchpocket to his mate Simon Nickpurse, "at least it can't get worse." As luck would have it this is precisely what was about to happen with the arrival of a man whose record has gone down in history as being found under 'Very Nasty Pieces of work'. This man was Captain Logan who I suspect today might have been diagnosed as being psychopathic or at least a little off centre. He was in charge from 1826 until his death in 1830. His rule was noted for its sadism and severe punishments were handed down for the most minor of infringements, such that he was universally hated. One of the main punishments aside from death was the lash and Logan was a big fan of using it and in 1828 he was recorded as having approved 11,000 lashes. What a jolly chap to have around. However, he was not alone in the usage of corporal punishment and by 1837 a Select Committee was set up to look into the use of transportation and the moral state of the colonies during which there was much evidence taken on the use of the lash. The report, published in 1838, showed that there was wide-spread use of the lash and these could be for the most minor offence as Isobelle Barrett Meyering in her 2008 thesis 'Contesting Corporal Punishment: Abolition, transportation and the British imperial project' pointed out in her discussion of the 1838 Molesworth Committee that was looking at the whole issue of transportation:

> 'The Committee did not have access to returns from New South Wales, but based on the figures for one month, estimated that over 108,000 lashes were inflicted in 1833 ... John Barnes, former surgeon at Macquarie harbour' [ordered] 'a man to be flogged because he did not take his hat off when he passed by Government House.'

Logan may well have been a sadist but the medal of for the biggest of all should perhaps go to Ernest Augustus Slade who, as Mayering describes it, felt floggings 'were not sufficiently harsh.' So in an act of supreme kindness he created a cat-o-nine-tails that had five lashes and more knots so that even if only 50 lashes were ordered under his benevolent eye this he declared, would be as if 1,000 had actually been inflicted.

As far as Logan was concerned convicts were so desperate to escape his clutches that according to David Bentley in an article for the Courier Mail on Logan ' … prisoners cast lots to slit one another's throats as a merciful release from torment.' There is some sympathy from a few about the way he acted not least as the number of convicts under his charge grew well over ten-fold and, some also argue, he was no worse than many others in his position before and after. Others point out that he was given an incredibly hard task of making Brisbane into something with limited resources (so limited that convicts had to use their hands as hoes for ploughing as they were not allowed horses or oxen). In 1828 Brisbane was hit by a drought and there was a huge rise in disease amongst the convicts with the result that more were ill than weren't. The Governor had wanted to move the penal settlement away but our man Logan stayed put thus 'saving' Brisbane for future generations to enjoy. The convicts must have popped a few corks to celebrate that decision.

Logan was a keen explorer and did much of this in the surrounding area. It was this that led ultimately to his death in October 1830 when on an expedition to chart the headwaters of the Brisbane River he was found with his head bashed in, very dead. No one knows who did it although nearly every account at the time and since says it was the local Aboriginal tribe, although the more objective articles suggest that if it was them they were probably encouraged to do so by convicts (there were by this time a large number living in the bush). His death was celebrated in song and verse. One such is called, with a huge does of irony 'A Convict's Lament on the Death of Captain Logan' which is also known in its shortened form as 'Moreton Bay'. The harshness that convicts faced under Logan is very evident in one of the verses where a prisoner describes Moreton Bay:

' … I've been a prisoner at Port Macquarie,
At Norfolk Island, and Emu Plains
At Castle Hill and cursed Toongabbie –
At all of these places I've been in chains,
But of all the places of condemnation
And penal stations in New South Wales
To Moreton Bay I have found no equal,
Excessive tyranny each day prevails.'

And on Logan's death:

> 'My fellow prisoners be exhilarated
> That all such monsters such death may find'

His death was little lamented and contemporary accounts describe how the convicts felt:

> ' … manifested insane joy at the news of his murder, and sang and hoorayed all night, in defiance of the warders.'

So the scene was set; Brisbane was not a nice place to have been incarcerated in. Worse still your chances of surviving a sentence there were not high either (Logan successfully managed to increase the death rate through working many to death as well as during 1828's famine reducing the ration). Much of what was Brisbane has long gone so there is little really to see to get a feel for what it must have been like in its earlier days. Most of the original buildings in the city were constructed of wood which unless treated had a habit of rotting in the climate and by the 1880's with the exception of a few most were gone, lost to history and time. Having now set the scene of it all being doom and gloom I ventured out to look round the city not knowing quite what to expect. When in this situation my travel tip is to always have at least one objective under one's belt that requires a bit a walk as you never know what you might pass on the way that might prick your interest. Of course if you are in Amsterdam's red light district then 'prick your interest' brings on a whole new meaning so adapt as appropriate.

It was an absolutely gorgeous day so I headed towards my 'objective', the Queensland Maritime Museum, which was located on the other side of the Brisbane River to where I was staying, in the Brisbane Graving Dock. I had thought as I approached it that I would stay for only a half hour or so as it looked pretty small from the vantage point of the Goodwill Bridge complete with coffee shop that overlooked it, as at first sight there seemed little to get excited about with only an old warship, a tug and an old lighthouse. However, I was here, it was there, it was a museum and because I like museums I was going to look into it. My love of museums has as a result incidentally meant that most of my friends are those who wear dirty anoraks, wear thick bottle glasses and carry their sandwiches around with them all the time in a grotty plastic bag, but at least they have a life.

As with almost every 'sight' that I had gone to so far whether museum or park, the place was virtually empty which to be honest I prefer as it gives me more time to just take my time without competing for the right view or having to wait to read the information card whilst listening to some annoying so-and-so's music from poor fitting earphones attached to their boogey box. I wondered out into the sun having paid my entrance fee and found that there was a bit more to the place than I had thought. The first thing I saw was a boat, the 'Happy II' that had been sailed from Canada to Sydney. Nothing strange about that as plenty have done this both before and since; however, I doubt if any have done it: a) solo and b) in a boat that is just over four metres long. The brave soul who did this was Howard Wayne Smith (he had already tried once before but been wrecked on 'Happy I') who duly arrived in Australia excited to have completed this epic journey and no doubt ready for a bit of 'R&R'. Now, it is my considered opinion that along with Health and Safety 'experts' the next lot of completely useless individuals are those public servants who have none of the following: a sense of humour, a sense of putting things into proportion or an ability to deal with certain events with a little flexibility. I say this not just because of my own personal experiences, but more because poor Mr. Smith was met with: "Have you got a visa to visit Australia?" or words to that effect.

Brilliant; the man has just sailed across the ocean and some peaked hatted jobsworth wants him to provide a visa. Unfortunately he had none, so not wishing to be churlish, customs thought about it and then asked for two grand for a bond to cover import duties. On the plus side he was given a tourist visa. It does end on a sad note though for Howard as he got kicked out of the country and eventually the boat was acquired first by HM Customs and then by the museum in 1988 where it has been restored and now rests proudly in all its shortness below the Goodwill Bridge. Behind this and facing the river were two enormous cannons that were clearly old (both had the insignia of King George III) and I was intrigued about how they came to be here, and what was their provenance so I approached one of the volunteers who worked in the museum and asked.

"Dunno mate; hey Rog, do you know anything about those cannons?" he said shouting into one of the huts that stood near the entrance.

"No" came the response.

Well this was going to be fun being in a museum where the people who worked here didn't know a huge amount about what was actually on show. As it turned out though after Rog emerged from one of the huts (STAFF ONLY) and greeted me with a big cheery grin things started to improve rapidly. I asked both of them what their connection was with the museum given that they were volunteers (it said so on their badges under their names just in case you were wondering how I knew; keen eyes you see). It turned out that Rog had served in Korea and that he was involved in working both at the museum as well as the local RSL. Jeff, the man I'd asked initially, was not ex-services but was very involved in the RSL as a helper to some of the old veterans of Second World War many of whom were immobile. As he said this I felt that Jeff had an immense respect and pride for these heroes of Second World War in the tenor of his voice. It was a pride that I had already encountered.

"There are only 16 left that can get around but the stories they have and the stuff that they had to put up with, like Rog, well it just gets to you, if you know what I mean. The trouble today is that kids have got no respect," Jeff continued whilst Rog lit a cigarette and nodded. "Look over there" he pointed to another hut where some gangly youths were standing idly with cigarettes protruding from their mouths and those jeans where the waist just about comes up to the knees "those little bastards have no respect. The only reason they're here is because they're doing community service. I heard the other day that a hoon had pissed on a war memorial. It's a bloody disgrace when you think about the sacrifices made so that they can live a free life. I'd bring back military service or send them to prison." I found out later that the memorial he was referring to was the ANZAC Shrine and Eternal Flame of Remembrance which I swung by later. It makes me sad to think that people act in this way when it may have been their own relative being commemorated only to have some low-life urinate on it.

I carried on my investigation of the museum leaving Jeff and Rog to their thoughts and the cup of tea that they had invited me to have with them. In the Graving Dock sat the tug ST Forceful as well as HMAS

Diamantina. Thanks to the Maritime Museum's wonderful handouts I can tell you that the word 'Graving' comes from the old French '*Grave*' which in turn became '*Graven*' in Middle English and meant gravel or pebbly shore; graving itself is an old term for cleaning a ship's bottom and coat with pitch. I boarded HMAS Diamantina, which has the motto 'Hic Regit Ille Tuetor' ('Whoever Rules Protects') and was named after the river of that name, which in turn was named after the wife of the then Governor, George Ferguson Brown. The last warship I had been on was the aircraft carrier USS Intrepid which is docked on the East River in New York. That ship is huge. To put this in perspective the Diamantina, the last river class frigate at 92 metres in length could have fitted into the USS Intrepid nearly three times. It did have something in common with the USS Intrepid in that it was built in the Second World War and saw service including being the ship on which the Japanese surrendered Nauru (an island that at the time was made up almost entirely of guano which must have been fun for those stationed there) and Ocean Island. Having wandered around and got an overload of naval history I re-emerged into the sun and bumped into another volunteer who was having a crafty cigarette before guiding some other tourist types around the ship. John (badge again!) had lived in the country since the early 1960's and was Australian through and through except that he wasn't. His early years had been spent in north London around Finchley and he still remembered it fondly. He loved Australia and all that it had on offer, but missed things like English football (although after the recent World Cup I can't see why), the climate (mad as a hatter this man!) and London. The reason for arriving in Australia was that his father worked with the company that worked with the Reserve Bank of Australia on changing the old Australian pounds, shillings and pence to decimalisation. It could have been called many names (Royal, Digger, the Kwid and so on) but eventually dollar was agreed upon and in 1966 it became the country's legal tender. John also let me into his little party piece which was as follows: When was the first dollar used in Australia? Was it a) in the mid 1960's or b) sometime earlier. The answer is (b) and involves our friend Governor Macquarie. Although the colony had money it had begun by the 1810's to run out of coinage. So Macquarie in a definite case of genius imported Spanish dollars, punched out the middle and thus doubled the potential number of coins in circulation with each called respectively the holey dollar and the dump. In fact in the first part of the colony's life currency was in such short supply that as Hughes points out there were:

' … IOUs and sliding coinage – guineas, johannas, guilders, mohurs, rupees, Spanish dollars and ducats … At one point in 1800, even the English copper penny was declared to be worth twopence.'

Behind the Diamantina was the steam tug 'Forceful' which is still in use today, ploughing up and down the river. Well I say 'today' but actually it wasn't. As had been happening with a number of my visits to places of interest there would be no sailing on this tug today as it was in the dry dock being repaired. It was a pity but I had had an enjoyable hour or so but it was time to move to the next site, the Old Government House (OGH).

When Queensland became separated from New South Wales in 1859 although it had a functioning political set up there were very few buildings that were either practical or in place to house its politicians and leaders. So bad was it that the first Parliament met in the Old Convict Barracks on Queen Street which for some is where they should have stayed given the abuse of the public purse and allegations of corruption and bribery in Australian politics today. The Governor's House was no exception as it was built in response to the need and today it is situated within the Queensland University of Technology campus. In all it housed eleven Governors from the time it was built in 1862 through to its closure at the beginning of the 20th century. It was designed by an Englishman, Charles Triffin, who had come to Australia in 1855 and who, by 1862, was the Government Architect. Built of sandstone from the Goodna quarry, the finished house was deliberately grand as befitted the Queen's representative and also because it was meant to symbolise the new found independence and hoped for future in the colony. It is today a much bigger place having been renovated and extended at some cost, but inside there is much of the old character left, including a sweeping double staircase in the main entrance area. This was not just a house but also a place of high office and of entertainment for the well-heeled the upper echelons of Australian society. It was the place to be seen and said much about who you were in Brisbane society if you were invited to one of the social events, the main one being the Birthday Ball held to celebrate Queen Victoria's birthday in May. Although this was a big house in terms of Brisbane at the time, balls as such were not held inside because unusually there was no ball-room for the Governor; perhaps he should have worn bigger underwear. Many parties would have been hosted here by the various Governors over the years from 1862 until it ceased to be the residency in 1910. Although the Queen's birthday was a a huge social occasion the really big event was in 1901 when the future King Emperor and full-time philatelist and all time bore George, Prince of Wales, visited as part of the celebrations of Federation. Pictures of this visit adorned the walls and the rigidity of the Victorian/Edwardian court can be seen with everyone dressed to the hilt in their 'Sunday' best with the slightly diminutive figure of George looking a tad out of place standing near to the Governor, Lord Lamington. Ironically perhaps it was this Governor who also oversaw the appointment of the world's first Labor Government, which was actually in favour of independence from the Britain. This was short-lived though as after just six days it was brought down on allegations of corruption. Some things *really* don't change

The house itself had a practical design to it because given that Victorian woman would have been decked out in all her finery, layered dresses and bustles their quarters were on the cooler side of the building. The building was also constructed along the lines of 'his and hers' with one side devoted to the Governor and his office and accommodation and the other side for the women and children. All the servants and flunkeys were housed at the back. It was all very hierarchical. Going back to the first incumbent in this house, Sir George Ferguson Bowen, not only was he the first Governor but he is to date the longest serving Governor. In some ways he was quite liberal supporting an elected upper and lower chamber in Parliament, supported immigration from other colonies like India, promoted education and introduced an entry exam to the civil service. He also believed that you couldn't do the job unless one rode and could shoot.

As I came out of the entrance back into the sunshine there was quite a commotion going on as some sort of dedication was taking place of a statue in the gardens. The local press and TV were there and various Very Important People were wondering around chattering away to each other in excited voices. Whatever was about to be dedicated (if that is the right word) was located just to the right of where I was now admiring the entrance to the OGH and as such proffered an opportunity for me to be on Australian TV. I would soon be famous for sure and it brought to mind my life-long attempt to be knowingly on television, the most vivid time being when I was nine years old and was in the audience listening to that superb flautist James Galway which was being filmed for a Sunday night TV programme called 'Aquarius'. Unfortunately that attempt failed as I was probably the only person not to appear on the TV which may have had something to do with my inane grin and wave every time the camera seemed to come my way. I have had success since though by appearing on Channel 4's news programme during the last United States presidential election, although as my wife remarked given that I was wearing a rather dirty mackintosh coat, had an umbrella up and it was in the shadows it could have been anybody. Just for the record it was me and I know this because the interview was live and I'd phoned my wife to turn on the TV and record it. So today I could make amends. I was ready, I was not completely dishevelled but more relaxed and I had adopted an air of serious authority, or in other words had a facial expression similar to Rodin's 'The Thinker'. What would I say when they interviewed me because that was bound to happen, after all I was the only under-dressed non-VIP in the immediate vicinity and therefore ideally positioned to do a bit of 'vox pop'. The bigwigs started to take their positions and the cameras started whirring. This was it. Fame at last, the voice of the common man on Australian TV and English to boot. I waited and waited all the while avoiding the mistakes of the past. Minutes passed and various short speeches were made and all the while I was standing and hoping that the camera would pan to where I, the lone tourist, was standing. Instead what I got was, "Excuse me mate, would you mind moving you're in the shot." Philistines!

I left in a bit of a huff to seek comfort in some food. After a sandwich lunch at a very pleasant pavement cafe ("What kind of bread would you like?" "What have you got?" "Brown" "Then that's what I'll have" "Good choice") I was keen to understand the history of the area better, my appetite whetted by the OGH, and made my way to the Royal Historical Society of Queensland (RHSQ) museum at the Commissariat Store which was one of the oldest surviving buildings in the city which had been built by convicts, being completed in 1829. Its main function then was to essentially be the main centre for storing everything that the penal settlement required from everyday equipment though to acting as an arsenal. Its life in that role was short-lived as by 1839 as the penal settlement was wound down it became an office building. Originally a two storey building it was added to in 1913 and in 1982 assumed its current role. I went in and fought my way past the crowds of people also waiting to have a look round. Oh all right I was alone and there was no one else aside from three weary looking individuals huddled around a table behind a glass door drinking tea. For a moment I wondered if I'd entered the wrong building or worse I had walked into a private building, although paying five dollars kind of gave the game away or else Mrs Miggins, or whoever owned this house, was pulling a fast one. However, my initial somewhat surreal concerns vanished in an instance when that now familiar greeting sounded from behind me: "G'day mate."

I turned round, shaken out of my tangential thoughts, and was confronted by a big grin from Matt. It's that helpful name badge again. I think everyone should wear one no matter who they are. I'm sure the world would be a much happier place and so much more friendlier although I suspect that may be a little fanciful of me. Matt continued: "Would you like to be shown round?"

I thought for a moment of an English museum and the kind of greeting one might get there also commonly known as silence with a grimace, the look of someone who would rather die than be helpful to you. But Australia had done it again and almost at once I felt as if I hadn't walked into a museum but rather as I'd thought first off, someone's house and I was a long lost friend. We were buddies. It's just so pleasant. Americans are very similar and every time, without exception, I have been to a museum there I have always found them welcoming. I immediately said yes – so much better to have local expertise than to try and decipher some of what was on show I always believe.

The first part of the tour started outside as Matt described the building and what it had originally been used for. He pointed out the retaining wall that was immediately behind the Commissariat which was the original one built by the convicts. I don't know why I was so amazed, after all where I live there are many buildings which are so much older than this, but I guess it was because of *who* built it rather than its age that had me thinking. An idea of the type of conditions the convicts would have faced is described by Hughes in 'Fatal Shore' and although he was referring to the work under Lieutenant Henry Miller who had taken his party up to the original settlement at Red Cliffe Point, the same would have faced those at Moreton Bay:

> 'Miller had the convicts working twelve hours a day, dawn to dusk. Horse, draught animals and ploughs were all proscribed … every inch of ground had to be inefficiently tilled with hoes, which kept breaking, and there was no animal manure. The convicts became afflicted with scurvy, and conditions were so squalid that they also fell victim to filth diseases like dysentery and trachoma.'

Everything that the convicts used from the tools they had to the stone and mortar used was all sourced or made locally with little or no mechanised help. The limestone alone came from Ipswich which is a good twenty or so kilometres from where I was standing today. As I looked around there was plenty of evidence that much of what was built was done painstakingly by hand, from the marks made by the adzes used in the timber frames to the marks on the sandstone. A little later when we were on the first floor Matt picked up a brick that was on one of the sills and asked me if I noticed anything. It wasn't like a modern brick: it was much cruder in manufacture and didn't have the usual groove in the middle one sees today. I studied it closely realising that missing that course on 'How to make a Brick' had been a big mistake. Matt pointed at a faint indentation: "That was made by a thumb or finger by the bloke who made this."

"Why?"

"Each convict was given the job of making a specific number of bricks a day and to prove that they had reached their target they marked it in various ways from hand prints through to writing. You see if they didn't do it then they could be lashed."

We moved to the ground floor which was filled with a series of models representing how the penal settlement would have looked in 1839. What was quite clever was that they were placed in exactly the spot they would have stood had the Brisbane River flowed through the ground floor but at a scale, for all you modellers out there, of 1:72. All the while as we walked around Matt churned out snippets of information about who these convicts were, about how the numbers by Logan's time were significantly higher than they would have been at the beginning which added to the strains of convict and master living together. In the corner of the room was a bit of real history – Andrew Petrie's workbench. This was the man who surveyed a very large part of this area of Australia and here was his workbench. I looked underneath it in the hope of finding some Georgian chewing gum but alas all I found was an old copy of 'Ye Playboy; Georgian Edition', well-thumbed of course. Alright so there was no porn but just imagine if there had been, what a discovery. Looking around at all the models did give me a feel of how it would have looked but not how it would have felt which was as I said no picnic. It was undoubtedly tough on the convicts, but it must equally have been difficult for those who lived here as part of the system, the guards and their families, the soldiers and other free people. I asked Matt what he thought it would have been like:

"It wasn't easy. On the one hand you have the convict population increasing along with all that entailed and then on the other you had the harshness of the environment. Much of what was built has gone as it was built in wood. As Brisbane grew following the end of the penal settlement in 1842 and the influx of new free settlers then new buildings were erected and, to me at least, it feels like the new inhabitants were quite keen to do away with as much of what had been here as it was almost like a bad smell. By the 1870's and 1880's much of what had been around had gone, although given the quality of some of the wooden structures by then it was hardly surprising"

"What about the convicts that were here, was there any hope that they could be free?"

"You have to remember that those sent here tended to be hardened criminals in the eyes of the law. They were ones where the original sentences they had been given were extended. You could be freed but that was hard, at least here."

"How?" I asked.

"By the early 1800's things called tickets of leave were instituted although it usually was directed at those who had been transported for seven years. Y'know the arch criminal who had stolen a hanky or something! Anyway, these tickets were given after a person had served about half their time if they'd been good; but until they'd completed their sentence they could be brought back." (It was under Governor Brisbane that these tickets of leave were formalised).

On the first floor were a number of glass cabinets all with stories to tell from the birth of Queensland to who had lived there, remembered through artefacts, busts, photographs of which the RHQS has over 68,000 and printed matter. There was also much evidence of what convicts would have had to put up with like the cat-o-nine tails through to the chains that they would have had to wear. It was a stark contrast to the much more genteel exhibition charting the impact of women in Queensland which was all about clothing, cream teas and all things ladies would have done. There was also a cross-bar from a set of gallows on display in one corner of the floor which caught my attention because it had three hooks for hanging which was just plain grim not least as it had been used to do just that. To be fair Queensland was the first State to abolish the death penalty in 1922 although the last person to have been hanged was Ernest Austin in September 1913 for rape and murder. His ghost is supposed to haunt Boggo Road Gaol where sentence was carried out. However Matt let me into a little secret:

"We didn't hang that many in this State, either before or after 1859; instead some of the nastier criminals were often sent down for trial in Sydney under Federal law and were hanged there. After 1922 any potential candidates for the rope were also sent there but those buggers stopped hanging people in 1939" he said with a smile as if to imply that maybe they should have carried on; all done in jest I'm sure.

I had noticed that there was very little on the original inhabitants of the area. Up until now the conversation had been about modern Australia as determined by the arrival in 1824 of the first convicts. I thought that this was somewhat anachronistic, after all this was the RHQS so surely there must be more to the story than what I'd seen so far. I asked Matt about this and was completely blown away by his answer:

"If you ask me a lot of what the Aboriginals talk about today as their history is really down to Petrie and his sons and what they wrote down which has been used by the local people today."

He said this not as a joke but just as a matter of fact; there was no malicious undertone to what he said. Instead this is what he believed. From an outsiders perspective I found this rather hard to take not least as I had already read much about the history of the first inhabitants. However, I had no way of challenging his view or where it had been created. I had no way I could prove he was wrong aside from saying "what a load of tosh! Have you read any books about their history?" but I felt disinclined to do so, after all he may have been right to an extent. It is a known that historical narrative can change through the generations as interpretations alter as times change. It may be that some of the indigenous peoples narrative has changed and was influenced by the white man but, on balance I'd like to believe that what I had read so far and was to read later was theirs, built on the fantastic spiritual Dreamtime world, and not someone who came to this country thousands of years after them. But even if it did have some Petrie-input surely it is still their history?

My head was beginning to ache with all this deep thinking so I moved on thanking Matt and the other possible sex addicts for their time (one of my surreal thoughts had been that this was a swingers house and they'd all been having a refreshing cup of tea before the next session. In my defence the sun was very hot and I was a little dehydrated or possible hopeful). I needed to change gear a little and decided that what I needed to do next was something that was of a much less serious nature. So what should it be? Maybe I could grab a beer and then go to the Treasury Casino & Hotel where in one of their deals I could check in, put on a tux, get three five dollar Match 'n' Play vouchers, 1,000 Qantas frequent flyer points and in the best James Bond tradition, gamble and win all night with a lady on each arm? Or I could go to another museum. Difficult one this, after all I do look a little like Sean Connery when not being George Clooney's double, so I could have pulled off the Bond bit, but that would require everyone having an incredible imagination, up to their eyeballs with mind-bending drugs and probably not 'all there' so to speak. So museum it was.

The previous evening as I was contemplating the world in my hotel room I had come across a little advert for the Queensland Police Museum, lured by the exotic sounding tag-line 'Discover policing in Queensland 1864 to the present'. Amongst the many exhibits were the shrine of horror and the simulated murder scene. How jolly exciting, so much better than a lady on each arm and of course so much more attainable! That had to be my next destination, a meeting with the fuzz, the filth, the pigs, yeah man I was hard, I was trouble and I was ready for them to bring it on. Come on! It was a bit of a schlep from the RHQS and, aside from the rather amusing sight of a Christmas tree with a solar powered star at its top and a Santa in shorts, not overly interesting as I had to walk most of the way along Roma Street which is one of the main drags in the City. By the time I arrived I was no longer hard, more like melted given it was still very hot and I couldn't wait to get indoors. The museum was located on the ground floor of the Queensland police headquarters so there was quite a bit of activity as I entered the building. As soon as I was through the doors I suddenly felt guilty of something. I always seem to have that paranoia which manifests itself when a member of HM's constabulary approaches me, it is because I have erred in my ways and they are about to arrest me for something like 'being fat and ugly in a built up area and causing a visual nuisance to other members of the public'. However, given that the entrance to the museum was off to the right of the main entrance I managed to escape arrest and what's more it was, glory be, free!

The museum charted the history of the State's police force from its establishment under Lieutenant David Seymour of the 12th (East Suffolk) Regiment of Foot in 1864 to the present. He went on to serve for over 30 years and so far is the longest serving Police Commissioner in Queensland. The first thing that I noticed, aside from the fact that all the mannequins had an uncanny resemblance to each other, even the female ones, was that amongst the original policemen there were indigenous people. The first force was made up of 150 white officers and 137 'natives'. Interestingly it was the latter who were primarily involved in the eventual tracking down of Kelly's gang in 1880. There was also one story which I found quite enjoyable which concerned the arrest and conviction for murder of a taxi driver by Arthur Halliday in 1952. In their investigations the police had interviewed dozens of witnesses and had built up a strong description of not just the car the murderer was driving but also his dog. It was the latter that ultimately helped secure a conviction but in a most peculiar way. The dog, which was called Peter, had died but was deemed a vital part of the prosecutions' case, so they had the poor mutt stuffed and then brought into court to prove that Halliday was indeed the murderer by linking him and the dog to the crime scene. It wasn't quite 'Lassie Come Home' but I have to hand it to the boys in blue for ingenuity.

I carried on, having had an overload of looking at sepia photographs and newspaper cuttings. I wanted to see 'The Shrine of Horror'. Would it be a sort of creepy homage to the worst that Queensland could offer from its criminal fraternity? Would there be some weird chap kneeling in front of it, candles burning, incense filling the air and chanting whilst rocking back and forth? Maybe there was an Australian version of Hannibal Lecter held behind bars? My imagination was going into overload. The excitement was building, beads of sweat beginning to form, I couldn't wait. Dramatic music played in mind, well actually from my headphones as Bach's Toccata and Fugue in 'D' Minor started playing. I turned the corner to face 'The Shrine of Horror', by now all a-quiver. And then there it was and my excitement evaporated as quickly as the morning mist being burnt off by the sun. No nutter bouncing off the walls, no candles and no Hannibal but instead just a list of some of the more unpleasant individuals and what they had done, to have graced Queensland's criminal history. Never mind there was still the popular (their words not mine) 'Simulated Crime Scene' where I could help solve the murder. Unfortunately, the only crime being committed that day was that of the exhibit with its somewhat tacky murder scene and mannequins that had seen better days. On the bright side as I reminded myself again it was free and I hadn't been arrested, so not so bad after all.

Back out into the late afternoon sun it was still like an oven but there were still two places that I wanted to see, the old Windmill and St. John's Cathedral. The former was situated at the top of Wickham Terrace and looked totally out of place in modern Brisbane. It no longer had any sails and stood rather forlornly as a reminder to days gone by. I had been told that although at the time of its erection in 1828 by convicts it was at one of the highest points in the town, there wasn't a huge amount of wind to power the sails so a solution had to be found to help in its job as a grist mill. Logan and his pals were not just sadists, but ingenious sadists as they added a treadmill to help power the sails, and depending on what type of convict was assigned the task, the treadmill had anywhere between sixteen and twenty-five people working as much as 14 hours a day to power the mill. It has an even grimmer side too when two Aboriginals were hanged in 1841 from the top.

By the 1860's it had assumed a new role as a signal station alerting all and sundry of the arrival of ships in the bay and this continued until the 1920's. It got a new name as a result, The Observatory. A panoramic photograph of Brisbane taken in about 1870 clearly showed the windmill then as being not just one of the tallest structures but very much in command of all that could be seen around it. It even acted from the 1890's as a fire observation tower and in another image taken towards the late 19th century it still had the advantage of views. The way that Brisbane then built up around it over the years, the windmill would have to be at least nine hundred feet tall today to even be seen from the bay, and to even be of any real use to fire observers using my thoroughly scientific estimates which are based upon an incredible understanding that I have garnered in recent years in the matter of calculating distance and height achieved whilst studying the theories of a Professor Rule-of-Thumb. It has one major claim to fame as it is the oldest industrial building in Queensland.

I wondered back down the hill heading towards the Cathedral but decided to take a quick detour and stop by the ANZAC Shrine and Eternal Flame of Remembrance. The Shrine had eighteen Doric columns that represented the end of the Great War and carved above were the names of some of the most famous battles fought. As a nation Australia lost over 61,000 dead in this war, or around 1.3% of the population of 1914, and a further 39,000 in the Second World War. On the latter, Brisbane played a significant role in the Second World War as a staging post for the Allied campaigns in the Pacific and hundreds of thousands of soldiers passed through the city, many of whom were American. Brisbane was not the size then as it is today, with just 330,000 inhabitants most of whom were very much colonial in their attitudes to life, including the local military. The influx of these Americans led to major social changes, not least the Americanisation of the city and this led to simmering tensions that came to a head on Thanksgiving Day, 1942, which is referred to as 'The Battle of Brisbane' which involved a mass fight between American and Australian soldiers that came out of what might be seen as a minor incident when an American military policeman had tried to stop a fight between Australian soldiers and ended up hitting one of them over the head with his stick, which as can be imagined didn't go down well with the less than pro-discipline diggers. The next day a G.I who had been having a few beers with some Australian diggers was asked for his pass, was slow in providing it, got hit over the head and was then defended by his new Australian pals. For the next two nights Australian soldiers then fought Americans, with the almost helpless police both civilian and military trying to bring calm. The garden that the ANZAC Shrine and Eternal Flame of Remembrance overlooked was also part of the memorial, and here there were bottle trees, a reminder of the country's role in the Boer War and palm trees that represented its role in the Middle East. There were also statues and murals that commemorated more recent conflicts from Borneo through to Vietnam. There were quite a few people in the garden as it was coming towards the end of the working day chatting and relaxing. I wanted to ask some of them what they thought about ANZAC square and what it meant to them but time was moving on and I wasn't sure if the Cathedral would be open still. I was also conscious of the fact that had I been sitting minding my own business on a seat in a London park and some overweight, red-faced sweating person had sidled up to me and started talking I may well have made a run for it or done one of those looks into space giving the pretence of being in deep thought or of being deaf.

I left to look for the Cathedral. Now a Cathedral as you will appreciate is usually a very large building. It is often defined as the principal church of a Bishop's diocese so you'd think that it would be quite hard to either miss or get wrong. Well not me, no sir! I have already told you that my map reading is less than brilliant, well it appeared that at this exact moment in time not only was this a lot worse than even I'd thought but my ability to spot the obvious had become non-existent. Let me explain. I had arrived at the Cathedral which was a tad smaller than I'd expected, but then this may have been because it had been built during the colonial era when things were on the whole smaller due to the lack or materials. However, on I pressed to the front entrance, undeterred because this was after all the Cathedral and there would be lots to see inside because as we all know churches in general are like Dr Who's Tardis, small on the outside but massive on the inside. I tried the door and my heart sank. It was closed. "Never mind" I thought to myself "I'll wonder around outside, maybe there will be someone there to ask some deep searching questions about the building". I walked around the building which, given its size, took what seemed a nanosecond and soon I was back at the front where as luck would have it, I bumped into man dressed in black save the giveaway sign for a person of the cloth, a dog collar. Excellent, here was my opportunity to become the Inquisitor General.

"Afternoon vicar" I said cheerfully "when does the Cathedral re-open?"

"It's open now" he replied beatifically.

"Oh. I couldn't see a way to get in. Have I made a mistake? Is there another entrance?"

"You wanted the Cathedral? St. John's?

"Yes, isn't this it?" and as soon as I said that our good man let out a loud guffaw. I thought this is a bit much from a man of God, I mean what about all that stuff on love and kindness.

"No, no. We are a church but actually St. John's is opposite – just turn around and you'll see it." He was still sniggering or at least if not actually that he was definitely enjoying this.

"So what is *this* church?" I asked somewhat sheepishly as only a person who now knows that they are looking decidedly stupid because as I was soon to find out it was very obvious that I'd completely cocked-up.

"This is the parish church of All Saints and it's the oldest Anglican church in Brisbane, dating back to the late 1860's if that makes you feel better" he said, smiling, as he wondered off no doubt to tell his friends that evening that he'd met the stupidest Englishmen in the world because as he said this and I turned to head in the direction he had indicated to me to get to the Cathedral, I passed a rather large and not exactly inconspicuous sign that said in big bold letters 'All Saints'. It was a shame that it hadn't been open because as it turned out when I looked into it later this church had quite a history of notables who worshipped here not just from Brisbane's 'Who's Who of Big Names' but also of Australia, such Sir Robert MacKenzie and Sir James Dickson who had both been Premiers of the State of Queensland.

I found the Cathedral easily because it was, well, as a Cathedral should be and thus not surprisingly quite impressive and decidedly larger than All Saints. Although the foundation stone was not laid until 1901 the design for the Cathedral by John Loughborough Pearson dated back to the late 1880's and was in the Gothic Revival style so loved by Victorians of the time. My guess is that when the town worthies were looking for builders erect the Cathedral they had been unable to find any Polish workers and had opted instead for Brits because over 100 years later this place is still not finished, although the totally uninformative guide told me that this would soon happen. I may have been mistaken to have asked this person because she had no badge on and when I left the Cathedral I had a nagging feeling that she was not the guide at all but some other visitor and that I had probably interrupted her in mid meditation. On reflection later the lack of badge was a big clue because as I had become accustomed to anyone who is involved in some form of tourist activity has a badge with their name writ large and usually the word 'Volunteer'. By now I was tired and so didn't stay that long and as there was little to get excited about from an historical perspective, I waved bye-bye to the non guide lady who looked back at me with a quizzical look that suggested she thought I have might been on a day pass from the local 'institution', signed the visitors book ('Very enjoyable, lovely. Will recommend Anglicanism, lots of love O.B Laden') and returned to Ann Street.

By now it was early evening and the shadows on the ground had a message to give which was that it was beer o'clock. It was time to sample some wobble juice, have a shower, change and then go to the casino. Or as actually happened find a Japanese restaurant, eat some delicious tempura and then go back to my room and the company of the cinema screen in front of the bed. Before I turned the lights out and thus saved the world from further global warming (why do all hotel rooms seem to have more lights in them than your own home?) I came across a story about the Brisbane Zombie Walk in aid of the Brain Foundation which looks to raise money for those with neurological problems, now in its fourth year. The idea of the zombie walk or as was then billed, 'zombie parade', had originated in California in 2001 as a bit of fun for fun's sake. By 2005 it had appeared in many other cities around the world, including Brisbane, gaining more and more participants. In 2009 the city hosted the largest ever recorded zombie walk with over 5,000 people lurching through the streets (walking sensibly is not permitted), many no doubt worse for wear. I turned the lights off and pondered for a while at the thought of seeing the strippers as zombies as was the case in 2009 and whether that was a legitimate fantasy or one that bordered slightly on the perverted. Tomorrow was another day in the car and this time I was off to visit an Australian friend who had worked in the UK and recently returned home and who lived in Pimpama which was just south of Brisbane. Zombies for brain disease – brilliant and so ironic!

CHAPTER 11

*I retreat into the rainforest in the mountains,
become a hippy for a day and end up
with some more convicts.*

DAY thirty two: December 5th

The day was another hot one, clear blue skies and a phone bill just short of the UK's GDP due to my use of the telephone in my room. I had assumed, not unreasonably, that if I used the hotel phone rather than my mobile to call Pimpama just a mere 50 kilometres or so south of the city and in the State of Queensland that it would be a 'local' call at local rates and thus cheaper. I'll know better next time because from what I could work out local meant the room next to mine. When I had finished expressing my displeasure at the bill by showing my 'angry face' whereby eyebrows are furrowed, there is a downturn at the sides of my mouth and a small amount of harrumphing emanating from deep within, the check-out clerk just grinned back with a vacant look that suggested very clearly she didn't care. She wasn't Australian so that may also have been a reason and according to her name badge, replete with Polish flag, was called Anna Mzcwaleskiachieskzy or something equally unpronounceable. So my mood was a little black to say the least and I was not a happy bunny when I got in my car which immediately got worse when the recycled sardine can I'd hired emitted an ominous rattle from its engine as soon as I turned on the ignition.

As with the other cities I had visited, Brisbane is plagued by a number of toll roads but luckily the Central Business District where my hotel was located was close to the toll-free South East Freeway that becomes the Pacific Motorway and so it was a quick drive from the city down to the turn off for Pimpama, at which point it then went completely wrong for me but a source of amusement for the gentlemen and ladies at the single shop come pub come petrol station on the Pimpama Jacobs Well Road as I drove back and forth trying to find the road that led to my friend's house; and no I did not stop to ask for directions because that would be just plain stupid and would mean admitting that I am weak and feeble. Eventually I managed to locate the correct road and sped on my way arriving shortly after in Pimpama which is set back from the main highway and is, in a word, pretty, surrounded as it is by beautiful countryside with a very pleasant village-feel about it. Pimpama is known in one of the local Aboriginal dialects as 'the place of the peewee' derived as it is from the word Peempeema and in another as the 'place of the soldier bird' from the word 'Bimbinbah' which has a nice romantic ring to it. The town was in the 19th century seen as one of the up and coming areas following the establishment of the Cobb and Co. Coach Company which terminated there before the road south was completed. The company was established by four Americans, Freeman Cobb, John Peck, James Swanton and John Lambert in 1854 initially to provide a service for the new gold fields but then as travel became more widespread and roads appeared, so the service expanded under a new owner, James Rutherford who was also American. Its last coach was in 1929 just before the Great Depression, however by now not only had they started using motorised transport but Pimpama itself had become what it essentially is today, a quiet community due to the construction of the highway. I bet those people watching me drive past for the fifth time didn't know all this, so I'm not so stupid am I?

Nick's house and garden were stunningly beautiful and, with the former set into the side of a small hill. As I drove up the steep drive the only thing to spoil the ambience was Nick's prized possession in the vehicular department, no less than a boy's muscle car, namely a V8 Holden (which could make him a bogan, of which more later). It was his pride and joy and I suppose I shouldn't have been quite so dismissive but, as I said to him as I got out my heap of metallic indifference "Nick mate" (note the use of the Australian familial greeting) "You're nearly 35 … " at which point I realised two things: 1) I immediately showed my age by saying this and 2) I was clearly the dullest human being on earth. We went into the house and I just said "Wow!" From the sun deck at the front of the house the views were magnificent with on the left in the distance Southern Moreton Bay Islands National Park, whilst to the right looking like something from a Sci-Fi movie were the skyscrapers of Surfer's

Paradise. At the back in the garden Nick had built a deck that was the perfect place for those sundowners save one thing, the probability that there were brown snakes and other nasties that might want to join one for a gin and tonic. Nick is another example of that almost stereotypical Australian who is so laid back, is so chilled to the point of almost being frozen and to boot a thoroughly decent bloke to hang around with. This is a man who takes each day as it comes and, to me at least, has got it right. It is a character trait which I had already identified as being very Australian and had been a feature of my trip so far. I did try to work out why there are so many who fall into this category not so much by asking (because then the answer would have been "no worries") but by looking at what was around me. Yes in a couple of places property was expensive but on the whole prices were much less than I'd have paid in the UK with the same specification. Then there was the fact that the pace of life just seemed slower but not in a backwoodsman way but more because there really was no hurry. I'd experienced the roads and, excepting getting out of Melbourne, traffic that was almost non-existent such that getting from A-Z was far less hassle and on top of that the scenery is breath-taking almost everywhere. Then there was the weather which afforded much more opportunity so it seemed to me, to get those endorphins jumping. So far I had not met one Australian who was unhappy with their life; they may have been bored but they weren't unhappy. I asked Nick's fiancée who was English and had moved here what she thought of the country and there was no doubt as to what she preferred, "Nick or no Nick". Okay she didn't say the last thing but that although she missed friends and family, Australia was for her. And why did she feel this? Ultimately it was for her that this was a country where most people could enjoy life to the full to the point that it was hard almost not to. I immediately empathised with what she said because not only had I seen this for myself first hand but I was seriously considering changing my name to Bruce and adopting a horizontal position as I too became more laid back and less stressed.

My Australian contacts in London had all, with no exception, expressed a desire to go back to Oz at some stage in the future 'for the lifestyle'. In May 2009, the Australian Bureau of Statistics published its National Health Survey that interviewed over 20,000 Australians on their state of being and health and the outcome was that the majority were both happy and that they felt in reasonable shape. In July 2010 AMP.NATSEM released a report 'The pursuit of happiness, Life satisfaction in Australia' in which it surveyed how people felt about life, love and their financial well being and its conclusion was that Australians were amongst the most happiest people in the world (the report does highlight some issues and not everyone is satisfied but the message was clear that on balance things weren't too bad).

After a quick coke Nick, his fiancée and I hopped into my car and headed to Southport for lunch at the local yacht club, leaving the dog behind to guard the house which was alright because he (the dog) was apparently still happy following his visit to Santa the previous day. To get to our destination meant going into Surfers Paradise. It is everything that I don't like and a much bigger version of Noosa but with an even bigger and greedier eye to the mass market. It was a high rise horror story. The Southport Yacht Club was on the other hand very pleasant and although I have never been in a yacht club in the UK I bet they wouldn't have allowed us in given that we were all three in shorts and T-shirts.

After I deposited them back at their house I then had quite a drive ahead of me to get to my night's destination which was O'Reilly's Rainforest Retreat situated in the heart of the Lamington National Park. Looking at the map the route from Pimpama looked a doddle and would take me into the Darlington Range and thence to O'Reilly's. I drove along deserted roads and through yet more spectacular scenery, turned off the main road at Coomera and then followed the road to Maudsland, which skirts the Nerang State Forest, before joining the Beaudesert Nerang Road that took me to Canungra, all the while climbing into the Darlington Range. By now the sun was fighting a losing battle with some very angry black clouds which gave the feeling of foreboding as I drove into the forested hills. The last part of the drive was spectacular but incredibly draining as the Lamington National Park Road wound up and up towards the Green Mountains and O'Reilly's, itself sitting in the McPherson Range. The last eight kilometres or so was absolutely incredible as I entered the rainforest itself along a single track road (this was the route of the original Stockyard Creek Track) where even if it hadn't been ominously overcast, it would have been dark, very dark. By the time I arrived the sky was beginning to spark and lightening had lit up parts of the sky so I quickly made my way to the bar area where I could sup a beer and get a glorious view of the park. Behind me the sky continued to be filled with lightening which came to earth in the distance; in front of me the sun had already set but the sky was a brilliant red and orange as if on fire, a sharp contrast to the rain leaden clouds behind. Sitting on the balcony, beer in one hand and camera in the other and with only four other people sharing this with me it was, in a word, magic.

I had missed 'happy hour' but that didn't matter as I was too knackered to drink much and following a light dinner (chips came with everything, including the chips) I went into the room that had a books, photos and newspaper cuttings that covered the history of the retreat. It was founded in 1911 by the O'Reilly family who back then were looking for land to become dairy farmers. By 1914 there was a track that allowed easier access to the land that the O'Reilly's occupied and it was around this time that the first tourists started to arrive, which in turn started the family's interest in what today is the Retreat, although the building of the guesthouse and accommodation was not until the 1920's, with an official opening in 1926. For the first tourists a visit was no mean feat and was certainly not for the faint-hearted as it took two days and it wasn't until the 1930's that a road appeared, but even then it was not all the way to the Retreat. The first visitors had been a hardy bunch but in fact the Retreat had no mains electricity until 1967 and no radio-phone until 1978. Today it has a luxury spa and all the amenities the modern day pampered tourist loves. And it is set in some of the most beautiful countryside I have ever seen, as I was to discover tomorrow.

The O'Reilly's were real adventurers, Australian adventurers of the top variety. One of their most famous entries in Queensland history was when Bernard O'Reilly led a team to try to find and then hopefully rescue the survivors of a Stinson plane that had disappeared somewhere in the bush in 1937. Although Bernard O'Reilly did not know about the crash for at least a week after it had occurred it was through him that two survivors were found and eventually brought out alive. The story was one of real heroics by all involved and the sheer logistics of achieving the rescue is a story that I believe is a key to Australians today: that of never giving up even when it looks like the most sensible thing to do.

Day thirty three: December 6th

Having arrived in the dark it wasn't until the following day that I got a real taste of the place. I had been woken up earlier than I would have liked by the loud noise of someone's radio blaring out that "It was going to be another great day" which given where I was, was somewhat unwelcome as it drowned out any noise that Mother Nature might be conducting through the plethora of birds that are native to the forests. I hope whoever it was goes deaf. O'Reilly's is not just remote but is also bang slap in the middle of the national park which is another world heritage site. I was beginning to lose count of the number of places that I'd been that were world heritage sites (I believe there are about thirty in all) in Australia but each time I was at one they just blew my mind for their sheer beauty. O'Reilly's had gone 'modern' in as much as it had moved into the 21st century with its amenities, a far cry from its origins. Here in the forest canopy I could do some shopping, enjoy the cafe/restaurant, stay in one of the lodges or hotel rooms or, and I loved this, partake of a luxury spa which of course is essential when communing with nature. I ate breakfast whilst sitting outside the O'Reilly's Mountain Cafe and Minimart next door to the O'Reilly's Mountain Gifts (there was a theme here I think), getting one of the best views I have had in a long time of the mountains covered in rich green forest and a sky devoid of clouds. I was in paradise yet again. Even better, and helping me with this experience was the almost total lack of human life, aside from the staff who all looked quite bored, or slightly hung-over as they were well into their beers when I'd turned up in the bar the night before. Back in London it was raining, miserable and the trains were running late. Good.

After finishing an exciting muesli, yoghurt and orange juice breakfast (a bargain at the equivalent cost of a new Series 3 BMW) I wondered back to the main lobby area and looked for something to do bearing in mind that I had to be gone by midday if I wanted to get to my next destination, Byron Bay, in good time. I'd pondered the previous evening doing the 'Morning Bird Walk' but had decided against it given that it started at stupid o'clock in the morning and may have been better called 'Wake the Birds Walk'. Given that the Retreat had daily programmes I was not short of what to do so decided that the less than strenuous sounding 'Rainforest Bird Walk' was the one for me. I turned up at the duly appointed hour and waited for my other naturalists to appear. I was alone. Just me and my guide, Dave who I found out had grown up around Walhalla and in his youth as he told me had been "a bit wild". The tour which was tabled to last an hour would be a somewhat personalised experience where Dave and I would cut a path through the rainforest fighting off tigers, lions and other animals that don't exist in the wild in Australia. The alternative was to follow the path that would take us through the rainforest with its many species of trees, bush, reptiles and birds that lived there. All jolly exciting and worth a shot.

Off we went and immediately things got interesting. There in the sun, bathing in the heat and curled up was a mullet. I was almost overcome with excitement. Here in the rainforest at O'Reilly's they had wild mullets, real wild mullets. Fantastic! Actually although it was a mullet it was not one attached to some bloke with tattoos and a girlfriend called Charlene, but rather a member of the skink family, the *egernia major*. I asked Dave why it was called a mullet, given that outside the human wearer I thought that they were fish and here we were 935 metres above sea level. Apparently, so Dave told me, a mullet is a bit smelly and when rattled emits a rather fishy odour although today I am pleased to report that Bob wasn't (I named him just for the fun of it). We moved on, all the while Dave pointing out different trees, birds (there are over 230 species in the park) like the fairy wren, thrush, robin and lots of others that had I been a member of the Young Ornithologist Club whilst at school would have remembered. Dave also pointed out which bird made which noise including the very aptly named whipbird, so-called because the male sends out a noise akin to a whip to be answered by the female sending out, wait for it, a noise akin to a whip. The noise, Dave told me, is a love duet. Anything with whips is probably more than my cloistered love life could take, but if the birds want to, well let them I say! We carried on until we reached a very weird site, the nest of the male bower bird. The female bird is quite promiscuous and will have her wicked way with any male and so the latter builds his nest, or bower, to make him look more attractive, filling it with everything from bits of plastic through to straws. The bower bird that built the one we were looking at had a strong liking for blue as everything was of that colour to make the nest even more attractive as if to say "look at me babe, I've got it all". To me it's a little like buying a red Ferrari when you have a small appendage (if you get the drift) and trying to pretend that it's bigger in order to attract some dippy female who has the IQ of "how much did you say you were worth", also known in the UK as a WAG.

As we came to the end of the tour I was interested to know a little more about why Dave worked here and what it was like living in the middle of nowhere.

"I've always liked working outdoors and even when I was in my wilder days I still loved being out of the city. I've worked in a load of other places, but here I feel it's a bit more special and I don't just mean the history of the place. There's a real sense of nature here that I like. It's also quiet even when the tourist season is in full swing. It's not that it isn't busy or anything but there seems to be less of a rush and more of a hum of contentment. Yeah, I think that's it, people come here stressed out and in a flash they relax. Why wouldn't you?"

"But isn't it a little claustrophobic here. You live, eat, breathe the place and in the evenings what do you do?"

"That's a fair point. You've got to be pretty sure that you prefer the quieter side of life here. I don't watch TV and read a lot so for me it's not really an issue. I've been here just over a year and am one of the longest member's of staff. There's a lot of cabin fever up here."

"How do you stick it?"

"Sometimes it's not that easy especially if the weather closes in, but at the end of the day it comes down to your expectations. I'm happy at the moment and haven't any intentions of leaving just yet, but who knows. What I will tell you is that if I do leave it would be to do the same thing again somewhere else."

I was only there for a night and the morning and so couldn't really get the 'feel' of the place as such, but I did notice that most of the staff there were young and more than one was on a work visa. But even if there was a sense of cabin fever it didn't come across in the bar the night before, the lobby today or even the shop; everyone had a smile on their face and were all very pleasant. Maybe it was the sun, or maybe they were just 'doing a job' in a part of the world that is staggeringly beautiful and that this was reflected in their demeanour. If I'd planned things a little better I would have liked to have stayed longer just to take in more of the atmosphere and also because I wanted to see if the bower bird managed to get laid. Before I left I watched a young Australian family complete with grandparents standing under a tree with king parrots happily feeding off their hands, perching on their arms and in one case, taking a rather large crap down dad's back. Up until that point it had been a rather nice image.

I was back on the road again, but before I left the area altogether I took Dave's advice and stopped to walk along the Python Rock Track, a 3.1 kilometre round trip as the sign told me when I arrived. The walk was mostly under the canopy of the rainforest full of trees of every type of which I now recognised just two, eucalypts and blackbutts. Still a few weeks earlier and I wouldn't have even recognised these so from small steps and so on. As I walked on, keeping an eye out for any of those nasties that might be lurking in the bush ready to pounce on me, I was again blasted by a cacophony of noise from the birds of the forest as well as my friends the cicadas. I got to the viewing platform remembering the stern advice on the Lamington National Park website: 'Please stay behind the barriers; crossing the barriers not only damages the fragile plants but could lead to a potentially fatal fall.' There are a couple things I like about this dire warning. The first is that the plants come first and the second is that they warn you not to climb over these barriers assuming that without this warning you would think it perfectly okay to venture over them even though it is an almost sheer drop of at least four thousand kilometres to the bottom of Moran's Gorge. It reminded me a little of the bag of peanuts that I bought a few days before that had the following caution on it: 'not suitable for nut allergy sufferers'. Who thinks these things up? After an uneventful walk during which I passed just six other people, a positive rush hour of humans, I reached the lookout. It was, in a word, breathtaking and not because I was puffed out. From where I was there was a magnificent view of Moran's Falls right next to O'Reilly's Mountain Retreat which was surrounded by the rainforest and to my right just more rainforest stretching endlessly into the horizon. I was slightly disappointed not to have seen a python but I think my chanting "handbag" probably kept them at bay. It was time now to get back in my car and head to Byron Bay and 'hippyland'. The drive back down was slightly easier partly because this time I knew what to expect and partly because it was light so I could see if there were nay hidden obstacles. All the way down the hairpin road were views that just defy description, suffice to say that 'magnificent', beautiful', dead wombat better avoid that, all came into my mind. Once I'd rejoined the main road there was little to really get excited about because by now unless it was really spectacular I was becoming noticeably blasé about what I was seeing. There was a brief bit of excitement when I drove through the sweet smelling smoke of a bushfire that had party obscured the road, but that was it. However, I was now back in New South Wales and as such a new time zone (however as a recommendation do not try to adjust your watch whilst driving) and now into the final leg of my adventure.

Byron Bay was first chartered by Captain Cook in 1770 and named after Vice Admiral John Byron who led a world tour (t-shirts and other souvenirs of this are available in all good stores and his next gig is at the O2 in London) in 1764–1766 aboard HMS Dolphin. The Aboriginal people might however disagree having lived here a tad longer than the white man. This part of Australia was home to the Bundjalung people (also spelt Bunjalong) and the tribes that lived here were the Minjangbal and Arakwal so they must have been pleased as punch to know that this area was not Cavvanba, or 'gathering place', as they called it, but Byron Bay. How silly of them not to know that; next they'll say that they were here first, as if. Cook was as we already know a man not short on descriptive words about what he saw, and one of the mounts that look over the bay he named Mount Warning, or as the Aboriginals called it Wollumbin or 'cloud catcher', given that the sea around is slightly treacherous to shipping with all the reefs and so being a Yorkshireman he used the most appropriate means to describe this to other mariners. Today, if our dear health and safety executive had their way then they probably would have named the mountain 'Mount Oh do be careful you might hurt yourself' and they would have banned all ships from the area, put a sign up saying that 'drowning is not permitted in this area without prior approval' and told everyone to dress up in bubble wrap.

I arrived mid afternoon and having crossed the railway tracks, entered the main street of the town and hippydom. This was a town that had definitely done a good job in reinventing itself from a grimy little industrial nowhere into something that was a bustling and thriving tourist hot spot which was described by Daniel Ducrou in his entertaining novel 'Byron Bay Journals' as:

> ' ... a joint passed between seven nations slouched around a living room. You are a flesh-lease on a beautiful beach, a lazy congregation of sun-worshippers basking in the mindless heat ... '

So that's what I should expect was it, along with the sex, drugs and all manifestations of human kind that he goes on to describe. Excellent as this was to be home for the next day and a half and I was looking forward to breaking out the caftan, shades, flip flops (sorry thongs), the head band and the psychedelic shirts and going round saying "Peace, man" to everybody. Now I know what you're probably thinking as you read this and yes you are correct. The problem with all this hippydom of course is that ultimately one has to be: a) stoned and/or b) in touch with one's inner self (and here that does not include playing with yourself). I was neither and the nearest that I can come to in terms of being 'with it' is when I let my hair grow slightly long so that it just touches the top of my shirt collar. I am not a stiff, far from it, but funky just isn't me. Never mind I was determined not to let this minor issue mar my stay. I was going to go native. Dude, I was going to chill out and become one with nature.

I parked 'the car', checked in and prepared myself for what the town could do for me. But first I had to walk to the iconic lighthouse in the scorching heat, with a hat on that didn't really let the air get to my head thus exacerbating how hot I felt and with clothing that would not have looked out of place in an old people's home, so as you can already deduce I stuck out like a sore thumb. As Noel Coward so eloquently put it ' ... mad dogs and Englishmen go out in the midday sun ... ' The walk to the lighthouse was going to be "a quick half hour", so I was told by the helpful lady behind the desk at the hotel and not too strenuous. By now you would have thought that I had worked out that an Australian half hour is not specific and can mean anything from the actual time to days and that their definition of not strenuous, as with Magnetic Island, is really a euphemism for 'take a survival kit as you're going to need it'. On the way I detoured onto the beach and climbed a large promontory that means I can now claim that I have been to the most eastern point in Australia. I fought my way off the beach through all the really ugly people with their fake tans and pretend bodies and resumed my walk to the lighthouse. By the time I arrived having walked for what seemed an eternity up hill, dripping with sweat, a good hour and half had elapsed but the sight that greeted me was well worth it. Standing tall overlooking the bay the lighthouse was a magnificent white, gleaming brightly in the sun, rising up from the fortress like structure that surrounded it, a feature that was really superfluous in terms of usefulness but suggested grandeur in keeping with the structure itself and the pride of all those dignitaries who attended the opening back in 1901. From this vantage point I could see as far as Brunswick Heads to the north, which was under a blanket of cloud providing another great contrast in weather, whilst to the south in the far distance was Ballina. Turning around with the sea behind me, I looked at Byron Bay itself, or at least that part of the town that was located in the thick wooded area and I've no doubt cost a fair few dollars to live in. As a good tourist I needed a photo of myself with the lighthouse behind me, but having as yet not mastered the art of the self-timer, I did the 'arms length shot' that always makes the sitter look more freaky than they would normally. Unfortunately in order to do this I had to get in the way of two German students (they looked young) who had arrived after I had started the process of taking my photo and had rather brusquely told me to get out of the way. I was surprised they didn't just put a towel on the lighthouse to reserve it for later whilst they went about annoying other people. Having upset Anglo-German relations I decided that rather than go back the same way I would venture towards the Captain Cook Lookout because, as I had been told by the that same very helpful lady back at my hotel the "views are really great". I should have known better. Either I completely missed the lookout or the views that "are really great" consisted of a lot of trees which blocked any potential vista. On the plus side it was downhill and completely devoid of any other living soul so I was able to enjoy an awful lot of trees and bush all on my own with the noise of a light breeze whistling (does a light breeze whistle? No matter.) in the canopy accompanied by the odd bird chirruping away and, I could have sworn, the tell-tell sound of a hiss which was either a snake or my shoes had been punctured.

Although the town itself, originally named Cavanbah until 1894, was not officially gazetted until the latter part of the 19th century, it was nevertheless by the 1840's a hive of industry which by the 1860's and 1870's included logging through to sugar cane. By the beginning of the last century dairy farming had also become big business and in the town itself there was a factory producing tonnes of butter and even during the Great Depression the meat industry survived and was actively recruiting. The town's history and that of the surrounding area was all about industry. The old black and white pictures of that time tell a story of hard work and toughness. There were no backpackers, six pack surfers or pony-tailed men with serious mid life crises. In those early days it was all about getting one's hands dirty as opposed today where the only dirt was going to be from applying body paint to a mate because apparently that's what went on here. By the 1970's the town had reinvented itself mainly as a result of the 1973 Aquarius Festival:

'Students and hippies flocked to the area for the festival ... and many just never left. Two decades of new settlers and alternative lifestyles began to repopulate the area ... '

However, it's the last sentence in this mini-history of the town that reinforces this image of a sort of laid back hippy-like culture:

' ... roll with the punches, roll in the hills, roll in the hay, roll with the waves or roll a joint.'

That evening I ate in and just vegetated in front of the television hoping against hope that the film I'd fancied watching would start on time. No chance, so off to bed and look forward to the new dawn, man.

Day thirty four: December 7th

Up with the larks and raring to go this morning and I was determined not to do anything that might affect my karma, man. You see, by now I was really into the swing of things and was, like, well cool. So I went for a run to the lighthouse and back dressed suitably for the 90 degree heat (rugby shorts and shirt) and in the process lost about nine stone. I did get some slightly weird looks from people as I trotted past them but apart from that felt good for having managed to achieve in forty minutes what had taken an age the day before. Changed again I was ready to have a proper look around and get a deeper feel of exactly what makes Byron Bay so popular and also why it has managed to stop becoming just another beach resort as has happened to so many other places along the Gold Coast. My first venture was to go right out of the hotel and away from the main drag past streets named after famous authors, Kingsley, Tennyson, Carlyle and McGuire. The last one is pending. What immediately struck me was that this was all very middle class with neat houses and gardens and little to suggest that anyone who might economically be struggling was living here. There was a mixture of housing but all of it was tidy and well ordered, almost as if the image that Byron Bay was the capital city of hippydom was actually a smokescreen to reality. I came across a huge grocer's shop that was housed in what appeared to be a large barn and was struck by how expensive everything was even by Aussie standards and how so much was organic. This was home to the well known creature that inhabits all cities and big towns, the 'Right on liberal' who invariably has two kids with preposterous names, advocates that everyone should recycle ("It's like the world is overheating don't you know; we have to like save the environment"), always votes in a box that says 'Anything but the Conservatives' ("The left really cares") and drives a 4x4 each weekend into the countryside because they are really total hypocrites. This shop was not catering for the hippy, this was catering for those with money who wanted to feel that by shopping here they were somehow putting something back in to the community whilst at the same time cocking a snoop at the large conglomerate supermarkets. Or it could have been because it was the local store and therefore more convenient than walking into the main part of town.

I headed back along the main drag of Jonson Street and passed all manner of shops from the brand names through to those with a more local feel. Dotted in between these were eateries catering for a less expensive pallet, all overflowing with youth. I stopped at one such place for lunch and felt conspicuously out of place and horribly old, not least as I had to change glasses to read the menu. I almost felt like saying: "I'll have the steak sandwich please, but can you liquidise it as I can't chew food anymore."

I half expected to have a youth like creature approach me to see if I wanted any assistance getting back to 'the home' and would I like it if he/she called Matron to say they'd found me. Jonson Street catered for all tastes, none of which were mine really. I didn't need any expensive jewellery, I don't smoke weed so no need for a bong, I don't surf, I had no need for antiques, didn't fancy clothing made from bamboo (a free panda with each purchase) and was getting an image in my mind as to what Byron Bay really was . Sure there were lots of people wearing clothing that was straight out of the heyday of the hippy movement. Sure there was a lot of skin on show and sure the atmosphere was very relaxed, but I didn't feel that this was hippydom. I'm no expert but when a shirt can cost 100 dollars it isn't the hippy they're looking to sell to, even the bongs, sorry cigarette holders, would have set me back a fair amount. The descriptions that some of these shops had in the Byron Bay Shopping Guide were, to me at least, a good indication of this more demographically upmarket attitude:

' … fashion business … using organically dyed bamboo fabric … '
' … our contemporary hampers are packed full of Byron Bay's finest quality gourmet foods … '
' … multi level carved glass from crystal to architectural … '
' … aims to bring you the best in eco friendly and organic products … '

Although this wasn't Noosa it certainly wasn't afraid of being pretentious either and as with 'bling town' so too here when it came down to the cost of buying a property because in Byron Bay in 2009 this was over twice that of the surrounding area. As in Noosa this in part reflected the fact that the residents of the town remain fiercely protective of where they live and have fought new development citing the environmental impact of building new houses (for example sewage and water) on the area. In 1973 the call was much more egalitarian and this was attractive to those whose lifestyle was perhaps more hedonistic. They're still there but in Byron Bay felt very middle class and is host these days to such events as the East Coast Blues and Roots Festival as well as Byron Bay Writers Festival. Many of the youngsters I saw (blond, well tanned and pretty darn sexy … and the women were quite nice too) looked like they came from wealthier families with their designer boards and swimwear.

I decided though that I needed retail therapy and that I should buy something that was more in keeping with Australia's past rather than its present. That could only mean one thing: something indigenous and that linked to the story of Dreamtime. As if by magic, or actually because I'd bothered to ask for one, I found a shop solely dedicated to selling Aboriginal arts and crafts. These shops can be quite tacky in that most of the stuff on display is invariably mass produced or is really too touristy and with little or no meaning to the people that it represents. Although the shop had some touristy things it was all quite tasteful with some pleasant ambient music playing quietly in the background and better still I was the only person in there and so with my 'Nosey Bugger' hat on I launched into some detailed and very searching questions.

"What are these stones meant to mean and who painted them?" I asked pointing to some painted stones which were in a basket.

"Local artists from around here did all of them and they're all hand painted and each one is unique and they relate to how those who paint them see the world through picture. All of these are images from the Dreamtime. This one here was painted by a guy whose name is Magpie and that one was painted by Scott Rotumah."

"Do they get paid much for this?"

"They get at least 50% of the profit we make."

"Do you see all this as being commercialisation of their history and culture?"

"Some might say that, but look you go to any museum today and there's always a souvenir shop that sells replicas of what you've just seen usually having been made in China. These stones, and a lot of what's in here, were crafted one by one. This is all about their heart and soul, what their culture is, the Dreamtime and the legends. It's important not just to them but also to the rest of us to learn more about who they are and what they see around them".

"Some have called this sort of thing as misguided charity ... " I was trying to avoid crossing the line between asking some rudimentary questions to some that were perhaps more insensitive. But Bill (name badge again!) responded without any anger in his tone:

> "That's true, but I don't see it as charity. This is about making sure we become more aware of what we are as a nation in Australia and of what that all means. This is one way to achieve it and the more people like you ask, the more we can get the message across."

He handed me some printed paper on which the two artists described why they do what they do. And it did as I read them in my hotel later that night. Magpie comes from the Bundjalung/Gugu-Yalanji whilst Scott comes from the Bundjalung. Both of them describe why they paint and it is very powerful stuff. Magpie's inspiration came from the ancestors. As I read this I noted that he didn't say 'his'. The more I read about

Dreamtime, the more I began to understand (I hope) that it was less about the individual per se, save the great spirits and more about the world in which a person lives and what they then take from it. We are just a part of it and not important as individuals. For Magpie the stories he has painted have come from the elders as he explained:

> 'My art style has come about through the power of word, singing and storytelling … I like to think that I look at life through my past uncles eyes … they have never really left; they remain with me in spirit.'

Scott's description was in a similar vein:

> 'My artistic inspiration comes from my younger brother who passed on his knowledge handed down to him from an elder from Western Australia. The traditional way in our culture – from generation to generation.'

I purchased some stones and as I went back in the street continued to think about what Bill had said. Looking back today to that conversation he was absolutely right that what he was doing and what this shop was providing was a good way to preserve a culture and to get people to take an interest in their own past and even if there is no direct link there is always one indirectly. I almost felt like greeting the next person with a "Jingi Wala", or "G'day" in the Bundjalung language, but I fear my pronunciation might have sounded more like "Ginga Wally" and that could have led to trouble. It was time to literally cross the tracks and see what was on the opposite side of town, away from the middle class shops and houses and where I had assumed would be much more of a down to earth part of town.

Once over the tracks everything changed and once more I had arrived in a different world. It was if I'd stepped across a time portal. There were no shops. There were no cafes or restaurants. In fact there wasn't a soul to be seen. It was a little eerie and I was alone with just some vocal birds and the wind which noisily blew through the pines that were all encircling a huge park. This park was clearly used for something as I could see markings all over it, suggesting that at some point in the year a market was held here. In the middle was a cricket square, although this was well passed its 'use by' date and I doubt very much that any game had been played here for quite some while. The houses that backed onto the field were still more akin to what I had walked past the day before in the main part of town, but somehow here they seemed lifeless. There was no buzz in the air, no atmosphere, nothing. It wasn't unpleasant as such and each house had a neat lawn and there were shrubs and flowers that would have been nice in any garden back home. It was just such an incredible contrast to the other side of the tracks in every sense. This part of Byron Bay was the bit that doesn't appear in holiday brochures because there was nothing here. I wondered if maybe this was the part of town that the older residents of Byron lived, having survived the rush of money much more apparent on the other side but as there wasn't anyone about I couldn't ask. Anyway it might have been slightly impolite in retrospect if I had found an old biddy and by asking them why they lived here and not where the money was it might imply they were a) poor or b) slightly lower down the social ladder. Best left alone I think.

However, Byron Bay did have a certain magic and charm to it on both sides of the tracks. It wasn't like Noosa trying to be really upmarket with all those designer labels and only being interested in the right demographic. Wondering around I saw enough internet cafes, organic food shops (although nowadays much more the home of the new middle class), campervans going along Jonson Street and parked up around the playing fields and plenty of backpackers to know that even with all its middle class attitudes someone could still have no money and enjoy the town. I liked it a lot and saw Byron Bay as a midway town that was not really a true hippy paradise but neither was it just suburbia full of coffee mornings and dinner parties. In Noosa I could see money on the people and yes Byron Bay has its fair share but much, much less ostentatious. I really liked it because of this and also because everyone looked happy or maybe they really were all stoned, but you know what, I thought "Good for them". In an article penned for the Times in 2003 under the wonderful title 'The hippie beach that chichi' by Rory McLean he talked about Byron Bay and summed it up:

> 'The Aussie kingdom come is Byron Bay, surfing mecca and "cashed-up" baby-boomer utopia, green heartland and honeymooners' hideaway; a hedonistic haven where the sun shines, the wide blue Pacific is always warm ... .cast a spell over me ...

instead of ranks of concrete towers, Byron has small, exclusive hotels and restaurants, neatly arranged among its pastel-shaded, tin-roofed bungalows … '

That evening I decided not to go out, eating my wonderful meal of burnt something accompanied by the best wine Australia could offer at less than twenty dollars, sitting on my balcony overlooking the old railway line that ran for 110 years finally closing in May 2004. I closed my eyes for a few moments in the silence (by now the cicadas were just a hum, a mere backing track to the world around me). The sun set through the trees opposite and for one instance I was transported to another time, when steam engines went back and forth transporting their goods from the jetty to the hinterland beyond; butter, whale meat and pork. The railway was built to accommodate the growth of industry in the town and was built relatively quickly and when it went 'live' was celebrated in true Australian style with lots of meat and beer, this was real history and I was getting mildly merry thinking about it.

As the evening air began to fill with biting bugs I went back inside, slightly worse for wear, and turned on the TV, bleary-eyed but content and although I remember little I was able to scribble in my notebook two words: fly spray. Why you are probably asking? Is it something that will have worldwide ramifications? Have I, James M McGuire solved that problem of the pestilent fly? Actually, none of these and it was for a much more mundane reason. As I sat there on the sofa, beer in hand, mind in neutral I watched an advert that brought me back to the growing realisation that Australians don't really worry too much about the niceties in the field of hygiene. The advert was about how to get rid of flies and started with some kids sitting around the kitchen table, eating lunch with flies acting like Kamikaze dive bombing them. Mum then appears in the kitchen with a fly spray called something like 'Killobastardfly' which she deftly sprays around the room. "Fair enough" I think in my somewhat addled state of mind, "good on yer" ('strine was beginning to become my Lingua Franca) "cheers" I said out loud raising a bottle (serving suggestion on the back for those with a simple mind: 'serve bloody cold') to the inanimate object that was the TV. At which point the little girl to whom mum had said that flies needed to die because of all the germs and diseases they spread, promptly gave the dog a bit of her food. At which point the dog then licked her hand and she then resumed eating her sandwich with her drool laden digits wrapped around her food, brilliant! Whoever wrote the script please let him or her take over health and safety back at home. Which is better to have, a dog that licks its gonads and then licks your hand or a fly that pukes on your food?

As a last point about Byron Bay I recently read that the town had been added to a list of 'No Go Zones' as reported in the Northern Star. This is a list compiled by Terry Ryder, a property analyst who focuses on what he sees as property hotspots and gives advice on which areas to avoid, these so-called 'No Go Zones'. Byron Bay made this list for 2010 for the following reasons: poor capital growth, volatile market and erosion. His view gives more credence to Nick Obaldiston's assertion that places like this are being 'loved to death'.

Day thirty five: December 8th

' ... and every torture was imaginable more was transported to Van Diemand's Land to pine their young lives away in starvation and misery among the tyrants worse than the promised hell itself ... were doomed to Port Macquarie Toweringabbie norfolk island and Emu plains and in those places of tyrany and condemnation many a blooming Irishman rather than subdue to the Saxon yolk Were flogged to death and bravely died in servile chains but true to shamrock and a credit to Paddy's land.' This is another extract from the Jerildrie letter dictated by Ned Kelly to Joe Byrne and mentioned in disparaging terms my next stop. I'd slept quite well last night, Byron Bay may not have gotten me stoned but it had worked its magic and I was in a very good frame of mind when I set off on the long drive to Port Macquarie. I had left quite early as I thought it would be worth a quick detour to a place called Evans Head for two reasons. First in my so far reliable guide of Australia's east coast it had been described as being 'worth a visit if you have time' and secondly because the tourist website 'Visit New South Wales' had painted a picture that spoke, and I quote verbatim, of ' ... an old fashioned beach town surrounded by national parks ... ' This was not to be missed and what's more it was only six kilometres off the Pacific Highway along which I was heading.

Evans Head was different to say the least. I wasn't sure whether the same time machine that had been with me in Byron Bay had once more done its trick. The town, or more like a village, was everything that I might have expected to see in the 1960's. The buildings were all squat two-storey affairs and the shops and cafes which lined the main square contained not one brand name or even a 'cool dude' surfing shop even though there were plenty of beaches to surf hereabouts. I sat down at a cafe and ordered some breakfast and looked at the people that were milling about. I estimated that the average age was north of fifty, and in the cafe where I was sitting, probably nearer seventy. There were no beach bums, no 'bling', no mullets or tattoos (or maybe the wearers of these were on to me and were hiding) and the cars parked in the square made mine look almost luxurious; this was a place that had been left behind by other Gold Coast resorts which was strange in many ways as apparently it was a major tourist destination, with the largest caravan park in New South Wales. And yet it remained unspoilt by commercialism and money. It was such a contrast to everywhere I had been so far, including Cooktown which was not dissimilar in many respects. Had I actually discovered the true Australia which wasn't about big shopping malls, expensive cars and branded clothing but instead was much quieter, even more unhurried and where life was the same today as it had been forty years ago. Maybe this is why so many of the younger generation want to travel before settling down and on coming back to the country tend, according to the demographic studies, live in more metropolitan areas. It was all very twee in some ways and not the least unpleasant. I like quiet and I like places that don't see a need to always change for the sake of change. The only blot to this almost idyllic setting was that nearby were two indigenous people who were, by the looks of their clothing, probably dirt poor. I had a sense of guilt rush through me, feeling that on the one hand I should get up and give them money whilst on the other hand worry that if I did, what would their reaction be? I was also worried that just giving them money when they weren't asking for it might seem patronising. I got up, paid my bill and left without doing anything save reminding myself once more that in Australia many still see that, even with the end to the Aboriginals total exclusion from society, a two tier system still exists. It didn't make me fill better or big, just a little sad.

I ate up and rejoined the road to Port Macquarie which historians believe was first settled by the Kattang Aboriginals. It was a pleasant drive, taking me past the Giant Shrimp, through Grafton, Coffs Harbour (which the previous month had 500mm of rain fall within 48 hours leading to flash flooding and road closures), past the Harbour's Giant Banana, along Bongil Bongil and Yarriabini National Parks and then having driven through Kempsey, into the town itself. As I came into town and neared my hotel I have to say my first reaction was to wonder if it was still a convict colony. The place looked grey and uninviting and was nothing like the other towns and villages that I had visited so far. My mood was not helped by the beginnings of an almighty thunderstorm that sent torrents of rain onto the pavements and roads with lightening flashing and thunder rumbling and made any chance of going out from the hotel on foot very unlikely. However, as I should have known, as quickly as it came, so it went and the sun once more peaked out through the clouds and signalled to me that it was time to get out of the hotel and take a look round. Just over the bridge from my hotel was one of those monstrous buildings that I would humbly suggest had been designed by someone with the aesthetic skills of Attila the Hun after a heavy days pillaging. Even with just a small amount of feeling for the area that person might have done a better job, but no, it was just a nasty huge lump of concrete that added nothing to the history of the town but instead gave it a distinctly run-down look so my initial reaction that I'd arrived at a not altogether attractive destination seemed confirmed. Even the history of the Port made it seem a miserable place even today.

Port Macquarie, named by Oxley in 1818 after Governor Macquarie, was established as another of those penal settlements for recidivist criminals although the first arrivals who came in April 1821, consisted of 60 convicts and 40 soldiers of the 48th Regiment, weren't themselves repeat offenders but were there to establish the settlement after which, if they behaved, they could gain their freedom. The Governor had asked Oxley who had already surveyed the area in 1818 and had noted at the time the lushness of the forest and an abundance of food including giant sharks, whether this location would be viable as a replacement to Newcastle further down the coast. The main reason for this was that the latter was not isolated enough for the type of criminal being sent there. The first landing took place a few minutes walk from where my hotel was located at the top of Clarence Street at what is now called Allman Hill after the first commandant, Captain Francis Allman. Just like Logan later at Brisbane, he too was a hard taskmaster and right up until the town ceased to be a penal settlement, successive commandants continued this harshness towards the convicts. Later in the settlement's life one convict, Thomas Cook, that Hughes quotes, wrote a book about his experiences 'The Exile's Lamentations: Memoirs of Transportation' in which he described one of the commandants as being especially brutal such that:

' ... he would make the Deaf to hear, the Dumb to speak, the lame to walk, the blind to see, and the foolish to understand ... '

Port Macquarie is a tourist destination today and as I set off on a trek around the bay that faced the Hastings River I wondered whether many people who stayed here knew of the hardships faced by the original white settlers let alone the indigenous people. As I walked along the harbour wall, nowadays called the 'Sundowners' Break wall', I noticed that every stone which made up the wall had been painted with various messages and pictures. Most just said who the 'artist' was and why they have visited the town with most done by those on schoolies week. I couldn't work out the oldest of these but it was an interesting contrast to think of those students spraying on their greetings to what those who first arrived here in 1821 cutting back the bush and erecting a stockade without the aid of large quantities of booze might have done. I looked for a stone that might have given me a clue to what these people had felt. Sadly there was none that said 'Having a wonderful time, flogging not too bad; Class of 1812' accompanied with a little smiley face. It did look rather out of place but some of the art on the rocks wasn't too bad and given that history is not static this wall told a story about what Port Macquarie had become today. I wondered who had begun this and what their motivation had been or were they just hoons who'd done some graffiti which had then been 'hijacked' to become a form of modern art by the middle class families and school kids that now came here.

The weather still threatened rain but I carried on regardless and ended up at the first burial ground that was established in 1821 in Port Macquarie which today is identified through a marker and is sited on Allman Hill. The hill was surrounded by holiday flats on three sides and the burial ground had long since gone but even with the holiday flats I felt an air of sadness (the first burial was of an infant girl) and a stillness and thought about the precariousness of life, the high mortality rate amongst infants of those early settlers and why anyone who had a choice would have wanted to come here. But then I thought that this is part of what makes Australia today; the stoicism of the early settlers (free or not), their resolution to build and to make a go of it and the determination to see it through. On then to the next point of interest which was the church of St. Thomas, an imposing red brick erection complete with tower and perched on a rise, and as I found out thanks to a very helpful leaflet, St Thomas' is the fifth oldest church still in use in Australia. As I've already said churches are a fascinating way to look at the past and as an aside this interest led me a few months ago to go into the church of St Mary-Le-Bow in London. This church has a direct link to Australia because there is a memorial to Admiral Arthur Phillip, the very same who led the First Fleet of 1788 and who was born close by (therefore a true Cockney as he was born in earshot of the bow bells!). It's a truism that it's a small world. Inside St Thomas's there was a distinctly musty smell and the decor was basic; there were no arches or expensive stained glass windows but rather a very utilitarian lay-out from that of the pews to the whitewashed one metre thick walls (under threat today from rising damp). The church itself was one of the first structures to be built in the new settlement and was completed in 1828, having taken four years to build and comprised of well over 300,000 bricks, each one with an indentation of a finger or hand of the convict that had made it. There was even a grave in the first pew of Captain Rollands who succumbed to sunstroke before the laying of the foundation stone and thus was literally in the body of the church.

There were a couple of volunteer guides by the door (this time I was in luck as they both had tags on their lapels telling me that they were guides, so no repeat of St. John's in Brisbane) and I approached one of them, Stan, and got chatting about the church and its construction. Built by the convicts it was constructed entirely by hand using local materials from the oyster shells in the mortar which came from the North Shore through to the cedar used in the roofing. Inside all the pews were set in the boxed style of the age, also of red cedar. At one end was the Walker Pipe Organ, made in England by J.W. Walker & Sons, and the only one of its type in the southern hemisphere. It is the smallest organ that they made and it was first played in 1857. I was quite intrigued to note that it only played thirty-three hymns and wondered if it could get a little tiresome after a while to hear 'Onward Christian Soldiers' for the umpteenth time. The church had been built here because at the time the hill it sits on was the highest point in the settlement. I thanked Stan for his time and climbed the bell tower on his suggestion as it afforded an all round view of Port Macquarie. I looked across at the houses and apartment blocks and once more had that sense that here was another place where a lot of the past still remained notable in the style of the buildings many of which I hazarded a guess were from over forty years ago, and of a population that was in no real hurry. As if to reinforce this impression that I'd had, later as I walked around the central area of Port Macquarie there were buildings such as the Art Deco looking Ritz cinema, the slightly dated (maybe jaded would be a better description) looking shops, a few more modern structures and then, wham, I was back to the original part of the town's life, of its convict history from the old Court House (1869) to the Port Macquarie Historical Museum. On the latter two I decided that I needed to look into them further because unlike Brisbane and the RHQS, these two establishments were chock full of information of one of the harsher penal colonies, or so my wonderful guide book assured me.

However, all this could wait until tomorrow as time was drawing on and I needed a beer and also some food, but what? I looked around when at 73 Clarence Street, Port Macquarie 2444, Australia, a sight that made my eyes widen, my heart beat a little faster, and my mouth begin to water, appeared which was none other than The Maharajah curry emporium. As I entered I could have sworn I heard angels singing hallelujahs and the sound of heavenly trumpets but actually it was the usual background music so reminiscent of Indian restaurants consisting of some Bollywood soundtrack, all very pleasant but not quite the divine music I'd imagined. It was heaven to me though as I tucked in to my first curry in weeks, savouring every morsel as it passed by lips into my mouth. I'd ordered heaps, enough to keep an army on the march, but damn it I wanted to gorge and it was delicious! When the waitress came back I enquired about business (the restaurant was empty, aside from me, the waitress and the chef). Given that this was a country in love with crispy fried duck, wonton soup etc, she sighed, then smiled and, I kid you not said: "If only we were Chinese."

Ok she didn't really say that but I know that was what she was thinking as she gave me the bill. Alright so she probably wasn't thinking that either but more likely "That is one fat and greedy Englishman". I finished up, paid and left a contented but saddened man. How can Australians really not be that hot on curry? Take my advice and give it a go at Port Macquarie, Woolgoolga or Laurieton.

Day thirty six: December 9th

Today was going to be another history lesson and given the weather looked less than welcoming I'd planned to do one walk and then stay mainly in museums for the day. First I needed breakfast and today was the day I was planning to try an Australian comestible that has iconic status in the country, no less a delectable than vegemite. I'd decided to do this because it was as Australian as the Kangaroo or Uluru, and not to have done before leaving would have been poor form; when in Rome and all that. Up until now on my trip I had been far too busy seeing which cholesterol laden delight I could force down my stomach to assuage the grumblings therein and to help mop up the previous evening's beer. I needed a change and had read that vegemite was good for a person for a number of reasons not least this delicacy has as its main ingredient beer. So I could have a pint of beer and accompany this with, well, a pint of beer on toast. Top marks to Australia I say! Added to this it is stuffed full of goodness and overflowing with vitamins, especially B. This is getting better and better. Without vegemite who would have known if electronic check-outs worked (in 1984 a jar of the stuff was the first to have this done in Australia). I shall put my order in forthwith. But, alas, as with all good things that sound too good to be true, so it is with vegemite. It is sadly not beer, but the yeast extract from beer that forms the basis of the spread. Not quite the same, really. And what was the upshot of this little experiment? Well you know when you think something is a really good idea and it turns out not to be, well I'm sorry Australia I did try some vegemite but can honestly say that having retched a couple of times as I tried to swallow it, I handed in the towel and ordered my usual heart-stopping concoction safe in the knowledge that if I keel over and die now at least I'll have eaten well. Anyway, as we all know real beer comes in cans or bottles, not in spreads.

I finished breakfast and prepared to go on to my first intended visit which was to be the lighthouse at the south eastern part of town which was called the Tacking Point Lighthouse and had been built in 1879. The promontory that it was built on was so named by Matthew Flinders who had sailed off this part of the coast in 1802 and who'd been getting bored waiting for HMS Lady Nelson to catch him up in his much quicker ship, HMS Investigator, complete with its 'go faster' stripes, that he did some tacking (nope I can't tell you what that means) waiting for her and the name stuck. However, and I am pleased to say fortuitously, having initially intended to walk there I bothered to just check the very helpful town map I had taken from the hotel and soon realised that this would have been a trek of some nine to ten kilometres one way so decided, quite sensibly, not to bother. I'd drive to it another time so looked for something else to do and so my first stop was to be the Historic Court House built in 1869 and in use until 1986 and a short walk from the cafe I was in. This was the only remaining building that was used by the government in Port Macquarie so it was going to be a very interesting visit as in the various leaflets I'd looked at there was history pouring out of every nook and cranny. It was closed. Of course it was, why wouldn't it be, I mean let's face it my record so far of finding places or buildings of interest to visit which were not open had become legend. It was supposed to be open today at least that's what the sign in the window said so maybe it would be later. All was not lost as almost opposite was the Port Macquarie Historical Museum which is housed in one of the oldest structures still in use in the town having been erected by 1840 originally as a shop and house by a free settler. The museum comprised of two buildings. The entrance to the first led me straight into what had been the parlour and where there was a raft of information about the settlement from its earliest days through to more recent times. Once I'd had a quick nose around the old house, which was tiny, I moved to the second building which housed all the exhibits. This took me through a history of not just the port but also some details on the original inhabitants, the Birpai, right through to some exhibits on the sugar cane industry (the first crop was raised in Port Macquarie). As I wondered back into the old house I mentioned to one of the volunteers that I had tried the courthouse but it was closed and did they know when it was going to open.

"I'd heard that one of the volunteers had got the hump about something and was refusing to open the place up. Silly bugger if you ask me" said Brian who was sat taking the money from visitors at the door. As I had Brian's attention I asked about how the convicts were treated here.

"Not much fun here. To start with these guys had already committed at least a second if not a third crime since they'd come to Australia so they were regarded with a lot a disdain by the authorities. These convicts were nasty types mostly and this was no holiday camp. They could get the lash just for having a piece of paper and if they fainted then the doctor who was always present would poke them until they came too and then the lashing could carry on."

"What if the convict had died whilst being lashed?" I asked

"Well this is where the official records and the reality differ. If a convict did die whilst receiving a lashing often as not, to avoid too much paperwork, the doctor or person in charge would put down 'infection'. No need for lengthy paperwork if that was the case."

"Did many die?"

"Quite a few but like I said the exact number is difficult to say."

"What other punishments did they receive aside from lashings?"

"Well there were the chain gangs with each bloke wearing a chain weighing as much as ten pounds. You imagine dragging that round all day, and then getting back to what passed for dinner. Having had maybe a pint of coffee, or something that passed for coffee and a slice of bread for breakfast, with lunch not much better although they did get meat though this was often rancid, they'd then be given more bread and coffee before they were locked up for the night. Life was unpleasant and hard." It was also interesting to learn from him that given that Port Macquarie had been built to replace Newcastle due to its then remoteness, so Brisbane was set up to replace Port Macquarie such that by the 1830's the more hardened criminal tended not to be sent here and free settlers began to arrive.

I thanked Brian and walked back on Clarence Street and followed the map he had provided me with that had some of the historic sites highlighted. Sadly there was little to actually see as I looked around but at least where a shop, office or cafe stood today I would know that is was where the first hotel had stood (New Inn), the Granary where convicts would walk on a treadmill to grind corn (appropriately perhaps today it is a police station), the female factory/prison where nails for use in St. Thomas' construction were made (today it is a Presbyterian Church) or the old Gaol (a hotel today for fee paying customers there voluntarily). One thing that had caught my eye was the Mid North Coast Maritime

Museum which promised to be a Pandora's Box of information about
the first arrivals back in the 1820's. It was a must on my 'list of things
to see, #305'. So down Horton Street once more past Oxley's camp
site of 1819, pass an enormous pelican that was about to eat a small girl
who was approaching it proffering bread (or herself), then via Oxley's
actual landing site toward the museum. It would be very hard to miss and
featured prominently in the Macquarie-Hastings Council website.

It all looked rather small, but never mind I bounded in and went
straight to Eric who was wearing a badge that said 'Eric, Volunteer' and
asked how much. Joy of joys it was free. However, I noticed something
rather quickly in that it was just me and Eric, together in just one room,
and a not altogether big one at that. I then had that horrible feeling I get
when I realise that I have been a complete idiot, because it wasn't the
museum. No. It was instead a single room which had a few details of the
lifeboat crews that had worked the river and sea around the port. That
was it. Short of going up to each photo hanging from the walls for minute
detail, I could see everything I needed by just standing in the entrance,
including some sepia pictures of old Port Macquarie. I felt a complete
bird brain and somewhat at a loss as to what to do. I needed to save
face and give the impression that I knew that this wasn't the museum,
but how? At this point we come once more to the ever constant male
dilemma of when to admit he is wrong and that as a result should perhaps
enquire as to the correct location of such and such a place. No chance of
that of course but all was not lost as Eric broke the silence, sensing my
predicament:

"Were you looking for the museum because if you were it is just up
the street from here; not too long a walk."

I did a double take suddenly wondering where I was. I don't mean
that I didn't know that I was in the wrong 'museum' or that I was in
Port Macquarie, Australia. No it was that Eric spoke with a very broad
Geordie accent which threw me for a moment. Was I in the north east of
England? I gathered myself and asked Eric if he lived here and given the
strength of his accent for how long. His was in interesting story and gave
an insight into what Australia meant to the older generation and, maybe,
was also a guide as to why people today look to come to Australia to live:

"Well I served with the Royal Navy in the Far East during the war and loved the onshore leave we got in Australian ports. It was a big change from home and the drabness. Anyway after the war when I was demobbed in 1949 I came back here and have never looked back. I lived in Papua New Guinea for a while working in civil aviation before moving back to Sydney before finally retiring here."

"Do you ever go back or want to?"

"Not now I'm too old and my family are all here really. I'm an Australian Geordie!"

"What made you stay?"

"You have to remember that Britain in 1949 was still recovering from the war and things like rationing were still in place and for someone like me who had travelled the world with the navy, I needed something more. It was a bit exotic to a young lad like me and I loved it, not the war mind you, but the travel. See the world for free. Australia just drew me in and having visited here a number of times in the war and knowing that the Aussies needed skilled workers as well I saw it as an opportunity and something that might change my life."

"And did it?"

"All except my accent" he laughed loudly, a man who was in my view truly content with what life and Australia, this 'lucky country', had given this to him.

I wished him well leaving him behind his desk with his memories and sauntered off to find the proper museum on Wilson Street. Of course, me being me I had to do a slight detour which was to see the Wesleyan Methodist Chapel on Horton Street. Hey, it's a church so was bound to be interesting and was a stone's throw from the maritime museum. The Chapel, erected by 1846, is another historical record of the settlement's early history and although it suffered a slump in attendance as did its Anglican neighbour after nearly two thirds of the town left following the end of the town as a penal settlement, it was revived and carried on as the central point of Methodist worship until 1964 when a new church was built although following restoration work in the 1990's it is now back in use. It was not a large building and inside it could best be described as cosy but I was interested to know more about why Methodism had been successful given that the Established church back in the UK was Anglican.

I asked Don, 'Volunteer', who was looking very earnest and thus must know the answer to this question.

"The Anglican Church was seen by many as being more for those in the ruling classes, the elite, less interested in the souls of those in the lower social orders. Its reputation in the Colony at the beginning was not great and you have to understand that back then it was at the time the only official religion. It wasn't uncommon for those tasked with bringing God's word to the masses not really being interested in 'saving souls' or who themselves were, shall we say, less than moral themselves."

"So why choose Methodism?"

"Many of the convicts who were sent to Australia were schooled, if that's the right word, in the non-established church. When John Wesley and his brother split from the Anglican Church, they created a new evangelical religion which had more appeal to the lower classes, many of whom were now being told that they too could be saved no matter who or what they were, something that the Anglican church refused to preach. You could say Methodism was less up its own backside" he chuckled. "The other thing is that it gave some of these convicts and free settlers a chance to poke two fingers up to the Establishment. This was *their* church and not the ruling classes'."

The first Methodist minister had arrived in Australia back in 1815, the Reverend Samuel Leigh, and although the church itself was split in the 18th century between the more Calvinist tradition and that of Wesley who followed a much more radical approach after the Dutch theologian Jacobus Arminius, what it had at its core was that it preached not just salvation but a re-birth. For many convicts, many of whom had committed petty crimes back in Britain, this must have seemed more attractive than the hell and damnation of the Anglicans and the loss of hope for all 'sinners'. Ironically, given that the British Establishment had used Australia as a dustbin for their criminal classes, it was the very same people as the representatives of this view under Governor Macquarie and others in Australia, who realised that allowing convicts to go unchecked in respect of morality would ultimately, in their view, be a de-stabilising influence. Macquarie may not have been an ardent supporter himself of non-conformists but he and his wife were strong believers in reforming criminals and some have said that the expression 'fair play' comes from this ethos so inviting religious leaders and teachers in would have fit into this thought process. On the centenary of the establishment of Leigh's ministry in 1815 an article was written in 'The Argus' that encapsulated the atmosphere of the time (this related to Sydney but was to be relevant as new penal settlements were created):

"It was a common thing to see scores of men and women and children before the magistrates for drunkenness and receiving sentences of six hours in the stocks, ten days to the cells,"20 days to the treadmill" or "50 lashes" … "

In the following year another piece in 'The West Australian' neatly summed up what the Wesleyan strand of Methodism brought:

"There could not be very high aspirations in low conditions, and the people who were eking out a miserable existence had nothing to stimulate their hearts and minds. Wesley brought to them a great and glorious evangel, the story of a personal salvation, that these people themselves might know that they were saved and justified … they were aroused from their sense of low ideals to a high pitch of enthusiasm."

It was the Methodist and other non-established churches that saw the initial benefits through their zeal and unlike the Anglican Church a person didn't have to be ordained to preach, which meant there were more to spread the message. For some, Methodism operated on a higher moral plane advocating, amongst other things abstinence from the demon drink. They also were quick to establish wider education for the lower classes (in May 1847 the 'Sydney Morning Herald' reported that in Port Macquarie a Sunday School was established by the Methodists) which, although this was beginning to happen widely back in Britain, was harder to achieve in Australia simply due to a lack of teachers.

Don recommended that I make a small detour and go up the road from here to something that in his opinion was of great importance and was just "a short walk". It was thus that I headed for another graveyard, this time appropriately called the Port Macquarie Historic Cemetery which took over from that on Allman Hill in 1824 and was officially in use until 1886. Taking Don's directions this involved a walk down to the end of Horton Street going south, then across the road at the Intersection of Horton and Gordon Streets. Having become acclimatised to the Australian definitions of "on time", "moderate climb", I was prepared for a fair old hike but this time Don was telling the truth, it was indeed very close. What Don had neglected to tell me was that to get to the burial ground required being run-down by the somewhat heavy traffic that occupied one of the arterial roads, Gordon Street, in Port Macquarie. Playing chicken was fun when I was young but not these days being overweight and much older (and I believe wiser although that is subject to debate still) person nearer to fifty years old than ten on top of which I was wearing flip-flops which were not designed for running across roads. It was therefore with much trepidation that I attempted to cross the road. I'd still be there I think if it wasn't for an altercation happening between two drivers who were disputing in very polite terms whose right of way it was. The words "shove", "it", "up", "your" and "arse" are I believe terms of endearment in Australia. I scooted across avoiding any unintended tyre marks.

Like the cemetery in Cooktown this one too was delineated along religious denominations and just as in Queensland many of the original 'notables' of the Port's early days were interred here, including the alleged illegitimate son of Napoleon Bonaparte, Dr. Fattorini and the daughter of Colonial Secretary Alexander Macleay who was the wife of Major Innes, one of the Port's most important early figures. What was interesting about this burial ground was that it had been mathematically drawn up. Having been inaugurated, if that is the right word, in 1824, it had become by the 1850's a bit of a mess so the local Church of England vicar asked the council if he could have it as an exclusive Anglican burial ground and in return he would maintain it. The council agreed but allowed other denominations some limited access. However, it was an exclusive club whereby the Anglican had two acres, the Catholics three quarters of an acre and the Presbyterians half an acre. I pondered this for a little debating whether the latter two religions were made up of predominantly shorter people and thus needed less space. I also wondered if at any stage in the arguments as to who had what someone had said "Over my dead body". On the Grand Opening of I presume a couple of new graves in 1860 were there people queuing to get in? Anyway the last laugh goes to Rosa, daughter of Abraham and Sarah Cohen who was Jewish and was also buried there, although I suspect that not much laughter was heard at the time, but you get the drift. The cemetery closed in 1886 with the bodies of over 1500 soles both convicts and settlers, but as my leaflet on the cemetery stated ' … further burials were reported after this date'. There's a little Burke and Hare to this if you ask me.

Of course by now I had forgotten all about the Mid North Coast Maritime Museum and decided to head back to the hotel. Fortunately

I found another less dangerous route back to Horton Street albeit somewhat circuitous via part of the Kooloonbung Creek Nature Park. Back at my hotel I hopped into the car and made haste as the afternoon drew towards evening to the Tacking Point Lighthouse. This required a drive through much of the southern part of the town and once more the streets offered up an eclectic mixture of housing, but with the most common invariably being single storey structures that were mostly of a fair size. There is money in this town and the demographic surveys done by the Macquarie-Hastings Council show that in the last few years the average income has risen, but unlike Noosa and Byron Bay, the average age profile remains dominated by the 55+ group, suggesting that there was a predominance of retirees. Tacking Point Lighthouse was a huge let-down. For a start it was tiny and on top of this it was, you guessed it, closed. The only thing I can report of interest is that in 1859 according to the Maitland Mercury a young lad, David M'Iver (sic) managed to almost blow his hand off by trying to light a fire using gunpowder! I wonder if he was at all a distant relative of the two men who had tried to get an action shot of the crocodile. I was glad I hadn't walked.

On the way I had passed a nature reserve on Pacific Drive, the Sea Acres Rainforest Reserve, so on leaving the lighthouse I went back that way in order to investigate, more as something to do than out of any real burning desire to visit another rainforest. After paying three years salary to gain entrance I was lucky enough once more to be given my own personal guide, Tony. I was getting very used to this one on one service almost as if I were some dignitary rather than just a rather smelly and sweaty tourist (deodorant was not working well by this time of day) with a pathetic stubble of hair on my chin pretending to be a beard. Tony it transpired had a direct link to the past through his great-great-great grandfather who had been a soldier in the 48th. I should have asked more about this but there was no time as we were off along the suspended rainforest boardwalk which was 1.3 kilometres long. Tony helpfully gave me a quick introduction to the Reserve outlining the sheer diversity of plant life as well as animal, bird and reptile life, including this little gem: this is one of the few habitats of the rare freshwater snail of which I know nothing more. As we continued the walk Tony was in 'naming things' overdrive like the bangalow palm, the giant water gum and the carabeen along with many others that I can't remember because by now I was overloaded. As we walked round he suddenly stopped and pointed to one innocuous looking plant with spiky leaves that was just over the edge of the walkway's fencing, and gently grabbing my arm said "Don't touch that" in what was quite an ominous voice. If I'd been twelve out of spite or just plain bloody-mindedness I might have touched it just to annoy him but instead asked why.

"It's poisonous and will leave you with a nasty burning sensation if you touch that it'll hurt like buggery for months to come. We've got a few in Australia but this is one of the nasty ones. Won't kill you though unless you're an ankle-biter"

Well that's a relief. Right, let me just revisit my list of things that can kill me in Australia. This country has spiders, snakes, sharks, fish and jellyfish that can all kill you and plants. Where will it end? Surely when I arrived in Australia there should have been someone there to provide me with the appropriate guide on dress code that involved wearing something akin to a biological warfare suits to avoid being poisoned the moment I left the airport.

Tony carried on talking and this time started to describe the medicines used by the Aboriginals, although rather curiously he wouldn't tell me which plant was used for what medicine telling me that it was not "policy at the Reserve" to do so. Instead if I was to obtain a legal high then I would have to sniff every plant and taste every leaf but I was short on time so instead I asked him how the Aboriginals knew which plant was safe and which wasn't.

"What they used to do, and still do in the bush today, was to touch their lips with the plant or wipe it under their armpit and see whether there'd be any swelling. If there was, then they left it well alone."

The visit done I looked at my map and saw that it was not far to a preserved slice of Australian history, Roto House. I arrived just as it was closing which would have been annoying had it not been for one of the ladies who was closing shutters and doors who on seeing me, beckoned me in and told me to take my time and look around. The house was a microcosm of Australian colonial life lived by a typical professional family of the period. It had been built in 1890 for John Flynn, a surveyor, and his family and was made almost entirely of wood from mahogany and Californian Redwood and all as a single storey, squat structure with a veranda that went all round the building. Each room told the story of the family or of their everyday lives and from one of the descriptions left for posterity by one of John Flynn's children, Nora, it was a lively place with dances and parties and also a place of beauty with the property sitting in lush surroundings. It was all very quiet today and the last Flynn had left in 1976 following which it had become a national heritage site. The Flynn family was not remarkable in the sense that any of them, including John, were significant historic figures, but this house that had been beautifully restored was a wonderful snapshot of the past of an 'ordinary' family, and I rather enjoyed it. As I looked out toward the car park from the front entrance I noticed a white cross under a huge tree and asked one of the ladies who had let me in what it was, assuming that it might have been for a pet.

"Desmond Flynn, one of John's sons, had a daughter who was stillborn and that's her grave under the Norfolk pine. It must have been difficult for his wife Elizabeth seeing that when she was here, but then there was I suppose a sense of closeness."

It was quite moving and with the clouds being so grey in the sky and a heaviness in the air, it had left me feeling a little down and full of pathos. Even a visit to the Koala Hospital didn't help as it was full of seriously ill or badly injured bears. I needed to be uplifted and that could only mean one thing, beer. As you will have gathered I am no stranger to the delights of the pint glass and am quite keen on tasting new varieties of falling down water and so it was that I found myself on an industrial estate on the edge of town on the Uralla Road looking at a nice, though rather unremarkable, white shiny warehouse with the following magic words on a board: 'The Little Brewing: Cellar Door Open'.

Like the White Rabbit in Haresville, this was also a family affair and was run by a husband and wife team, Kylie and Warwick Little who were passionate and very proud of their beers. I asked them how hard it was to break into the Australian beer market, given that lager-style beer was the preferred tipple and this was dominated, as in the UK, by the big brands.

"It's not easy. Basically to get things really going you need to get your foot in the door of a company that has a franchise across the country or the state or you could sell out to larger brewer as some have done. It gives you distribution sure but less control and I'm not sure we want to do that; after all you lose your independence. We do get orders from across the country and we are building up a following but it's still all hands to the pump. "

That evening I sat down with a steaming takeaway from a Chinese and my bottles of Wicked Elf Pale Ale, which was delicious, and watched a programme on Australian lifeguards' manly and womanly feats. I thought about a similar programme filmed in the UK and had this image that instead of some lithe young lad or lassie running into the water to save some unfortunate from drowning, without concern for themselves, there would probably be a completely pointless human from Health and Safety testing the water's temperature first to make sure it wasn't too cold, then putting any lifeguard through a work assessment test and then checking that they're wearing approved clothing by which time the swimmer would probably have drowned. My thoughts once more re-engaged with the television and I do have a couple of questions for those brave Australian lifeguards:

What's with the bathing caps?

Why do the men wear such small and very tight trunks – you know it makes the rest of us feel, well, inadequate.

I dozed off imagining myself as some bronzed lifeguard, muscles rippling and girls dripping off of me whilst heroically and effortlessly saving the lives of swimmers in trouble. Sometime during this semi-consciousness I think I had David Hasselhoff giving me the kiss of life whilst Pamela Anderson looked on. Why is it that even in my dreams I get it the wrong way round although he was one heck of a kisser.

Chapter 12

*The end is in sight, but first I must drink lots of wine with
the Hunters and then try not to get lost in
the Blue Mountains.*

DAY thirty seven: December 10th

The drive today would take me through the southern part of New
England to wine country. There is a debate as to where New England
officially starts and ends but I was told that the route I was to take along
the Pacific Highway, then across from Taree inland towards Gloucester and
thence south to the Hunter Valley, the 'home' of Australian wine, skirted the
southern part of this region, so write to Miss J Fredericks, Port Macquarie,
NSW, if you disagree. It was to be quite a long drive but promised to be one
that would allow some meaningful scenery viewing as well as the chance to
stop at a couple of towns that had featured in my guide book, Gloucester
and Paterson. As I continued my journey south I was becoming a little
travel weary and my mind was beginning to wander quite a lot. I don't
mean I was off with the fairies or losing my mind but rather that I started
ruminate on a lot that I'd seen or heard, but at the most trivial level. For
instance I wanted to know why it is that I was everyone's 'mate'. Back home
it is one of the more irritating use of language I find (ok I use 'mate' when
drunk, as in "you're my best mate, I really love you" but that is permitted).
Let's face it I make friends as easily as Rudolph Nureyev could have played
front row for London Irish, but here I seemed remarkably popular. I had
stopped for breakfast in Gloucester and, Greg (no badge but he did say "Hi,
my name's Greg …), who had served me my cheese flavoured scrambled
eggs on a brick-sixed piece of toast along with a slug of decent coffee had
said, when handing me my change to which I had responded "Thanks", " …
no worries, mate". At this, more out of someone to talk to (I was lonely) I
asked him why Aussies say 'mate' all the time,

"Aww that's 'cos were nice!" he smiled a brilliant white smile, and then added (as I looked vacantly at him, jaw slightly agape in anticipation of a slightly longer answer) "Goes back to the First World War I think, Gallipoli when it was all about looking after each other. I reckon today though it's just the way we do things. Y'know like g'day and fair dinkum. It's 'strine'!" He also reckoned that it was a connection to the convict past, so of course I, being of a curious nature, looked into this further as I ate breakfast. It appears that it actually has a much longer history than that, way back to those first convicts who shared the hardships not just of transportation but also life once they reached here. In fact it is a deep rooted part of an Australian's very being, something that every one of them is proud of and which features heavily not just today but in folklore. Henry Lawson, one of Australia's true patriots, summed it up this in his 'Triangles of Life and Other Stories'

'True mateship looks for no limelight. They say that self-preservation is the strongest instinct of mankind; it may come with the last gasp, but I think the preservation of life or liberty of a mate – man or women – is the first and strongest. It is the instinct that irresistibly impels a thirsty, parched man, out on the burning sands, to pour the last drop of water down the throat of a dying mate, where none save the sun or moon or stars may see … '

So that's one puzzle solved. I took my empty cup and plate back inside to Greg. I didn't say "thanks mate" as it doesn't sound quite the same in my Home Counties accent. Instead, as I am a man of the world in touch with my everyman self, I just said "Ta." Doesn't have the same ring to it, does it.

On the road again I was now starting to move back in time travelling through Dungog, a town that can date itself back to 1824 with the first land grant, and which was to become a focal point for the lumber industry with our weird looking friend, the Sydney Opera House, being a recipient of wood in 1972 from here. I carried on through land that had been developed by free settlers who had been allowed to move out of the Sydney area in the 1820's following the move from Newcastle to Port Macquarie of the penal settlement in 1825. Aside from the buildings in the towns themselves there was little to show for this part of the country's history. It's definitely not like the old world where I can be driving along and all of a sudden there, off the side of the road, is a ruined castle or, as in the case of France, some Frenchman peeing in full sight of the traffic, and much of this is because, as with my discoveries in Brisbane, so much was originally made of wood which just didn't last. It's a shame in many ways as I would have liked to have seen an original homestead but it was not to be. I drove on through Paterson which was originally the area where the Gringgai Aboriginals lived until the white settlers arrived and booted them out and was named after Colonel William Paterson who came by in 1801. I stopped for a coffee and found a small unassuming cafe, ordered my latte and sat down, my mind a blank, staring out at nothing in particular. Paterson does have a claim to fame as I discovered on the web the previous evening. It was here that one Mary Anne Bugg was tried for being a bushranger in the 1860's. Although this in its own right was interesting given that virtually no females were bushrangers, what was more exciting was that she was the wife of Frederick Ward, alias 'Captain Thunderbolt', a notorious villain who was supposedly shot dead by the law but rumour had it that it wasn't him but his half brother, Harry and that Fred was last seen riding off into the sunset, as it were. Did he survive and assume a new identity or was that it? Little was heard of him afterwards aside from the odd sighting where he was with Elvis Presley and the Big Dipper enjoying a cool one. But the legend lives on as there is a road named after him called Thunderbolt's Way. I just can't see us back in Britain naming one of our roads something like Dick Turpin Highway but for Australians this attitude to admiring the underdog, the anti-hero, the men and women of folklore, is not so much for their more grisly crimes, but for their two-fingered salute to authority and today it can still be seen in the way they act and talk. These are people whose antecedents were schooled the hard way and they're proud of this. We British of course are far too law-abiding to want to do anything like naming a road after a convicted felon which, given the cost of driving today which is itself nothing short of highway robbery, is a pity.

I passed through Cessnock and turned west into the Hunter Valley itself. Here I come, ready to sample the delightful wines of the region using my extensive knowledge of the grape which usually means necking a few glasses of the white and red stuff, nodding sagely, sniffing the glass and making that slurping noise tasters do on before falling over. I am actually such a philistine when it comes to wine not least on the etiquette of just having a little in the glass to taste which to me is a complete anathema and

I will always helpfully tip the servers hand in order that they can pour a full glass for me. I'm sure that is how it should be quaffed or whatever the term is for drinking the grape. I found my bed for the next two nights in the hamlet of Pokolbin, albeit with a degree of difficulty that once more showed that when I'd been offered a GPS back in Port Douglas I perhaps should have accepted rather than saying: "Thanks, but I have a map" whilst thinking to myself, in a semi-Neanderthal " … and don't need to spend the UK's entire GDP on something that given my excellent navigational skills will add nothing. I am a man who hunts, mates and fights. I have no need for a piece of electronic gadgetry. Ugh." I bet the lady at the counter, who was charming I may add, was probably thinking "What a total drongo. He'll be sorry … " Well Gill, if you are reading this you were right and I was wrong, but like I said "Ugh!"

Day thirty eight: December 11th

The day started well with the sun blazing away in Sydney. The only problem with that though, was that I wasn't in Sydney but a good few kilometres north. Here there were some ominous looking grey clouds which the sun was fighting hard to peek through. The Hunter Valley, so I had been reliably informed, was spectacularly beautiful when bathed in sunshine so the clouds were a huge disappointment but at least it wasn't raining as yet and so I decided that the best way to get around and off road was to hire a bike. As luck would have it there was a hire shop near where I was staying although the desk clerk had warned me when I enquired about it the night before, that I should get there early to avoid disappointment as "Biking is very popular especially amongst the tourists". There was an advantage of hiring a bike as well; this is wine country and where there is wine there has got to be tastings. It would be nuts to drive, but cycle, well why not. I located the bike hire shop to find that not only was I the only person there but that the shop had enough bikes to supply the Chinese PLA. The choice was huge and duly kitted out with mountain bike, helmet, water and map I set off to 'drink in' the region. The history of the Hunter Valley is once more very closely linked to the first free settlers breaking out from Sydney and although it is the oldest wine region in the country, its original potential was seen in timber which then became farming, both sheep and wheat. Although wine was being produced in the 1820's it was on a very small scale. By the 1850's new varieties of vine were being cultivated thanks to James Busby, 'the father of Australian wine' who had brought many cuttings with him from his travels not just from the old world but also from South Africa. This may seem odd given that the latter too was a relatively new British Colony, but not so when the history of the influx of Huguenot exiles from France in the late 17th century who brought with them their wine-making skills, is taken into account. Other notables were men like William MacCarthur and his brother James. From all accounts William was a hard taskmaster forbidding anyone (i.e. the workers) from eating the grapes and making them work up to fourteen hours a day; what a jolly fellow he must have been to work for. Still it was all worth it as I discovered when trawling through The State Library of New South Wales' guide to the Hunter Valley's wine history which had the story of when in 1988 the English wine writer Hugh Johnson tasted some red wine made some time between 1825–70, from the MacCarthur estate and declared it to be 'sumptuous … of enormous richness.'

As I cycled around on near deserted roads on a bike that, along with my not too ungenerous bulk, weighed a ton I thought of the first settlers who had arrived here on the few routes that were around then. It was not until early 1820's, thanks to Howe, that a means to get to this part of the world was achieved through a route from Windsor and thence to Singleton along what is now called Putty Road. It can't have been much fun travelling with all the kit needed to survive as well as having to keep an eye on not just possible attack from the Aboriginals, tribes such as the Darkinung, Wonnarua, Awabakal, Worimi, or Geawegal, from escaped convicts (the Hunter River was discovered in 1797 by Lieutenant John Shortland whilst he was looking for escapees) but also the convicts that had been assigned to you to help build the future. The richer you were apparently the better 'class' of convict was to be had. Roll the calendar forward to 2009 and the whole place was, in a word, neat. All the vineyards were well kept and all, or nearly all, of the wineries had an almost French feel about them, reminiscent of the Loire, through the design of the buildings to the very fact that everywhere I looked there were vines. By now the sun had won its battle and had made an appearance resulting in the air beginning to feel decidedly warm which in turn resulted in me having a thirst that could only be slaked through imbibing the noble grape, white or red or both it mattered not one bit. In fact anyone offering me a tasting could put it all in one glass for all I cared. Bring on the wine, sir; fetch hither the grape of Bacchus! Just before I continue this part of my adventure I would like to point out that I have been on wine tasting tours in South Africa at Stellenbosch, Boschendal and Takara as well as the Loire Valley in France and each time managed to drink at least a bottle or more without having to pay, because you see it was all free, or at least each little glass was. And being brought up with a strong sense of manners the very thought of spitting it out was just not the done thing. It was all rather amusing as the sales person would stand there pouring out small tasters hoping that as a result of this and the subsequent impact on my palette I would part with a huge amount of money and six crates of Chateau Le Something or Other, 1999 which, had they known that I was taking a leaf out of the Roman Soldier's Phrase Book, 'Nemo dat quod non habet' or 'no one gives what he does not have', and in my case money, they would probably have thought better of. Unfortunately this cunning plan had a fatal flaw here. As hard as I looked, and I did a lot of cycling both on and off road, including what initially seemed a rather pointless trek up Pokolbin Mountains Road (no wineries as I found out) but which turned out to provide a panoramic view of where I was staying, I had noticed a problem. This problem was having a devastating impact on my idea of the perfect day where the odd glass of Shiraz, Sauvignon Blanc or maybe a Riesling or even a rich Merlot would be had along with an obligatory cheese accompaniment. No matter where I looked none had that key set of words 'Free Tasting', which given my decision to cycle was a bit of a bummer. I manfully rode on past names that I know from back home such as Lindeman's (founded originally in 1842 on land called Cawarra), Wyndham and Rosemount as well as others I'd never heard including the rather splendidly named Cockfighters Ghost Wine. The last one gives much to the imaginative mind, or in my case, the puerile mind.

On a more serious note, the settlement of the Hunter Valley had a devastating effect on the Aboriginal tribes. The Arwarbukarl Cultural Resource Association calls the period before European settlement BC or Before Cook and provides an insight not just to the tribes that lived here but also the devastation that was brought upon them such as disease which soon spread with smallpox being the major killer. The numbers killed were huge and figures of between 30% – 50% have been cited as estimates of how much of the indigenous population succumbed. Added to this was the often indiscriminate manslaughter and dispossession of many whose ancestors had lived on this land for millennia. But here I was cycling around and although there is much evidence of the early European settlements through historical markers or signs these had only oblique references to the indigenous tribes. It was strange, but maybe I was looking in the wrong place although when researching the Hunter Valley I noticed that most of the websites or books that waxed lyrical about the wine industry, there was a cursory mention, maybe a couple of paragraphs, on who was here before, that is of course the Aboriginals. It was also written as if there had been a quick assimilation between those that came and those who were already here, almost as if Mills & Boone had come up with it. It's hard not to think that even today history is being sanitised and that the depredations suffered by these people have been reduced to a footnote of history. Although Australia has 'recognised' the Aboriginal people as being not just citizens but also rightful owners of their own traditional land in the last 40 years, it was not until 2008 that, representing Australia's non Aboriginal population, Kevin Rudd the then Prime Minister issued an apology to the 'Stolen Generation' for the wrongs visited upon them since the First Fleet, and notably the forced separation of children from their parents which went on for close to 100 years only ending in 1968. Was this better late than never, I wonder? On a more recent event, 222 years after the First Fleet, Australia elected its first Aboriginal MP which although doesn't seem much when compared with the ethnic diversity back home in our Parliament in the UK, should nevertheless be applauded.

It was continuing to get hotter by the minute and by now I had become a mobile sauna, which, I can assure you, is an unpleasant sight at the best of times. I was also getting more knackered and thirstier (my water ration had run out pretty early as I had expected to be slightly sozzled on ample free wine by now) and a little saddle sore so I returned to the rental shop, the one where I has been advised that there would be such a rush of customers that I may not get a bike unless I went early.

"Been busy?" I asked breezily

"No, mate, you've been the only bike rider today; it's been real quiet."

I could have stayed in bed longer and not worried about getting here so early and let's face it I need as much beauty sleep as I can get. On the plus side he only charged me for two hours even though I'd been out closer to three because "It was easier ... " but didn't actually explain than what as he finished his sentence there, but then again this was Australia where something that costs close to a dollar is usually rounded up or down given that they don't have any small denomination currency. This country was continuing to grow on me. I liked a similar system in the US where people place their pennies on a small plate on the counter so that if someone is short of a penny or so then the shopkeeper just uses these 'spares'. This would never happen back home; I can just see myself going into a shop and saying that I was short a couple of pence and could they, the shop, effectively sub me the rest. I'd be marched out accompanied by the sounds of raucous laughter along with a suggestion of how to 'travel and have sex' at the same time. I went back to my little hacienda and after a quick shower I got into the car to explore the less well known wineries and some of the hamlets that dot the area that lay further inland to the south west of Pokolbin. One town I wanted to see was Wollombi ('the meeting of the waters'), not least as all those travel books and websites I'd looked at prior to coming to Australia had suggested that 'if you are travelling in the area you must visit Wollombi'. As you may recall I have been a victim of this type of invite already on the trip (Melbourne: Fitzroy Gardens and Fairies Tree) but deep down I'm a trusting soul and so taking a deep breath I looked at the map in front of me which showed that it would be about five finger nails and half in distance (I always use my index finger on a gauge of one nail to ten minutes – very reliable) from Pokolbin and set off.

The first place of significance on the way was Cessnock, an old mining town that can trace its history back to the 1820's and is named after a castle of that same name back in Scotland (in the early days of European settlement in the Hunter Valley there were a large number of settlers who were of a Celtic persuasion). As part of the history of the Lower Hunter Valley's coal mining industry it was an important town as it was one of the first places to be associated with the new coal industry in the region in the mid 1850's, although the economic benefits of what lay underground had to wait almost twenty years before wholesale extraction took place. The coal industry lasted some seventy to eighty years and at its peak employed thousands of workers in the surrounding area. The closure of the pits has left Cessnock looking worn down today with a distinct feel that its best days are behind it.

The contrast to the more opulent wineries up the road to here could not have been starker. Leaving Cessnock I stopped at a memorial that was a little way back from the main road that had been in erected in commemoration of the 21 miners who had died in the great Bellbird mining disaster of 1923 which presaged the launch of mining safety governance in Australia and then continued to follow the road towards Wollombi, meandering slowly through countryside that was given over to vines and farming with, in the distance the mountains of the Yengo National Park looming tall and verdant into the now blue sky. I'd read that around here wildlife was teeming such that you could not actually drive on the road but would have to walk over the tops of all the koala bears, wallabies and kangaroos which were so plentiful that they acted as a moving mammalian carpet of fur. Well all I can say is that today must have been a half-day holiday because the closest I came to anything with fur was flattened across the road in front of me (although quite tasty accompanied by fries, a béarnaise sauce and a fine merlot).

Passing through Crawfordville and Millfield and then Sweetmans Creek I approached Wollombi and the first thing that struck me as I crossed the small narrow wooden bridge and was in Wollombi was that I'd left 2009 and was in a 19th century town complete with a pub, a sandstone church, a school, a courthouse, a general store, an inn and some wooden framed houses; there was no sign of modernity outside of the road and the telephone wires. And it was silent aside from the low murmuring that was coming from the drinkers outside the pub. Lunch was called for and as I sat eating this sitting on the veranda of Gray's Inn I tried to see the town as it would have been when it was first being put on the map which meant that I would have been sitting on a rock (the Inn was built towards the late 1840's) whilst watching convicts working under a hot sun in conditions that were, to say the very least, harsh, laying the foundations for what was to become the Great North Road. In fact no other village existed at the start of the project of building a road to connect Sydney's Hawkesbury district to the Hunter Valley and beyond, which by the 1820's and 1830's had become an area of rapid European colonisation and expansion. Wollombi owed its existence to the fact that it was at the junction that took the traveller north towards Broke, or north east towards Cessnock. Having eaten a splendid sandwich and drunk a coffee that kicked a punch (a double, double espresso I believe)

I walked the short distance to the Courthouse which was a 'must see' item. It was closed; of course it was, why would I have expected it not to be? Almost opposite was a church and so I crossed the road hoping that it would shine a light on some of the locals many of whom would have been immortalised on those memorial tablets that festoon the walls. It was closed. There was a pattern emerging here but no matter in front of the church was a stall selling those hippy style hessian shirts and some local craft; maybe I could get a run-down about the history of the village both then and now. Nope, it was closed for lunch. In fact so far aside from the few people outside the pub, me and the three people at the Inn, there was no one else around. It was almost a ghost town. Next to the Inn was the General Store and this was open so in I strode in and entered what I initially thought was a museum as nearly everything looked like it was from a different and much older era, including a couple of the customers who were chatting animatedly to the storekeeper. I waited a couple of minutes to see if I could get a word with any of them but the conversation was by the sounds of it quite important and involved a Debs and Malcolm and something to do with what he/she had been doing with Ron. The conversation was in full swing and by now I knew that Australians don't stop in mid-flow even if there is another customer and as I couldn't wait for what could have been an eternity I got back into the car and took the northern route towards Broke, following the Wollombi Brook, which is in Cockfighter Country. Honest. Actually Cockfighter was the name of one of the horses in Howe's expedition to this area in 1820 and nothing to do with some hidden male talent but it still makes me smile even today as I write this.

Time was moving on and somewhere in the world the sun was below the yardarm and this meant only one thing and tonight I was going to really push the boat out and spend large on a decent bottle of the local 'vin de choice' to be drunk slowly over dinner at a BYOB restaurant. What would it be though? I needed some ideas and so stopped off at the general store in Pokolbin where there was a wine merchants and thus clearly a place of vine-related education. Given that my knowledge of wine is limited to red, white, pink and most importantly 14% volume, I am happy to take advice but am very wary of looking a total idiot. The best way to hide ignorance I find is to head for a shelf of wine, pick out a bottle, look down on it, smile and gently nod to myself before replacing it and then repeating three or four times with other bottles. I may even ask the wine merchant for his or her view and nod again, making sure that there is a chin stroke involved as well as an arched eyebrow, the sure sign of knowledge. The genius of this is that the wine merchant will then usually leave me alone recognising in me a fellow wine expert who is just reaffirming through the advice given their own view. So imagine my joy as I walked in and the wine merchant, grinning from ear to ear, said, "G'day, can I help you?"

I'm not prepared for this upfront approach. He should have waited at least until I'd had a look at a couple of bottles. I had no answer. I was bereft of words. I was stumped. My plan had gone to pot. And then it got worse: "What you looking for? We've a wide selection from the Pokolbin area, reds, whites and some really lovely sparkling"

"Um, um … something light please. Do you have any Gris de Gris" I'd got him fooled. I could see he now thought that the podgy bloke in front of him knew his wines. Gris de Gris is for me a holiday wine best drunk when in Southern France and is probably best described as being a pale pink but best of all it costs around four Euros per bottle at most, and at that price is lovely. He was bound to have some here, not least if there was rosé on offer. My confidence soared. We were brothers, fellow wine aficionados.

"Sorry. What was that again?" He asked, looking slightly puzzled.

"A Gris de Gris, you know a light pink wine?" This was beginning to look bad.

"Well I've personally not heard of that … " ("Blast" I thought, "my cover is blown") " … but I do have some nice rosé. Is that what you're after?"

I sheepishly said yes. There was no point in the pretence now. He knew it and I knew it. I was a fake, a fraud and man whose knowledge of wine was actually down to pot luck.

"Well here I have some … (he pointed to a rack of wines that started at a price equivalent to my monthly mortgage payment) … or … " he had noted the sweat and nervous tick I had developed " … I've got these bottles in the wine bin at twenty bucks each."

I quickly gave him the money and put the bottle into my backpack in a manner more in keeping with someone buying porn and not wanting to have it on display for all to see and left. I could feel his contempt for me as I left the shop. This was wine country and I had too all intents and purposes taken a metaphorical dump on all that it stood for. Still twenty dollars for 13%, yes 13%, in Australia is good value my friend and by the way I'm not too proud to retreat with some honour.

That evening for dinner I planned to go to Harrigan's Irish Pub following a recommendation from a friend back in Sydney and which I could not just walk to but also do this by going via a rather pleasant venue called Hunter Valley Gardens which was an all singing all dancing place of entertainment with gardens, restaurants, shops, accommodation and function rooms. I would have stopped but I was after a decent pint of beer and some basic Australian fare which Harrigan's promised to have. Well it would have done had the kitchen not been badly damaged so there wasn't therefore any food. I'd walked a good forty-five minutes so I thought I'd at least have a beer but the place was teeming with people and the noise suggested that a good time was being had by all with laughter in high abundance and quite a bit of fruity language as I tried to find the bar. But I was getting quite excited because it was at this point that my mullet-tattoo-metre almost exploded. They were everywhere, under tables, on tables, swinging from the rafters, everywhere! I exaggerate a little but who or what were these people? Was this a new tribe? Was this a mullet and tattoo reunion party?

Most of the ladies were sporting low slung but breast enhancing dresses, showing tattoos pretty much of the same design situated just above their gluteus maximus, wearing ridiculously high heeled shoes and enough make-up to keep the local Avon sale's lady in clover for decades. Their gentlemen friends almost to a man sported frizzed hairstyles with an obligatory mullet and clothing that would look good in the sports section of the local athletics shop or act as some sort of reflector on the road (lots of shiny shine). In the car park there were huge 4x4's, Holdens all with massive engines and the newer low slung UTE's everywhere I looked. Not wishing to ask one of the revellers what was going on I quietly asked a fellow Neanderthal who had a badge that said 'staff', and who was dressed all in black with wires protruding from his left ear and with a grimace on his face suggesting that he was probably sucking a lemon or had very bad piles, what this was all in aid of. "Bogan wedding" he grunted, the grimace becoming ever more pronounced to the point I thought he was about to explode or else he might have been smiling, but it was hard to tell.

I beat a hasty retreat from the pub back up towards the more salubrious surroundings of the Hunter Valley Gardens for some food, but keen to know more about this strange new creature, the bogan? I needed a local expert (for all I knew the bogan could have been a native to this area) to find out more and so later that evening whilst chatting to a couple of Aussies over dinner I broached the subject. Well chatted over dinner is perhaps a bit a too suggestive given that they were eating and all I was doing was getting myself a beer from the bar. I was also slightly confused as to what a bogan was versus a hoon but all was clear after a quick chat with my new chums. They explained that to most Australians a bogan is the Australian equivalent of the US redneck (or, I would guess in the UK, a chav). Bogans have a strong affinity to mullets, tattoos, a preference for strange first names often spelt in peculiar ways but with a huge commonality in pronunciation, a sartorial bent to have shiny clothing, a tendency to have the latest home entertainment systems (on credit) and who tend to be show-offs through the use of bling or other materialistic things. My new chums also intimated that a bogan is not overly bright and the women have a tendency towards being blessed with a lot of children but not always from the same father. However, unlike the anti-social hoon who uses his car as compensation for the lack of a trouser snake and technically can be from any part of the social ladder, the term bogan was more of a derogatory descriptive of a complete social class, almost they said a class within a class, the latter being predominantly working class. Back in the UK I got another interpretation from one of my Australian friends who had been, in his youth, mullet-headed and tattooed, and said that many of the older bogans, like him, were in fact those who were in their late teens and early twenties as heavy metal took off in the late 1960's, through the 1970's and early 1980's. Whatever the real definition there was no doubt that the gathering here this evening fitted neatly into the first stereotypical definition. Well I'm glad that was cleared up. Still who cares? The bogans at Harrigan's hadn't been causing any problems that I could see and there were lots of Sharons, Sharrons, Shayrons and Waynes, Wanes and Waines running about having lots of fun all dressed just like their mums and dads. How sweet!

After a fine dinner I retired to my room to drink a couple of glasses of my expensive Australian wine. I'd been looking forward to this – here in the Hunter Valley drinking one of the local brews looking out at the remains of the day which by now was pitch black. No one had told me that this country gets dark really quite early which can be a tad awkward when walking back from a restaurant full of good food and beer on an unlit road with, knowing my luck, a high probability that some deadly something was about to jump out at me and bite my leg off. I eased the cork out of the bottle which made a mouth watering 'pop' releasing a pleasant aroma. That's pretty much as far as my abilities to describe wine goes so the only thing left was to quaff. It was delicious and the first glass went down quickly. A smack of the lips and another poured at which point I thought that for once I'd educate myself a little as to what this gem of a wine was. The label told me that it was local, which I already knew, and on the back it gave the usual serving suggestions along the lines of 'goes well with fish' or 'perfect with a light lunch'. For people like me it should really also say 'perfect after you've already drunk a lot of alcohol already'. My eyes strayed to a small label that was just below these helpful hints. Now if you like wine and like me know little about the making of it aside that it involves vines, grapes, vats and bottles you will share my surprise at what was written thereon. I may well have been a wee bit tipsy but this wine, you see, had as part of its ingredients fish extract, charcoal and egg. No I was not blurry eyed and although it was quite a palatable wine I couldn't help thinking that I could taste a bit of haddock as I supped away.

Day thirty nine: December 12th

The following morning I got up quite early with a slightly sore head and still feeling that I'd had kedgeree the night before, got into the car and headed to my final destination, the Blue Mountains. The mountains played a key part in Australian European history and although they had been explored by men such as John Wilson, Francis Barrallier and William Paterson it was not until 1813 that they were crossed by Gregory Blaxland, Lieutenant Lawson and William Wentworth. Many of the earliest explorers tended to be landowners or at least men of position and were often referred to as 'cockies' which sounds exactly as it means as many of these men were self-assured and cocky and not to be confused with the other 'cockie' who was a dirt poor farmer who spent his life trying to grow crops only for cockatoos to come in and plunder the field. They were also referred to as 'nobs' and here this is not to be confused with the National Organisation of Beaters and Pickers Up, also known as NOBs. Being the 'cockie' he was, Blaxland recorded his journey in his log in the third person (this is a quote by taken from Flannery in 'The Explorers'):

' ... they had sufficiently accomplished the design of their undertaking, having surmounted all the difficulties which has hitherto prevented the interior of country from being explored, and the colony from being expanded ... ' and it had been an incredibly arduous journey with progress slow such that by the time they returned as he goes on to report 'Their provisions were nearly expended, their clothes and shoes were in very bad condition, and the whole party were ill with bowel complaints.' Perhaps that chicken vindaloo they'd had the night before wasn't such a good idea.

This was the real start of European expansion west and the Governor, Lachlan Macquarie, was keen to know more so he sent the explorer and deputy surveyor George Evans to not just verify what Blaxland had done but to see how much further he could get. In this he became the first European to cross Australia's Great Dividing Range and in doing so he had shown conclusively that the land beyond was ripe for expansion and cultivation. The National Library of Australia has a cutting from the Sydney Morning Herald from the spring of 1814 written by Macquarie expressing not just his gratitude to Evans but also to Blaxland and his team but also highlighting one of the key reasons why these expeditions were so important:

'The greater part of these plains are described as being nearly free of timber and brushwood, and in capacity equal (in Mr. Evans' opinion) to every demand this colony may have for an extension of tillage and pastures for a century to come.'

By 1815 thanks to William Cox, also known as the 'Road-builder' and it now appears a distant relative of that other Neighbours stalwart Jason Donovan, a road was in place and, along with the discoveries of the others, helped to pave the way for the development of the Hunter Valley and beyond. Cox from all accounts was quite a decent bloke and was regarded as being more humane than many of his contemporaries who were in authority. Anyway, Katoomba, where I was headed, was bang in the middle of all of this. In order to get there I decided that the best route would be to go west towards route 69 (not that there is anything remotely sexual about this choice) which connected Singleton to some of the outlying areas of the old colony such as Windsor, Richmond and Paramatta, although I would only go as far as Kurrajong before then heading to Katoomba. As I drove along the scenery just became incredible with green everywhere dominated by tall eucalypts standing proud against the clear blue sky; my chums the cicadas were also back in force making enough noise to wake the dead, but I didn't care as I began to climb higher into Wollemi National Park, home to the so-called dinosaur tree, the Wollemi Pine (for all you gardeners out there *Wollemia Nobilis*) which is millions of years old and one of the rarest in the world. This park is an incredible wilderness that just brims with life and is home to a large percentage of Australia's flora and fauna. It is also the first part of what in 2000 was designated the Greater Blue Mountains World Heritage Site which comprises eight national parks in all.

As I passed Wollemi to my right, to my left driving along what was a ridge I had Yengo National Park, home to Mount Yengo one of the most spiritual places of the local peoples. Here the Great Spirit Baime is said to have stepped on the top of the mountain making it flat after he had completed his creation. In the Dreamtime, or Dreaming, there is the story of the Creation which starts with the awakening of supernatural beings who were living underground, half creature and half human known also as the Totemic Ancestors, who then created all things from the animals that roam, everything in and on the earth, man through to the sun, moon and stars. Each creation has a meaning and a spirit. For example the sun is female and it is her daughter who lights up the sky everyday only to go back underground at the end of the day because she wants to rejoin her mother in the west. The spirituality of these stories varies but there is a common thread or a crossover in many. Of utmost significance to the Aboriginals is that these spirits, the Totemic Ancestors, having returned to sleep after their work was completed, often became features of the land and are seen as sacred to Aboriginal people only to be visited by those who have been initiated in the ways of Dreamtime. This has led to disputes between those Aboriginals who hold to their beliefs and those non-Aboriginals who don't, with perhaps the best example being the arguments between the traditional owners of Uluru, the Anangu people, and the tourist industry about whether it is right for people to be climbing the rock. There is a feel to Aboriginal descriptions of the world around them which makes the more scientific way to describe the relationships between animals, man, plants or to look at the mechanics of say the wind, the earth or even the planets which may well be fascinating seem rather dull. For us, the so-called cultured and educated for example, the moon is just that, the moon. It orbits our planet, comes out at night and is replaced by the sun (or in the case of the UK, cloud/rain) by day. To the Aboriginal people there is much, much more to this and it is celebrated in the rituals of dance and word today most importantly at corroborees. As I passed Mount Yengo somewhere in the wooded hinterland I remembered what I'd also read and that it was declared an Aboriginal Place, the largest in New South Wales, by the State Government in April 2009 and has specific importance to the Wonnarua, Awakabu, Worimi and Darkinung who the Department of Environment and Climate Change recognised at the same time as being the traditional owners. I wondered as I drove along which spirit was watching me.

I came to Kurrajong, a small but decidedly wealthy-looking small town where I stopped for some lunch. As I sat there munching away on a delicious tuna sandwich I tapped into the town's website to see if there was much to look at before I turned inland towards Lithgow and thence to Katoomba. Kurrajong was one of the towns that was selected for re-settlement for returning veterans of both World Wars and was described by Mr. W.S Arnold, the Superintendant of Soldier Settlement Scheme (sic) in glowing terms 'to all who would seek the tonic of pure air and the exhilaration of beautiful scenery, the call of Kurrajong is simply irresistible.' As the sixtieth fly dived bombed me I was not quite sure that at that exact moment in time I'd have agreed with him, but it was nevertheless pleasant on the eye and quiet. One coffee and obligatory belch later, a quick nose around the high street (which was a little passé) and I was back in the car, driving west along the Bells Line of Road, also know more boringly as State Route 40, still with the Wollemi National Park on my right, but significantly now to my left, the Blue Mountains National Park. The road out of Kurrajong through to Bilpin and down through Berambing was packed with houses that were not for those on a small budget. In Bilpin a modest four bedroom house could have set back the average worker over ten times the national average wage. In return, though, the occupants did get an idyllic part of the world to live in, albeit with the ever present threat of forest fires.

I was making good progress and so decided that rather than turning south at Bell towards Mount Victoria and on to Katoomba I would go into Lithgow because I had read in my ever reliable guide that there were 'places of interest'. Let me say this from the outset, Lithgow is not an attractive town. It has an industrial past, was named by Oxley after the first Auditor-General of New South Wales, has lots of historic sites including the 'must see' Small Arms Factory which just for clarity is not about people who have short arms but about guns dating back to the early days of European settlement. I decided that I would double check just to make sure and pulled up outside the very pedestrian looking building in which the museum was housed. Well blow me down and stand me up again because it was closed on Saturdays and looking at a rather curled piece of paper taped to door for most of the week. I just loved my guide book's accuracy. There wasn't much else to see, everything looked like it had been shut for the season or else a major epidemic had erased all human existence because there was virtually no sign of any life. Even the birds had seemingly chirruped their last before I'd arrived. I needed a plan B and remembered that on my way into Lithgow I'd passed the Zig Zag railway at a place called Clarence. I checked the guide book and nothing, not even a passing reference. That was a good sign as it suggested that as no one from the publication had visited this or thought it worth to mention as a 'must see' it was bound to be open. I turned round and headed back up the steep gradient out of Lithgow and drive the few kilometres to the railway terminal at Clarence. I turned off the highway into the massive car park which was empty, a veritable Marie Celeste of car parks one might say. This didn't look good for the railway being open. This was also clearly the end of the line (the giveaway was that the line ended, so no real detective work required on my part). The station was a relatively small wooden affair and like all enthusiast-run steam railways was decorated with posters and signs that harked back to a bygone era. And even better it was open. I was completely alone aside from the staff, one of whom was shuffling up and down the platform dressed as,

I presumed, a station-master from the 19th century (it may have been that's how he dressed everyday but I didn't want to pry) whilst the other was sat behind what was the ticket office/cafe/shop counter.

I was curious to know more, especially if I was to part with my money, as to what this was all about and what, more to the point, was on offer. I approached the shuffler who turned out to be George and who was indeed the station master. He was quite pleased to see me as I think business might have been quite slow to this point and quickly said hello telling me that he worked here at the week-ends as a volunteer whilst during the week he worked in an office "shoving paper around". So I asked him about the history of the railway and it was as if I had released him from a vow of silence as he then started to give me the story in a tone that could be described as 'excitable'.

"The Zig Zag dates from 1869 and was built in order to be a link between the city and the developments that were taking place in the coal and iron industries around Lithgow and the surrounding areas. It was a real beaut' in engineering terms and really does zigzag from here into the valley below. At the height of the railway Clarence was one of the busiest points on the line with trains all over congregating in this one spot as they waited their turn to move down the valley or into Sydney. At its peak Clarence had a population of over 3,000, it was real busy but it didn't last long as by 1910 they'd built tunnels through Mount Sinai and linked Sydney to Lithgow and beyond and thus no longer required this railway. Because of this it fell into a state of disrepair until some enthusiasts formed the Zig Zag Railway Co-Op with the intention of putting it back on the map, which was officially opened 106 years to the day that the original line went into service. Where we are now was opened in 1988. Today we take tourists from here all the way to where one of the original steel smelters was sited at Bottom Points. There's a story about one of the earlier visitors to the railway back in around 1880 who described the journey as 'a descent into Hades' as they saw the flames and smoke from the smelter." Now breathe, George.

George also told me that originally the State Government were not interested in providing any funds to the restoration so all that was here was done through private means. As he had been talking a young family had appeared and as with all things different, the children were all talking at once in excited voices asking dad when the train was coming in, how long would it be, where did it go, what time would it arrive, which stations did it call at and so on. It is a fact that young children when really excited about something have the attention span of a gnat and I was listening to a perfect example of this as dad answered the same questions, albeit cleverly rephrased, with the patience of Job. The train eventually arrived and by now the passenger manifold had grown to myself, the young family, a slightly dirty looking individual who I would venture to guess was probably a train spotter and a couple of oriental tourists. All aboard and we were away and immediately over the intercom a soulless voice started to tell the story of the railway as George had with me. I did learn that none of what was running today originated from New South Wales, the engine being built for the Tasmanian Government Railway whilst the carriages were originally from the suburban lines in and out of Brisbane. As the disembowelled voice flowed forth my suspected train spotter was scribbling away furiously in his notebook such that I was a little worried it might burst into flames. He looked very pained with his tongue protruding from the bottom left hand side of his mouth amidst all this frantic activity. I was about to ask him whether he'd considered using a Dictaphone as can now be seen frequently at London Bridge Station when I suddenly had a thought. What if he had been looking at me and was in fact writing in his note book a description of me; the people watcher being watched. I stopped looking at him and gazed out of the window as the train pulled out of Clarence.

The disembowelled voice who I'd nicknamed Bruce for no other reason than I believe in stereotyping to avoid any ambiguity then announced that the railway consisted of a number of loops and that in order to get to the valley floor the train would pull in half way down to allow the engine to switch ends. Bruce also told me how many tunnels there were and how many viaducts we would cross. All jolly interesting and accompanied by the most spectacular views not just of the valley but also the railway itself. It was fun for all the family, and worth an ice-cream on arrival in 'Hades', where the flavours were orange or orange so, being in good cheer, I asked for a 99' only to have the volunteer, Fred (love those name badges still) reply without batting an eyelid "One orange 99 coming up … " handing me an ice lolly which, given the heat, instantly evaporated. Notebook man was now furiously photographing everything with a passion that would make any Japanese tourist proud although I'd not want to be at one of his 'and this is what I did on holiday' get-togethers (" … and this is a very exciting picture of a double bogey twin headed piston cylinder type 4–0–4 rotating steam engine … "). We all climbed back onto the train and puffed-puffed our way back to Clarence, or more accurately we chugged-chugged as this was a diesel engine (and not a double bogey twin … .) due to the fact that as a result of the drought conditions, all steam locos had been grounded. Thinking about this are trains grounded given that they are already on the ground as it were? Maybe they are quarantined? I must get out more!

It was now mid afternoon and I needed to check-in and find my beer for the evening so I headed back towards Bell, down to Mount Victoria (very pretty and where I had a very enjoyable and highly fattening cream tea two days later) and then west again through the pretty town of Blackheath, visited in 1815 by Macquarie who gave it its name, and finally Katoomba itself, known to the local indigenous people by its Aboriginal name, 'Kedumba' ('shiny falling waters). The region where the town sits is the ancestral home of a number of language groups and tribes, the Gundungjarra, Wanaruah, Wiradjuri, Darkingung, Darug and Dharawal who had roamed the land for tens of thousands of years. This was my final destination of the trip and I was both sad because it was all coming to an end and yet at the same time quite excited, as much by my expectations of what the Blue Mountains had to offer, but also because on the 16th I was going home and would be back with the family in time for Christmas. However, things didn't start well. For whatever reason, call it romanticism or just a lack of research, I had envisaged staying in a quaint town, surrounded by mountains and forests, birds singing away in the trees and the gentle breezes of late spring keeping the heat down, sitting on a balcony outside my room from where I could slurp mojitos and beer, whilst watching the sun set behind the mountains. It was, in fact, going to be the ideal place to unwind, relax, enjoy some decent food and walk or cycle the trails. At first I was damned if I could find the hotel as I arrived into Katoomba's outskirts along Route 32, the main arterial route that takes the traveller from Sydney all the way to Adelaide, South Australia a mere 1658 kilometres away. Just to put this into some sort of perspective it would be like driving from Lands End in the south west corner of England to the Shetland Islands' capital Lerwick on the assumption I had either an aquatic car or that said vehicle was a really a divinity and could drive on water and yet in Australia if I'd done the distance I'd still have at completed only about 40% of the total trans-Continental route. From an historical perspective this stretch is better known as 'The Great Western Highway', albeit originally named the Great Western Road by Macquarie in 1815, and was the very road that was built by William Cox. Adding to the sense of being lost was the multi-lane layout of the highway (actually just four lanes, two westbound and two eastbound but in Australian parlance a super-highway) which had a fair bit of traffic, much of which comprised large trucks or camper vans going all over the place (I might have been a little tired at this point but that's what it felt like). Surely my hotel was somewhere much quieter than this, tucked away I felt sure in some sort of Eden and hence the difficulty in locating it. Not to fret it wouldn't be long before that idyll became my reality. And then I saw it and my first thought was surely not. There's this road and there's my hotel, my supposed serendipity which might just as well have been on the highway itself and probably would have been had it not been perched precariously on a small hillock. My heart sank. This looked horrible. Knowing my luck I would no doubt have a room that faced the road (which I indeed did have), and that it would be just one big noise-fest. This was to be my last taste of Australia, surely not!

I drove up the steep drive into the hotel, parked and festered away in the car muttering unmentionable things about the travel company and how incompetent they were, given what I'd specifically requested, and that they'd put me in the middle of nowhere that would result in almost certain death to get to anywhere as to get to Katoomba town centre meant crossing the highway and seemed thousands of kilometres away. Still muttering I checked in and enquired how many days travel I still was from Katoomba and should I take provisions before I left, only to be told:

"Easy mate; all you have to do is go down the driveway you came in on, turn right, walk maybe a kilometre, cross the road by the lights and you're there. Ten to fifteen minutes at most."

The news was good and my mood, although still not great, had improved enough that I merrily skipped up the stairs to my room, but in a very heterosexual fashion. Maybe things were better than I had expected after all. I dumped my cases and set off for the town centre. Looking into the history of Katoomba, the name of Kedumba was first mentioned in 1828 according to Jim Smith in his article 'New Insights into Gundungurra' in a Crown Survey carried out by Robert Dixon. He goes on to trace the development of the name from then to its current form and how this was championed by James Henry Neale. Originally the town, or at least the station, was named 'Crushers' in 1874 because of the noise made by the crushing plant (and my thanks here go to various websites of modern day crushing companies for enlightening me as to what these plants do; *most* interesting and a recommendation for all fellow anorak wearers and those others like me for whom life is just so exciting) which provided metal that was used in the construction of the Permanent Way. However, in 1877 the present name was adopted. Katoomba was also just over the midway point for Blaxland and his team, arriving here thirteen days into their expedition, although then it was no more than a blip on the map and would have probably had an Aboriginal name. On the Great Western Highway there was 'The Explorers' Tree' which is a salute to them and their achievements. It was also a place that our intrepid explorer George Evans visited and there is an historic marker that commemorates this just outside some government buildings. On the marker, aside from explaining the relevance that it had was a quote from Evan's log book describing the scene on the 2nd January 1814:

> 'At a quarter of a Mile is a Tract of Forest Land underneath this Ridge, the centre a marsh, I judge leads to the Riverlett which apparently runs between some high hills about a Mile West; beyond are Mountains considerably higher that what I am now on; the road is through thick brushes and over pieces of sharp Granite Rock. Halted in a Valley of good feed and water.'

Today, he'd have been run over by one the large trucks passing along the highway a mere ten metres away if he'd ventured forth. It was odd to imagine that standing here as I was dressed in a natty t-shirt (one of those that men of a certain age wear because we think it looks cool and 'with it' and can be 'in' with the kids), sandals and shorts, just under two hundred years ago at this very spot was one of the great Australian explorers looking around and I think probably wondering if he'd make it back to Sydney. Unlike him though, the only concern I had was that the beer was cold and the food was hot that evening. As I walked over the railway bridge and into the town itself, the past was still evident in the design of the buildings around the centre of town, many of which looked functional rather than places of fun (even though one I passed just before the high street appeared to be a rather grotty looking night club) to the very grand looking Carrington Hotel where the wealth earned in mining could be spent. The buildings were mostly two storey affairs, solidly built and in that style so prevalent of the colonies with many predating not just the Second World War, but also the First. They'd all retained their character, including the grandly named Palais Royale which had been built in 1896. They also reflected a reality that many of the towns in Australia have which is that their past is more glorious than their present which, for me, is actually preferable as it allows history to be seen and not replaced by some faceless lump of concrete and glass stuffed full of offices. However, unlike Lithgow which felt like it was gasping for air to stay alive with little activity, human or otherwise, (either that or everyone was around John and Jan's for their famous 'let's invite the entire town' barbecue), Katoomba had a vibrancy even though I'd read that it was past its prime. The streets were busy with day-trippers grabbing an early beer and dinner (Sydney and its suburbs were no more than 120 or so kilometres away), young backpackers trying to find the cheapest food outlet, locals meeting friends for a night on the town and families out enjoying a stroll in the late afternoon sun. Restaurants and cafes were beginning to fill up, after all it was nearly seven in the evening so almost closing time and yet there was no sense of urgency in anyone. Having been in the country now for close to six weeks it felt perfectly natural, as if in some sort of slow-motion sequence from a film, to be a part of this relaxed approach to life which was utterly removed from what it was like back at home. I popped into the local booze shop, liberated a few beers and a bottle of wine, complemented the shop assistant on the town which she personally took credit for, and looked for somewhere to have dinner and decide what to do in for my last two days in Australia.

Day forty: December 13th

It was another glorious day as I set forth to conquer the Federal Pass from Leura in the west to the eastern part of Katoomba at the Golden Stairs. My decision had been reached the evening before when I'd been given a guide/map by one of the staff at the bar I'd had a couple of beers in. My new chum, let's call him Mr. Liar (I'll explain why later although it starts to become obvious) said that if the weather was kind then this would be an experience never to forget and not too demanding. To be precise he summed up the walk as: " … .going down a lot of steps, walking a ways in the rainforest which was pretty flat, past the old mine workings where the railway is and where you can go back up or on until you get to Golden Stairs. It'll be a breeze."

"But" I said pointing at the entire route and showing him "the guide suggests that it will take around six hours to do all that"

"Aww, that's only if you walk slowly. I reckon you're done in maybe three, maybe four hours at most. If you're chicken you can finish at the mine by going back up there into town."

"Are you sure?"

"Sure I'm sure" he said laughing that hollow laugh which sounds more like a sneer but is a tad politer, but still suggesting that I was chicken.

Chicken, me, perish the thought after all I was an explorer, a fearless warrior of the wild and this was a challenge to what remained of my manhood (I've been married a long time you see). It was only three to four hours so I thought "Fair enough", as that would also allow me time to visit, what the town guide described as the 'Quirky, clean Katoomba toilets …' that included a list of highly recommended toilets to visit. I can't say that I have visited many toilets that are defined as quirky but I do remember going to some trendy bar in Soho in Manhattan where all the toilets were unisex and the way to know if they were occupied was simple as the door would be frosted (door closes, frosts up; door opens de-frosts). When I needed to avail myself of the facilities after I'd had one or two 'cocktails' as our American cousins would say I merrily forgot that these loos were unisex and because of that closing the door properly. The face on the lady as I came out was one I'd like to believe of awe given the unexpected flash she had seen, but I know deep down it was probably more of shock. The other thing about not spending all the day on the go was that it would also give me some time to perhaps just spend an afternoon unwinding with a glass or two of grape juice to catch my thoughts and, for really the first time on this trip, do nothing. Well that was the idea and to me and, based on my new pal, Mr. Liar, very achievable.

I looked at the map again and felt reassured. Even the online bushwalking information service said that the walk was 'moderate' and that with all the wonderful scenery suggested that it would be a relaxing, marginally strenuous, walk in the woods. In fact the only thing that could possibly go wrong aside from the weather turning nasty was if I met the Australian version of Sasquatch or the Abominable Snowman, which is referred to as a 'Yowie'. The Yowie has its fans as with the other two and there are many articles, books and websites dedicated to the sightings of these strange creatures and, in some, serious discussions of an anthropological nature how they are linked to one of the apes' ancestors, Gigantopithecus which according to The Museum of UnNatural History was discovered by Professor Gustav von Koenigswald and … :

' … was the largest primate that ever walked the Earth. He would have risen 9 to 10 feet high if he choose to stand up on only his hind legs, and probably weighed about 600 lbs (A few scientists suggest the largest of the males might have weighed almost 1,200 lbs.). In comparison, the largest gorilla stands only 6 feet tall and weighs about 300 to 400 lbs.'

Another website appropriately named 'Australian Yowie Research', informed me that as early as 1790 the earliest white settlers had reported seeing large creatures, but even before them the Aboriginals across the Continent told of stories of these huge ape-like beings although they had different names for them depending on the region. I knew one thing for sure if it I met him or her then the only thing I'd be thinking is whether I could run faster than Usain Bolt. The first part of the walk went smoothly because from my hotel and through Katoomba the road down to Leura descended to the edge of the cliffs that loomed up out of the Jamison Valley. Even when I took the steps down from Merriwa Street into the canopy of the Leura Forest and thence towards the Dardanelles Pass it was easy. Progress was quick such that I even had time to have a banana and drink break at a picnic spot complete with gazebo that had had some photographs of visitors from a different era all, it appeared, dressed for church but like me keen to explore. Given that I was beginning to feel the heat more and had begun to operate as is my wont like a human sauna looking at these sepia pictures made me think that the people in them were completely off their trolleys dressed like that. As I sat there I looked at the map and looked at what I'd covered so far and how much time it had take so far and felt quite good with myself although I did note with a little trepidation a warning that came with the map: 'It's rare to encounter a snake on a track as they usually know your coming and stay clear … ' well that's a relief but … 'if you are stupid enough to harass one or pick it up, I'm on the snake's side' How dumb have you got to be to pick up a snake? Oh, that's right, be like that lady from Fraser Island and think that the legless thing slithering in the bush is a lizard that has had an unfortunate accident.

Tourism has been a feature around the valley for well over 100 years, but with the focus being at the cliff tops where Victorians and then Edwardians could stroll around and admire the fantastic scenery that confronted them. Federal Pass' life began in 1900 and took the more spirited walker from Katoomba Falls to Leura Falls. This though was just the beginning because in 1901 James McKay became the Chief Ranger and it is really thanks to him that Federal Pass was then extended to where it is today and it is down to him that some of the most ambitious parts of the walk were completed even in the face of some strong opposition along the lines of "You're nuts", but more on this in a moment. As I walked through the dense undergrowth, surrounded by huge ferns, pines and tall eucalypts I continued following the signs to 'The scenic railway', past the intersection at the Dardanelles Pass and the base of the Three Sisters. Just before this I had passed what had been one of the single most ambitious projects on this trail, the Giant Stairway. Conceived prior to World War I as a means to connect Echo Point above to the Jamison Valley below it was then abandoned as being a barmy idea, but eventually was finished and opened in 1932. The Sydney Morning Herald for the 3rd October 1932 carried the story as the Premier, Mr. Stevens did the honours:

'The stairway has not been misnamed. Hewn from the rock of a perpendicular cliff 1000 feet high, its 800 steps and runways take one to the Jamieson Valley below. At the bottom, it connects with the Federal Pass, almost midway between Katoomba and Leura, thus bringing the pass within easy reach of the visitor. Mr. and Mrs. Stevens and their children did not descend the 800 steps, but they went far enough to convince them of their rugged beauty and the magnitude of the task … Later, Mr. and Mrs. Stevens, with other visitors, stood for some moments on the look- out, just above the first step of the stair-way' (and) 'met Chief Ranger McKay, who conceived the idea of constructing the stairway, and carried it out. It was a proud day for this veteran of the mountains. He told the Premier how people used to laugh when he mentioned his proposal; how he persevered and hacked the first footholds from the cliff; how a former council ordered him to cease work; and, finally, how he achieved a long-cherished ambition. So dangerous was the work that on occasions he had to be roped to prevent him falling to certain death below. "The real McKay," one visitor observed after hearing a few details of the task.'

I was a little tempted to ascend the stairs but decided against it and carried on walking, rounding the Dardanelles Pass and joined the Federal Pass below the Prince Henry Cliff Walk. I was surrounded by enormous trees dominated by eucalypts and thick vegetation which made viewing across the valley quite difficult but that didn't matter as I was having fun. I soon came to the original start at the Katoomba Falls and crossed Cook's Crossing and walked on to the Turpentine Tree which pointed me towards the Furber Steps which was where the mine was located, an important slice of local history. I'd made really good progress so far not least as I tend to walk fast unless my wife is with me when, as a last gesture of my almost forgotten independence when I could do what I wanted, I walk slowly.

Along this part of the walk and as I came to where the mine was, I had come across a few other adventurers and as we came close and then passed there was much nodding as we politely, yet silently, acknowledged each other, because that's what tourists do, nod. Well at least that's what we do in an area which is clearly tourist heavy or, as I prefer to call it, 'neutral territory'. Here the art of talking to another person or at least verbally acknowledging their existence seems to be superfluous, unnecessary even. So what exactly is this 'neutral territory'? Just before I explain this perhaps a little contextualisation is required. In all my travels to foreign climes I always felt that by learning some rudimentary phrases it helped me to get by and avoid too much embarrassment, from the very important like "Where the hell am I" to the essential "Please don't point that gun at me or my leg will fall off." One of the best ones that I learnt from a guide book given to me about Cape Town was "Where is the liquor shop?" There is a serious point to this though and that is not to stick out like a sore thumb in some of the less salubrious parts of the world because I, the tourist, may be the only one and thus potentially a vulnerable target. Even the simple "Hello" can suffice I find as it often puts others at ease resulting in a faint smile, or else, given that my pronunciation is probably terrible, it is a look of bemused concern that I might be the village idiot. This approach does have its potential pitfalls as a story I was told years ago by a friend of mine demonstrated. Her father, not known as a polyglot, decided that as he and his wife were off to France he would learn to say the French colloquial word for "Hi". My friend who speaks the lingo like a native taught him the right word, or so she thought. He returned after his fortnight away and rang his daughter to express his disappointment that, having learnt the word, all he'd got were black looks from the local French. She related that her subsequent conversation with her father went something like this:

"What word did you use Dad? Was it the one I told you?"
"Yes, of course."
"What did you say?"
"Well I said what you told me, salaud"
"Salaud?"
"Yes, salaud. That's right isn't it?"
"If you'd said 'salut' then yes, but sadly you have just spent two weeks questioning their legitimacy."

We can debate for hours whether this was a deliberate faux pas by him or based on fact but it does bring me back to this nodding business in the 'neutral territory'. Simply put this is an area that is specifically just for tourists and where we are in the majority. It is a comfort zone where we are one herd and thus less likely to be attacked by some deranged local. Not only that, at most tourist sites if we need to know something then English, however basic, is invariably the lingua franca, both written and spoken. Given that English is still the world's most used language and most people speak a smattering that is enough at least to get by and invariably sufficient to understand what is written on the various information boards that are all over tourist spots. As such there is no need to learn any other complicated language or talk even. The outcome of all of this is that instead of conversation there is a lot of polite nodding because we are in this 'neutral territory' and we are all tourists doing a touristy thing and if we want to know something we only have to read it. It is a far cry from asking directions of a local. We are safe, cocooned in our own tourist world where everything is easy to follow if written or, as with the Zig Zag Railway, piped through a rather old intercom system for all to hear and learn. There are some exceptions to this theory of mine, most notably in Russia where it seems that unless one speaks Russian, then one is doomed to reading a lot of Cyrillic text without the faintest idea what it means. English — fat chance. And whatever else happens, don't even think about asking one of the many Babushka's that sit around in museums doing what appears to be absolutely nothing as they won't even acknowledge a person's existence and may actually eat you.

The old mine workings, located at Orphan Rock, are today 'a tourist hotspot for any visitor to the Blue Mountains'. Well that's what my guidebook told me. What it failed to tell me was that here at the bottom of the cliffs half, if not all of Japan's population, had arrived making easy movement a little difficult as cameras flashed and poses were made, all doing the Churchillian 'V' for victory sign as their picture was taken. The mine was founded in the 1870's by John Britty North who originally came to Australia in 1852 having been born in the West Country back in the UK. In the Australian Dictionary of Biography he comes across as a determined individual:

> 'In the 1870s with Robert Henry Reynolds, whom he later bought out, he began to mine for coal in the Jamieson Valley near Katoomba. Once, without machinery and with only a few men, he hauled a 4-cwt (203 kg) block of coal 1100 ft (335 m) up the slopes to exhibit it in Sydney where it secured for North a government contract. An exacting employer, North had over a hundred men at his Katoomba Coal Mine which in 1878 he registered as a company.'

As I looked around me it was hard to believe that here in this heavily wooded rainforest that any industry had taken place. There was a slightly tacky exhibit located in one of the old openings but little else except the scenic railway. This was originally used to haul the coal from the mine workings to Katoomba at the top of the cliffs. Following the closure of the mine the scenic railway was established. Now I have once or twice braved roller-coasters with all that entails (breakfast out, lots of screaming and a general admission that this was about the stupidest idea I'd had in ages) and here was a chance to not just end my walk but also experience the 'thrill' of riding up in this contraption some 450 metres at an alarming, well to me, angle of 52 degrees. My decision as to whether to take this was tempered by the fact that the queue to ascend was quite long so I contented myself walking around the boardwalk that took me into the rainforest and offered a variety of viewing areas to see the creatures that lived here. As I looked hard at the forest and saw the square root of nothing I had a sneaky feeling that they must have all gone on holiday with their chums from the Sea Acres Rainforest Reserve back in Port Macquarie; trees and ferns aplenty but not one furry or slithery thing to be seen.

Rejoining the pass and remembering the challenge from Mr. Liar I resolved to continue to the Golden Stairs, after all I was still making good progress. The sign pointing the way to my final destination said it was 3.5kilometres, a doddle and surely no more than 40–45, maybe 60 minutes at most I calculated assuming of course that what was up ahead was as had been written on the guide, 'moderate'. The route hugged the cliffs to my right, passing the odd old mine workings, and once more I was achieving a good pace and had I been called Dorothy and had as company a cowardly lion, a heartless tin man and brainless scarecrow I'd merrily sing that "we were off to see the wonderful Great Stair of Katoomba", because at this point all seemed right with the world. The sun was casting its shadows through the trees, it was warm but the breeze was pleasant, my heart was light and I could taste that first drop of cold white wine or deep, fruity red. However, Mr. Liar omitted to tell me of one slight snag on the Federal Pass that had come about in 1931, namely the landslide just after Malaita Point. I only had about 1.5kilometres to go, which had the path not suddenly become an exercise in rock scrambling, would have taken minutes. And scramble is exactly what I was now doing and though the view was undeniably superb I was too intent on both avoiding a potential fatal slip or, just as bad, a bite from some nasty rock hugging snake. This was not fun, not even enjoyable and was taking a lot of effort. As I struggled over yet another mini mountain one of the skinniest persons I think I have ever seen appeared as if from nowhere.

Frankly he would have been difficult to spot even if I'd been looking. Even his walking stick was fatter than him. Worse still he wasn't even perspiring and had a smile on his face and, as he got nearer, leaping from rock to rock like some mountain goat he cheerily greeted me with:

> "G'day mate, lovely walk. Mind you it's a little steep that way" he said pointing in the direction I was heading "but what great views though watch your footing – it's easy to fall!"

I didn't respond because for that split second I blamed him for everything including Mr. Liar, the map, that bushwalking guide telling me it was a 'moderate' walk that could now kill me (yet another potentially lethal thing in this country) and because, as he was an Australian, I felt like telling him that it was his bloody fault. Churlish yes, indeed a little childish but I would have felt better. However, I opted just to glare at him to avoid, yet a scene. My anger was not made any better by that fact where he had just come from and where I was heading had clearly been easy for him, yet here I was sweating so much that there was a real possibility that I'd be mistaken for a newly discovered waterfall whilst he was the total opposite. In his eyes I could sense that look of worry that comes over someone when they realise that a potential faux pas had been made. In this case my glare and silence may just have alerted him that there was an 'atmosphere' and that the quivering fat thing on the rock in front of him may well be slightly deranged. He quickly moved on, leaping like the damn mountain goat he was from rock to rock whilst I looked ahead of me and just thought "Why?" My agility can be described, at best, as being static to non-existent and I had a horrible feeling that things were going to get a lot tougher. It was lucky I hadn't read the cautionary tale I came across later about the dangers of the Federal Pass (and again I would emphasise the word 'moderate') which came from the Sydney Morning Herald in an article dated Friday 25 May 1934 as I might have not even have got this far:

> 'Thelma Partridge, 20, of St. John's Avenue, Gordon, fell 150 feet down a steep slope in the Federal Pass, near Katoomba, yesterday. Her life was saved by a large tree, which stopped her from falling down a cliff below. She was seriously injured ... The track was

rough, and her foot slipped on a wet stone. She attempted to regain her balance, but fell over the edge. The steep slope was covered with loose stones, stumps, logs, and bushes. They bruised her body as she was dashed against them, but they interrupted her progress to some extent and probably saved her life. She attempted to clutch the bushes as she rolled past them. A large tree about 150 feet from the path blocked her fall and she crashed against it. Her back, chest, neck, hands, arms, and legs were badly injured, and she suffered concussion.'

An hour later I reached my destination, the Golden Stairs and realised that the horror of the landslide, from which I was still alive, was nothing compared with what was about to happen next because of course I had to ascend to get back to the town. I don't know what I'd expected, after all the way down at Leura although long didn't seem particularly steep. Forty minutes later, almost on hands and knees and some 850 metres higher than where I'd been I was at Glenraphael Drive and on my way back. Total time taken, excluding the detours, had been six hours, two more than expected, and what's more what Mr. Liar had failed to mention was that from where I was to where I needed to be, namely my hotel, was going to take the best part of the rest of the afternoon and early evening. I was not best pleased but carried on and found the main road that followed the cliff which provided various spots to take happy snaps of the valley and mountains. By now I had nothing left to sweat out and needed to get some liquid inside me before I collapsed in a heap on the road. I grumbled to myself that knowing my luck if I did collapse I would probably get picked up by some local hick who, mistaking me for a Yowie of restricted height but large girth, would have had me stuffed and placed on the floor in front of the fireplace. As I soldiered on I recalled the scene from that great war film, 'Ice Cold Alex', where Captain Anson (Sir John Mills) leads a small group of evacuees who have escaped from Tobruk by driving through the German lines and is motivated all the while by the thought of an ice cold lager once they reached their destination (apparently this was filmed first thing in the morning, it wasn't hot and not particularly pleasant) and thinking that I too needed to find a place of ale or at the very least somewhere that had liquid refreshment of any kind. The good news for me was that this turned out to be Scenic World where, had I been good with both heights and cable cars I could have ridden the Scenic Skyway a mere 270 metres above the ravine below. Some years ago when on a team-building trip to Switzerland we climbed a mountain and then descended on what can only be described as one of the worst thirty minutes of my mortal existence as we (the team, not the royal we of course) went down on a cable car suspended in outer space as far as I could work out. I was left a quivering puddle of humanity on the floor of the cable car only to be then told when it arrived at the stop that we had to catch another, but this time it was one of those ski lift things that leaves the rider dangling precariously above the ground. The whole journey took what seemed a lifetime and I swore that I wouldn't ride a cable car or ski lift ever again, unless it meant promotion because then of course the suffering would be for a sensible reason, which is why the Scenic Skyway was out of the question.

The lady in the refreshment kiosk suggested that I go on to Echo Point to witness "one of the wonders of Australia". Given that I was knackered and wishing that I was in a bar with a bottle of wine the thought of walking too much further had as much appeal as shoving a conga eel down my pants. Mr Liar's three to four hour walk had lasted nearly seven hours so far and even if I went back from here I was looking at another fifty minutes or so at least. But she did say it would be worth it and she was very pretty and I thought why not so off I went following the Prince Henry Cliff Walk which afforded glimpses of the Blue Mountain range along its way. But this was nothing to compare with what I saw next. There have been times in my life when something will stick in my mind because the memory is just so incredible, good or bad, but here it was the former because Echo Point was just incredible. As I left the path and came onto the viewing area, with not a cloud in the sky, I was almost blown away by one of the most spectacularly beautiful sights I have ever seen ranking alongside other greats like walking around Mount St Helens in the US, going up Mount Ventoux in the Auvergne region of France and, of course, me in a pair of Speedos. In front of me were the Blue Mountains and the valley from which they rise in all their splendid glory. The air was warm, birds were singing away competing noisily with my ever present friend the cicada and there was a gorgeously sweet smell that filled my nostrils coming from the pine and eucalypt trees. If I was into jaw-dropping then now would have been the time to do this. In front of me, stretching as far as the eye could see was forest and mountains with, and this was the icing on the cake, a blue haze hovering above them. The blue, from which the mountains get their modern name, is a natural phenomenon that comes about due to the oils in the eucalypts evaporating in the heated air. Much of what was in view was linked to the Aboriginal Dreamtime stories. Directly in front was King's Tableland, known to the Gundungurra as Muggadah and which to them is associated with a person's consciousness, the Jamison Valley itself (Gedumbah or Godoomba), Mount Solitary (Korrowal or 'the strong one'; to some Aboriginals it is also home to the Jogung giants), Mount Colong (or wombat), Mount Jellore, Mount Gibraltar (the highest in the Southern Highlands) and Ruined Castle (apparently it looks like one) that once was the connection between Narrow Neck and Mount Solitary. There was a wonderful story about the Three Sisters, which were large rock formations that rose up from the valley floor. In this story there were three sisters called Meehni, Wimlah and Gunnedoo who were in love with three men from a rival tribe but any thought of marriage was strictly taboo. So the wise man, Kuradjuri, turned them into stone with the intention of returning them to human form once the brothers had been defeated. Alas he was killed and thus the Three Sisters remained as they were today. There was another story at the visitors/gift shop/cafe/massage parlour just up from Echo Point. This involved their father Tyawan and the Bunyip. This story told of Tyawan leaving his three daughters behind a rock each time he went away to hide them from the Bunyip. Unfortunately Meehni woke the Bunyip as she tried to scare away a centipede which had alarmed her, resulting in the former looking to get revenge having been awoken from his sleep. Tyawan returned in time to use his magic bone in order to turn his daughters to stone, then turned himself into a lyrebird to escape the Bunyip but in the process loses the bone and is today still trying to find it. The sisters await his return to turn them back from stone. So much more romantic than knowing what these great rocks are made of in geological terms (which I can't tell you as I haven't bothered looking it up).

As a postscript in the late 18th century the Blue Mountains were called Carmarthan Hills and then Lansdowne Hills, but the name was changed as the blue haze that rises from the oil of the eucalypts made it logical to rename them as they are today. As I looked out at the panorama in front of me listening to all my fellow tourists all making the same appreciative noises in their own tongues, at least I assumed they were unless they'd read about Yowies and were slightly concerned at the sight of me dripping with sweat and with forty days of facial hair looking far from tidy and thus anxiously asking each other what to do. It could also have been that Mr. Spindly Man who'd been the brunt of my glare had already been through and warned them that I was potentially a little unstable and they were discussing ways of escape. Whatever it was in an instance I forgave Mr. Liar because this view was worth a thousand others. I have a video of it and still today can't believe how incredibly beautiful it was. Having said that, if I ever see him again I'd still like to punch his lights out just because!

Day forty-one: December 14th

The weather had overnight been transformed and today there was a steady drizzle falling and with the cloud cover being so low that visibility was very poor, making any meaningful sightseeing difficult so I made my way into Katoomba to have breakfast and see what the guide book recommended. Breakfast was fun. Having ordered eggs on toast with sausages I was a little disappointed to note that the latter were not on the plate when it arrived. What should I do? This was a major diplomatic incident, an error of the utmost gravity. My response needed to be firm and to the point. However, at this point we come once more to that age old tradition of the Englishman who doesn't actually know what to do next. Here's how it goes: the food arrives and it's any of the following from being cold, missing something as with today or just plain horrible. There is a grumble of dissatisfaction from said Englishman to his fellow diners, assuming he has company, about how annoying this all was and how frankly it was all very unacceptable. Nods of agreement all round from the men at least, whilst the women tell said Englishman to get the server back and tell him or her about it. Said Englishman says he will but only at the end of the meal after all he doesn't want to spoil everyone else's enjoyment, but grumbles all the while. With the food suitably finished the server then reappears to clear away the plates asking whether everything was ok. At this point, and I've experienced this first hand, any other nationality in the world without exception would declare war on the restaurant and curse the chef (in fact they would not even wait until the meal had ended). However, said Englishman just smiles meekly and responds "Lovely thank you" as the women at the table look at him in disgust. Today, I was that Englishman as I manfully ate what was in front of me without mentioning anything to the server even though he was right behind me at the counter. "Everything alright, mate?", "Lovely thank you" I said in response, paid and left the cafe. I know it's pathetic and I really can't explain why this happens, it just does, but I'd still like to know who had my sausages and if they were nice.

Given the weather coupled with the fact that I was still quite tired from all my exertions the previous day I wasn't too disappointed that any major walking was not likely to happen. Instead it would have to be mostly driving today with my first point of call to be the Toy and Railway Museum at Leura, Lithgow (again) to see the Small Arms Museum (again) and also Eksbank House, then on to the English themed town at Mount Wilson, followed by the Megalong Valley and then lastly take another look at Echo Point. Leura, the name is Aboriginal for 'lava', was the town next to Katoomba and if the sun had been shining was worth a long visit in its own right (so my Blue Mountains guide told me) but not today given the drizzle was now a steady rain. The museum was easy to find as it was quite close to where I'd set off the previous day on my epic journey. I parked the car and approached the entrance to 'Leuralla', an imposing family mansion that would have looked at home in the Home Counties back in the UK. It was designed following the concept of 'organic architecture', the creation of Frank Lloyd Wright, which looks to blend a building into its surroundings (as he termed it 'form and function are one'). Leuralla is the second house to have been built on this site as the first had burnt down and it was the home of the Evatt family of which the most famous was Dr. H.V. Evatt. In the Doc Evatt Memorial Room there were photographs that told the story of Evatt who was one of Australia's most celebrated politicians and who, amongst his many roles, was Attorney General, a High Court Judge and perhaps most significantly the Secretary General of the UN in 1949 when he was very closely involved in the creation of the Universal Declaration of Human Rights. Quite a dude all round as my kids might say. I wonder if I'll have a room dedicated to me when I depart this mortal existence and if so what would they it? Jimmy's Fat Retreat? The 'who was he' room?

As I walked into the entrance hall it immediately brought back childhood memories of being back in my grandparents' house with all its wooden panelling and floors and with that unique smell of wood polish (French of course) that I could happily sniff all day along with a side order of creosote and hot tar. The lighting gave off an ambience that was warm and welcoming and I half expected my grandmother to sound the gong for lunch (we were very posh you see) and then my grandfather appear, pipe at a slant, with his gin and angostura bitters in hand, ready to do battle with the roast of the day. He was a great one for taking any joint or roast bird and performing a battle of wills with it as he tried to cut it into portions, mainly because as was often the case my grandmother had forgotten to cook it properly or, as at one Easter, the turkey was still frozen inside. I was brought back down to earth with a bump when lady who was sat behind a small desk enquired as to whether she could help me. I paid and started to look round. This mansion was a toy collectors' paradise with cabinets full of toys dating from close to a century ago when lead and tin were perfectly acceptable even if the former had a tendency to potentially shorten a child's expected lifespan to the very near past, whilst the walls and shelves were covered in posters, friction and battery models. There were so many famous brands from not just my own childhood but that of my parents like Triang, Marx, Dinky, Meccano (I could never do these as my ability to do the simplest type of model making was always doomed to failure as any attempt when shown to parent would be met with "Yes, darling, very good, but what is it?"), Barbie dolls and Ken, Steiff Bears, Kathe Kruse porcelain dolls from the 1920's, Japanese robots from over fifty years ago and so on. It was glorious and escapism at its best. Each room had a different display but still retained the character that this house would have had when lived in, whether it was the comfy leather chairs, the fireplaces, the light fittings or the music room complete with rose motifs everywhere and a Bechstein Salon Grand from 1912, the date when Leuralla was completed.

The gardens are quite historic and dated back to the beginnings of the house and originally had been the work of the Searle Brothers from Sydney and then, in the 1920's, that of Danish born Paul Sorensen who went on to become one of the most highly respected horticulturalists in Australia. The gardens were full of 'Sequoia, Maples, Cedar, Linden, Copper Beech, Chestnut, Ash, and Oaks' along with 'Rhododendron, Dogwood, Camellia and Azalea groves … tulips, daffodils, bluebells …' I didn't of course know this as I've already told you my knowledge of plant life wouldn't occupy the back of a postage stamp and would still have room for transcribing War and Peace, but the Leuralla guide tells the visitor all. It was a pain that the rain was still with me as the pictures in the guide showed how lovely this place was with the sun out. The gardens were home to the railway collection including a full sized replica of an engine rather oddly coming out of a tree. For a dollar I sent the LGB (Lehman Gross Bahn) around the Matterhorn; I could almost smell the edelweiss and glühwein, or it could just have been the dampness. In a large outbuilding was housed an impressive collection of model trains from 'Hornby, Märklin, Lionel, Basett Lowke and Bing' which sounds more like the team sheet for a six-a-side tournament, all whizzing round a track with each having the livery of whatever company they were operating under including four British lines one of which, Southern Railway is the provider of my enjoyable daily commute to London. On the side of the building there were various signs that had come from some of the more local stations most of which had very British sounding destinations.

Leuralla hosted many famous people but there was one story that made me realise that I'm a mere plebeian and that there are people in this world whose importance and station in life is far superior to mine. In 1954 Queen Elizabeth visited the house and as part of her visit she was to visit Echo Point, so named as you may have guessed already because it is supposed to echo when you shout. The town big-wigs were keen to impress the Queen and invited her to have a go in order to show her, and Phil the Greek, just how impressive Echo Point was. Now this meant that they had to be sure that it would do what it was supposed to do and that the royal voice would indeed echo. So they had a cunning plan which involved posting people around the area below the lookout to be the echo 'just in case'. Now I'm no genius but I've worked out that this plan had a fatal flaw which is this. The Queen is a woman and to be precise an Englishwoman, whose voice is what many would term 'plummy' and has a slight nasal sound so as she stands at the is edge of Echo Point and says "Cooee" what would have happened if the stand-in echoes had to leap into action? How would they have known which of them was supposed to respond? Were they sufficiently 'English' to have been able to "Cooee" back in exactly the same tone? I also had this vision in my mind that there might have been a rogue stand-in who had perhaps republican sympathies and instead of the polite "Cooee" had instead responded as only a true Australian can by saying "Bugger off". That would have been much more fun but luckily that didn't really happen as there was an echo and so much celebration was had by all and I've no doubt knighthoods and OBE's were awarded to all. I do hope that someone told the stand-in echoes to come back out of the bush after the royal party left or do you suppose they might still be there, their skeletal remains standing (or sitting) with bony jaws poised to shout "Cooee" cradled in skinless hands. I didn't try to get an echo whilst I was there because frankly I think it would have made me look a bit of a wally when there were so many people there. I wonder how the Queen felt.

The sun had started to make an effort to come out and so I decided that it was time to move on and off to see Mount Wilson because it looked as though it would be a rather nice detour (it was some way off the main road) in my guide book which was then reinforced by an article in 'The Age', February 8th 2004 in which it was described thus:

'The experience of the town is the experience of its gardens, its avenues of trees and its walking trails and picnic areas ... walks to Wynne's Rocks Lookout, the Cathedral of Ferns and the Waterfalls Picnic Ground all offer excellent views ... '

With clouds now bowing to the inevitable, so my spirits lifted as I left Leura and turned back towards Mount Victoria and thence to Bell, turning off the Bell's Line of Road and on towards Mount Wilson. The Bell's Line of Road was so named after Archibald Bell who was another one of those first explorers to come over the Blue Mountains and as with its southern counterpart, the Great Western Highway followed an old Aboriginal path. Looking at some old photographs of the road which had been built in earnest after the end of the First World War, it was reminiscent of those I'd seen for the Great Ocean Road in Victoria. In both cases the risk to life and limb must have been immense and not for the faint-hearted. The road up went on for eight kilometres and became quite twisty making it slow going. However it would be worth it I told myself. The views would be stunning. That's what 'The Age' had said and the sun was still just about out. Not only that the early residents were a who's who of late Victorian Sydney, a place of high society and this town had been built by them and thus would be a real reflection of those times. I reached Mount Wilson and drove down The Avenue which was the main street which was lined with huge trees when as if by magic, the sun disappeared and as if on cue, the rain returned. At the same time the clouds just fell out of the sky creating a thick mist, giving the whole place an eerie still feel, akin to one of those horror movies where a load of teenage Americans get chopped up whilst camping in the middle of the boondocks where it's all misty and spooky, thus adding to the suspense. I could see nothing and even though Mount Wilson was an undoubtedly beautiful place (reference: 'The Age') and had a very English village feel about it, none of the gardens were in fact open. And even if they had of been, it was now bucketing down so I turned the car around, took one photo of the thick mist, and started to motor back towards the main road. However, all was not lost because Mount Wilson was also home to the Turkish Bath Museum, a heritage listed building and well worth visiting according to, yes my guide book. Except today I couldn't because, and this really was no real surprise, the place was closed.

Things were definitely not going well and in a bit of a huff I decided that further indoor exploration was required and so decided to revisit Lithgow's museums. Lithgow was as it had been when I was first here although because of the weather much more depressing, and still no one around. Still never mind because I'd be inside at two 'recommended' attractions, of which Eksbank House was to be the first visit. I'd read all about it; built in 1842 for Thomas Brown, one of the key industrialists to have lived in Lithgow at that time, it was now home to a museum that details the story of not just the town but also its industrial past, just my cup of tea and perfect on a rainy day. I duly pulled up outside, gathered my gear together and rocked up to the front. And there was the sign that I dreaded, 'Closed. Only open Wednesday and Sunday'. Never one to be defeated and determined not to be upset I felt sure that the Small Arms Museum having been closed on my first visit would be bound to be open. I mean it couldn't be closed every day, could it? I pulled up on the opposite side of the road. It looked very quiet, but no matter this was a weekday and thus I reasoned it was therefore unlikely to be busy. I walked up to the door and in another shocking discovery I saw the sign 'Closed'. I heard something snap and realised that it was me, and my anger swelled up. I was to say the least a little peeved I mean what is the point in having a museum that seems always to be closed, answer me that Lithgow Town Council? Maybe, and this is a suggestion only, you lot might want to put a big sign up at the town boundaries telling anyone who enters Lithgow that the town is actually closed! I was not a happy bunny as I climbed back into the car and headed back to Katoomba.

I took the southern route back with the intention to dump the car at my hotel and go into town to have that beer/wine that I'd not had the day before. As I drove along the Great Western Highway and my mood began to brighten a little, I saw a signpost for the Megalong Valley which given that at that precise moment I was out of non-alcoholic ideas seemed worth visiting, not least as it promised a chance to do some bush horse-riding, which, although it was by now late in the afternoon, could make up for a somewhat disappointing day. Descending into the valley along a very windy road, narrowly avoiding a hiker who had decided for some reason known only to himself to walk down the middle of the road (and for information purposes only you get less points if the pedestrian makes themselves an easy target), the sun once more began to come through the clouds warming the damp ground which started to steam giving off a sweet smell of pine and eucalyptus. The name Megalong is believed to be Aboriginal for 'Valley under The Rock' and it wasn't hard to see why. Once on the floor of the valley the cliffs rose up maybe a thousand metres or more as if touching the sky itself and as the sun lit the sides of the sandstone there were colours in every shade of brown interspersed with shaded areas where the odd Yowie was no doubt looking at me and wondering how his cousin below in the valley had learnt to drive. The Megalong Landowners Association notes that the valley first appears in modern Australian history in 1838 when George Aspinall received a grant of land which was called the 'Megalong Station' or 'Medlow Station'. The whole area was an attractive proposition to early settlers because the soil, a mix of basalt and shale was, from both an agricultural and industrial perspective, attractive. Tourism also followed although the hotel that started this all, the Hydro Majestic at Medlow Bath that overlooked the valley and which was built around 1903 and was also Australia's very first health spa was today in a state of disrepair which was a shame. I'd already passed it a couple of times already and there was a real belle époque feel about it and it would not have been out of place in somewhere like Évian-les-Bains on Lake Geneva in France. I read that in 1922 this historic hotel had nearly been destroyed in one of the worst bushfires to hit the Blue Mountains, when most of the west wing was consumed. It had also been a hospital during the Second World War and had been the last place ever visited by Sir Edmund Barton who'd been the first PM of the Federation given that the poor sod died here. Not much of a health spa for him perhaps. One other fact about Medlow Bath, and which I rather enjoyed, was that it had, at one point been the love capital of Australia, which was not a reference to all that free love stuff in the 1960's but because as tourism in the Blue Mountains really began to boom in the 1920's, so newlyweds would come to Katoomba for their honeymoon.

As I drove along the valley, I passed evidence of the old mining industry at the Megalong Australian Heritage Centre which was closed and there wasn't a soul to be seen. So no horse-riding then, but then I should have known that the place was likely to be closed. I'd scored a hat trick. It was too early to go back to the hotel and yet there was nothing more to do here aside from drive aimlessly around and try to run over any other hikers which though fun can get boring after a while. So what to do? Now I am a strong willed person and always believe, as was taught to me in my youth, that no alcohol should be consumed before the sun was below the yardarm. Luckily being in the valley meant that this was now the case so beer it was then and so without much inner questioning I turned round and headed back up the valley towards the Great Western Highway and thence to Katoomba with its bars in my mind. I passed the hiker who was walking towards where I'd just left and wondered if I should stop the car and just warn him, maybe even offer to give him a lift somewhere. But hang on Australia has in the recent past been noted for the plight of one or two hitch-hikers who have come off second best. If I stopped my car, maybe the hiker would worry that I was one of those who 'did away' with their companions. He could also have been a loner who had recently escaped from some high security prison and was waiting for some poor sap like me to stop and give him a life only to find that I was his next victim. Anyway that's what I thought to myself as I sped past him just as he waved or was he asking for a lift? Better safe than sorry as my old mother would have said as I reversed back over him. Fifteen points, not a bad score.

As I arrived back in Katoomba the sun was continuing to play hide and seek with the clouds and though just about visible everything once more had become decidedly gloomy. After my experiences the day before I was keen to have another gander at the magnificence of Echo Point and maybe get a whole different perspective of the place under this sunny-cloudy sky. I'd been to the Grand Canyon once when there had been a fierce lightening storm going on with hail the size of large gobstoppers falling around me whilst in the near distance the sun shone through giving the place an awesome majesty. I was hoping that I'd get a similar experience today. As neared Echo Point down Lurline Street and then onto Echo Point Road the pea-souper that that had covered Mount Wilson had obviously decided that it needed to also be here because all that could be seen was, well, nothing. The cloud cover was dense. Apart from me there were two rather upset students who'd travelled up from Sydney that morning to see the Blue Mountains before their flight back home the next day. Having a slight sense of guilt over leaving the hiker in the lurch (I didn't really reverse over him, no it was full frontal), I offered to show them the video I'd taken yesterday. I'm not sure how I'd react if some man who looked slightly dishevelled (given I'd not shaved for over a month though my 'beard' couldn't be described as particularly hairy, more patchy) and probably whiffed a little approached me if I were a young lady and offered to show me a video. Run? Spray him with pepper spray? Call the police? Look to participate in the sequel (after all these were the *Blue* Mountains)? But this was Australia where everybody is friendly and we were on 'neutral territory' so they said that, yes they'd like to have a look and so I showed them, got arrested and spent three days in jail. I still have the film on my phone and look at it almost every day, partly because I still have no friends and partly because it just makes me wish that I could be there every day. Good deed offsets bad deed and everything is now right with the world. As we stood there in silence looking out into the greyish void I remembered again of the dangers of this wonderland and how people had got lost and been found days later having died or, as in the case of the British backpacker Jamie Neale, been found having spent days lost. But it seems that this potential for tragedy has ever been thus as an article in the Sydney Morning Herald from Friday 31 July 1931 noted:

'After having been lost in the bush near Katoomba all night, Jack Barton, 20, and Miss Beryl Humphries, 21, two visitors to the town, arrived in Leura shortly after 1 pm today. They had been members of a picnic party which went for a walk to the Federal Pass yesterday. After refreshments at the Amphitheatre they said that they would wait and follow the others later.'

I walked back to the car and thought that I definitely needed a beer and plan my last full day in the 'Lucky Country'.

Day forty-two: December 15th

The rain from yesterday had gone when I emerged from my room and, although I was slightly hung-over due to an outburst of irrational exuberance on my part the previous evening which involved a rather large amount of ale, some (well lots) wine, a rubber duck and a basting spoon, I was keen to make the most of the day. Unlike nearly every day on this trip though I was slightly at a loss as to exactly what to do, given that Lithgow was probably still closed, Mount Wilson was too much of an effort and I'd done the walk. The night before I'd read more about the mining industry in Katoomba and decided that what I needed was to get a feel of this in a way that hadn't been so evident at Orphan Rock. John Merriman in a piece entitled 'Coal and Shale Mining near Katoomba' provides a nice potted history of what had been a big part of not just Katoomba's history but also that of the Jamison and Megalong valleys. In short as early as 1841 coal had been evidenced in the Blue Mountains, followed by oil and kerosene shale, the latter discovered by Campbell Mitchell on the Megalong side of what is today called the Narrow Neck Peninsular. The industry had both its ups and downs but by the turn of the century shale mining had all but stopped. However, as I'd glimpsed the day before in the Megalong Valley evidence still existed and the Narrow Neck Peninsular was a part of this history so that was what I had to do and a bike was the best way to do this.

Hiring a bike is in my view a precarious business wherever I am in the world. I've had the experience of riding to the top of the mountains that surround Lake Tahoe only to have a puncture and have no repair kit thus resulting in a seven mile walk back downhill, of hiring a bike in Arizona that consisted of one gear in 100 degree heat ("But Jim, it's a dry heat". So is an oven, but I don't willingly stick my head in that!), the heavy ones I'd already ridden up in Queensland to the one in France which was the piece de resistance, where the actual wheel split. Look I accept that I'm rather on the large size, but honestly it wasn't me and I have yet to hear it happening to anyone else. The trouble is that as with all hire bikes it is a known fact that they are all invariably rubbish, poorly maintained and invariably rusty. If they had been cars they wouldn't pass an M.O.T. The bike shop come rental shop in Katoomba was therefore a refreshing change because here the bikes for hire had gears that worked, brakes that braked along with wheels that weren't buckled and above all bikes that weren't from the age of the boneshaker. The only snag was and I'm being a tad picky, was the rental price that nearly had me wondering if I'd actually bought the bike. After ringing my bank to see if my credit was still good I agreed to part with my money and in return was provided with a rather nice looking machine, complete with pump and puncture repair kit which, for a rental is about as common as an honest politician.

The route that the shop proprietor had given me was around 35 kilometres there and back (assuming that I wanted to go right to the end of the Neck) and should take no more than 3–4 hours and was 'moderate'. Does this sound familiar? I am a keen cyclist at home and quite happily will do that amount of time on a bike covering many kilometres in the process but that's with the full kit on and crucially that bit of padding that allows a certain amount of dignity when dismounting, the padded cycle short. Without a pair of these the next thing is how cushiony is the seat and this was not in evidence so little protection as it were against all the bumps that I was bound to come across given all I was wearing were shorts, a light raincoat and not much else. I set off towards the Neck in the sure knowledge that their estimate of time and distance was this time realistic and, just as with the walk, it all started well as to get to the start it was mostly downhill. The Neck from tip to toe was about 13 kilometres and is the dividing range between the Jamison and Megalong valleys. It looked a doddle as I approached the first hill, not a problem, not even a puff or bead of sweat. I was in my stride. I was like the great Miguel Indurain winning another hill climb in the Tour de France (although he was a supreme athlete and I had more in common with Bibendum, otherwise known as Michelin Man) , moving along with an ease that just made everything feel rather relaxed. The air felt damp from the early rain and there was little noise aside from the odd bird call but no cicadas just for once. Maybe they don't like the damp. Then, what's that saying 'it's too good to be true', things suddenly took a turn for the worse just after I passed the emergency vehicles' locked gate because from here the track began to become a mix of steep inclines and small declines as I climbed higher up and towards the end of the Neck. Just like the descriptive of Mount Wilson, though, I knew that it would all be worth it because as the man back in Katoomba in the bike shop had told me "The ridge allows great views from there and you will be able to see the expanse of the Jamison to your left and that of the Megalong to your right". Somewhere in the skies above the Wondjina, or cloud and rain spirits as they are to the Aboriginals, had decided that the whole area should be shrouded in low cloud and mist. I have a photo of my epic ride, looking quite 'fit' if I may so ladies, with the background (in this case the Megalong) behind me, except that for all intents and purposes I could have been on any track in Anywhereville given the weather. It was a bit disappointing and to top it all if there had been mining activity up here it was well and truly hidden. I reached a bushfire lookout platform which wasn't quite the end of the track but, by now somewhat deflated I decided to call it a day and head back to town.

On the way I stopped just to see if I could see the Megalong valley and was this time in luck as for a fleeting moment the mist and cloud parted to reveal a dark green canopy of trees stretching into the distance. It was down in the valley that the nomadic Gundungurra would come for food and to set up camp whilst the weather was good, that was until they were moved into permanent settlements by the Europeans, like the Katoomba West Mission in the Megalong itself. The Europeans looked to instil a Christian, educated and so called civilised view of the world on them because that was what Victorian Britain was doing at home and thus, by extension, its colonies. Their view of morality was at times perverse but it was this that drove them to make the indigenous people abandon their traditional ways. Nowadays there is little evidence that the Aboriginals were here at all, the mission having long gone and their nomadic lifestyle no longer so much a feature of today's world. It's all rather sad really that there were no pyramids, no Stonehenge's, no castles that could be explored telling of their history. Of course there are cave paintings in Australia, but most of these are well off the beaten track and often as not in areas that are not open to non-Aboriginals. One of the last Aboriginal's who'd lived in the Megalong was Billy Lynch whose father, also Billy, had been quite a character as, according to the Australian Dictionary of Biography, he'd been a member of an All

Aboriginal Team cricket team, a 'lost tourist tracker' as well as a one man food stall. Lynch was the product of a liaison between an Irish-born convict and a women from the Gundungurra and his life showed up one of those contradictions that I'd come across in the past. As a half-caste he was neither Aboriginal nor white, but from what I could gather lived as both giving his children both Christian and Gundungurra names. He and his family became part of not just the community in Megalong but also through a son, landowners. There was it appears an acceptance by the white community that 'Billy' was 'one of them' in stark contrast to Bennelong. It was notable that Billy played cricket which is as English as tea and crumpets and wet weather and, like rugby was to be, had been taken to all parts of the Empire as it was seen as a civilising game by the great and good at home. However, I wonder if he and his team mates were treated as some sort of exhibit, a freak show almost, as the Aboriginal cricket team that toured England in 1868 nicknamed 'The Indigenous Tour', had been.

The journey back to the hire shop was a relatively quick affair. I dropped the bike off and paid for the bike pump I'd lost (about the price of a new BMW Series 6) that is probably still hiding somewhere on Narrow Neck Peninsular and drove back to the hotel for a quick shower and rest before going to the last item on my 'list of places worth a look at', Mount Tomah which is part of the Sydney Botanical Gardens. As I have already alluded to my knowledge of greenery is decidedly limited and although Mrs. McGuire is a keen fan of gardening and all things garden centre, for me the only real benefit of a garden is to have a bit of outside space to put a comfortable garden chair in, add a table and then beer. So you might be surprised that I'd chosen to go to Mount Tomah at all, but actually I was quite keen because it was more than just a garden, it was another link to the history of the Blue Mountains. By the time I left Katoomba the weather had become a lot less inclement with a watery sun poking through the clouds although there was still a threat of rain and it was now quite chilly. The road to Mount Tomah today is an easy route and passes through some beautiful countryside, but when it was first visited (or more to the point when the area was) the road would have been much more basic and far from comfortable to travel on even by car. By the early part of the 20th century things were much better as the Sydney Morning Herald pointed out in an article from April 1928 which gives a great description of what the traveller might expect:

'From Kurrajong it winds – the 'Old Bell Road' – through orchard and forest, and over sudden gullies brimming with the rich verdure of these regions; a road which is perhaps the most beautiful of all that traverse the eastern portion of the mountains ... ' the writer then goes on to tempt the reader further ... 'The floral and scenic attractions of this area are not its only ones. Its fauna is almost as remarkable as its flora, and especially alluring are the birds ... ' which are then listed from the lyre bird to the bower bird and the many different parrots.

As I drove today, aside from a wider road and coming from a different direction, it could just have been 1928. There was one sentence that brought a smile to my face and that was a great social comment on the times and also highlighted the popularity of the four wheeled combustion engine:

'Nor is it in any way difficult of access to the motorist, indeed and who is not a motorist today?'

When I got to Mount Tomah, originally called Fern Hill but then changed to the Darug name for a fern, I was, by the looks of the near empty car park, going to have the place virtually to myself. Mind you I had a nagging feeling that perhaps this was going to one of those "This could be rubbish. Well I'm here now, I might as well have a quick look because it won't take long and then do something else" attractions. The gardens were begun in 1934 by Alfred and Effie Brunet (what a wonderful name) as a business selling cut flowers and specialist shrubs to Sydney florists. But the Brunets were green fingered to the point of being the greenest of green fingered people in the whole State because from this humble start the gardens today are home to 5,000 different species of plants and trees which I have listed in the appendix in alphabetical order and in Latin as I'm a purist. One of life's great puzzles to me is why there is a near universal use of Latin names in science. Why not Etruscan or Ancient Greek or Ancient Arabic or even good old Anglo-Saxon? Why was Latin picked and who started it? I reckon it was some up-his-own-derriere scientist who in order to outdo his fellow scientists and look more intelligent suddenly decided to use Latin. Imagine a garden in which two gentlemen of science are walking. The year is a long, long time ago:

"Dr. Richards look at that beautiful yellow flower over there. I think I shall call it a buttercup because it looks like a cup that might hold butter which as we know is yellow."

"Ahem, methinks you are mistaken sir, I think you'll find it's actually a Ranunculis repens."

"You really are a complete fundus"

The garden covered twenty-eight hectares and was laid out in segments, each designed to tell a story whether it be learning more about some of the early botanists who scoured the planet collecting seeds and samples to then try to propagate them in Australia or via the Gondwana walk that tells of the formation of the Continent. I did walk this path and am pleased to report that it had a Wollemi pine, that dinosaur tree I'd not seen in Wollemi National Park. The whole garden was all rather good and the half hour that I'd originally thought would suffice became an hour and then an hour and a half. The link to Sydney came in 1972 when the Brunets officially gave the gardens over to the Royal Botanical Gardens, Sydney. Actually there is an older connection because a Mr. Allan Cunningham visited here in 1824 and by 1837 he was the Superintendant of the Sydney Botanic Gardens. After an official opening in 1987, it was the following year the site of the first bi-centennial event in Australia. As part of the entrance fee I was given access to 'The Jungle' which pre-dated the gardens and was originally a small area of rainforest consisting primarily of ancient sassafras and coachwood and which was saved by a group of businessmen who purchased it in 1929 mainly it appears as a tourist attraction, but these were clearly men of distinction because when it was opened the ceremony was conducted by Governor Admiral Sir Dudley DeChair. In all the rainforest they bought was around 280 hectares. The original cost was over two thousand pounds, a hefty sum in those days, and part of the Sydney Morning Herald article from April 1928 I noted above was also a backhanded promotion for the ten pound shares someone could buy to help pay this debt back. Back then a person driving from Sydney and arriving here would have been able to stay in their car and drive through here. By the mid 1930's the Jungle was falling on hard times due to the Great Depression and it was only in 1993 that is was rescued to become what it is today. In 2008 the 33 hectares of the original Jungle were purchased from the owners and exactly 80 years to the day it was re-opened to the public. The walk took me past the lilly-pilly, pines and coachwood trees, the huge gum trees and so much more. There was also the wonderfully named Wonga vine. It was all very jolly, with the highlight being a giant sassafras tree, or more accurately a circle of trunks that had belonged to a single tree. I half expected a trio of witches to appear and ask me if I was happy to be the next Thane of Glamis or Thane of Cawdor and even maybe king hereafter. It was all quite Shakespearean the atmosphere.

And then that was it. I'd finished my walk and given the time of day to all intents finished my adventure of a lifetime. I'd finished. There was no more to see. There were no fanfares to signal this, no one cheering or slapping me on the back, no one even to tell me this. Even the charming old dear in the entrance kiosk was too involved in taking to Edna on the walkie-talkie that she had nothing to say, although Edna really ought to see the doctor from what I could gather. It was as if for a moment everything stopped as I looked at the view from the top of the pond for the last time. All the memories of what I'd done flashed through my mind giving me both a sense of elation that I'd done all of this, but also a sense of sadness that it was all over. Tomorrow would be a drive to the airport, dump off my hire 'car' (not really a real car just a lump of metal with wheels attached), sit in the lounge, catch the plane – remembering that it was Bangkok not Singapore – and then home. I didn't even fancy a going to some swanky bar that evening to celebrate, but instead bought some food from the supermarket and a few beers and stayed in my room waiting for that film that was supposed to start at nine but actually could have been anytime in the next two days.

Day forty-three: December 16th

My drive today was without any real drama. I had thought about what would be a good way to end my trip but by now I just wanted to be home with my wife and kids. There was a part of me that wanted to do something that would act as the really memorable part of the trip, but it was in the minority. I'd looked at my road map and thought about going to Sans Souci or Monterey, both of which had memories for me (the first being historical as it was Frederick the Great's favourite palace and the latter from Highway 1 in California, one of the best trips I have ever done. Yes I know I need to get out more but so what). In the end I did stop at a beach at Brighton-Le-Sands which afforded two views. The first was in front of me on the sand where there was stretched a very well-honed sunbather with perma-tan reminding me that this was a country where lying on the beach with not much on was ok as the weather was great as opposed to back home where aside from a wind-break and fifty blankets, woollen clothing was a must. The other view was a poignant one. When I was living in Boston I used to walk down to Fort Independence and watch the planes leaving and arriving at Logan Airport, just as I was doing now as Sydney's international airport was across the bay, thinking about life in general and wondering if the travellers in those large silver birds were on their way to an adventure, or like me now, were about to return from one. I didn't linger for too long as by now I was in the mood just to return the car and wait for my departure. I have always been a little like this on my last day of any holiday in that for me it is to all intents and purposes over, so why wait any longer before checking in to the ferry or plane. Even so it was with a slightly heavy heart I headed for the airport.

I dropped my 'car' off with the most cheerful man I think I have, and possibly will ever, meet. To say that he was happy would be an understatement and I firmly believe if major drug companies were to tap his blood, they would be able to cut back R&D spending by billions. It was as if all my experiences of the Australian character had gathered into one person almost to say "Look what you're going to miss". In all I counted at least ten "No worries mate" as I told him what a heap of total rubbish the car had been. All that remained, aside from checking in, was to settle the tab on the 'car' hire back at the hire desk. There were no more sights to see and so my mind was now adjusting to my going home and being back with my family. I was in a good mood. Yes the heavy heart was there in that I'd miss the freedom, the people, the weather but I, and some might find this strange, quite like my family. I walked into the airport and located the car hire desk. At which point it suddenly felt that the last six weeks was about to be erased, the bonhomie, the laid back-ness, the mate-ness, absolutely everything. You see I had met the sister, or a close relative, of that stroppy woman from when I'd checked for mine and Chris' trip to Fraser Island. I sidled up to the counter and handed the paperwork on the car, big smile on my face.

"You're late" was the response from the Arctic winter land in front of me.

"Pardon me?"

"You're ten minutes late returning the car so I have to add another full day's hire to the cost." By now it was so cold that icicles had formed on icicles.

"And how much is that?" I enquired thinking that it would be pennies.

"Eighty five dollars"

"Eighty five dollars! You're kidding aren't you I mean I was only ten minutes late?"

"Yes and no"

"I'm not paying it."

"You've got no choice, you were late."

Mentally I was working out that the effective hourly rate for this car was 510 dollars an hour based on my ten minutes of my tardiness and thus over 12,200 dollars for the day or the cost of a second hand car. I explained this to 'madam' who just blanked me. It was 'Time for the manager'.

"I'd like to speak to the manager please."

"Sorry you can't as she's busy."

My parents brought me up to be polite. At school it was rammed into me as if my life depended on it. In fact throughout all my days on this planet I've striven to be polite. But now this, a person whose only modus operandi in life seemed to be as a complete and utter waste of space was severely testing this, so it was time to turn on the old McGuire charm; time to be Mr. Debonair, Mr. Tactful. After all I'd just spent six weeks 'chilling out' so why should it matter that I'd another eighty five dollars to pay and the manager was busy. But you see that was the problem. After six weeks of travel it had come to this.

"I don't care how bloody busy she is I want to talk to her now!" I said in as forceful a manner I could short of causing a major international incident.

At this point Sharon, or whatever her name was (to be honest I didn't care), nonchalantly looked at me, giving me the 'evil eye' and picked up the phone. She turned her back to me as she spoke to whoever it was at the other end of the telephone. After a couple of minutes she replaced the receiver and, turning back towards me, smiled and said: "She's busy and says just forget it."

And that was all she said as she handed me my final bill, without the eighty five dollars added and you know what I thanked her as if it was really my fault and somewhat sheepishly went off to check-in. When I arrived to have my passport stamped showing that I'd left the customs officer asked me where my entry stamp was. At which point another potential international incident was in the brewing. When I'd entered the country I'd been chatting merrily away to the customs office who had been telling me how she had found it so hot the day before that the A/C wasn't even keeping her cool that she forgot to stamp my passport. As a result, as this new customs officer told me, I was technically illegally in the country. At this point the most obvious reaction would be of blind panic. Would I be arrested, carted off to some detention centre and become someone's 'cell *biatch*'? What would my wife say? Did the British Ambassador need calling? But, with a sense of panic still in me I asked "Oh, is that a problem?", to which she smiled and said "No worries mate, have a great flight." As I entered duty free two thoughts came to mind: firstly even though 'Sharon' had been a little awkward the outcome was nevertheless what I'd come to love about the country where it seems stress takes a very distance second place to enjoying life and then secondly at customs. If I'd been in the UK and there had been a issue with my passport/papers the last thing I'd have been told to do was not to worry. I'd well and truly finished, there would be no more check-ins at hotels, no more concerns about the four-wheeled scrap box and no more wondering around without really caring about time or even where I was. I'd travelled to the other side of the world, driven over 7,350 kilometres, flown another 2,360 odd kilometres, cycled, run, walked and swam another billion and drank Australia dry. I'd stayed in more hotels than in the last decade and seen more places than I have done back home, and loved every bit of it.

CHAPTER 13

So the big question then: are all Australians convicts with mullets and tattoos?

THE easy answer is to say of course they are and that they should just accept it but then I'd be lying. The fact is that there *are* too many mullets and tattoos but really, who cares? But then getting designer tips from me is like Einstein trying to explain the offside rule in football. There is a sense that the past is in some ways still the present in parts of Australia but it is done very well. No one I'd met went on about life being "groovy man" or said "like" after every word as if they were some throwback to the 1960's. No, the feeling was much more about the pace of life rather than what era they were in and it was good. I liked that I couldn't get food after 8pm. I liked that even if I really wasn't, superficially I was everyone's best mate. I liked the familiarity of the country and of everywhere I went being greeted by "G'day" or "No worries". I'd miss that, I'd miss the chumminess of all I'd met and above all I'd miss having decent weather for more than three minutes a day. In the UK we seem always to pre-judge someone even if we don't really know them which translates itself often as not into some in-built aversion to anyone who is not able to speak the Queen's English but here in Australia I could have spoken Martian and still be greeted like a long lost relative.

There is no hurry in Australia, but not in any mañana sense but rather as if life is for living to the full but to be done enjoyably. To explain what I mean I recall having a coffee in Melbourne opposite Victoria Market (a place that sells everything conceivable) and whilst sipping away the lady, who ran the cafe, was in the process of closing for the day. I asked her if she wanted my cup which was still half full. "No, you're alright love; when you're ready". No hurry. No immediacy. Things could wait. Nothing needed to be done in haste and, once I got used to it because you really have to if you don't want to go bananas, began to prefer it to the hurry-up way that we do things in the UK.

It is also a country of wonderful anachronisms. Take the railways. I was fascinated to learn that when the 'Iron Horse' first appeared on the scene in around 1854 it was at a time when each of the then existing colonies (they weren't States until after the 1901 Federation) very much viewed themselves inwardly, almost as if they were in some ways a country in their own right and which had only two things in common with the other colonies which was language and answering to the Imperial government back in London. So of course when it came to constructing the railways they were all different. For example, Victoria did not have talk to New South Wales about what it planned to do in respect of a railway gauge and, when Queensland in 1859 became independent from its southern neighbour, it too looked to do its own thing and adopted its own. Although the country did have, by the late 19th century, a railway network that allowed people and goods to travel across the Continent each state had different gauges such that in Australia there were three. In the same country! Even into the 20th century matters were unresolved and a person that had a mate, for example, living in the east when he or she was living on the west would have to change trains at least six times. It took over 100 years for a train service to be in place just to get from the north to the south because of these differences. I might think that this is plain daft but the reality is symptomatic of the nature of an Australian, of an independence of mind that is in of itself very admirable however illogical it may seem.

This is also a country that has public figures who are renowned for straight-talking which to the untrained ear could be a little disconcerting, not least if you have been brought up in the British system of inwardly having mutual loathing of each other but outwardly showing the utmost politeness. It may not be to everyone's taste but it's very refreshing. There are many examples from Tony Abbott, also known to his critics as the 'mad monk', who became leader of the Liberal Party as I was travelling and who referred to the climate change talks in Copenhagen as akin to the Munich Agreement because, in his view, climate change was 'absolute crap' and said of Julia Gillard (who was elected Labor leader in 2010) that she had a 'shit-eating grin' back in 2008. Then there is Paul Keating the ex Prime Minister and Labor Party leader with his many, many gems including these two which I particularly liked: 'What we have got is a dead carcass, swinging in the breeze, but nobody will cut it down to replace it' on John Howard, then Prime Minister, and on Andrew Peacock, a Liberal politician ' … if this gutless spiv, and I refer to him as a gutless spiv … ' Whilst in Queensland I read about the influence of their erstwhile leader, the political maverick, New Zealand born Joh Bjelke-Peterson who had had a long career in the National Party before eventually becoming the state Governor for nineteen years until 1987. His views were very to the point whether on conservation (not a big fan; he quite liked the idea of building roads through rainforest) to his strong religious sense of right and wrong (according to John Harrison of The University of Queensland his was 'an evangelical pietist of a kind much more akin to the 18th century Moravians …) or social policies (not overly progressive). The result was that he was referred to in some quite blunt ways as remembered by the Sydney Morning Herald on his death in 1989:

> '(He) is a Bible-bashing bastard – the man is a paranoic, a bigot and fanatic' according to Gough Whitlam in 1974 a year before Bjelke-Peterson put him out of office. For ex Labor Party president, Barry Jones 'He is the Ayotollah of the north.'

This approach has a lot to do with the Australian character. In simple terms they either like you or, if they don't, make it pretty clear. It also suggests another quality that this country seems to have in spades and that is a people with tough skins which I would suggest has a great deal to do with their ancestry whether through forced transportation or else arriving in the country to make a better life but where in both cases it was important to know who you could trust to make things easier.

Australia was known for a long time, and by some still is, as the 'Lucky Country' as it was seen by those freeman and women who emigrated here as being a land full of promise with plenty of land (never mind the fact that almost anything could kill you of course) and an abundance of commodities, from precious metals through to coal and timber, which may seem a little ironic given that its original role was as a penal colony for British society's less desirable elements. Many of those who were sent here involuntarily also saw opportunity in this country to build a new life. This sentiment is echoed in a novel 'For the Term of His Natural Life', by Marcus Clarke published in 1874 just six years after the last convict ship where he provides a real sense of who was sent and how raw Australia would have been then. But there was one sentence caught my attention the most:

'It was customary on board these floating prisons to keep each man's crime a secret from his fellows, so that if he chose, and the caprice of his jailers allowed him, he could lead a new life in his adopted home, without being taunted with his former misdeeds.'

One of the questions that I have come away with since returning to the UK is whether Australia is still finding out about itself and is a question that I asked myself when researching this book? I would say yes, and that there is more to come. In the northern half of Queensland there has been a serious debate about secession from the south over concerns that those in the north western parts were being under-represented. It seems unlikely and maybe it was just a publicity stunt as pointed out by Senator MacDonald at the North Queensland Government Association conference, but the main driver was population growth and its impact. In 1967 the northern part of New South Wales in what is part of New England almost became an independent state. Australia is still growing and as we have seen even more recently with talks about caps on immigration this has become a serious issue. The debates about becoming a republic continue, although currently these are less than they were under Paul Keating, but it feels that it can't be long in coming. However, underneath all of this there is a uniquely Australian attitude to who they are. On the one hand I felt that they were largely at ease not just with themselves but also with others, accepting that the ambivalence to Aboriginals is still there but for me at least not in any overtly nasty sense, whilst on the other there is still this feeling that they need to be seen as more than just stereotypes from a convict class, the cultural creep I talked about earlier.

In some ways the summary of Australians by Anthony Trollope who travelled there in the 1870's and whose views were published under the title 'Australia and New Zealand (Chapman and Hall, 1873) which were generally seen in a negative light by the Australian press sum this up much better. It comes from his lecture that he gave in Melbourne, the infamous 'blowing' lecture, when he said the following (which I have taken from Flannery's 'The Birth of Melbourne'):

' ... these stories are soon received as works of fine art much cultivated in the colonies, for which the colonial phrase of 'blowing' has been created. When a gentleman sounds his own trumpet he 'blows'. The art is perfectly understood and appreciated among the people who practise it. Such a gentleman or a lady was only 'blowing!' You hear it and hear of it every day. They blow a good deal in Queensland – a good deal in South Australia. They blow even in poor Tasmania. They blow loudly in New South Wales ... but the blast of the trumpet heard in Victoria is louder than all the blasts ... '

Although this may seem to be a back-handed compliment it continued to cause angst amongst Australians even upon his death in 1882. But for me he was right. This is a country that is justly right to 'blow its trumpet'. In any event the overall antipathy to Trollope was, according to Nigel Starck in his article 'Trial by media: Anthony Trollope in Australia' presaged on a couple of statistical errors he made as well as referring to them, twice, as braggarts which is in my view wrong. Yes there is no doubt that they are boasters, but certainly not empty, and let's face it when it comes to sport where they excel absolutely fair. Australia has many problems as any growing society has and these also include a hang-up about their past. However, there was no one I met in Australia and no one I know in the UK who is not proud to be an Australian, who is not proud to wear the green and gold (personally I think they need to get some sort of colour designer in) at a sports event, wind up every Pom how awful the weather in the UK is, how the word 'bugger' is theirs because "we used it first" as my little Australian chum told me (well yes if you'd been around in the 16th century and had been referring to ' Bulgarus' or non Catholics in Bulgaria but let's not split hairs), go on about the beeches with sand and sun everywhere, is so relaxed that you can't be entirely sure that the Dutch didn't leave a 'little something' behind and remind us continually that Kylie Minogue is Australian. In fact "I'm an Australian and proud of it" is much more likely to be heard than "I'm British and proud of it" nowadays.

I like Australia, I like Australians. I admire much of what they stand for and their approach to life. I will still shout abuse at the TV whenever I watch the cricket or rugby, but you know what, I would be happy to break bread (actually prefer beer but you know what I mean) with them anytime, especially if they are paying and we have won. I never had a really cross word with anyone I met or for that matter had someone express real anger over something. Above all they are a friendly people willing to tell you what is what with no mixed metaphors and with a smile. I will leave the last word though to the people to whom the land original belonged and which explains how the indigenous people see themselves which I've taken from the Aboriginal Australia Art and Culture Centre and, to me, sums up something quite poignant and something that Australia today is beginning to understand:

> 'Our people, of course, did not use the word "Aborigene" (from the latin ab, origin meaning "from the beginning:" (sic) to refer to ourselves before the coming of non-Aborigenes. Everyone was simply a person.'

Acknowledgments

My thanks go to all those who helped me in writing this book especially James and Sandra whose hospitality was kindly taken in Melbourne, to Nik and Gina who gave me a perspective of a returning Australian and his English wife, to Loughlin and Matt for reading through my first draft from an Australian perspective and providing constructive criticism; thanks to Jane, an Australian who has discovered France and Champagne, to Charles for his thoughts as the son of an immigrant, to my father for his comments and to the encouragement I received from so many people. I would also like to thank Mark who tried to persuade a well-known publisher that I was the next Bill Bryson, to Ed 'The Agent' for his tips on what not to do, to Dan for the introduction, to Tom and Tom's father and to Paddy. Above all this book would not have been possible without the support from my family for which my grateful thanks.

Bibliography:

In the course of writing this book the sources that I used included internet sites, newspapers, tourist guides, academic works, books and local guides. The bibliography is divided into two parts; 1) books; 2) newspapers, newspaper articles, magazines and websites.

Books

1. 'Australia: A Biography Of A Nation' by Phillip Knightley, Vintage Books 2001
2. 'The cultural cringe' A.A. Phillips Melbourne University Press 2006
3. 'The Explorers' ed. Tim Flannery Grove/Atlantic, Incorporated 1999
4. 'Atlas of the British Empire' ed. Dr. C.A. Bayly Hamlyn 1989
5. 'The Birth of Melbourne' Tim Flannery Text Publishing Company 2004
6. 'Down Under' Bill Bryson Doubleday Publishing 2000
7. 'The Commonwealth of Thieves' Tom Keneally Vintage Books 2007
8. 'Fatal Shore: A History of the Transportation of Convicts to Australia 1787–1868', Robert Hughes Vintage Books 2003
9. 'For the Term of His Natural Life', by Marcus Clarke Penguin 2008
10. 'A concise history of Australia' Stuart Macintyre Cambridge University Press 3rd Edition 2009
11. 'A Certain Grandeur: Gough Whitlam's Life in Politics' Graham Freudenberg June 2009 Penguin
12. 'Gallipoli' Andrew Moorehead Wordsworth Editions, 1998
13. 'The Rebel Chorus. Dissenting voices in Australian History' Geoff Hocking, The Five Mile Press Pty Ltd 2007
14. 'Walhalla graveyard to cemetery' Yolanda Reynolds Genepool Publishing, 2007.
15. 'A Voyage to Terra Australis' Mathew Flinders Project Gutenburg, August 2004

16. 'Dulce et Decorum' Wilfred Owen, Poetry of the World Wars ed. Michael Foss Michael O'Mara Books Limited 1990
17. Princess K'gari's Fraser Island: a history of Fraser Island' Fred Williams, Fred Williams Enterprises
18. 'In the Wake of First Contact: The Eliza Fraser Stories' Kay Schaffer ,University of Adelaide Paperback January 1995
19. 'The Byron Journals' Daniel Ducrou, Text Publishing Australia 2010
20. 'A Rudimentary Exposition on the Induced Magnetism of Iron In Sea Going Vessels And its Action on the Compass, In Different Latitudes, and Under Diversified Circumstances' William Walker, R.N Piper Brothers & Co., Paternoster Row, Charles Wilson (Late Charles Wilson and Norie), Leadenhall Street 1853

Newspapers, newspaper articles, magazines and research pieces

The National Library of Australia is the source for all Australian newspaper articles of the 19th and early 20th centuries and for the James Cook Endeavour Journals. There is also reference in many places to the Australian Dictionary of Biography. I have also used articles from many newspapers which included The Age, The Sydney Morning Herald, Brisbane Times, The Times (UK), The Guardian (UK), The Queenslander, Sydney Daily Telegraph, STYLE Living Magazines, Sunshine Coast Daily.

1. 'From a Berlin bunker to a Noosa beach: the secret life of Hitler's secretary' The Weekend Australian August 2005 by John Lehmann and Natasha Robinson,
2. 'The Labor Trade in Melanesians to Queensland: An Historiographic Essay' Doug Munro; Journal of Social History Vol. 28, No. 3 (Spring, 1995), pp. 609–627
3. 'Gold Coast desalination plant a billion-dollar rusty white elephant': Mike O', Connor 'The Courier-Mail June 28, 2010
4. 'Schoolies worse than footy hooligans as arrests up on last year' Jeremy Pierce The Courier-Mail November 2009
5. 'Work starts on Fraser Coast RV village' Homebase ReView September 2010

6. 'The sayings of Premier Joh', The Age April 20th 2005

7. 'Seachange: Risk for a Better Life': Nicholas Osbaldiston Paper presented to the Social Change in the 21st Century Conference, Centre for Social Change Research Queensland University of Technology – 27th October 2006

8. 'Australia's sugar industry' Robert F. McKillop Published by Light Railway Research Society of Australia Inc

9. 'Barrier Reef Australia' ; Great Barrier Reef Marine Park Authority 2008 report

10. 'Overstaying Their Welcome: Cane Toads in Australia' Tina Butler, mongabay.com April 2005

11. Cane Growers Association, Queensland

12. 'Grey Nomad Volunteers: New partnerships between grey nomads and rural towns in Australia' Annette Maher, Rosemary Leonard, Helen Hayward-Brown and Jenny Onyx University of Western Sydney and University of Technology Sydney 2009

13. 'Effects of tourism on Fraser Island's Dune Lakes' Wade Hadwen, Angela Arthington, Stuart Bunn and Thorsten Mosisch, CRC for Sustainable Tourism Pty Ltd 2004

14. 'Faith in the Sunshine State: Joh Bjelke-Petersen and the Religious Culture of Queensland' John Harrison, ABC News based on his 1991 thesis

15. 'Friends of Noosa Report – February 2010': Bob Ansett

16. 'Contesting corporal punishment: Abolitionism, transportation and the British imperial project': Isobelle Barrett Meyering October 2008, Department of History, University of Sydney

17. 'Queensland's shameful management of the Fraser Island World Heritage 'randomKaos' John Sinclair July 2010

18. 'Dingos of Fraser Island' John Sinclair May 2001 Fraser Island Defenders Organisation

19. 'The hippie beach that chichi – Sun, sea and shabby-chic surfers' Rory McLean The Times Online October 26, 2003

20. 'Contesting corporal punishment: Abolitionism, transportation and the British imperial project' Isobelle Barrett Meyering, October 2008

21. A Convict's Lament on the Death of Captain Logan' oldpoetry.com

22. 'Colony and Empire, Australia's Subservient Relationship with Britain', Thomas Ross NATIONAL REPUBLICANS and Aussie Educator

23. 'The AMP.NATSEM Income and Wealth Report Published July 2010

24. 'Triangles of Life and Other Stories' Henry Lawson, Melbourne: Standard Publishing, 1913

25. 'No Go Zones' by Terry Ryder, founder of Hotspotting.com.au; quoted from the Northern Star, 9th June 2010

26. 'Blue Mountains Local Studies: January 2011' John Merriman, Local Studies Librarian © 2011 Blue Mountains City Library

27. 'Trial by media: Anthony Trollope in Australia' Nigel Starck, Australian studies in journalism no. 17, pp. 2–16 2006

28. 'New insights into Gundungurra place naming' Jim Smith taken from 'Aboriginal place names: naming and re-naming the Australian landscape Canberra' : ANU E Press and Aboriginal History Inc, c2009. xxi, 496 p. : ill., maps ;

29. Sea Change: Re-Inventing Rural and Regional Australia: Peter Murphy in Transformations, No. 2 (March 2002)

30. Australian National Dictionary Centre

31. UK's Office of National Statistics

32. Museum of London

33. Australian Geoscience

34. World Travel and Tourism Council

35. Australian Bureau of Statistics

36. British Met Office

37. The Samuel Johnson Sound Bite Page

38. Lloyds TSB

39. Guinness World Records

40. Centre for Government of Queensland

41. Oxford Dictionary

42. Centre for the Study of Sexually Transmissible Diseases, La Trobe University Melbourne, in 1997

43. Queensland Tourist Board; Queensland Travel

44. The Aboriginal Art and Culture Centre in Alice Springs

45. FIDO (Fraser Island Defenders Organisation, also known as 'The Watchdog of Fraser Island') for numerous articles within this book

46. Australian Dictionary of Biography Online, Copyright 2006 Published by the Australian National University

47. Noosawiki

48. Noosa Official Guide – Operated by eGuide Pty Ltd © 2010

49. Australian Finance Group (AFG)

50. National Seachange Council
51. Australian Cancer Council
52. Sunshine Coast tourist information website
53. Queensland Treasury
54. Brisbane History
55. National Health Survey: Summary of Results; State Tables, 2007–2008 (Reissue): Australian Bureau of Statistics, May 2009
56. The State Library of New South Wales
57. Arwarbukarl Cultural Resource Association
58. The BBC
59. The Museum of unNatural History Copyright Lee Krystek 1996.
60. Aboriginal Australia Art and Culture Centre Alice Springs
61. kurrajong.org
62. Fianna: A guide to Irish Ancestry
63. insults.com,
64. World Gambling Review in 2009
65. Robert Burns 'Rogues in a Nation' courtesy of 'Burns Country'
66. City of Sydney's Barani History of the Indigenous People:
67. Grey London poll 2003
68. State Library of Victoria 2004
69. living.australia.com
70. Outback Australia
71. Project Gutenberg
72. Buzzle.com
73. The Centre for Government of Queensland
74. Austrailian Traveller Magazine